THE POLITICS OF BUREAUCRACY

The Politics
of
Bureaucracy

SECOND EDITION

B. Guy Peters

University of Pittsburgh

Longman
New York and London

For Matthew and Sarah

The Politics of Bureaucracy, Second Edition

Longman Inc., 95 Church Street, White Plains, NY 10601
Associated companies, branches, and representatives
throughout the world.

Developmental Editor: Irving E. Rockwood
Editorial and Design Supervisor: James Fields
Production and Manufacturing Supervisor: Ferne Y. Kawahara

Library of Congress Cataloging in Publication Data

Peters, B. Guy.
  The politics of bureaucracy.

  Includes index.
  1. Public administration. 2. Bureaucracy.
3. Comparative government. I. Title.
JF1501.P43 1984   350   83–12059
ISBN 0–582–28317–5
ISBN 0–582–28316–7 (pbk.)

Manufactured in the United States of America
Printing: 9 8 7 6 5 4 3   Year: 91 90 89 88 87 86

CONTENTS

PREFACE

This second edition of *The Politics of Bureaucracy*
continues the basic approach used in the first edition. There is still an emphasis
on the role of the public bureaucracy in making public policy and on the
institutional politics of policy making. There is also an emphasis on the importance of institutional structures for explaining policy outcomes in the public
bureaucracy. Finally, like its predecessor, this revised edition emphasizes accountability and control as central concerns of public sector management.

However, much new information has also been added. There is an entirely
new chapter on public budgeting. This is of necessity a broad overview, but
it does highlight common problems of budgeting and the ways in which different
countries have approached them. In addition, a new section of chapter 4 gives—
again somewhat broadly—some basic structural information about the civil service systems of several major countries. Greater attention is also given to the
work on implementation, a highly popular topic with students of administration.
Finally, I have striven to fit the changing nature of the world and of academic
analysis of that world into the framework that I used in the first edition.

I am grateful to many people for helping me to complete this edition.
Several colleagues have made useful comments on the first edition, which I
have attempted to integrate into this edition. These include—but are not limited
to—Alfred Diamant, Dennis Dresang, Martin Heisler, Patricia Ingraham,
George Jones, Bert Rockman, and Richard Rose. My colleagues at the Center
for Public Policy Studies, Tulane University, and especially Don L. England
bore many burdens to allow me the time to finish this and other projects.
The University of Manchester, through a Hallsworth Fellowship, provided time
to finish the manuscript. Mr. Brian Putt and the other residents of Broomcroft

Hall provided a congenial environment in which to work and live. Last, and certainly not least, my family put up with a ridiculous schedule for several years while this and other projects were under completion.

B. Guy Peters

INTRODUCTION

Government is increasingly a part of the daily life of the average citizen. Once relegated to the rather basic tasks of delivering the mail, policing the streets, and defending the nation in time of war, the modern government provides an array of goods and services too large to enumerate here. Moreover, governments now regulate a large number of actions that once were left to the whim of the individual and the free market. Many activities that were virtually unknown thirty years ago are today the subjects of extensive governmental regulation, if not outright governmental ownership and management. Television, atomic energy, and large-scale commercial aviation are only three of a number of possible examples.

This increase in the government's work load does not mean that government is more popular. If anything, the public image of government is more negative—especially in industrial countries—than it has ever been. Almost paradoxically, the more government does, the more negatively it is regarded. The sheer size of government and the associated taxation, combined with the publicity given its failures, have reduced the faith and possibly even the allegiance of citizens.

Before dealing with the failures and problems of government, let us first ask a more basic question: How does government manage this expanded work load? The best answer is that it is largely done by public administration, by those mythical bureaucrats generally blamed for most of government's failures. Administration and bureaucracy are apparently almost as old as government,

1

but they have become an increasingly significant part of the governing apparatus of virtually every country in the world.[1] Despite this apparent importance, we probably have less systematic information concerning this aspect of government than any other. Elections, political parties, legislatures, and the courts—the glamorous parts of the political system—have been analyzed extensively. These components of government provide a vast quantity of readily usable data for the researcher. Administration, on the other hand, is far from glamorous, has been generally considered nonpolitical in most Western societies, and has appeared to defy adequate quantification and theoretical analysis.[2]

If our knowledge of administration in any one country is inadequate, then our lack of knowledge of the comparative dimensions of administration is appalling. We still apparently lack the conceptual and operational basis to make sense of a large number of scattered and disparate findings.[3] This volume seeks to provide one relatively well-integrated viewpoint that will be useful in the development of a more adequate knowledge of comparative public administration.

THE IDEA OF PUBLIC ADMINISTRATION

At the outset, it is vital to define what is meant by public administration, and particularly to differentiate the commonly employed "bureaucracy" from the more general term of public administration. Most public administrative agencies are indeed bureaucratic, but the correspondence is by no means complete even in those agencies that do display bureaucratic tendencies.

In the main, public administration can be described as:

1. In functional terms, the process of rule-application; that is to say, the process through which general social rules are converted into specific decisions for individual cases.[4]
2. The structures of government whose primary function is to perform the functions outlined in (1).

This definition may appear somewhat restrictive. However, we are interested in the political and economic functions of administrative agencies even when they are not performing strictly administrative functions. For example, the political interactions of administrative bodies in the budgetary process are only tangentially related to the application of rules, but they are essential for the survival and maintenance of organizations that perform the administrative functions.[5] Thus, the study and analysis of public administration have come to include a good deal more than what is considered strictly "administrative." For example, either through necessity or the abdication of other institutions, administrative agencies have become major rule-making bodies in both developed and less-developed societies.[6] They also perform a number of functions that might ordinarily be considered judicial. We shall be concerned with these, but mainly to the degree to which they elucidate the structural and functional aspects of the principal administrative roles.

Here it is necessary to further differentiate traditional bureaucratic notions concerning administration from this somewhat looser definition.[7] The meaning of bureaucracy has been broadened in popular parlance, and in some scholarly writing, to include any administrative organization. We shall use bureaucracy somewhat more strictly to mean:

> organizations with a pyramidal structure of authority, which utilize the enforcement of universal and impersonal rules to maintain that structure of authority, and which emphasize the nondiscretionary aspects of administration.[8]

Several scholars have gone to some length in detailing the various components of Max Weber's conception of the ideal type of bureaucracy, showing that the components are not of necessity interrelated in actual organizations.[9] We shall largely accept these analyses and therefore adopt a conception of bureaucracy much less stringent than that of Weber or of the commentators on Weber.[10] At the same time, however, not every public organization should be considered bureaucratic. For example, even in industrialized societies organizations that serve the chief executive, such as the Executive Office of the President in the United States, have patterns of authority and decision making more similar to that described by Weber as patrimonial than to that described as bureaucratic.[11] Other organizations have adopted "modern" approaches to management, emphasizing the personal involvement and self-actualization of organizational members.[12] Nevertheless, the vast majority of public organizations have a number of bureaucratic elements that tend to structure their performance. In dealing with the social and cultural aspects of administration, we shall point out how certain value systems and systems of social organization contribute to the effectiveness of the hierarchical forms of authority, while others tend to cause a reexamination of that type of management.

COMPARATIVE POLITICS AND COMPARATIVE ADMINISTRATION

The first major point to be made here is the conception of public administration as an integral part of the political system. Therefore, the analysis of public administration is amenable to much the same type of analysis as comparative politics in general. As such, we shall be examining David Easton's "authoritative allocation of values" but be looking at it as performed in bureaucratic structures rather than in legislative, executive, or judicial structures.[13] The process of decision making is perhaps better hidden in bureaucracies, but decisions are made there. We shall be seeking to ferret out the manner in which they are made and the effects of those decisions on the political and social systems.

This equating of public administration with politics may appear quite logically to some readers as common sense. Still, a long intellectual and governmental tradition in most Western societies attempts to separate the two functions. For example, Woodrow Wilson wrote:

> Administration lies outside the proper sphere of politics. Administrative questions are not political questions. Although politics sets the tasks for administration, it should not be suffered to manipulate its offices. The field of administration is a field of business. It is removed from the hurry and strife of politics; it at most points stands apart even from the debatable ground of constitutional study. It is a part of political life only as the methods of the counting-house are a part of the life of society; only as machinery is part of the manufactured product. But it is, at the same time, raised very far above the full level of mere technical detail by the fact that through its greater principles it is directly connected with the lasting maxims of political wisdom, the permanent truths of political progress.[14]

As long as it was assumed that administration was a simple nondiscretionary action, it was useless to think of administration in the more general context of the political system.

Fortunately for our understanding of the political process, the artificial dichotomy between politics and administration has been eroded in both the scholarly and the popular literature. As the work load of government increased, more and more decisions were of necessity made outside the "political" branches of government, and in the administrative branches. It became increasingly apparent that government decisions were not all made in the hallowed halls of the legislature; rather, a good number of them were made in the less impressive but more numerous halls of administrative office buildings.[15] Likewise, in the scholarly literature, the increasing use of systems theory and structural-functional analysis tended to emphasize the interconnectedness of politics and administration rather than their separation.

It is the thesis here that the artificial separation that developed between politics and public administration has been eroded to some degree but has not disappeared entirely. Analysis of public administration and its comparative role in public policy formation will probably further erode that barrier. We will examine administration as an integral component of the decision-making structure of government, and, further, discuss the linkage developed between administration and those structures that we would normally regard as "political." This inquiry should demonstrate that what appears to be administrative may actually be political, and that those who make administrative decisions do so for political reasons. The politics involved are the protection and promotion of organizational interests rather than the promotion of one political party or another, but they are politics nonetheless.[16]

COMPARATIVE POLITICAL THEORY AND COMPARATIVE ADMINISTRATION

As we begin our examination of comparative public administration, we should expect guidance from two large and important bodies of literature in the social sciences. One of these is the vast literature on comparative politics; the other is the even more vast literature on organization theory and public administration. Each of these bodies of literature makes a contribution to the discussion that follows, but each also has several serious shortcomings for our purposes.

As the literature on comparative politics has developed from the 1950s onwards, it has gone in two directions that have not been particularly beneficial for the comparative study of public administration. The first of the directions might be called the "scientific approach" to comparative politics, although that term does not fully capture the nature of this change or its impact on comparative administration. In general, the scientific approach has focused on the political system as an organizing concept, and has placed special emphasis on the environment of government and inputs from that environment into the political system.[17] Thus, unlike the more traditional study of political institutions, the emphasis of much of contemporary comparative politics has been placed upon voting behavior, political attitudes, the activities of interest groups, etc. This change in the focus of comparative research was very refreshing in an area of study that had become concerned almost exclusively with formal structures and constitutional aspects of government, but there was something of an overreaction against the traditional background. When stressing the importance of input mechanisms, theorists tended to disregard the importance of formal institutions of decision making, for example, administration. The decision-making institutions of government became the famous "black box" into which inputs entered and from which outputs emerged, almost by magic. Thus, knowledge of formal institutions and the processes of policy making (known as "throughputs" in the jargon of the time) tended to be superceded by the more quantifiable concerns such as voting behavior and political attitudes.[18]

Interestingly, although there was presumed to be a linkage between inputs entering the political system and the outputs that emerged, some time passed before comparative politics gave much attention to analyzing those outputs. Only as the "postbehavioral" movement gained strength, with its emphasis on the activities of government, was there significant interest in the study of governmental performance.[19] Now, as the concerns of both academic analysts and ordinary citizens have come to rest more on the performance of government, the focus of inquiry has been shifting back to institutions, with the public bureaucracy being the institution most clearly associated with performance.

The second dimension of development in the literature on comparative politics that has affected the study of administration has been termed "political economy." This approach focuses on the structural arrangements in advanced, industrial societies and attempts to relate the performance of those governments to the structural arrangements.[20] In general, this approach has been based upon neo-Marxist or critical theory premises, with "late capitalism" being the most significant structure affecting government. Regardless of the ideological orientation of this work, its emphasis on the macro-structural aspects of modern governments has obscured consideration of the nature and performance of public bureaucracies almost as thoroughly as did the "scientific" paradigm. Variations in patterns of recruitment, organization, and behavior, which are all so important for understanding variations in bureaucratic performance, occur at too low a level of generality to be of much interest to those employing the political economy approach. Further, to the extent to which these phenomena are of interest, they are almost entirely as dependent variables, rather than as independent variables that might explain differences in policies or efficiency.[21]

The above characterization of the two dominant approaches to comparative political analysis should not be taken as an undifferentiated attack upon all work in comparative politics during this period; indeed, some important contributions to our understanding of comparative administration appeared in those years. In particular, the activities of the Comparative Administration Group in the 1960s were crucial in keeping alive interest in comparative administration, and especially in beginning to apply some of the conceptions of administration that had been developed in the industrialized countries to the then emerging countries of the Third World. Likewise, the work of Fred Riggs, Ferrell Heady, and others were explicit attempts at developing theoretical approaches to comparative administration that would meet some of the canons of the scientific approach to comparative politics, while at the same time preserving concerns with institutions and structural factors.[22] Further, the development of the methodological sophistication and empirical research techniques associated with the scientific approach have enabled those interested in institutional decision making to approach such institutions from new and theoretically important directions.

An argument could be made that public administration is the one area of government that is most susceptible to meaningful comparison and the development of middle-range political theory. In the first place, public administration is assigned relatively common tasks in almost all political systems. Most fundamentally, it is expected to translate the authoritative decrees of legislatures or other lawmaking bodies into action. In addition, public bureaucracies themselves are assigned significant lawmaking roles, as well as important roles in advising political leaders. The mechanisms whereby public bureaucracies perform these tasks may be given different titles, but the tasks are similar and quite comparable.

In addition to the relatively common tasks, the structures within which administration is conducted are also relatively similar. At least on the surface, the structure of a public organization in the United Kingdom is not a great deal different from one performing a similar function in Upper Volta. This relative similarity allows us to assess the possible effects of relatively small organizational differences. Further, it allows us to assess the effects of a number of cultural and environmental factors on the behavior of administrators.

Finally, public bureaucracies have the advantage that they almost always will have a formal structure, which need not be true of important political actors on the input side of the political system. Thus, it is easier for the researcher to specify exactly the subjects of research, and to locate those individuals in a structure of interactions with other actors. It is, of course, undesirable to concentrate entirely on formal structures, given that the majority of industrialized countries have developed important quasi-official and coopted private organizations that are important for the implementation of public programs.[23] Likewise, the informal structures that exist even within formal structures are crucial for understanding actual patterns of organizational behavior.[24] The formal structures do, however, constitute an important place at which to begin the inquiry. Such a convenient starting point may not exist for other relevant policy actors.

In summary, while comparative political analysis may not have been particularly kind to students of comparative administration, comparative administration can repay that absence of concern with positive developments. The (relative) similarity and identifiability of administrative tasks and administrative structures permit the researcher to specify relationships and to explore similarities that would be more difficult for other political institutions. What is needed, however, is a realization that this form of institutional analysis, albeit combined with more behavioral analyses, is important for the development of comparative political theory.

ADMINISTRATIVE THEORY AND COMPARATIVE ADMINISTRATION

The second major body of literature that should influence the study of comparative public administration is the general literature on public administration. But even that would be a narrow delineation of the field, for to some extent the entire literature on organization theory and management theory in both the public and private sectors has some relevance for comparative administration. While the debate continues as to whether public and private administration really are different, or merely subsets of a broader phenomenon, it is clear that developments in organization theory and management theory in the private sector certainly do have some relevance for governmental organizations.[25] Further, it can be argued that by ignoring more general developments in organization theory, practitioners and students of public administration run the risk of locking themselves into a rather outmoded and potentially ineffective approach to organizations and management. Innovations in the private sector may well have to be adapted to meet the special requirements of the public sector, but government can ignore those innovations only at its peril.

One of the most important of these developments has been the contingency approach to organization theory.[26] This approach attempts to match the characteristics of the environment of the organization and the mode of production within the organization to the most appropriate structures. Such a theory would therefore argue that organizations performing different functions (prisons versus research laboratories as extreme examples) and operating in different environments (information levels, for example) should be designed differently.[27] This appears to be an obvious point, but it is one that frequently escapes the notice of government officials who tend to construct all public organizations as neat pyramids governed by Weberian principles. The simple admonition of the contingency approach is also frequently ignored by academic analysts of public administration who continue to rely upon the "proverbs of administration" for guidance in understanding public administration and advising government officials.[28]

The contingency approach to organizations should have a great deal of applicability in comparative administration. Considerable variation in organizational structure and performance may be explained by factors central to the contingency approach. The principal difference in the application, however, is that the wide range of variations in both environmental factors—the affluence of Western Europe as compared to the poverty of Third World countries—and the demands placed upon the organizations may be too great to develop anything more than gross generalities about the relationship of those two factors to structure. Also, there is the very great problem of the effects of diffusion on organizational structure—the number of former colonies that have adopted French or British administrative models, for example—so that any attempts to develop theoretical propositions concerning the relationships of these factors may be suspect.

As well as important developments in organization theory, there have been important developments in the study of public organizations themselves that can aid in improving the understanding of comparative public administration. The most significant of these are the increasing emphasis on the study of implementation and the associated interest in the multiorganizational nature of most administration.[29] Some may argue that implementation is no more than a new word for what students of public administration have always studied. The implementation approach, however, has placed increased emphasis on the changes that a piece of legislation may undergo as it is translated from a document to a working program. Such a perspective combines an understanding of formal administrative practices with an understanding of the political realities of administration in the public sector. Great hopes are indeed dashed in Oakland,

and elsewhere, and it is important to understand why this happens and perhaps what can be done to prevent it.

The implementation perspective also highlights the multiorganizational nature of public administration. There is a danger of viewing public administration from the perspective of the "single lonely organization."[30] That is, there is a danger of assuming that a program is implemented by a single organization that is solely responsible for its success or failure. In reality, a number of organizations and their interactions go into determining the success or failure of a program. Some of these are "central organizations," or the central staff organizations concerned with such areas as budgeting, personnel, and legislative clearance.[31] Other relevant organizations will be other line agencies that administer programs affecting the program in question. For example, the success of an agency delivering a health program is affected by the activities of other agencies delivering housing, nutrition, and educational services. Finally, especially in federal political systems, the interaction among organizations at different levels of government produces a number of different implementation problems, especially when the different governments are controlled by different political parties or are pursuing quite different goals in a single policy area.[32]

The implementation perspective and the associated concern with the multiorganizational nature of implementation structures have been of some importance in developing theory in comparative public administration. Just as administration itself is an identifiable and relatively similar structure cross-nationally, so too is the need to develop a process to translate authoritative decrees into action. The barriers that must be overcome are in many ways similar regardless of the national setting, but each has its unique contribution to make in the understanding of the general phenomenon. Explaining implementation cross-nationally then allows the development of theoretical approaches to the problems, as well as offering opportunities for more practical learning based upon the success or failure of implementation in other national settings.

Comparative public administration is a specialized branch of administration taken as a more general area of inquiry. The development of organization and management theory at a general level can assist in our understanding of comparative public administration, but we should not expect all the answers to come even from that fertile field. The public nature of administration and the need to understand the social, cultural, and political settings of organizations make the enterprise of comparative public administration somewhat special. The borrowing from more general managerial approaches—something we would consider necessary for the development of the field—must therefore be done quite carefully and with a proper concern for contextual and situational factors. If this borrowing is done carefully, then comparative administration should be able to repay the loan with a more complex analysis of the relationship between environment and administration, and between processes and structures of organizations.

ADMINISTRATION AND PUBLIC POLICY

In this volume the relationship between public administration and public policy will also be examined. As noted, the intellectual history of the study of public administration has tended to cloud this relationship severely. This has been unfortunate because administration, like all aspects of government, is principally interesting and important because of what it does for and to the people in the society. Government and politics can be good, clean (?) fun to observe and discuss, but ultimately we must ask: So what? In this case, there is a ready answer to that potentially devastating question. It is simply that the political system is involved in making public policies that in turn benefit some people in the society and disadvantage others.[33] Laws against murderers disadvantage people who enjoy violence and advantage people who want to get home safely every day. Nevertheless, all laws are meaningless unless they are enforced, and this is where public administration comes into the picture. The administrators—including the police—are charged with putting the laws of the legislature or the ordinances of an executive into effect.

In fact, one could reasonably argue that the manner in which the laws are enforced gives them their true meaning. If laws are administered differentially for various segments of the society (for example, ethnic minorities, youths, lower-class individuals), then the application of the law has given a different meaning to the piece of legislation than was intended by its drafters. This conversion by decision making on the part of administrators of the legislative output of the nation to actual operational rules is of great interest when we examine administration. A good number of these operational rules will be written down as administrative regulations and the like, but a number will also be simple traditional or habitual actions on the part of administrators. Thus, the standard operating procedure of many police departments is to stop and question only certain types of individuals. This may be justified from their perspective by a certain probability of the occurrence of crimes by certain social groups, but it points out that the probability of being questioned by the authorities is not determined by laws concerning vagrancy, etc., but rather by the actions of individual administrators. This is certainly not true only of the police as administrative or enforcement personnel. Blau, Lasswell, and Almond have shown that it is also very likely to occur in social services where the receptionist and similar screening personnel determine who has the possibility of receiving aid.[34] More recently, Goodsell and also Katz have demonstrated the importance of the personal encounter between the citizen and the public administrator in the delivery of services.[35] Those people whom the "screeners" initially reject have no possibility of receiving aid, while those who get by this initial step have some relatively good possibility of receiving aid.

This leads to another point to be made in discussing the role of the administrative apparatus in public policy. Often, the lowest echelons of the administration have the most to do with the outputs of administration. Thus, it is often the cop on the beat, as opposed to the commissioners, chiefs of police, or other upper-level personnel, who determines what the operational policy is going to be. Or the receptionist at Blau's public-employment office makes many crucial decisions for the agency, as did the field agents in Blau's analysis of FBI agents.[36] As a general rule, it is necessary to discuss and to understand the operations of the lowest level of administration in order to fully understand administration. Unfortunately, most of the literature on administration deals only with the upper echelon. This is understandable; according to the organizations' charts, these are the positions that exercise formal authority and control, and formally make policy. Much of this emphasis is no doubt misplaced. The upper levels are certainly important to understand, but not to the exclusion of the soldiers in the field who daily confront the problems about which the upper officials make policy.

Following from this point is the assumption that the outputs of the political system will have two basic components. The first is an objective component, that is, what the political system actually provides the citizen in the way of gratifications and deprivations.[37] Thus, we can examine the net sum of gains and losses that the individual receives from being a member or subject of a certain political system. There is also a subjective component. This concerns the style in which those gratifications and deprivations are delivered to the individual. Individual citizens will value services according to the amount of services that they receive and also according to the way in which they are treated in the delivery of those services. This has become most apparent recently in the delivery of social-welfare services in a number of societies. Despite the fact that most developed countries have rather extensive systems of social welfare, many clients and critics of these systems argue that although economic citizenship is granted to the individual, the demeaning manner in which the services are administered tends to deny the client his "social citizenship."[38] Basically, the receipt of social assistance sets the individual apart as a special type of person who is somehow less worthy than his peers. This holdover from the economic liberalism and social Darwinism of the nineteenth century has been most apparent in the United States but has also been manifested in a number of other societies with better developed systems of social welfare.

Administration is extremely important in the development of the objective component of public policy. It is, however, most crucial in defining the subjective component of public policy. Public administration, and especially the lower levels of that administration, actually deals with the clients. Thus, for most clients, what government is and does may be personified in the actions of lower-echelon administrators. Their style in handling clients, the courtesy and consideration they show, as well as their competence, can do a great deal toward defining the role and the respect of the political system in the society. Thus, a great deal of emphasis must be placed on this admittedly vague matter of administration. Some interview studies of clients of public agencies have shown that there are substantial differences in the evaluation of services and the evaluation of the style of administrative personnel.[39] At present this evidence is unsystematic, but there is good reason to believe that this is a directly measurable phenomenon. In any case, we shall be concerned with the interpersonal side of administration in the delivery of services to clients. Just as previously pointed out with respect to inputs from the society to the political system, the administration also serves as the major point of contact on the output side of government, and as such it is important in actually delivering services and in the interpersonal aspect of service delivery.

In summary, administration and policy, instead of being discrete phenomena, are actually interrelated. In both an objective and a subjective manner the nature of the administrative system can influence the policy outputs of the political system. Administration does make policy, although these policies are not always written and promulgated in the same manner as the rules made by legislatures and executives. Moreover, the operational rules developed by administrators can be more telling for the actual outcomes for individuals than are the formally promulgated rules. In addition, administrators are the major personal contact between citizens and their government. As such they define a large percentage of the objective outcomes of the policy process. While the objective component of administration and policy is certainly important for the individual, the subjective component cannot be ignored and may actually be more important in developing attitudes of loyalty, commitment, and affection among the citizens for their government.

AN OVERVIEW

The remainder of this book is divided into nine chapters. Chapter 1 provides an overview of the increasing involvement of government in the lives of its citizens and demonstrates the increasing involvement of the administrative system in providing services. This is supplemented with a discussion of the general sources of administrative power in dealing with the society and with the remainder of the political system. The second chapter deals explicitly with cultural foundations of administration. The study of comparative administration obviously involves these differences, and an attempt will be made to catalog some of the probable effects. As well as needing economic and cultural support, the public bureaucracy also needs personnel. The third chapter discusses the recruitment of personnel, especially in the light of models of representative bureaucracy. The fourth chapter describes four major administrative systems, used as examples frequently throughout the remainder of the book, and then proceeds to review several classical questions in administrative organization and to relate those questions to the policy choices of bureaucracy. The fifth and sixth chapters are discussions of the interaction of political and administrative officials in policy making, while the seventh concentrates on one special aspect of that interaction—the budgetary process. The eighth chapter discusses problems of administrative responsibility and the need to control the seemingly uncontrollable bureaucratic structures that characterize modern public administration. A number of approaches have been tried and proposed for accomplishing this difficult task; their effectiveness as well as their cross-cultural transferability will be evaluated. The final chapter discusses the challenges facing public administration in the 1980s and the 1990s, and the possible means of addressing those challenges. At this point the conclusions that can be reached about public administration across cultures are quite limited, but it is necessary to ask the proper questions, with the possibility that some of the answers will be able to withstand a more rigorous examination.

NOTES

1. S. N. Eisenstadt, *The Political System of Empires* (New York: The Free Press, 1963); Charles Tilly, ed., *The Formation of National States in Western Europe* (Princeton: Princeton University Press, 1975).
2. See Nicholas Henry, *Public Administration and Public Affairs* (Englewood Cliffs, N.J.: Prentice-Hall, 1975), pp. 3–32.
3. Some notable attempts in that direction have been Ferrell Heady, *Public Administration: A Comparative Perspective*, 2nd ed. (New York: Marcel Dekker, 1979); Mattei Dogan, *The Mandarins of Western Europe* (New York: Halsted, 1975); Joel D. Aberbach, Robert D. Putnam, and Bert A. Rockman, *Bureaucrats and Politicians in Western Democracies* (Cambridge, Mass.: Harvard University Press, 1981).
4. See Gabriel A. Almond and G. Bingham Powell, *Comparative Politics: A Developmental Approach*, 2nd ed. (Boston: Little, Brown, 1978).
5. See chapter 7.
6. See chapter 1.
7. Anthony Downs, *Inside Bureaucracy* (Boston: Little, Brown, 1976), pp. 24–31.
8. Max Weber, "Bureaucracy," in *From Max Weber*, H. H. Gerth and C. Wright Mills, eds. (New York: Oxford University Press, 1946).
9. Stanley H. Udy, Jr., "Bureaucratic Elements in Organizations," *American Sociological Review* 23 (1958): 415–18; Helen Constas, "Max Weber's Two Conceptions of Bureaucracy," *American Journal of Sociology* 63 (1958): 400–409; Richard H. Hall, "The Concept of Bureaucracy: An Empirical Assessment," *American Journal of Sociology* 69 (1963): 32–40. An interesting treatment oriented entirely to the public sector is Christopher Hood and Andrew Dunshire, *Bureaumetrics* (Farnborough, England: Gower, 1981).
10. Thus, we will be looking at any and all formal organizations involved in the implementation of public policy and the delivery of public services. See Alfred Diamant, "The Bureaucratic Model," in *Papers in Comparative Public Administration*, Ferrell Heady and Sybil L. Stokes, eds. (Ann Arbor: Institute of Public Administration, 1962), pp. 79–86.
11. See Roger B. Porter, *Presidential Decision-Making: The Economic Policy Board* (New York: Cambridge University Press, 1980).

12. For a review of participation and related approaches to management, see William B. Eddy, *Public Organization Behavior and Development* (Cambridge, Mass.: Winthrop, 1981).

13. David Easton, *The Political System* (New York: Knopf, 1956).

14. Woodrow Wilson, "The Study of Administration," *Political Science Quarterly* 2 (June 1887): 209–210.

15. In the United States this is referred to as writing regulations. In the United Kingdom it is referred to as "secondary legislation" or as writing statutory instruments. See James O. Freedman, *Crisis and Legitimacy* (New York: Cambridge University Press, 1978).

16. Graham Allison, *Essence of Decision* (Boston: Little, Brown, 1971).

17. See Martin O. Heisler with Robert B. Kvavik, "Patterns of European Politics: The 'European Polity' Model," in *Politics in Europe*, Martin O. Heisler, ed. (New York: David McKay, 1974), pp. 27–89.

18. *Ibid.*

19. See George J. Graham, Jr., and George W. Carey, *The Post-Behavioral Era: Perspectives on Political Science* (New York: David McKay, 1972).

20. Ian Gough, *The Political Economy of the Welfare State* (London: Macmillan, 1979).

21. But see N. Poulantzas, *State Power, Socialism* (London: New Left Books, 1978), pp. 223–229.

22. Fred W. Riggs, *Administration in Developing Countries—The Theory of Prismatic Society* (Boston: Houghton Mifflin, 1964); Heady, *Public Administration: A Comparative Perspective;* Ramesh K. Arora, *Comparative Public Administration* (New Delhi: Associated Publishing House, 1972).

23. See chapter 5.

24. The classic statement on the importance of informal organization is F. J. Roethlisberger and William J. Dickson, *Management and the Worker* (Cambridge, Mass.: Harvard University Press, 1939).

25. Nicholas Henry, *Public Administration and Public Affairs*, pp. 15–18.

26. Paul Lawrence and Jay Lorsch, *Organization and Its Environment* (Cambridge, Mass.: Harvard University Press, 1967); Charles Perrow, *Organizational Analysis: A Sociological View* (Belmont, Calif.: Wadsworth, 1970).

27. An important statement of this design problem is Amitai Etzioni, *A Comparative Analysis of Complex Organizations* (New York: Free Press of Glencoe, 1961).

28. Herbert A. Simon, *Administrative Behavior* (New York: Macmillan, 1957).

29. Jeffrey L. Pressman and Aaron B. Wildavsky, *Implementation* (Berkeley: University of California Press, 1973); Merilee S. Grindle, ed., *Politics and Policy Implementation in the Third World* (Princeton: Princeton University Press, 1980); Benny Hjern and Chris Hull, eds., *Implementation Beyond Hierarchy*, special issue of the *European Journal of Political Science*, 1982.

30. David O. Porter and Benny Hjern, "Implementation Structures: A New Unit of Analysis" (paper presented to American Political Science Association Annual Meeting, 1978).

31. Colin Campbell and George J. Szablowski, *The Superbureaucrats: Structure and Behavior in Central Agencies* (Toronto: Macmillan of Canada, 1979);

Colin Campbell, *Governments Under Stress* (Toronto: University of Toronto Press, 1983).

32. See, for example, Fritz W. Scharpf, Bernd Reissert, and Fritz Schnabel, "Policy Effectiveness and Conflict Avoidance in Intergovernmental Policy Formation," in Kenneth Hanf and Fritz W. Scharpf, eds., *Interorganizational Policy Making* (Beverly Hills, Calif.: Sage, 1978), pp. 57–112.

33. Or, as Lasswell put it, politics is about who gets what, when, and how. Much the same could be said of public administration.

34. Peter M. Blau, "Orientation Toward Clients in a Public Welfare Agency," *Administrative Science Quarterly* 5 (1960): 341–61; Gabriel A. Almond and Harold D. Lasswell, "Aggressive Behavior by Clients Toward Public Relief Administrators," *American Political Science Review* 28 (1934): 643–55.

35. Charles T. Goodsell, ed., *The Public Encounter: Where State and Citizen Meet* (Bloomington, Ind.: University of Indiana Press, 1981); Elihu Katz and Brenda Danet, *Bureaucracy and the Public* (New York: Basic Books, 1973).

36. Thompson bases an important analysis of organizations on the increasing separation of authority and expertise, with authority remaining at the peak of the organizational pyramid, and expertise—and experience in the field—at the bottom. See Victor A. Thompson, *Modern Organizations* (New York: Knopf, 1961).

37. Karl deSchweintz, "On Measuring Political Performance," *Comparative Political Studies* 2 (1970): 503–11.

38. T. H. Marshall, "Citizenship and Social Class," in *Class, Citizenship and Social Development* (New York: Doubleday, 1965), pp. 89–126.

39. R. Lewis Bowman, Eleanor C. Main, and B. Guy Peters, "Clients in the Atlanta Model Cities Program" (Report, Emory University, 1971); Goodsell, *Public Encounter;* Katz et al., *Bureaucratic Encounters* (Ann Arbor, Mich.: Institute for Social Research, 1975).

CHAPTER 1

THE GROWTH OF GOVERNMENT AND ADMINISTRATION

We began our introductory chapter with the statement that government has become a pervasive fact of everyday life, and that in addition public administration has become an especially pervasive aspect of government. This chapter will attempt to document briefly that generalization—if indeed any documentation is required. The "growth of government" has become both an object of scholarly research and a rallying cry for political activity. Any number of explanations have been offered for this growth.[1] Likewise, the expansion of the public bureaucracy has been viewed as either a by-product of the general growth in the public sector or as a root cause of that growth.[2] The arguments concerning this phenomenon are too numerous to discuss here, but it is important to place contemporary public administration in some context, and the increased concern about the size of government is an important factor shaping the current debate about public administration.

THE MODERN PUBLIC SECTOR

The above paragraph was written as if the "size of government" could be clearly and unambiguously measured. In fact, it is a fundamental feature of contemporary government, especially in industrialized societies, that the boundaries between government and society—between what is public and what

16

is private—are increasingly vague. As a consequence, any attempt to say unambiguously that government is growing or shrinking is subject to a great deal of error and misinterpretation.

Several examples of the difficulties in measuring the public sector may help to clarify this discussion. One obvious example is the role of the tax system in defining the impact of government on the economy and society—an impact that is not adequately assessed by most measures of the size of government. In the United States, for example, subsidies for housing through the tax system (primarily the deductibility of mortgage interest and local property taxes) exceed direct government expenditures for public housing by 150 percent. Likewise, although the United Kingdom has an extensive program of council (public) housing, tax relief for owner-occupied housing still amounts to over £1 billion.[3] Similar tax concessions are available to citizens in the majority of other industrialized societies, and housing is but one of many concessions that are granted.[4] All of these tax "loopholes" influence economic behavior and amount to government influencing the economy and society just as if it taxed and spent for the same purposes. Tax concessions are not, however, conventionally counted as a part of the "size" of the public sector as expenditures would be.

Government loans are another means through which government can influence the economy without ostensibly increasing the size of government. In the majority of industrialized countries governments make loans to their nationalized industries that are repaid only rarely, but that commonly do not show up as a component of public expenditure. The involvement of government is even more subtle when, as in the United States, administrations offer to guarantee private loans to companies that are in financial difficulties.[5] Such an arrangement involves the direct expenditure of little or no public money but, again, produces a significant influence on the economy.

Finally, not only do expenditures fall on the boundary between the public and private sectors, but whole organizations do as well. There has been a significant increase in the number of quasi-public organizations in most countries during the postwar era.[6] In order to provide organizations greater flexibility in making decisions, or to subject them to greater market discipline, or to protect them from potentially adverse political pressures, or simply to mask the true size of government, organizations have been created that straddle the public-private fence. In some instances these are created anew as government enters a policy area for the first time, for example, the Corporation for Public Broadcasting in the United States. In other instances these are organizations that have existed previously as a part of government but that are "hived-off" to a quasi-independent status, such as the Manpower Services Administration in the United Kingdom. In addition to the obvious measurement problems these organizations create, they give rise to even more important problems of accountability. As they have been divorced from government to some extent, the conventional political means for enforcing accountability (see chapter 8) may not be applicable, with the resultant opportunities for abuse of powers by these organizations.

Although we now know that it is difficult or impossible to measure the growth of government definitively, we can still gain insight into the changes that have taken place in the role of government by examining figures for public expenditure. This is the most widely used measure of the relative size of government and represents perhaps the most visible portions of governmental activity. A particular clue can be found in the relationship between government expenditure and Gross Domestic Product (GDP), a standard measure of all the marketed goods and services produced in an economy.

As can be seen in Table 1.1, there are marked differences among nations in the proportion of GDP devoted to public expenditure. The major differences are between the less-developed and the industrialized nations. Even the less-developed country with the highest level of public expenditure (Kenya) spends much less as a proportion of GDP than does the United States, which spends the least among the three industrialized countries. Of course, a sample of only six countries is prone to great error, but similar findings would be borne out were there a much larger sample of nations. In addition, there are differences among the industrialized and the less-developed nations. Sweden spends 71 percent more as a proportion of GDP than the United States.

The rate of increase in public expenditure appears higher in the less-developed countries than in the industrialized countries. India more than tripled the proportion of GDP devoted to public expenditure over the thirty years from 1950 to 1980, while Colombia more than doubled its percentage. Kenya

TABLE 1.1
PERCENTAGE OF GROSS DOMESTIC PRODUCT
GOING TO PUBLIC EXPENDITURE[a]

Country	1950	1960	1970	1980
United States	20.0	27.5	30.3	33.4
United Kingdom	35.3	33.1	33.2	42.2
Sweden	23.6	28.7	37.1	57.2
Colombia	7.0	8.4	16.2	14.9
Kenya[b]	—	11.5	16.2	20.4
India	5.8	11.4	14.1	18.0

SOURCES:

United Nations, *Statistical Yearbook* (New York: United Nations, annual).

United Nations, *Yearbook of National Accounts* (New York: United Nations, annual).

Organization for Economic Cooperation and Development, *National Accounts of OECD Member Nations* (Paris: OECD, annual).

[a] Gross Domestic Product at market prices; total public expenditure, including transfers.

[b] Kenya did not exist as a nation state in 1950.

TABLE 1.2
PROPORTION OF GROSS DOMESTIC PRODUCT
COMING FROM PRIMARY SECTOR OF
ECONOMY (AGRICULTURE, FORESTRY, AND FISHING)

Country	1950	1960	1970	1980
United States	7	4	3	3
United Kingdom	6	4	3	2
Sweden	10	7	4	3
Colombia	38	32	26	26
Kenya	—	38	30	30
India	50	47	41	31

SOURCES:

United Nations, *Statistical Yearbook* (New York: United Nations, annual).

United Nations, *Yearbook of National Accounts* (New York: United Nations, annual).

Organization for Economic Cooperation and Development, *National Accounts of OECD Member Nations* (Paris: OECD, annual).

almost doubled its percentage of public expenditure in GDP in the twenty years from 1960 to 1980. Sweden also doubled its proportion of public expenditure, but public expenditure in the other two countries expanded much more slowly, increasing by only 20 percent in the United Kingdom.

Part of the reason for the relatively lower rate of public expenditure in the less-developed countries is that so much of their Gross Domestic Product comes from agriculture and especially subsistence agriculture, as is apparent in Table 1.2. This means that there are fewer "free-floating resources" in the economy that are readily taxed. A cash transaction is easier to tax than someone simply growing his own crops in order to eat or trading by barter.[7] If we calculate the rate of public expenditure in relation to the secondary and tertiary sectors of the economy (manufacturing and services, respectively), we get a somewhat different picture of the rate of public expenditure in the less-developed countries. Using this calculation, Table 1.3 shows that Kenya and India spend almost as much in relation to Gross Domestic Product, or readily extractable Gross Domestic Product, as does the United States. Thus, the less-developed countries do tend to make rather substantial public expenditures when the difficulties of resource extraction are considered. In the terminology of Almond and Powell, since the extractive capabilities of these countries are weak, so are their distributive capabilities.[8]

These data, while only illustrative, point out that government is a big "business," and it is growing. Even in the less-developed countries with their smaller public sectors, a minimum of one dollar (or whatever monetary unit) in seven goes into public expenditure. In the United States—the least expendi-

TABLE 1.3
PUBLIC EXPENDITURE AS A
PERCENTAGE OF READILY EXTRACTABLE
(SECONDARY AND TERTIARY SECTORS)
GROSS DOMESTIC PRODUCT

Country	1950	1960	1970	1980
United States	21.5	28.6	31.3	34.4
United Kingdom	37.5	34.5	34.3	43.2
Sweden	26.2	30.9	38.7	59.0
Colombia	11.3	12.4	21.6	20.0
Kenya	—	13.1	22.9	29.1
India	11.6	21.5	24.0	27.6

SOURCES:
United Nations, *Statistical Yearbook* (New York: United Nations, annual).
United Nations, *Yearbook of National Accounts* (New York: United Nations, annual).
Organization for Economic Cooperation and Development, *National Accounts of OECD Member Nations* (Paris: OECD, annual).

ture-prone of the developed countries—this figure is one dollar in three. However, we much remember that when government spends money, it is not shoveled into a hole somewhere in Washington or Nairobi; the expenditures provide education, hospitals, highways, police protection, and the whole range of government services that most citizens require. Further, especially in the less-developed countries, these funds can be used to promote economic growth.

THE GROWTH OF GOVERNMENT

Forgetting for the time being that the concept of "government" cannot be measured in quantitative terms, we can proceed to inquire just why this institution—or set of institutions—has been appearing to increase in size and power. There are almost as many answers to that question as there are scholars concerned with the subject, but several fundamental approaches to the problem exist relating to the growth of the public bureaucracy.

Entitlements

One of the dominant explanations for the growth of government is that governments extended a variety of "entitlement programs" to their citizens during bountiful economic times and have been unable to rescind those entitlements as the economy has become less buoyant. Examples of these programs are social security, public health insurance, housing subsidies, etc. These programs are especially difficult to curtail when they are supported by an earmarked tax that gives citizens the impression of actually purchasing something akin to an insurance policy. Programs of this type constitute a major portion of the expenditures of government in the 1980s—approximately 40 percent in the United States, 43 percent in the United Kingdom, and 46 percent in Sweden.

Entitlement programs in and of themselves would not necessarily produce increases in the relative size of the public sector were it not for the demographic shift occurring in almost all industrialized societies. These societies are aging, with a higher proportion of the population retiring each year. In addition to pensions, the elderly tend to consume more medical care per capita than do younger people so that expenditures for public medical-care programs are also likely to increase as populations age. The shifts in the age structure of industrialized countries is quite rapid. For example, in the United States, which remains a relatively young country (just over 12 percent of the population over 65 as compared to 16 percent in Sweden), the over-65 component of the population is increasing more than twice as fast as the population as a whole.

Fiscal Reasons

The nature of public sector economics also tends to increase the size of the public sector relative to the rest of the economy. This proposition was advanced in its most extreme version by Adolph Wagner and has come to be known as Wagner's Law.[9] The basic idea is that as the economy of a nation grows, a larger proportion will be devoted to the public sector. The logic underlying this proposition is that as the economy grows, the basic subsistence needs of the population will be met, and as a consequence money for private consumption will have declining marginal utility. A number of empirical studies have found only slight support for this contention, and some scholars—most significantly John Kenneth Galbraith—have argued that public expenditures tend to the lowest acceptable level rather than increasing along with economic growth.[10]

A second financial explanation for the relative growth of the public sector was advanced by Peacock and Wiseman.[11] They argued for the existence of a "displacement effect," whereby public tolerance for taxation increased during times of stress, for example, a war, and after the end of the crisis, government would use newly created revenues to fund new programs. Thus, the public's acceptance of taxation was displaced upward during each successive crisis, allowing those within government to develop new policies and programs. Although this "ratchet effect" has a certain plausibility, it would appear equally plausible that politicians or other governmental decision-makers could reap an equally large benefit from reducing taxes rather than creating new programs.

The third fiscal reason for the expansion of the public sector has been called "Baumol's disease," or more technically the Relative Price Effect.[12] Government is a labor-intensive "industry," and as such gains very little from the application of capital expenditures. The majority of the tasks performed by government, such as delivering the mail, teaching school, or policing, have their costs reduced very little by the introduction of any but the most extensive technological advances. All this means that in an inflationary period the costs of government services will increase more rapidly than the costs of other types of goods and services, assuming that public sector pay remains on an equal footing with private sector pay. Thus, in order to provide the *same* level of services, the costs of government will *increase*. At one time the British Treasury estimated this relative price effect to be 0.7 percent per year.[13] That is, just to provide the same level of public services, public expenditures would have to increase 0.7 of 1 percent. In ten years, with compounding, this would amount to an increase of almost 8 percent. This basic fact of life in government leaves two options: increase expenditures or cut services, neither of which is very palatable to politicians in contemporary governments.

The Political Process

The third reason for the increase in the size of government might be termed the "Pogo phenomenon." That is, "We have met the enemy and it is us"; or government grows because citizens demand more services from government. This expression of demand is rarely, if ever, through mass political means but rather derives through the role of pressure groups and their access to government.[14] Pressure groups have every incentive to press their demands on government. They can receive a special, concentrated benefit for their members—farmers can collect higher subsidies, businesses can acquire greater tax concessions, and the elderly can achieve higher pensions. The costs of these benefits are dispersed widely across the population, so that forming organizations to combat these pressure groups is difficult. As Lowi has pointed out, the public sector may be appropriated for private purposes, all funded by taxpayers' money.[15] These developments approach the "tragedy of the commons," in which behavior that is perfectly rational for the individual, or in this case the group, becomes extremely dysfunctional for the society as a whole.[16]

Decline of Late Capitalism

One explanation for the growth of government in advanced, industrial countries has been the "decline of late capitalism." This approach is rather obviously based upon Marxist or neo-Marxist principles.[17] It argues that the inherent contradictions of the capitalist system—most notably that the removal of profits by capitalists reduces the overall growth and productivity of the system—forces governments to attempt to patch up the system by increasing public expenditures, especially for welfare programs. However, as more and more money is spent for social purposes, there is even less that can be used to maintain the economic viability of the societies. The public sector will increase relative to the productivity of the entire economy, but ultimately the socio-economic system is doomed to come crashing down from the weight of its own contradictions.

This explanation for the increasing relative size of public expenditure has obvious ideological overtones, but interestingly, this analysis is in many ways similar to the analysis offered by conservatives. Both Marxists and conservatives might argue that social expenditure will slow the rate of economic growth, although one argues that this is because of profits and the other that there are too few profits. Further, in both ideological systems, social expenditures are a major cause of the decline of the economic systems in question.

The Public Bureaucracy

Finally, the public bureaucracy—our major focus of inquiry—has been cited as a cause of the growth of public expenditure and of government generally. One of the many stereotypes of the public bureaucracy is of an acquisitive and expansive set of organizations. This view is perhaps most forcefully expressed in the work of William Niskanen.[18] He argues that bureau chiefs—these are assumed to be permanent civil servants—are budget maximizers, and that they will use their control of information and their ability to mask the true costs of producing the public services they provide in order to increase their budgets to points far above the level necessary. In his model, Niskanen has the legislature with little or no ability to control the bureaus, and as a consequence the costs of government increase very rapidly. The solution offered to this problem is to create something approximating a market, with multiple bureaus competing to provide the same service.

This elegant economic analysis is based, however, upon several very shaky assumptions. The first and most basic is that bureaucrats have incentives to maximize the size of their bureaus. The individual bureaucrat would have little to gain personally, given relatively inflexible pay scales with pay to some extent based upon longevity rather than organizational size.[19] It is true that those at the bottom or middle ranks of the organization may be able to advance more rapidly due to new positions being opened, but the bureau chiefs—the budget maximizers in Niskanen's model—would themselves gain little or nothing. In fact, increasing the size of the bureau may only generate managerial difficulties for the bureaucrat, an outcome that would conflict with the other prevailing stereotype of the bureaucrat as interested primarily in minimizing difficulty rather than maximizing budgets.

And even if this model was descriptive of the United States bureaucracy for which it was developed, it is doubtful whether it would be as descriptive of other countries. This is primarily because the independence accorded to bureaus in the United States is by no means typical of countries where the cabinet departments are more dominant. Likewise, the career for civil servants outside the United States is less within a single organization. As a consequence, individual civil servants may perceive their careers more within the public bureaucracy as a whole rather than in the one organization. Such a perception will then produce an emphasis on the creation of trust and dependability rather than the hiding of costs to produce growth.

Summary

Government has grown. By whatever measure we would want to apply, governments spend more money and constitute a more pervasive influence on the lives of citizens. The reasons advanced for this growth are numerous, including those enumerated above. Some support as well as some contrary evidence can be found for each of the reasons advanced. What may be happening, in fact, is the confluence of all of these above reasons; there is no single cause for the growth of government, but rather a large number of factors. And growing along with government, the public bureaucracy has become a more important institution.

THE GROWTH OF ADMINISTRATION

The public bureaucracy is an increasingly influential governmental institution. As Krislov put it:

> Bureaucracies are the late bloomers of modern political structure. They grew silently, inexorably in the underbrush—seldom noticed, little analyzed. Convenience and necessity, not ideology and legitimacy, are their life-blood; they are not loved and respected, but rather tolerated and depended on.[20]

The increasing power of the public bureaucracy is indicated by growing levels of public employment, as well as by expenditures for general governmental purposes. On a less-quantified level, the growth of bureaucratic power has been documented, discussed, and damned in a number of places.[21]

In these discussions several alternative stereotypes of the public bureaucracy have been developed. On the one hand, bureaucracy is seen as a leviathan seeking to increase its powers and operating as an integrated, monolithic institution. On the other hand, bureaucracy is pictured as a court jester; a fumbling, bumbling set of uncoordinated agencies that at best muddle through and at worst make absolute fools of themselves. The examples of the apparently foolish behavior of bureaucracies have been assembled in several places and include contradictory programs, meaningless memos, and other assorted blunders. So as one federal agency (OSHA) requires backup sirens on construction equipment, another (EPA) bans them as violating noise-pollution regulations. Each month Senator William Proxmire presents a "Golden Fleece" award for the silliest government grant. In the United Kingdom, a nationalized industry has had to go into court several times to get approval for a program that has been blocked by a local government for environmental reasons, and the failure to coordinate activities has resulted in public organizations digging up the same street dozens of times in a two-year period. The examples of bumbling proliferate, and the negative stereotypes of bureaucracy persist in the popular mind.

Our understanding of both quantitative and qualitative trends in policy formation leads us to the conclusion that we must understand public bureaucracy in order to understand policy in contemporary political systems, and further that the power of the bureaucracy is increasing steadily. Our task here is to provide an explanation of these changes in the relative powers of institutions. To that end, we argue that the reasons for this change are primarily four: the quantitative growth of public problems and concerns, the qualitative growth of those concerns, the failures of two alternative institutions—the legislature and the political executive—to cope with the changes in the policy-making environment, and bureaucracies themselves.

The Quantitative Growth of Public Concerns

To say that the scope of government has increased because there are more things done in the public sector is tautological, but it is important to note the vast array of things now done by collective action that were either unheard of, or the subjects of private action, twenty years ago. The developmental scheme proposed by Rose is one indication of this as government added first resource-mobilization activities and finally social activities to its array of functions. One bit of his evidence, reproduced in Table 1.4, shows how these functions have increased in several European nations. Thus, as well as increasing in the *level* of activity, for example, the size of the budget, government is also extending the *range* of its activities.

The increasing complexity of modern economic and social life is one obvious reason for the increase in the range of governmental activity. This complexity is a function of the technological content of modern life, in which telecommunications, atomic energy, rapid commercial air service, space travel, and the mechanization of most production are but a few examples of dramatic increases in technology that impinge upon the citizen as consumer and voter. Further, increases in the rapidity of communication and transportation, and an increasing concentration of people in urbanized areas, have required collective

TABLE 1.4
GROWTH OF GOVERNMENT: NUMBER OF AGENCIES

| Period | States | Functions (average number) | | | Total |
		Defining	Resource Mobilization	Social	
19th-century origin	22	5.7	1.7	1.1	8.5
20th-century origin	9	4.8	3.7	1.9	10.4
1913	25	5.9	4.0	1.6	11.5
1936	31	5.7	4.7	2.4	12.8
1972	32	5.6	9.1	4.4	19.2

SOURCE:
Richard Rose, "On the Priorities of Government: A Developmental Analysis of Public Policies," *European Journal of Political Research* 4 (1976): 247–89, tables 1 and 2.

decisions on matters that in simpler societies could be handled by individuals. Thus, in terms of economics, the externalities of individual behavior have tended to increase as the size and concentration of the population have increased.[22]

Not only have the externalities of individual behavior increased; so, too, have the perceptions of those externalities. Unfortunately, little research exists to document changes in perceptions of this sort, but by using somewhat softer evidence we can get some idea of the attitude changes. Such evidence is given by the increasing organization of individuals in a number of nations attempting to get regulation of things such as environmental pollution, deceptive and unsafe business practices, land use, and even economic foreign policy. Likewise, society is increasingly unwilling to allow individuals to live below certain minimum standards, so that the vast array of social functions represent, if not a perception of increased externalities, at least some concern for the ability of collective action to improve the lot of fellow citizens. Thus, modern society produces situations in which mechanisms of collective action are perceived as virtually necessary for a high quality of life. These necessities are apparently recognized by much of the population, although variably by both classes of individuals and by nations, and the bureaucracy has become the institutional manifestation of those necessities.

As well as real or perceived externalities, changes in modern social structure have tended to place pressures on government to intervene in society. For example, the rapid increases in female participation in the labor force have produced demands for public day care, after-school programs, and other programs to assist working mothers. Also, the increase of leisure time enjoyed by most people has resulted in demands for more public recreational programs. Less positively, the "breakdown" in family life in many Western nations has resulted in programs designed to deal with disturbed, displaced, and delinquent youths.

The society has not been standing still, and government has become *the* means of addressing problems of social change.

The Qualitative Growth of Public Concerns

As well as the increasing externalities of modern life and popular desire to have some regulation of economic and social problems, the technological content of life—already alluded to—has definite implications for bureaucratic dominance in decision making. Increasingly, the things that government is called upon to regulate are matters having significant technological content. This is true not only of things involving the natural sciences and engineering, but also the developing "social technology." Experts in government tend to be concentrated in the bureaucracy, with few legislative or executive structures employing their own experts. As the concerns of government are increasingly influenced by the available technology, the public bureaucracy, as the possessor of the public's share of that technology, comes increasingly to the fore.

As well as influencing its relationship with other political institutions, the level of technological sophistication of the bureaucracy has also influenced relationships with the society. As programs such as atomic energy and space exploration have developed—requiring enormous capital investment, high levels of staffing, and some national security concerns—few if any private institutions would be capable of engaging actively in the problem area even if they were legally able. This leaves government as the sole supplier of certain technological services. Private concerns that seek to engage in these technologically sophisticated activities—for example, a utility company building an atomic reactor—must seek the guidance and, more importantly, accept the regulation of the public bureaucracy. Further, research and development activities are diverted from what might be valued in the private marketplace into directions dictated more by political and bureaucratic demands. The "spin-offs" of these research efforts may have positive values for the citizens, but the interest here is in the change of location of the impetus and direction of that research from the private to the public sector.[23]

Institutional Weaknesses

The remaining reasons for the increased power of bureaucracies in contemporary political systems are institutional, related to the characteristics of bureaucracy as a political institution and the characteristics of other political institutions that are competitors for power. This competition is rarely overt, but it does have the effect of delineating the power relationships among institutions and the nature of the policies that are likely to be adopted. This section focuses on the weaknesses of the traditional decision-making institutions in government and discusses the characteristics of bureaucracy that make it a powerful actor in the policy process later.

The Legislature   The legislature has been the traditional locus of rule making in democratic political systems, and most nondemocratic systems use a legislative body to legitimate their actions to their own people and to the outside world. Given this traditional and normative role of legislatures, it is necessary to understand why they are apparently losing, if not the formal powers of decision, at least the actual role-making powers within many political systems. The gainer in this decline of legislative powers is generally the bureaucracy.

Rather obviously, the quantitative and qualitative growth of governmental concerns has contributed to this decline in power. Legislatures, by placing their organizational effort into discussion, debate and elaborate procedures for the full and open consideration of viewpoints, consequently limit their ability to consider more than a handful of issues in any one session. For example, in the period of 1970–1974 the British Parliament passed only an average of fifty-eight bills per session; approximately twenty-nine of these were bills consolidating and clarifying existing legislation, or changing administration.[24] The issues that legislatures consider may be the most important issues or may set very broad parameters of policy, but this still leaves a very large quantity of detail to be filled in by administrators. Further, the qualities valued in legislative recruitment, popular elections, or advancement within the legislature are rarely those needed to handle technically complex materials in large quantity.[25] The nonlegislative careers of most legislators are hardly those that would prepare them for such tasks except in terms of legalistic problems.

Going along with the questions of recruitment of legislators are questions concerning the structure of the institutions. Relative to the bureaucratic agencies that they must confront, legislative bodies are understaffed and underspecialized. Even when well-developed systems of legislative committees exist, as in the United States and West Germany, the members of those committees have any number of other duties that prevent their specialization in narrow policy areas. Further, few legislative bodies are lucky enough to have specialization in committees to begin with, so that policy consideration in those bodies is often a haphazard thing. Finally, even when legislative committees exist as highly specialized bodies, rarely do they have independent sources of information to draw upon in considering policy; they must rely upon information gathered and processed by a bureaucratic agency, which presumably has some interest in a particular outcome.

Finally, the relative instability of legislative bodies as compared to the bureaucracy places the legislature at a disadvantage in any power competition.[26] Even in societies that have not had high levels of governmental instability or frequent elections, legislators and legislatures are certainly more transitory than bureaucracies. Thus, a certain uncertainty surrounds the conduct of legislative business, and an opportunity arises for bureaucrats to engage in tutelage to new and inexperienced legislators. Further, the bureaucracy can always try to wait out the legislature, hoping that at the next election the people or parties in charge will change their minds, or not be there at all.

Some have argued that the desire for stability, or at least for stable personal careers, is accelerating the decline of legislatures as decision-making bodies. Fiorina and others have argued that as legislators have sought to maximize their chances for reelection they have found that the best way of doing so is to serve the constituents well, for example, helping with citizens' grievances and providing "pork-barrel" benefits, rather than making statements about national policy issues.[27] Strong advocacy of a policy runs the risk of offending voters, while effective constituency service can only benefit voters. Thus, the safe path for the legislator is to vote when he or she must, but to concentrate on service.

The Political Executive   Many of the problems of legislatures are also found in the political executives of contemporary governments. This is especially true for parliamentary systems in which executives suffer from the instability of regimes and must frequently rely on policy staffs of the legislature, such as they are. This has been described as the "problems of party government" and reflects the difficulty of any political executive imposing its will upon the ongoing administrative offices.[28] There are three particular problems that political executives have in seeking to impose their wills.

The first is a lack of skills relevant to understanding the policies that must be made, and a lack of time required to understand and manage those policies. Political executives must rely on their civil servants to shape policy and advise them about the operations of the ministry. Headey, for example, calculates that of the fifty-one appointments to departmental ministerial posts in the Wilson government of 1964–70, only five had any substantial prior knowledge of the policy area, with another five or six having some background in the area.[29] In the 1970 Heath government only four original appointees could claim specialist knowledge, with four more having some background.[30] Britain may be less well served than other countries in this regard, but hearings for cabinet posts in the United States, as well as cabinet reshuffles in any number of countries, would indicate that a knowledge of the policy area is by no means a prerequisite for a cabinet appointment.[31]

Lacking any specialized knowledge, it would be helpful if those in the political executive had sufficient time to spend in running their departments. In fact, most spend a "dog's life" in their ministerial posts.[32] Again, this may be especially evident in parliamentary systems, and even more particularly in Britain. Suleiman points out that revision of the French constitution preventing ministers from also being parliamentarians has greatly aided French ministers in running their ministries.[33] Likewise, the norms of other parliamentary systems concerning hours and the time spent in the legislatures may ease political burdens substantially.[34] Even in political systems in which political executives are not members of the legislature, they are political figures and must spend time in public appearances, receiving delegations of interest-group representatives, and other political activities, with a consequent drain on the time available to contemplate policy questions. Thus, the minister remains at a disadvantage in attempting to understand and control the work of full-time and relatively specialized civil servants.

If the disadvantages of time and skill were not enough, the political executive also is seriously outnumbered in his attempts to impose external political goals upon a bureaucratic structure. Compared to the size of most administrative bodies, the number of political appointees who are imposed upon the top of the organization is quite small, but the appointees are expected to control all activities within the organization. This number is, of course, variable by political system; the United States and France, for example, have considerably more political appointees than the United Kingdom. But the numbers still pale in comparison to the size of the full-time bureaucracy.

Finally, the need for civil servants to accept the will of their political masters and actually put into effect a partisan program is another obstacle to effective political control. Although few civil servants systematically sabotage or even obstruct the stated program of a minister, they still have their own departmental or ideological concerns, which may impede the smooth flow of work. From all that is known about human nature and behavior in organizations, it is unlikely that civil servants who disagree with, or are genuinely neutral toward, a policy will administer it with the same alacrity and vigor as they will a policy they like. Further, given the handicaps under which many ministers labor, civil servants are frequently able to control the agenda of the minister sufficiently so that few programs actually hostile to the interests of the civil service will be considered. The need for a neutral civil service has been discussed even in societies such as the United Kingdom that have a strong tradition of impartiality.[35]

The tendency of administrators to drag their feet, or at least not administer vigorously, will be exacerbated in situations of high politicization both of particular policies and of the society in general. For example, when a political system is divided communally and changes occur in the composition of the political leadership, frequently this may require the reshuffling of many senior civil servants so that the two may have the ability to cooperate somewhat effectively. Perhaps the most general point that can be made is that civil servants have little to gain by close cooperation with politicians. Their careers are largely untouched by politicians, and it may in fact be a detriment to be too closely identified with a particular political party or politician—especially if they lose office.

The Nature of Bureaucratic Institutions

Although bureaucratic institutions should not be blamed for (or credited with) the growth of the public sector, they do have some influence on the redistribution of powers away from elective institutions and in the direction of the bureaucracy itself. We will not adopt the totally cynical view that agencies are concerned only with the growth of the agency budget, but neither can we adopt the more naive view that agencies are concerned entirely with the performance of their constitutionally and legally designated tasks.[36] The truth probably lies somewhere in between. Further, attempts at bureaucratic "empire building" may be closely related to the desire of the agency to survive and also to perform functions that it considers essential to a high quality of life for the society. Thus, despite the obvious attempts of the Pentagon at times to increase the military budget to feed its own needs, it is only fair to say that officials in the Department of Defense sincerely believe that they are supplying an essential service to the society. Or, as Cleaves wrote of the Chilean bureaucracy:

> Derogatory comments on bureaucracy's tendency to consolidate its power (e.g., empire building, prestige accrual) are value judgments to the extent that they are not examined in context of the agency's need to increase its capacity for goal-oriented behavior.[37]

In addition, the model of bureaucratic dominance in policy making assumes that agencies will compete over scarce resources—the budget—and for control of policy choices. This competition would appear to limit the extent to which any integrated bureaucratic governance might emerge, given that the bureaucracy would tend to behave as a set of competitive entrepreneurs rather than as a unified political force. However, it can also be argued that bureaucracies are competitive primarily when their core interests are threatened; they rarely engage in conflict at the edge of their "policy space."[38] Likewise, in the budgetary process they can perhaps be best seen as satisfiers, rather than maximizers, again seeking to ensure survival of the organization rather than the domination of a policy field. Perhaps the best analogy would be with the balance of power in international affairs in which all actors involved attempt to gain security through limited or tacit cooperation rather than overt competition.

Even if the bureaucracy as a whole does not constitute a unified political force, it may still constitute a formidable force within individual agencies. We have already noted the ability of the permanent staff essentially to determine the agenda for their presumed political masters. This becomes especially important in the presence of an agency ideology concerning proper agency goals and proper means of attaining those goals. Through the ability to control information, proposals for policy, and the knowledge concerning feasibility, the bureaucracy is certainly capable of influencing agency policy, if not determining it. It requires an unusual politician to be able to overcome this type of control within an agency.

Thus, we can view the bureaucracy as being in a powerful position in competition with its ostensible masters. Having control of information and of the instigation of policy alternatives, having an expert knowledge of the subject matter, and having a ministerial or departmental ideology concerning the manner in which the subject matter should be treated, the bureaucracy can control decisions actually adopted by the partisans at the top. Further, competition between agencies, which might serve to limit such powers, is usually confined to a small number of issues in which the basic interests of one or more agencies overlap. Within its purview, each agency remains supreme and consequently can dominate or influence its own political masters.

COUNTERTRENDS IN GOVERNMENT GROWTH

Lest we think that all goes well for the statist position in modern society, we should mention several important countertrends that tend to restrain the growth of government and of the public bureaucracy. One obvious fact has been the "taxpayers' backlash" and the associated strength of more conservative political parties in the late 1970s and 1980s. This has been manifested in events such as the passage of Proposition 13 in California to limit the property tax and the elections of Margaret Thatcher, Ronald Reagan, and a bourgeois government in Sweden (1974–82). Also, the strength of tax protest parties such as the Progress Party (Mogens Glistrup) in Denmark and the Anders Lange Party in Norway illustrate the political power of groups seeking to dismantle some of the structure of the contemporary welfare state. It is debatable whether these reactions are against government in general, or only against certain aspects of taxation and expenditure. Wilensky and Hibbs and Madsen have argued that visible, direct taxes, rather than taxation in general, are what populations are protesting by these votes.[39] However, for whatever reasons, words like "privatization" and "deregulation" are now common parlance in political circles that a decade ago may have been discussing new programs.

In addition to expressing their concerns by voting for political parties favoring reduced taxation, citizens have taken more direct action. The amount of increase in tax evasion is a matter of some debate, but there is general agreement that there has been such an increase.[40] The rejection of the legal claims of government to their money may be taken as an indicator of a more general rejection by citizens of the government's claims on the society in general.[41]

Associated with changes in behavior have been changes in attitudes. Table 1.5 shows that citizens are expressing less support for government and for the public bureaucracy in particular. By the late 1970s there are solid majorities against increased public expenditure in each country for which we have data. These majorities are particularly strong in the United States, but it is interesting to note that citizens of two of the most advanced welfare states—Denmark and Sweden—also show reservations about increased expenditures and taxation.

TABLE 1.5
CITIZENS' EVALUATION OF GOVERNMENT

	1962	1963	1964	1965	1966	1967	1968	1969	1970	1971	1972	1973	1974	1975	1976	1977	1978
United States																	
Percent agree, "Government wastes a lot of tax money"			48		61		61		70		67		76		76		80
Percent agree, "Income tax too high"	47				52	58		66				64	69	72	73	69	70
Percent confidence in leaders of executive branch					41					23		19	28	13	11	23	14
United Kingdom																	
Percent prefer current level rather than more spending			23	48					51			47					48
Sweden																	
Percent agree that social reforms have gone so far that states should reduce rather than increase							41	52									
Percent agree that social welfare system is too expensive and should be cut back						34						60			60		39
Denmark																	
Percent agree that politicians are too lavish										85		91		84		77	

SOURCES:
Douglas A. Hibbs and Henrik Jens Madsen, "Public Reactions to the Growth of Taxation and Government Expenditure," *World Politics* 33 (1981): 413–35.
"Opinion Roundup," *Public Opinion* 1 (July/August, 1978): 30–31.

TABLE 1.6
CITIZENS' EVALUATION OF PUBLIC SPENDING

	1968	1973	1974	1975	1976	1977	1978	1980
United States								
Government spends								
too much for:								
a) foreign aid		70	76	73	75	66	67	71
b) welfare		51	42	43	60	60	58	60
c) defense		38	31	31	27	23	22	—
d) helping blacks		22	21	24	25	25	25	—
e) urban problems		12	11	12	20	19	19	—
f) education		9	9	11	9	10	11	9
g) health		5	5	5	5	7	7	—
United Kingdom								
Government spends								
too much for:								
a) defense	37				21			19
b) national health								
service	21				12			4
c) education	18				15			5
d) roads	8				23			6
e) old-age pensions	2				3			1

SOURCES:
"Opinion Roundup," *Public Opinion* 1 (July/August, 1978): 32.
"Opinion Roundup," *Public Opinion* 6 (April/May, 1983): 27.

These majorities against public expenditure tend to vanish, however, when particular expenditures are discussed. In Table 1.6 we see that when citizens are asked about programs in the United States and the United Kingdom, there are majorities for cutting only two programs. Likewise, people who voted for Proposition 13 in California were in the majority in favor of cutting only one program—welfare.[42] The hostility expressed to public revenue collection and expenditure may therefore be quite shallow, and when the positive benefits created by government are remembered attitudes may differ.

SUMMARY

This chapter should help preface what is to come in the remainder of the book. It establishes one crucial part of the environment within which contemporary public administration functions. This is that government in the late twentieth century is very big government, which makes the job of public administrators much more difficult. In the first place it means that any organization being managed is likely to be a large organization with complex interrelationships with other public and private organizations. Even small local governments now require skilled management to be effective and efficient.

The second problem that arises is a constraint on resources available to the administrator: real resources, for example, money; and the "policy space" in which to function in making new policies. Anything an administrator is likely to want to accomplish may involve him or her in a conflict with other organizations over money and over "turf." With limited resources, the conflicts that arise over the use of resources become more intense.

Finally, citizens are ever more wary and watchful of government in general and the public bureaucracy in particular. The majority of public administrators do not "flee" from accountability for their actions, but the level of concern of citizens may make doing the job more difficult. Also, even in societies where public service has been a respected profession, the "bureaucracy" is increasingly a negative symbol of what is wrong with the country. This negative image cannot help but harm morale.

NOTES

1. For a review see Patrick D. Larkey, C. Stolp, and M. Winer, "Theorizing about the Growth of Government: A Research Assessment," *Journal of Public Policy* 1 (1981): 157–220.
2. See pp. 23–24.
3. J. R. A. Willis and P. J. W. Hardwick, *Tax Expenditures in the United Kingdom* (London: Heinemann, 1978).
4. See Stanley Surrey, *Pathways to Tax Reform* (Cambridge, Mass.: Harvard University Press, 1973).
5. Andrew S. Carron, "Fiscal Activities Outside the Budget," in Joseph A. Pechman, ed., *Setting National Priorities: The 1982 Budget* (Washington, D.C.: The Brookings Institution, 1981), pp. 261–9.
6. Anthony Barker, ed., *Quangos in Britain* (London: Macmillan, 1982).
7. S. N. Eisenstadt, "Bureaucracy, Bureaucratization, Markets and Power Structures," in *Essays on Comparative Institutions*, S. N. Eisenstadt, ed., (New York: John Wiley, 1965), pp. 172–215.
8. Gabriel A. Almond and G. Bingham Powell, *Comparative Politics: A Developmental Approach* (Boston: Little, Brown, 1966), pp. 195–6.
9. See Richard A. Musgrave, *Fiscal Systems* (New Haven, Conn.: Yale University Press, 1969), pp. 69–90.
10. John Kenneth Galbraith, *The Affluent Society*, 2nd. ed. (New York: Houghton Mifflin, 1969).
11. Alan T. Peacock and Jack Wiseman, *The Growth of Public Expenditure in the United Kingdom* (Princeton: Princeton University Press, 1961).
12. W. J. Baumol, "Macroeconomics of Unbalanced Growth: Anatomy of Urban Crisis," *American Economic Review* 57 (1967): 414–26.

13. H. M. Treasury, *Public Expenditure White Paper: Handbook on Methodology* (London: HMSO, 1972).

14. William Spangar Pierce, *Bureaucratic Failure and Public Expenditure* (New York: Academic Press, 1981), pp. 60–68.

15. Theodore J. Lowi, *The End of Liberalism*, 2nd. ed. (New York: W. W. Norton, 1979).

16. Garrett Hardin and John Baden, eds., *Managing the Commons* (San Francisco: W. H. Freeman, 1977).

17. James O'Connor, *The Fiscal Crisis of the State* (New York: St. Martin's, 1973); Ian Gough, *The Political Economy of the Welfare State* (London: Macmillan, 1979).

18. William A. Niskanen, *Bureaucracy and Representative Government* (Chicago: Aldine/Atherton, 1971).

19. See L. L. Wade, "Public Administration, Public Choice and the Pathos of Reform" (University of California, Davis, mimeo, n.d.)

20. Samuel Krislov, *Representative Bureaucracy* (Englewood Cliffs, N.J.: Prentice-Hall, 1974), pp. 40–41.

21. But see Charles Goodsell, *The Case for Bureaucracy* (Chatham, N.J.: Chatham House, 1982).

22. Charles H. Wolf, Jr., "A Theory of Non-Market Failure: Framework for Implementation Analysis," *Journal of Law and Economics* 22 (1979): 107–40.

23. Albert D. Biderman, "Social Indicators and Goals," in *Social Indicators*, Raymond A. Bauer, ed., (Cambridge, Mass.: MIT Press, 1973), p. 43.

24. Ivor Burton and Gavin Drewry, *Legislation and Public Policy in the 1970–74 Parliaments* (London: Macmillan, 1981), p. 112.

25. Richard Rose, "The Making of Cabinet Ministers," *British Journal of Political Science* 1 (1971): 393–414.

26. A. Grosser, "The Evolution of European Parliaments," in *A New Europe?*, Stephen A. Graubard, ed. (Boston: Little, Brown, 1964).

27. Morris Fiorina, *Congress: Keystone of the Washington Establishment* (New Haven: Yale University Press, 1977).

28. Richard Rose, *The Problem of Party Government* (London: Macmillan, 1974).

29. Bruce Headey, *British Cabinet Ministers* (London: George Allen and Unwin, 1974), pp. 83–109.

30. Ibid.

31. In her hearings for confirmation as secretary of housing and urban development, Carla Hills Anderson stated she knew little if anything about housing policy but expected to learn in office. *New York Times*, 25 February 1975. A rather similar exchange took place when Richard Adelman was being considered as a disarmament negotiator in the Reagan administration.

32. E. Marples, "A Dog's Life at the Ministry," in *Policy-Making in Britain*, Richard Rose, ed. (London: Macmillan, 1969), pp. 128–31.

33. Ezra N. Suleiman, *Politics, Power and Bureaucracy in France* (Princeton: Princeton University Press, 1974), pp. 164–70. Suleiman argues, however, that the nature of the party system is more important than the structural arrangement in determining relationships between ministers and civil servants in France.

34. For example, until recently the respective analogues of the Question Hour in France and West Germany have been easily disregarded by the government. In several parliamentary systems the Question Hour does not exist as a check on the executive.
35. F. F. Ridley, "The British Civil Service and Politics: Principles in Question and Traditions in Flux," *Parliamentary Affairs* 36 (1983): 28–48.
36. Robert D. Putnam describes these as the classical and the political bureaucrat. See his "Political Attitudes of Senior Civil Servants in Britain, Germany, and Italy," *American Political Science Review* 3, no. 2 (June 1973): 257–90.
37. Peter S. Cleaves, *Bureaucratic Politics and Administration in Chile* (Berkeley: University of California Press, 1974), pp. 310–11.
38. Anthony Downs, *Inside Bureaucracy* (Boston: Little, Brown, 1967).
39. Harold Wilensky, *The Welfare State and Equality* (Berkeley: University of California Press, 1975); Douglas A. Hibbs and Henrik Jens Madsen, "Public Reactions to the Growth of Taxation and Government Expenditure," *World Politics* 33 (1981): 413–35.
40. See, among others, Edward L. Feige, "The Other Economy: How Big Is the Irregular Economy," *Challenge* (November/December, 1980): 6–10; "Le Travail Noir en Europe et aux Etats Unis," *Intersocial* 61 (1980): 3–16.
41. Richard Rose and B. Guy Peters, *Can Government Go Bankrupt?* (New York: Basic Books, 1978).
42. Jack Citrin, "Do People Want Something for Nothing?: Public Opinion on Taxes and Government Spending," *National Tax Journal* 32, Supplement (1979): 113–29; Peter Taylor-Gooby, "Two Cheers for the Welfare State: Public Opinion and Private Welfare," *Journal of Public Policy* 2 (1982): 319–46.

CHAPTER 2

POLITICAL CULTURE
AND
PUBLIC ADMINISTRATION

Citizens do not interpret the behavior of their government in a vacuum. They are equipped by their society with an image of what constitutes good government and good administration. This "picture" of good government is actually comprised of a set of rather complex cognitive and evaluative structures that tend to be (relatively) common among all members of the society. We refer to these generally shared psychological orientations as *political culture*. [1] Although at times this common culture is directly imparted to children through civics courses and patriotic exercises, the acquisition of a political culture is usually part of the more general process of learning about the society. Thus, just as the child learns the prevailing norms concerning economic behavior, social interaction, and child rearing, he or she also learns how to understand and evaluate politics and government. This process of learning political values and political culture is referred to as *political socialization*. [2]

We have already seen that the social and economic systems of a country place boundaries on the actions of government, and more specifically public administration. Political culture is equally important in setting boundaries, although the boundaries are less tangible than those determined by economic conditions. By defining what in government is good and bad, the culture may virtually mandate some actions and prohibit others.

Despite the seemingly abstract and vague nature of these cultural boundaries, governments can violate the prevailing political norms only at risk. This is true no matter how antiquated and vestigial this element of the culture may be. This is not to say that a society's cultural values are immutable. Culture is subject to change, and there is a constant interaction of culture and politics that redefines the role of government. For example, the latitude of action allowed governments at present would have been unthinkable before two world wars, one major economic depression, and a cold war fundamentally altered popular perceptions of the role of government.[3] Nevertheless, at the same time that the scope of government has been allowed to expand, some of the other values supporting a democratic political system, such as freedom and equality, have remained important, or have actually increased in importance to citizens.[4]

The remainder of this chapter examines the effects of political culture on the nature of the public administrative system. The comparisons made are of two varieties: (1) between political systems, commenting on the differences in administration in different countries, which may be a function of differences in their cultures; and (2) within systems across time.

ADMINISTRATIVE CULTURE

For our purposes, we can think of culture as existing at three distinct levels: societal, political, and administrative. The conceptual relationship between these three levels can be seen in Figure 2.1. Notice that all three types

FIGURE 2.1
CULTURE AND PUBLIC ADMINISTRATION

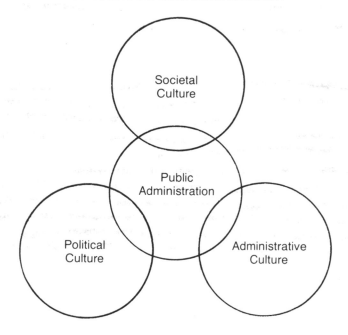

of culture—societal, political, and administrative—influence the conduct of public administration. Very general value orientations in the society will influence the behavior of individuals in formal organizations, as well as the manner in which those organizations are formed. The political culture will in part structure the relationships between political and bureaucratic elites, and between the population and the bureaucracy. Finally, the general orientation of the society toward management and impersonal authority in formal organizations will also affect the behavior of public officials. Public bureaucracies are sometimes portrayed as running roughshod over their societies, but they are bound by many thin but strong bonds to their societies and their values.

General Societal Culture

Let us first look at several aspects of societal culture that affect the performance of administration. The first of these concerns the basic question of the acceptability of "bureaucracy" as a means of large-scale organization in the society. A culture will have a basic set of evaluations of bureaucratic structures not only in government but also in any large-scale organization. Likewise, those societies that tend to adopt bureaucratic forms of management for one type of enterprise will tend to adopt bureaucratic means for all types of enterprise. In discussing some aspects of these patterns, Bendix made the distinction between entrepreneurial and bureaucratic societies.[5] Great Britain is used as an example of an entrepreneurial society. The development and management of British enterprise has traditionally been an entrepreneurial action, despite the rather early acceptance of corporations and limited liability. The style of management tended to remain personal, the development of a rather extensive administrative apparatus notwithstanding. The administration of public policy in Great Britain would appear to follow many of the same entrepreneurial channels. Despite the development of the bureaucracy in Whitehall, the manner of functioning of public administration appears to be decision through personal bargaining and negotiation rather than through a bureaucratic imposition of authority. This process is evidently carried on in an informal, personalistic manner based on personal acquaintances and personal trust.[6]

The opposite of this entrepreneurial approach to administration is the institutionalized bureaucratic style of administration that has characterized Germany. This is, of course, a common stereotype of the culture of Germany (either East or West) but is also rather descriptive of styles of administration. Bureaucracy is the dominant form of social organization, just as the informality of the committee is the dominant form of organization in Great Britain.[7] This is true not only in government but also in economic, social, and cultural organizations. Likewise, authority and status relationships have been described as dominating the more general form of social relationships, including family relationships.[8] In such a society, bureaucracy and its emphasis on authority relationships is a natural and acceptable form of public organization. This is considerably less acceptable in a society more oriented toward personal and informal decision making as in the United Kingdom, or the even more extreme case of the United States.[9] This is especially interesting given that the societies are equally concerned with the equal application of the rule of law to individual citizens.[10] However, the increasing role of bureaucrats in policy making appears to be creating stress within the government of the United Kingdom, while it is accepted quite readily in Germany.[11]

Bendix was discussing primarily differences among Western industrialized nations, but there are perhaps even more significant differences between that set of nations and the non-Western and nonindustrialized nations. In general, the non-Western world is less accepting of the use of bureaucratic methods than is the Western world. Attempts to import this Western concept into the non-Western world have often resulted in the adoption of formal aspects of bureaucracy but the circumventing of procedural norms. Riggs, in his discussion of the use of bureaucratic methods in underdeveloped countries, talks about the "sala" model of administration—having the form of a Western bureaucracy but actually filled with individuals operating according to more traditional norms of family and communal loyalty. Even in an economically developed albeit non-Western society such as Japan, the norms of personal loyalty tend to supplant any bureaucratic reliance on authority, achievement, and rules.[12]

Related to societal acceptance of bureaucracy as a means of organization is the acceptance of impersonality and universality of rules. Parsons has discussed this characteristic as one of his five pattern variables describing general patterns of cultural development.[13] Bureaucracies depend for their smooth functioning on the acceptance of impersonality and universality of rules. If rules must be renegotiated for each individual, bureaucracies become not only inefficient, they become superfluous as well. Bureaucracies have been developed to provide consistency and universality in the application of rules demanded by law as well as "modern" conceptions of fairness.

What sort of cultural systems tend to support this bureaucratic concept of universality and impersonality of rules? It can be associated with what we will call *rationalist*, or *deductive*, cultures.[14] These have become characteristic of most developed countries but are especially well developed in continental Europe. These cultures tend to emphasize the deduction of specific statements from general statements. It is only a short step from this type of argument in the general social culture to the bureaucratic style of decision making, in which decision about an individual case is made on the basis of deductive reasoning from a legal premise. This is to some degree manifested in the legal system of codified law, which attempts to detail every aspect of the law and thereby to minimize the need for personal discretion. In these cases, if the deduction of the specific is performed correctly, there is no basis for argument. Both client and administrator can accept the adequacy of the ruling. The client may not always like the ruling made by the administrator, but the correctness of the impersonal nature of the application is difficult to question within such a cultural context.

The rationalistic culture may be contrasted with the *pragmatic*, or *empirical*, culture that has been said to characterize the United Kingdom and much of Northern Europe.[15] In these cultures, generalities are derived from a series of individual decisions. This type of culture is perhaps best typified by English (and American) common law, built up from centuries of individual decisions. This culture is not so amenable to the development of bureaucracies or to impersonal decisions. Each case is, to some degree, a new case, and the particular individual circumstances may be sufficient to modify or overturn an apparent generality. Here, administrative and legal decisions are almost inherently personal, and, although precedent may rule, each case may be contested on its personal merits. This should not be taken to mean that the United Kingdom and the United States do not have bureaucratic organizations. By almost any definition of bureaucracy this would be a foolish statement. Rather, there will tend to be less rigidity and impersonality accepted in these more inductive cultures than would be true in the more deductive continental systems. The concept of individuality and individual rights, as one component of the more empirical culture, tends to make the job of the bureaucrat more difficult and forces more attention on specifics rather than on the generalities of the case.

Katz and Eisenstadt point to an interesting case in which the norms of impersonality developed by a bureaucratic system are undermined by an influx of clients unaccustomed to those norms.[16] Israel was settled initially by Jews of European origin accustomed to the norms of impersonal and universal rule applications. These same norms were not held, however, by later waves of immigrants from the Eastern branches of Judaism. Socialized into the largely personalistic and barter cultures of the underdeveloped nations, the new settlers were unwilling to accept even the most basic universal rules, for example, that everyone who rides the bus should pay the same fare. Moreover, these immigrants were to constitute a major portion of the caseload for a number of social-service agencies in Israel. Interestingly, both the clients and the administrative structures found it necessary to modify their behavior in order to accommodate to the strains on their usual behavior patterns. The immigrants tended to adopt some of the basic ideas of impersonality, but the administrators also became more aware of personal differences among clients. Caiden found rather similar conflicts between the older immigrants to Israel, who were prepared to operate in a Middle-Eastern style, and the native-born sabras, who were more oriented toward impersonality and bureaucracy.[17]

The above example brings to light two important aspects of the relationship of culture and administration. The first is the "barter" nature of the cultures of most of the underdeveloped world.[18] These nations present a variety and richness in cultural patterns, while impersonality and universality of rules remain largely attributes of developed and Western societies. In the non-Western world, all decisions are assumed to be subject to influence through personal bargaining and negotiation. Thus, any formal rules promulgated by the bureaucracy constitute merely a place to begin the bargaining. Likewise, Riggs has noted that societies in transition from traditional societies to modernity, which he terms "prismatic," adopt a style of decision making that he refers to as "double-talk."[19] He notes:

> Even more typically prismatic is a law which provides for one policy although in practice a different policy prevails. A rule is formally announced but is not effectively enforced. The formalistic appearance of the rule contrasts with its actual administration—officials are free to make choices, enforcing or disregarding the rule at will. We have already seen that over-conformity and nonenforcement of laws is typically prismatic. It makes possible prismatic codes which, while appearing to promulgate a rule, in fact permit a wide variety of personalized choices by enforcement officials. . . . Apparent rules mask without guiding actual choices.[20]

Thus, we can imagine a rough continuum of cultural orientations toward impersonality and universalistic rules ranging from the barter cultures described by Riggs and others to the highly rationalistic attitudes of continental European countries. On such a continuum, the pragmatic culture of the United Kingdom might be close to a halfway point. That is, compared to many non-Western political systems, the political culture of Great Britain would appear quite accepting of impersonal rules. When compared to other advanced and industrial countries of Europe, however, the culture of the United Kingdom is more personal and less bureaucratic than most other nations at similar levels of development.

The second point emphasized by the Katz and Eisenstadt research is interaction in the setting of the norms of administration. We have been stressing the importance of the lower echelons of administration and of contact with clients. Not only is this type of contact crucial for the client, it may also be crucial for the organization in the definition of its policies. Here we have the case of the organization modifying its basic orientation toward clients and toward administration on the basis of a problem in applying rules to specific clients. We can argue that at least formally the organizations could have continued to apply rules impersonally. In this case, however, the organization chose to innovate and innovated successfully to meet client needs. Organizations willing to make this type of innovation will be more successful in the long run than organizations that maintain rigid bureaucratic procedures even in the face of nonbureaucratic clients.[21] Evidence in this respect is limited, but it is important for the effectiveness of administration.

In summary, we have examined two aspects of the cultural values of society that are potentially important for understanding public administration. This is only a sample of these types of values, but any further enumeration runs the risk of being somewhat tedious. It would further distract attention from the more important relationships of the political culture of a society to the functioning of public administration. To the examination of these political aspects of the culture, and their relationships to public administration, we now turn our attention.

Political Culture and Administration

In discussing political culture, we are concerned with the specific orientations of individuals toward politics as one type of social action and societal decision making. Public administration is a part of government and may therefore best be analyzed from this more politicized perspective.

Unfortunately for our purposes, the analysis and classification of political culture have been concentrated largely on the input side of the political system. Thus, attention has been given to attitudes and values concerning political participation, democratic procedures, political efficacy, and political involvement.[22] Much less attention has been given to classifying the orientations of citizens to the institutions of government, and to the outputs of the political system. In this respect, our knowledge of popular conceptions of administration is even weaker than our knowledge concerning people's feelings concerning legislatures, the political executive, and perhaps even the courts.

There is an increasing body of information about the ways in which citizens evaluate their public bureaucracies, especially in industrialized societies, as illustrated in Table 2.1. How these data are evaluated may depend upon whether one thinks the glass is half empty or half full. On the one hand, given some of the exaggerated statements made about the incompetence and venality of public officials, the ratings of public officials are generally rather good. On the other hand, the ratings are not as good for public sector employees as for private sector employees. Even for fairness, which should be the public sector's strongest point (see chapter 8), the public sector did not generally rate as high as the private sector.[23] Further, some of the evidence suggests that actual contacts with the public service, even if favorable, have little impact upon attitudes; the evaluation of the public sector appears to be culturally determined, as much as determined by the actual performance of government.[24]

The evidence of citizens' attitudes toward the public bureaucracy is spotty in the developed countries, but it is extremely difficult to find for less-developed countries. Almond and Verba examined the administrative competence of citizens in five countries, including Mexico.[25] They sought to determine the degree to which these citizens feel capable of influencing administrative decisions. There was considerable variation among the countries, with over half the respondents in Germany and Great Britain feeling capable of exerting such an influence, while only 8 percent of Mexican respondents felt their protests would make any difference. Eldersveld, Jagannadham, and Barnabas, building on the work of Janowitz, Wright, and Delany, have been able to make some comparisons between citizens' attitudes toward administration in the United States and India.[26] Although the Indian sample was more willing to work in public jobs

TABLE 2.1
POPULAR EVALUATIONS OF PUBLIC BUREAUCRACY

A. Fairness (percentage of those answering)

	United States (Government)	Canada	
		Government	Business
Good and Very Good	43.8	68.9	84.4
So-so	29.2	21.1	10.6
Bad and Very Bad	27.0	10.1	4.9
Total	100.0	100.1	99.9

B. Government vs. Business (United States)

	Government Better	Same	Business Better	No Answer
Considerate	11.5	47.8	37.5	3.2
Fair	18.8	33.6	44.5	3.1

C. Public Employees Are . . . (percentage responding yes)

	United States	Australia
Too Numerous	67	54
Working Less Hard than Business	67	63

SOURCES:
David Zussman, "The Image of the Public Service in Canada," *Canadian Public Administration* 25 (1982): 63–80.
Daniel Katz et al., *Bureaucratic Encounters* (Ann Arbor, Mich.: Survey Research Center, University of Michigan, 1975).
The Bulletin (Sydney), 20 August 1977.

than private jobs, their general evaluation of public administration was much less positive than that of a sample in Detroit. The Indians felt that they were treated badly in their interactions with administrators and had a cynical view of corruption and favoritism in the public bureaucracy of India. This may be accounted for, in part, by the "prismatic" nature of India and of Indian administration, but it also points out that, despite Levy's findings, Americans are not entirely negative concerning their administrative structures, especially when compared to the attitudes of citizens of underdeveloped countries.[27]

Leaving aside for the time being a lack of much direct evidence concerning popular orientations toward administration, we can undertake a more analytical discussion of the effects of political culture on administration. This should begin with some of the possible dimensions for analysis. As mentioned previously, the majority of analyses of political culture have dealt almost exclusively with political participation. Thus, Almond and Verba speak of parochial, subject, and participant cultures on the basis of the willingness of the individual to participate on the input side of politics.[28] Almond and Powell use cultural secularization as one of their three variables to describe political development.[29] Although this is a broad concept, one of the primary components is an orientation toward politics involving manipulation and the attainment of individual goals through political action. We do not want to paint with too broad a brush, however. Some discussions of political culture have been concerned with problems of authority and of governmental institutions. Nettl has used "constitutional" and "elitist" as the two basic dimensions of his analysis of culture, with these two dimensions defined largely by the authority relationships within the society and polity.[30] This is therefore somewhat similar to Eckstein's discussion of authority as a crucial dimension of the analysis of political culture.[31] Likewise, Elazar's discussion of the dimensions of political culture in the United States rather explicitly involves a discussion of the cultural acceptability of certain types of public policies.[32]

Dimensions of Political Culture

There obviously have been a number of attempts to classify political cultures. Perhaps the most useful general categorization of the dimensions of political culture has been provided by Lucian Pye in the introductory essay to *Political Culture and Political Development.*[33] He develops four dimensions for the examination of political inputs, dimensions that are also useful for our analysis of the administrative aspects of government.

Hierarchy and Equality   The first dimension is hierarchy and equality. Most administrative structures have a hierarchical structuring of personnel and authority in a formal organization, and cultural values concerning authority and impersonality of rules are important here. Several more basic political questions also come to mind when we think of hierarchy and equality in administration.

First, what are the means of recruitment into administrative positions? Parsons has used the terms "ascription" and "achievement" to describe how societies recruit people to positions.[34] In an achievement-oriented society, an individual's place in society is determined by ability. Advancement in society is determined by what the individual can do, not by who he is. Ascriptive societies recruit individuals to positions in society (and administration) on the basis of ascriptive criteria—class, status, race, language, caste—and the individual's position is determined by these largely immutable personal characteristics. As one would imagine, achievement criteria have generally been linked with "modern" society, while ascriptive criteria have been linked with "traditional" society. As discussed by Weber, as well as most other commentators on administration, bureaucracy and administration are inherently modern and achievement-oriented components of the political system.[35] Voters may choose a traditional elite to rule the country, but the bureaucracy would (in theory) still select the best people regardless of socio-economic position or other ascriptive characteristics. This is true in theory, but the actual application of the principle varies markedly from society to society.

Equality in the recruitment of administrators is discussed at length in chapter 4, but some comment is necessary at this juncture. Equality of recruitment has been most thoroughly examined in the United Kingdom. Kingsley's seminal discussion of representative bureaucracy in Britain found that the middle classes are heavily overrepresented in the higher civil service.[36] The study was, however, ambivalent concerning the effects of that overrepresentation. It is probable that even bureaucracies recruited on the most achievement-oriented basis possible would still display this same dominance of the middle and upper classes because of the correlation between social class and the ability to take standardized tests, success in school, and so forth.[37] Nevertheless, the degree of equality or inequality in recruitment can be seen as a function of egalitarian norms in the society.

Equality is especially important given the composition of the clientele of most public bureaucracies. While a number of administrators are concerned with business and industry, agriculture, foreign policy, and defense, the majority of the clients of public agencies are from the relatively disadvantaged segments of the population. Thus, we come to the common situation of middle-class administrators attempting to provide solutions for working-class problems. While there may be a common national culture, there may still be differences among social classes in their values.[38] This problem is especially important when class lines coincide with ethnic, linguistic, or other cleavages. On this basis, some have advocated the recruitment of administrators on a quota basis to ensure that administration accurately reflects the society it is attempting to govern. This solution, of course, can easily be interpreted as running counter to the concern for achievement-oriented recruitment.

Equality raises a second question for administration. As previously stated several times, bureaucratic organizations as they have been known in Western societies have involved the use of hierarchical authority. Superiors in the organizations have always attempted to exercise their authority to tell subordinates what to do. Various cultural groups have been more willing than others to accept this authority. Crozier points to distinct differences in the acceptance of authority among French, British, American, and Russian organizations.[39] He points out that French organizations are plagued by the inability of many of their members to accept authoritative commands from a superior, while patterns of deference in British culture made such an authoritative command quite acceptable. Massive changes in orientations toward authority have taken place in Western societies, but many of the problems and differences cited by Crozier persist.[40] Likewise, several studies of administration in developing societies point out that orders from a superior may be obeyed as a function of the personal following of that individual, rather than from an acceptance of the authority of the position.[41] Despite these differences, acceptance of authority has declined in all developed nations. This may be seen as a part of the new individualism of the "postindustrial society."[42] Alternatives to the traditional hierarchical structuring of organizations have been proposed with such titles as "dialectical organizations" and "collaboration-consensus" organizations.[43] These, and myriad other proposed reforms, have had in common the replacement of authority with spontaneous forms of organization based on the equality of the members within the work group. The leaders and the led would be replaced by groups of collaborators.

Some of the most important efforts in the direction of equality in organizations have taken place in industrial management. Going under the general label of "industrial democracies," some organizations have replaced the leadership of the foreman with joint decision making by the work group. For example, workers at the Volvo and Saab plants in Sweden have been able to choose their own work leaders and own working pace and times.[44] A number of companies have also imported mechanisms, such as "quality circles" from Japan, in an attempt to create greater involvement of the workers in their jobs and improve the quality of the products.[45] Finally, in West Germany and Scandinavia companies are required to give places on their boards of directors to representatives of workers, and this practice has been proposed for other industrial countries.[46]

These new forms of organizational management pose a unique problem for public organizations: the role of the client in relationship to the organization. Public organizations tend to be "people-processing" organizations in which the product has the same sorts of human needs as the producer.[47] As such, the position of the client as either subordinate or participant must be defined by the organization. Few public organizations could afford the luxury of making the client an equal partner in the decision-making process, no matter how normatively desirable such a form of organization might be to some observers (and clients). At the same time, the organization does have the opportunity and ability to involve clients in some aspects of decision making concerning their cases and the general functioning of the organization. The evidence coming from the first decade of the postindustrial society indicates that clients are increasingly unwilling to accept a passive and subordinated position in the organization. Just as do the employees, clients seek self-actualization and some control over their lives. This plea for equality will probably present public organizations with some of their most pressing problems. This is especially true given that one of the reasons for maintaining an unequal status for clients in participatory terms is to maintain greater equality in the outputs that are provided to clients.[48]

Liberty and Coercion   Closely allied with hierarchy and equality is the dimension of liberty and its opposite, coercion. As a gross generality, most of the societies discussed here have been undergoing changes in their value systems favoring decreased economic liberty and increased liberty of expression and social action.[49] It is often the bureaucracy that must decide the limits of both types of liberty and also determine how much coercion is acceptable in enforcing these decisions. This is, of course, true for economic regulatory agencies, but we often fail to remember that the police are themselves one of the most ubiquitous forms of administration. We can make the argument that the stability of a democratic society may depend upon the degree of value consensus among the enforcers of those rules and the majority of the citizenry. As numerous student activists during the late 1960s demonstrated, and continuing protests against racial inequality, nuclear weapons, and environmental degradation have continued to demonstrate, there is apparently a great deal of value dissensus, at least across generational lines, with respect to the amount of liberty felt to be desirable and the amount of force deemed necessary to enforce one side of that argument.

Despite the above-mentioned outbursts, the application of direct physical coercion is becoming less frequent in modern societies. On the other hand, the application of indirect coercion is becoming an increasingly frequent and controversial technique of political control. Here we are referring not only to the potential use of psychological devices to exercise thought control, in the manner of an Orwell novel. Rather, we are speaking of the ability of administrative agencies to impose their wills on citizens without the opposition of those citizens. This is done in a variety of manners, the most common being the claim of efficiency and the appeal to technological criteria in decision making. It has become increasingly difficult for the average citizen, or even the exceptional citizen for that matter, to dispute the decisions made by a technologically competent and well-insulated bureaucracy. Government has therefore become an amalgamation of large organizations making decisions on their own terms and forcing them on individuals. Emmette Redford has said:

> The first characteristic of the great body of men subject to the administrative state is that they are dormant regarding most of the decisions made with respect to them. Their participation cannot in any manner equal their subjection. Subjection comes from too many directions for man's span of attention, much less his active participation, to extend to all that affects him. Any effort of the subject to participate in all that affects him would engulf him in confusion, dissipate his activity and destroy the unity of his personality. Democracy, in the sense of man's participation in all that affects him, is impossible in the administered society.[50]

We, and Professor Redford, may be guilty of overstating the case, but the possibility of administrative tyranny is apparent in even the best-administered modern societies. Here we comment on this only as a dimension of culture and leave the analysis of possible solutions to chapter 9.

Furthermore, while the possibilities for manipulation are certainly great in the administered or postindustrial state, we must not lose sight of the fact that the degree of control exercised over the individual through noncoercive means may be as great in traditional society. Thus, the period of mass democracy and liberalism of the early and middle twentieth century may merely be a point of transition between two more "totalitarian" forms of government.[51] In the traditional society, this use of nonphysical coercion is justified on the basis of religious or ideological dogma. In the postindustrial society, it is justified through appeals to efficiency and technology, which constitute the dogma of the modern society striving for cumulative social and economic rationality. However, the increasing levels of education of the population, and the consequent subjective competence to participate in political decisions, may generate increasing conflicts and tensions within postindustrial societies.[52] This is manifested in part in conflicts over the siting of nuclear power plants.

Loyalty and Commitment The third dimension of political culture mentioned by Pye was loyalty and commitment, referring mainly to the terminal community to which the individual gives his or her ultimate loyalty. For many traditional societies and even for some developed societies there is little identification with others outside the family. Even where the commitment to the family is *not* paramount, loyalties to language, religion, caste, or ethnic group diminish individual commitment to the national political system and produce the potential for political unrest and instability.

The implications of a lower level of national commitment for administration are profound. This is especially true when those commitments are to subnational groupings outside the family. First, the existence of this type of social cleavage will tend to direct power upward toward the bureaucracy. Political decision making in situations of extreme cleavage is a difficult if not impossible process, although some countries of Europe have been developing structural and behavioral mechanisms to circumvent the problem.[53] In most cases, however, either immobilism or the necessity of imposed decisions will limit the effectiveness of legislative or executive decision making. In these cases, the public bureaucracy may be the only effective decision-making body in the nation. Moreover, if the bureaucratic ethos expressed by Weber and others that the bureaucracy is above politics is successfully inculcated into the population, the bureaucracy may be able to function effectively.[54] It can present the image of acting independently and rationally and at the same time make important policy decisions for the society when more conventional democratic institutions are inoperable. Certainly France in the Fourth Republic and modern Italy would fit this characterization, as would a number of underdeveloped countries.[55] As becomes apparent, however, the erosion of these conceptions of bureaucracy may limit the future effectiveness of the bureaucracy in immobilist or fragmented societies. The bureaucracy ceases to be an impartial arbiter of justice and becomes the object of manifest political appeals.

A second implication of the segmented nature of many political cultures for public administration concerns the relationship of administrator and client. As in discussing the relationship of social class to recruitment, so here we must give attention to differential hiring by ethnic groups. This is especially true if one subculture tends to dominate other subcultures. In such cases, typified by the domination of Protestants in Northern Ireland and the English-speaking community in Canada, the implications are not only for civil unrest but also for day-to-day tension.[56] One aspect of this tension between groups is the usual position of the dominant culture personnel in administrative agencies administering programs designed to aid people from the subject culture. As with social class, we find that the majority of administrators come from the dominant cultural groups in a society.[57] On the other hand, a disproportionate share of their clients tend to come from the subject cultures. This not only contributes to the underlying tension between the groups, but it may also place limits on the effectiveness of the administrative structures. Most public administration is people-processing. It involves the communication of desires and demands from client to administrator, the making of some decision on the part of that administrator, and the transmittal of that decision to the client. This is obviously a communication process, and as with all communication processes, it involves the use of common values, symbols, and cognitive structures.[58] This consensus does not necessarily exist between members of different subcultural groups. In these cases the probable result of interactions between administrators and clients is not the development of effective communication and empathy, but rather hostility, resentment, and the reinforcement of existing prejudices. This will be especially true when the program involved is a social program affecting the values of the client and administrator. The majority of direct evidence in this regard comes from the study of interactions of different social classes, but if we generalize, we can agree with Sjoberg, Bremer, and Faris concerning the "critical role of bureaucratic organizations in sustaining social stratification."[59]

Trust and Distrust: A Theory of Bureaucratic Power   The fourth and final aspect of political culture is the level of trust and distrust among the population. In our discussion of this dimension of culture, we attempt to develop a theoretical explanation for the differential development of the power of administration in different political systems.

We argue that differences in the rate of growth of administrative decision-making powers in modern countries are not due entirely to random or irrational forces, but instead are at least in part related to patterns of political cultures in these societies. The patterning of trust in the political cultures may play an important part in this explanation. To begin with, let us distinguish two separate components of social or political trust. The first of these components is a trust in individuals, as opposed to personal cynicism. This is conceptualized as the degree to which individuals in the society believe that others outside their immediate family can be trusted, as well as having a generally benign view of human nature. This trust of humanity is not at all evenly distributed across cultures. Almond and Verba offer some of the best direct evidence of this variation. In their survey they found that 55 percent of the Americans,

49 percent of the British, but only 7 percent of the Italians in their sample indicated that they believed that "most people can be trusted."[60] Rather similar distributions of trust and distrust were found on several other items. Social distrust has been well described in the French context by Wylie, who notes that many of the French feel that

> since all individuals are on the whole malicious and since society never tames the deeper self, every individual is actually motivated by hidden forces which are probably hostile.[61]

The importance of this attitudinal variable in the political culture for the growth of administrative power is that the lack of social trust removes the possibility, or at least the probability, of informal and self-regulative activities. In more trusting societies, these types of activities can be used to supplement the activities of government in regulating relationships within the society. In political systems such as the United States, the United Kingdom, or Scandinavia, where social trust is high, nongovernmental alternatives to public administration emerge quite readily.[62] Individuals feel that they can safely form organizations and allow those organizations some control over the lives of the members. Some rather obvious examples of this are the use of bar and medical associations to regulate some important aspects of public policy. This can be further evidenced by the comparative powers of labor unions in these societies in the regulation of economic affairs. Thus, in cases where high levels of trust among individuals exist, we may expect a large number of otherwise public functions to be performed privately.

Using the willingness to form associations as one indicator of trust among individuals, we again find high levels of variation by countries. For example, Almond and Verba found that 40 percent of the Americans and 30 percent of the British preferred outgoing leisure-time activities, most of which involved some type of group membership.[63] In contrast, only 7 percent of the Italian sample and 11 percent of the Mexican sample preferred activities of this type. A survey of French respondents, reported earlier, displayed equally low interest in outgoing activities (11 percent preferring activities involving any sort of group membership).[64]

Another indicator of the willingness to form groups may be taken to be the proportion of the work force that belongs to labor unions. Unions have emerged as probably the principal organizational groups in Western society, especially in terms of their influence on the political system. Thus, if we look at the proportion of the economically active population involved in these organizations, we get some indication of the organizational skills and interest of the respective populations, as illustrated in Table 2.2. Here we see that the Scandinavian nations, the United Kingdom, and Australia display disproportionately larger percentages of memberships than the other nations. We have already mentioned the high levels of interpersonal trust in the United Kingdom, and the organiza-

TABLE 2.2
PROPORTION OF ECONOMICALLY
ACTIVE POPULATION
WHO ARE MEMBERS OF TRADE
UNIONS

Country	Percent
Australia	46
Austria	50
Belgium	46
Canada	26
Denmark	39
Finland	34
France	15
West Germany	31
Italy	18
Netherlands	27
Norway	41
Sweden	60
Switzerland	41
United Kingdom	41
United States	23

tional propensities of the Scandinavian countries have been noted frequently.[65] The two most interesting aspects of this table are the low proportions reported for France and Italy and the low figure reported for the United States. As we have been seeing throughout this discussion of trust, Italy and France have low levels of social trust among their populations. This low trust is manifested here in low levels of organizational activities. Not only is this a quantitative indication of the lack of organizational propensity, but qualitative studies also indicate weakness within the organizations that do exist.

Given the findings concerning attitudes of social trust and the use of outgoing leisure-time activities, somewhat higher levels of union membership might be expected among Americans. This is apparently an isolated manifestation of a lack of interest in joining a particular type of organization, rather than a more general indication of the propensity to join organizations.

A second aspect of trust is trust in government and political institutions. Here we are especially interested in the degree to which an individual believes that the "political" structures and politicians, as opposed to administrative structures, are worthy of trust.[66] Also involved in this conception of political trust, or its reverse of political cynicism, is the idea that politicians will take the citizen's viewpoint into account when making decisions. The implications of this type of trust for the development of administrative power are perhaps more obvious than the implications of generalized social trust. If the majority of the population, or even a significant minority, does not trust the government and politicians to be fair, honest, and impartial, then government will have at best a very difficult time in ruling the country. Decisions of a highly distrusted political system will be difficult for the population to accept as legitimate. The assumption would always be that some sort of corruption, deception, or favoritism was involved in the decision.

As with the social dimension of trust, we find considerable variation across cultures on the level of political trust. Almond and Verba present some directly comparable evidence as to the distribution of this trait. When respondents in the five countries involved in their survey were asked if they believed themselves capable of influencing local and national regulations, 75 percent of the American and 62 percent of the British respondents felt that they could influence national regulations, while only 28 percent of the Italian respondents felt that they could exert such an influence.[67] Also, in a study of political socialization in France, the Netherlands, and the United States, Abramson and Inglehart compared the trust expressed in a child's father and in the head of state.[68] In the Netherlands and the United States, the children were very slightly more trusting of the political official; in France, the children were much more trusting of the father than the representative of the political system. Rather high levels of political trust have also been reported in the Scandinavian countries and in the Low Countries.[69]

Trust in government has been in decline in most industrialized countries since the time that Almond and Verba did their research. Nowhere has that decline been more precipitous than in the United States, where the traumas of the Vietnam War and Watergate followed so closely on one another. For example, in response to a question on whether they could expect the government in Washington to do the right thing all the time, most of the time, or only some of the time, 77 percent of Americans in 1964 said all or most of the time. By 1976 that percentage had dropped to 34 percent.[70] Looking at the problem the other way, 22 percent of a sample in 1964 said that government could not be trusted to do what was right, while in 1978 70 percent said government could not be trusted.[71] Of nine major institutions in society asked about in 1979, the executive branch of government ranked next to last in people's confidence; only organized labor was lower. In 1966 the executive branch was tied for fourth.[72] Thus, as mentioned previously, political cultures can change, although it is unclear whether the decline in confidence expressed in government in the United States is a long-term phenomenon or only a short-term reaction to a series of specific events.

Trust and Administration   We have now developed two different dimensions of trust—trust in individuals and trust in government. These two dimensions can be interrelated in a typological formation, as shown in Figure 2.2. In this typology, we attempt to explain different levels of political power and of affect of the population toward administration from the positions on the two trust dimensions. In referring to political power of the administration,

FIGURE 2.2
RELATIONSHIP OF DIMENSIONS OF
SOCIAL TRUST TO ADMINISTRATIVE POWER

Trust in Others

		High	Low
Political Trust	High	Low Administrative Power	Moderate Administrative Power (positive effect)
	Low	Moderate Administrative Power (negative effect)	High Administrative Power

we mean the decision-making power of the public bureaucracy relative to other decision-making bodies (for example, the legislature) in the political system, which over time has increased.

The second dependent variable in this typology is the affect felt by the population toward the administrative structures. It is basically difficult to love a bureaucrat, barring the outside chance that he is a member of your immediate family. Yet there are instances in which the general patterns of orientations toward the administrative structures are at least benign and actually somewhat positive. This may be only a grudging respect for the administrative and technical abilities of the civil service, but it is still a positive view of administration.

As shown in Figure 2.2, we do not include all possible combinations of the two dependent characteristics of the typology in our predicted outcomes. Instead we have chosen to hedge our bets and have labeled two of the cells as having moderate administrative power. This is, however, something more than a simple hedge and is related to some characteristics of the political and social systems in question. Following is a discussion of each of the four cells of this typology, with an attempt to explain and justify our predictions.

The first cell is comprised of societies that have high levels of interpersonal trust and high levels of trust in government. Here will be found the weakest administrative structures. In these political systems the normal "political" branches of the political system are reasonably successful in ruling the country and tend to maintain a strong hold on their decision-making prerogatives. They are able to make and enforce rules without excessive assistance from their public bureaucracy. At the same time there are successful decision-making bodies outside government that are capable of performing a number of regulatory functions.

The most obvious example of a nation that would fit into this category of high interpersonal trust and high political trust is the United Kingdom. Here, the Cabinet and to a lesser extent the Parliament comprise an effective political decision-making body.[73] As Nordlinger points out, the level of political trust is sufficiently high in this system to allow the political decision-makers extreme latitude after an election.[74] The population thus expects to exert a direct political control on its elected officials only at the time of election. Also, there has been traditionally a good deal of regulation and self-regulation by organizations within the society. Perhaps the best example of the reliance on self-regulation is the very low level of government involvement in regulating labor-management disputes. At various times Conservative governments have proposed and implemented some labor legislation, but it has been quite meager even when compared to the United States.[75]

This cannot be taken to say that the British bureaucracy is entirely dormant and uninvolved in making public policy. There has been an increasing concern about the role of the civil service in making policy in Britain.[76] However, unlike a number of other political systems, the Cabinet and Parliament have not been relegated to the role of a virtual rubber stamp for the administrators, and the traditions of parliamentary control of ministers and their ministries have tended to prevent takeovers by bureaucratic authority experienced in other regimes, for example, France. The United Kingdom therefore remains a political system with a relatively low level of administrative power and control.

At the opposite extreme are several European countries and a number of societies in the Third World that have neither trust of the political system nor interpersonal trust. In Europe, this pattern can be attributed to France and Italy, and it fits probably a majority of the Third World, especially those nations with ethnic diversity that have been unable to build effective national institutions.[77] In these nations, there is little or no basis for the construction of effective extragovernmental organizations that could be useful in the regulation of some economic or social affairs. A number of authors have noted the relative weaknesses of these organizations in France and Italy.[78] These societies are certainly not devoid of interest groups, but the groups that exist tend to be fragmented and effective largely as defensive groups. They further lack the firm normative and political commitment on the part of their members that is so characteristic of groups in other societies.

The political systems of these countries are relatively weak. The weakness certainly diminished in France under the Gaullists but has appeared to reassert itself during the first years of the Mitterand government. Politics has tended to be characterized by fragmentation, ideological argument, and "blockage."[79] This is in part a function of the institutions themselves and in part a function of the values of the societies that stress family and individual roles rather than the role of the government. Thus, the population is less willing to accept the decrees of government than the needs of the family or the guidance of the local patron. In these cases, the bureaucracy may be required to step in to fill a power vacuum in the political system. The country must be run somehow, and the logical heir to powers ordinarily held by Parliament or the Executive is the bureaucracy. Unfortunately, perhaps, this pattern tends to be self-reinforcing. As more power and decision making pass to the bureaucracy, the popular image of government as authoritarian and impersonal is reinforced. This further reduces the legitimacy of the political system in the eyes of the population and further prevents the legislative and executive bodies from becoming effective rule-making bodies. Thus, a cycle of bureaucratic domination tends to perpetuate itself, being broken mainly by "charismatic personalities" who are capable of producing effective political action either through or around normal political channels.

The similarity between the situations of France and Italy and some of the countries of the Third World is rather striking. The new nations tend to lack interpersonal trust among the population.[80] This is often traceable to the predominance of ethnic cleavages in the society and the use of protective as opposed to promotional groups. Each segment of the society tends to protect its interests against all others, rather than offering an alternative means of social decision making. Likewise, the long history of colonial rule and the lack of a social and economic infrastructure usually associated with democratic government have made the bureaucracy and the army the two logical contenders for power in these societies.[81] As well as being the choices by default, the bureaucracy and the army also have some of the characteristics of modernity that would qualify them for the management of developing economies and societies.[82] Both institutions tend to have had relatively extensive contacts with more modern nations and to have values and attitudes that conform more closely to those of the modern state than do those of other political elites. Thus, just as with the developed countries of France and Italy, the bureaucracy in the underdeveloped world fills a power vacuum when it exists. One question that remains is whether this will be a continuing phenomenon or whether the underdeveloped countries will be able to develop the political and interpersonal trust that a large proportion of the developed world has been able to generate.

We move now to the two cases with mixed degrees of trust. These have been characterized as having moderate levels of administrative power, but they differ in the affect felt by the population toward the administrative system. The first is the case of low interpersonal trust and high trust for government. This would appear to be typical of the "consociational democracies" of the Low Countries, Austria, Switzerland, and (once) Lebanon.[83] In these societies, strong cleavage between religious and linguistic groups in turn produces relatively few feelings of interpersonal trust. Lorwin notes that in Belgium:

> Flemings know little of Walloons thinking; Walloons know little of Flemish thinking. People of each side therefore tend to see and resent the others as a solid bloc arrayed against them.[84]

Likewise, Dutch political sociology has emphasized the "pillarization" of their society with the three major groups (Protestants, Catholics, and the nonreligious) vertically integrated and having relatively little contact with members of other "families."[85] Mass communications and secularization are reducing this isolation of groups, but significant separation remains.

These societies obviously have the ability to develop the immobilism and the conflict that has been characteristic of French and Italian governments. Fortunately, however, there is a well-developed sense of mutual trust among the elites of each of the "families," as well as a general feeling of political trust for the government.[86] Thus, although vertically integrated, compromise and interaction at the elite level enable the political system to function effectively. It is also able to function with only a moderate level of administrative power. The legislative bodies are fragmented politically but at the same time have formed coalition governments with the continuing support of the population. This feeling of trust and respect for the government is carried over into the generally positive feelings of the population toward the administrative structures.

The final set of nations are those with relatively low trust in the political system but high levels of interpersonal trust. This pattern would appear to be displayed in the United States. The political culture of the United States has traditionally been one preferring individual and group action to governmental action.[87] A number of functions that might be performed by government, or at least with extensive governmental intervention, are still performed privately in the United States. The most notable example of this is health care, although a number of other professions and businesses have retained the right to administer their own affairs and make decisions that in other societies would be considered a matter of public concern.[88] Despite this, survey evidence has shown that Americans at least expect fair treatment from the political system, although this expectation is not so high as in the United Kingdom.[89] Moreover, when compared to levels of interpersonal trust, the government comes out a rather poor second. Thus, if we use the level of interpersonal trust as an "expected" level of trust, the level of trust found for government is low, and getting lower.

Whether or not the United States can be said to be indicative of this pattern, what are the consequences for administrative power? In the first place, we may expect a moderate level of administrative power. The use of nongovernmental organizations for a variety of regulatory tasks lessens the work load of the administration; at the same time, the relatively bad image of the political arms of government forces a number of questions to be decided administratively rather than politically. The "political" branches of governments tend to be so weighted down with checks and balances that the bureaucracy must again be called on to fill something of a decision-making vacuum. This is apparent in part in the widespread utilization of regulations written by the bureaucracy in place of other legislation and in the difficulties that some presidents have experienced in trying to control the administrators whom they nominally commanded.[90] But, even given the relative powers of the public bureaucracy, the general viewpoint of Americans vis-à-vis the bureaucracy is negative. Americans may have some respect for individual administrators, but the dominant theme of the culture is perhaps all too well indicated by George Wallace's desire to throw the "bureaucrats and their briefcases" into the Potomac River.

In summary, a relatively simple typology of variations in the levels of trust among the population toward two different social objects—individuals and the government—can be useful in explaining differences in the degree of administrative power in modern governments. This typology and its conclusions are rather obviously an oversimplification of a complex reality. A number of other cultural and political factors must be taken into account in the final explanation or prediction of administrative power. However, the relatively high correspondence between the predictions of the typology and this descriptive analysis of representative political systems offers some credence to the relationships hypothesized.

CULTURE AND THE INTERNAL MANAGEMENT OF ORGANIZATIONS

Up to this point we have been examining the relationship between the societal and political cultures and the role prescribed for the public bureaucracy; that is, observing what the bureaucracy does within the political system rather than the manner in which it chooses to perform those tasks. We now turn our attention to the question of the impact of culture on the internal management of complex administrative organizations. This is the third broad type of culture discussed at the beginning of the chapter and is a complex topic worthy of several volumes in itself. However, only two topics will be discussed here: the relationship between superiors and subordinates in an organization; and the cultural basis for the motivation of workers. As with most other topics in this book, we are especially interested in the effects of these internal management practices on the policy outputs of the public organization.

Culture and Authority

The definition and acceptance of the authority of one individual by another is a function of culture and society. As with virtually all cultural norms, there are individual interpretations of the norm, and hence individual variation, but certain modal patterns emerge. The use of impersonal and "rational-legal" authority as a means of controlling individuals, as suggested in formal models of bureaucratic management, is a culturally determined concept. First, it is intimately connected to the social cultural patterns of the West, and even then to a rather small segment of Western thought. This managerial strategy, to be successful, would require the support of a generally hierarchical and bureaucratic society. A culture that stressed the ideas of individualism and personal equality would find it difficult to support such a system of management.

Weber has presented the classical discussion of the sources of authority in society.[91] Much the same can be said of patterns of authority in organizations. Weber argued that authority had three sources: tradition, charismatic personality, and rationality. The first was taken to characterize most traditional societies. The authority exercised by an individual in government or in an organization (such few as might exist) would be a function of the individual's position in the traditional hierarchy in the society. This hierarchy is ordained by some alleged divine connection, or it may be a function of property, but the source of authority is not subject to any rational challenge. Charismatic authority is a transitional variety of authority. The source of authority is the force of personality of the individual. Weber spoke of this largely in terms of social leadership, but the same category could apply to organizational leaders who were capable of commanding respect and obedience through the force of their individual personality.[92] Weber notes that over time charisma tends to be institutionalized and to be converted into rational-legal authority. In this third class of authority the individual willingly accepts the authority of his superior simply because of the hierarchy of the organization or society. Thus, if the superior is in a superior position within the organization, that is sufficient to provide the individual with authority. In Simon's terms, the subordinate willingly suspends judgment and accepts the direction of the superior.[93]

Much management thinking is still bound to this Weberian conception of rational-legal authority, and of the right of the superior to command the subordinate. This, in fact, would appear to be one of the major causes for discontent in most large organizations in the Western world today. The cultural values of these societies have changed decidedly in favor of the right of people to decide their own futures. Workers, especially younger workers, are seeking involvement in decision making. This has largely been phrased in terms of the management of industrial enterprises, but much the same can be said of public organizations. The lower echelons of these organizations are also seeking new forms of management that will allow participation by those affected by decisions. This is often taken to include clients as well as the lower levels of administration.

Another challenge to hierarchical authority is expertise. The appeal of technology and expertise in modern society is almost hypnotic in its effects. Expertise has become a new basis of charisma for leaders of an organization. The problem is that this source of authority often (usually?) conflicts with the rational-legal basis of authority. Victor Thompson has argued that this divergence between expertise and formal authority is the fundamental problem of modern organizations.[94] Authority is concentrated at the top of the organizational pyramid while expertise is concentrated at the bottom. The conflicts intrinsic in such a situation are obvious. In public organizations expertise is often not only technical, but is also direct knowledge of the clientele and their problems, which is considered unimportant by those in the upper levels of the organization. The conflict, over both knowledge and values, in such a situation is virtually unavoidable.

The problems of authority and management in underdeveloped nations are rather different. The acceptance of hierarchy and rational-legal authority in these cases is formalistic at best. This pattern of authority conflicts with the traditional basis of authority in most other relationships. Even under colonial rule, the traditional authority structure was often borrowed by the colonial power for its own uses,[95] and attempts to modernize place new strains on traditional power structures. In many cases, the ideology of modernization would require the destruction or bypassing of older systems of authority. The destruction of this authority has created a vacuum that has been difficult to fill on the basis of rational-legal authority. Riggs notes the formalism of administrative structures in these societies, with apparent rationality in the pattern of organization, but a general reliance on traditional criteria of decision making.[96] Pye notes the same formalism in the bureaucratic system of Burma.[97] Thus, modern institutions may often serve as a thin disguise for traditional practice. In addition, charismatic leaders have supplied another major source of authority both for government as a whole and for public bureaucracies.

In fairness, however, it is not only the administrative structures of Third World countries that contain vestiges of traditional and charismatic authority. Many "central agencies" in developed countries are based upon the personal leadership of an individual.[98] Individuals remain a part of those organizations so long as they have confidence in, and the confidence of, the person in the executive position—be it president, prime minister, or whatever. Organizations with this personal authority constitute a small but crucial component of the administrative structures of most countries.

Culture and Motivation

How do you activate workers to join an organization and to produce once they are members? To some degree, this is a part of the prior question of authority, in that Weber tended to assume that authority was itself a sufficient motivation for performance.[99] Beyond this seemingly naive expectation, how can the manager of a public organization activate his subordinates to do their jobs effectively? Answers range from the use of physical coercion, either real or threatened, to involvement in decision making. In each case, the choice of motivational strategy will be to some degree a function of the culture of the society. In general, we can think of four basic motivational techniques that are available to managers. The first technique, if it may be given such a euphemistic title, is coercion. Fortunately, the modern world has largely left behind the period in which direct coercion might be used as a means of gaining organizational compliance. The use of indirect or implied coercion is still an actively used technique, however. The coercion is rarely physical but involves other types of deprivations to the employee. In particular, this involves the loss of prestige, status, and acceptance through either loss of office or demotion. Newspapers carry stories of the deportation of disfavored administrators to the country's functional equivalent of Siberia (for example, Cut Bank, Montana, in the United States). While this is certainly better than a public flogging in most people's minds, it can still be a severe deprivation in both physical and psychological terms.

A somewhat more subtle form of coercion is the use of ideological or religious doctrines as a motivating force. Perhaps the two most famous examples of this are the Protestant ethic and the thoughts of Chairman Mao. The former religious and ideological doctrine has been cited as one of the principal reasons for the development of Western industrial society.[100] By equating success in business or profession with Salvation, the Protestant ethic constituted an important motivating force for the growth of Western business and commerce. Even now, when direct belief in the correlation of success and divine election has waned, the culture of the West has been sufficiently influenced by this doctrine that success is valued as a good in itself.

The thoughts of Chairman Mao, although less widespread, constitute perhaps the best example of the use of a secular ideology as a motivating device. Exhortations to progress, development, and efficient production through this ideology were an important if not crucial factor in China's economic development. This was true despite a number of economic inefficiencies dictated by the doctrine. On a more personal basis, the desire to fulfill the thoughts of Mao and to please him and the people of China served as important means of motivating the individual. As with the Protestant ethic, the threat of coercion has been internalized by the individual. The deprivations for the individual are more often than not internal, so that personal pressures of compliance constitute the major motivation for the individual.

It should be noted here that the use of ideology and religion can be at once a very expensive and a very inexpensive means of motivation. On the one hand, once the ideology is accepted by the population, it requires largely symbol manipulation in order to be effective. This is certainly less expensive than having to pay people money to motivate them or to involve them in decision making. Thus, as with any cultural device, the ideology of a society (or organization) provides a set of symbols that can be manipulated by those in power. The ideology also provides a set of psychological deprivations for the individual for failure to comply with the ideology. At least psychologically, the manipulation of symbols can constitute something approaching coercion. Ideology used as a means of motivation becomes expensive when it restricts forms of action available to the organization.[101] One of the defining characteristics of an ideology is that it prescribes and proscribes actions for individuals and groups that in turn limit the flexibility of action for the organization and society. Political leaders have been quite adept at justifying virtually any policy in terms of the dominant ideology, but this is costly both in the time required and in the probable weakening of commitment by some individuals. The same types of problems are encountered when attempting to change an ideology to meet changing social conditions. Thus, an ideology can be an exceedingly inexpensive motivational method in the short run, but it may impose a number of long-range costs. The rational assessment of the net benefits of this motivational strategy will therefore depend upon the discount attached to long-range costs as well as the level of short-range demands.

The third motivational technique available to managers is monetary reward. Probably the prevailing concept of management in Western societies has been that monetary rewards are a sufficient inducement to gain the compliance of workers with the demands of the organization. The importance of money as a means of management and motivation is that in many ways it is the cheapest means of motivation, particularly in administrative organizations. Here, the main "product" is not goods or services, but rather it is decisions. If the majority of the work force can be motivated through their paychecks, then the need to allow their participation in decision making is eliminated. This will allow greater latitude of action for decision-makers than can be found in ideological or involvement systems of management. This type of motivation was, in fact, a major assumption of Weber's ideal-type of the bureaucracy.[102] It makes bureaucracy virtually a neutral instrument that can be used for almost any purpose by its managers. While this assumption is rather obviously overstated, the latitude granted to managers through monetary motivation is an important consideration for any manager. The choice, however, is probably not individual but cultural.

The question of the latitude of decision making brings us to the fourth source of motivation. This is the involvement of the workers in decision making in the organization. The use of this method of management has varied across time more than across cultures and is generally considered to be a product of the "postindustrial" or "postwelfare" society.[103] In general, this method of management employs the ability of the worker to perceive that he has greater control over his life and work as a means of motivation. Studies of motivation have shown that the major source of motivation for professional and white-collar employees is the individuals' ability to perceive that they are doing something significant and the ability to feel that they could control what happened to them in their jobs.[104] Given the level of education and training required for most administrative jobs, the same type of motivational structure can be expected among administrators. Moreover, the ideology of participation is apparently increasing in importance as an increasing number of workers at all levels of administration demand an influence in the decisions made that affect them. This development is rather obviously in contradiction to the ideal-type bureaucratic model and to a significant body of literature in public management stressing the importance of executive control and the duty of leadership at the top.[105]

One interesting aspect of this increasing demand for involvement is that it has spread not only among administrators, but also among the clients of administration. Thus a new force has to be taken into account by management, and managers must think of motivating the clients of the organization to gain their compliance in much the same way that managers must think about motivating workers. The inducements are not only of the monetary (services) variety, but now also include involvement in decision making.

With both workers and clients, involvement is an expensive means of gaining organizational compliance. It reduces the latitude available to a manager and provides possibly very little in return. Unlike an ideology that can be readily used in "normal" times to satisfy employees, involvement requires a constant redefinition of goals and priorities. And, as with ideological change, these types of changes are generally quite costly to the organization in terms of both time lost and personal costs to the losers in the struggle. In public organizations, this also involves a redefinition of some aspects of public policy that may require negotiations of other political institutions. Thus, the losses in continuity of programs, in the reanalysis of priorities, and in the personal reshaping of work priorities make the granting of involvement an exceedingly expensive means of motivation. Nevertheless, in some cases it may be the only means of motivation that will be successful. Increasingly, organized labor has sought to negotiate means for becoming more involved in plant decision making; some countries, for example, West Germany, have developed mechanisms for co-management of firms.[106] Teachers and other professionals in government demand to have their professional judgment considered when making policy. We should expect that even in times of economic difficulty labor negotiations will be directed at the problem of participation as well as wages.

We should not be totally negative concerning the use of involvement as a motivational device. In terms of human values it is probably the best means of management devised. Furthermore, it may be one means of solving Thompson's dilemma concerning the comparative misplacement of expertise and authority in organizations. In the short run, this means of management has been successful, although its long-range effects have yet to be gauged. Involvement with little real consequent change for the individual may actually be an alienating experience. Given the demands of the present culture, however, the demands for involvement can no longer be denied.

We have, to this point, avoided the traditional notion of the motivation of the public servant being solely the public interest. This was not done to denigrate the long service of a number of committed individuals in organizations.[107] Thus, we view the majority of individuals in public organizations to be little different in their motivational structure (but perhaps in their value structures) from individuals in any other organization. The idea of the public service would, therefore, be classified analytically as just another of the many ideological convictions that have motivated individuals in organizations.

SUMMARY

This chapter has attempted to show the influence of patterns of political culture and general cultural values on the operation of the administrative system. We have examined this influence as it affects not only the outputs of the administrative system, but also the internal management of the organizations. In both cases, we find that culture has a significant impact on the behavior of public administration. Unfortunately, the assessment of this impact had to remain at a somewhat impressionistic level because of the lack of much hard evidence on these relationships.[108] One of the main problems with the concept of culture, and especially of political culture, is that it generally tends to be a vague and amorphous concept that can be twisted to include virtually anything a researcher wishes. We hope we have avoided this pitfall as much as possible and have presented the evidence in as unbiased a manner as possible. But we are the products of our own culture and see the world from our own perspective. It is difficult if not impossible to escape the imperatives of a culture taught to us from birth. Any significant progress in the field of relating cultural values and their effects on administration (or other aspects of politics) must come from a more complete empirical delimitation of culture and an examination of its dimensions. Hopefully, this discussion has been a step in the direction of analyzing the potential and probable effects of culture so that more informed empirical analysis can test for these effects.

NOTES

1. Lucian W. Pye and Sidney Verba, *Political Culture and Political Development* (Princeton: Princeton University Press, 1965).

2. For a recent review, see David O. Sears, "Political Socialization," in Fred I. Greenstein and Nelson W. Polsby, *The Handbook of Political Science*, vol. 2 (Reading, Mass.: Addison-Wesley, 1975).

3. Just as with expenditure levels, major public events may have a "displacement effect" on the more general sphere of government activity. See Alan T. Peacock and Jack Wiseman, *The Growth of Public Expenditure in the United Kingdom*, 2nd ed. (London: George Allen & Unwin, 1967), pp. 27–28. For some contrary evidence see B. Guy Peters, "Public Employment in the United States: Absolute Change and Relative Stability," in Richard Rose, ed., *Public Employment in Western Democracies* (Cambridge: Cambridge University Press, forthcoming).

4. Ronald Inglehart, *The Silent Revolution* (Princeton: Princeton University Press, 1977); Alan Marsh, "The 'Silent Revolution,' Value Priorities, and the Quality of Life in Britain," *American Political Science Review* 69 (March 1975): 21–30.

5. Reinhard Bendix, *Work and Authority in Industry* (New York: John Wiley, 1956).

6. Hugh Heclo and Aaron Wildavsky, *The Private Government of Public Money* (Berkeley: University of California Press, 1974).

7. Sidney Verba, "Germany: The Remaking of Political Culture," in Pye and Verba, *Political Culture*, pp. 151–54; Kenneth Dyson, "West Germany: The Search for a Rationalist Consensus," in Jeremy Richardson, ed., *Policy Styles in Western Europe* (London: George Allen and Unwin, 1982): 17–46.

8. Verba, "Germany." Verba does point to significant long-term changes in the family structure. See also Kendall L. Baker, "Political Participation, Political Efficacy and Socialization in Germany," *Comparative Politics* 6, no. 1 (October 1973): 73–98.

9. All industrialized societies have definite bureaucratic aspects, in both the denotative and connotative sense of the word.

10. Kenneth H. Dyson, *The State Tradition in Western Europe* (Oxford: Martin Robertson, 1980).

11. Hugo Young and Anne Sloman, *No, Minister: An Inquiry into the Civil Service* (London: BBC, 1982); Peter Kellner and Lord Crowther-Hunt, *The Civil Service: Britain's Ruling Elite* (London: Macdonald, 1980).

12. Robert E. Ward, "Japan: The Continuity of Modernization," in Pye and Verba, *Political Culture*, pp. 27–82; Taketsugu Tsurutani, *Political Change in Japan* (New York: David McKay, 1977), pp. 26–31.

13. Talcott Parsons and Edward A. Shils, *Toward a General Theory of Action* (Cambridge, Mass.: Harvard University Press, 1951), p. 77.

14. Giovanni Sartori, "Politics, Ideology and Belief Systems," *American Political Science Review* 63 (June 1969): 398–411.

15. Ibid.

16. Elihu Katz and S. N. Eisenstadt, "Some Sociological Observations on the Response of Israeli Organizations to New Immigrants," *Administrative Science Quarterly* 5, no. 1 (June 1960): 113–33.

17. Gerald E. Caiden, *Israel's Administrative Culture* (Berkeley, Calif.: University of California, Institute of Government Studies, 1970).

18. Riggs refers to this as the "bazaar" nature of these cultures. Fred W. Riggs, *Administration in Developing Countries: The Theory of Prismatic Society* (Boston: Houghton Mifflin, 1964); S. Heginbotham, *Cultures in Conflict: The Four Faces of Indian Bureaucracy* (New York: Columbia University Press, 1975).

19. Riggs, *Administration in Developing Countries*, pp. 200–202.

20. Ibid., p. 201.

21. See S. N. Eisenstadt, "Bureaucracy, Bureaucratization and Debureaucratization," *Administrative Science Quarterly* 4 (December 1959): 302–20.

22. This has been true not just of studies of political culture, but of most contemporary comparative politics. See Roy C. Macridis, "Comparative Politics and the Study of Government: The Search for Focus," *Comparative Politics* 1 (October 1968): 79–90. See also, Jorgen Rasmussen, "Once You've Made a Revolution Everything's the Same: Comparative Politics," in George J. Graham and George W. Carey, eds., *The Post-Behavioral Era* (New York: David McKay, 1972), pp. 71–87.

23. David Zussman, "The Image of the Public Service in Canada," *Canadian Public Administration* 25 (1982), pp. 63–80.

24. Ibid., pp. 70–76; Daniel Katz et al., *Bureaucratic Encounters* (Ann Arbor: Survey Research Center, University of Michigan, 1975).

25. Gabriel A. Almond and Sidney Verba, *The Civic Culture* (Princeton: Princeton University Press, 1963), pp. 70–73.

26. Samuel J. Eldersveld, V. Jagannadham, and A. P. Barnabas, *The Citizen and the Administrator in a Developing Democracy* (Glenview, Ill.: Scott, Foresman, 1968).

27. S. J. Levy, "The Public Image of Government Agencies," *Public Administration Review* 23 (March 1963): 25–29.

28. Almond and Verba, *Civic Culture*, chap. 1.

29. Gabriel A. Almond and G. Bingham Powell, *Comparative Politics: A Developmental Approach* (Boston: Little, Brown, 1966), pp. 57–63.

30. Peter Nettl, *Political Mobilization* (New York: Basic Books, 1967).

31. Harry Eckstein, *Division and Cohesion in Democracy* (Princeton: Princeton University Press, 1966); "Authority Patterns: A Structural Basis for Political Inquiry," *American Political Science Review* 67 (1973): 1142–61.

32. Daniel J. Elazar, "The States and the Political Setting," in his *American Federalism: A View from the States* (New York: Crowell, 1966), pp. 85–104.

33. Lucian W. Pye, "Introduction: Political Culture and Political Development," in Pye and Verba, *Political Culture*, pp. 3–26.

34. Parsons and Shils, *General Theory of Action*.

35. H. H. Gerth and C. Wright Mills, *From Max Weber: Essays in Sociology* (New York: Oxford University Press, 1946), pp. 198–200.

36. J. Donald Kingsley, *Representative Bureaucracy* (Yellow Springs, Oh.: Antioch Press, 1944).

37. See, for example, OECD, *Social Objectives in Educational Planning* (Paris: OECD, 1967); George Busch, "Inequality of Educational Opportunity by Social Origin in Higher Education," in *Education, Inequality, and Life Chances* (Paris: Organization for Economic Cooperation and Development, 1975), pp. 159–181.

38. One view of the difficulties created thereby is given by Edward Banfield, *The Unheavenly City* (Boston: Little, Brown, 1970). A very different view is given by Gideon Sjoberg, Richard A. Bremer, and Buford Faris, "Bureaucracy and the Lower Class," *Sociology and Social Research* 51 (1966): 325–37. See also Richard Sennett and Jonathan Cobb, *The Hidden Injuries of Class* (New York: Vintage, 1972).

39. Michel Crozier, *The Bureaucratic Phenomenon* (Chicago: University of Chicago Press, 1964), pp. 213–36.

40. See, for example, Michel Crozier, *On ne change pas la societé par décret* (Paris: Grasset, 1979).

41. Lucian W. Pye, *Politics, Personality and Nation Building* (New Haven: Yale University Press, 1962); Edgar L. Shor, "The Thai Bureaucracy," *Administrative Science Quarterly* 5, no. 1 (June 1960): 66–86. Though clearly not underdeveloped, Japanese administration has the same tendency toward per-

sonal followings and cliques. See also, Heginbotham, *Cultures in Conflict;* N. Abedin, *Local Administration and Politics in Modernizing Societies: Bangladesh and Pakistan* (Dacca: National Institute of Public Administration, 1973).

42. Inglehart, *The Silent Revolution.*

43. See Orion F. White, "The Dialectical Organization—An Alternative to Bureaucracy," *Public Administration Review* 39 (January–February 1969): 32–42.

44. See Charles H. Gibson, "Volvo Increases Production Through Job Enrichment," *California Management Review* 15 (Summer 1973): 64–66. Nils Elvander, "Democracy in Large Organizations," in M. Donald Hancock and Gideon Sjoberg, *Politics in the Post-Welfare Society* (New York: Columbia University Press, 1969), pp. 302–24.

45. *Organizing for Higher Productivity: Analysis of Japanese Systems and Practices* (New York: United Nations, 1982).

46. Thomas Kennedy, *Industrial Relations in Europe* (Lexington, Mass.: D. C. Heath, 1978), pp. 173–96.

47. Jeffrey M. Prottas, *People Processing: The Street-level Bureaucrats in Public Service Bureaucracy* (Lexington, Mass.: D. C. Heath, 1979).

48. See chapter 8.

49. Inglehart, *The Silent Revolution.*

50. Emmette S. Redford, *Democracy in the Administrative State* (New York: Oxford University Press, 1969), p. 66.

51. This is certainly the feeling one gets from the spate of "crisis" literature. See Michel Crozier, Samuel P. Huntington, and Joji Watanuki, *The Crisis of Democracy* (New York: New York University Press, 1975).

52. Samuel P. Huntington, "Post-Industrial Politics: How Benign Will It Be?" *Comparative Politics* 6 (1974): 163–91.

53. Arend Lijphart, *The Politics of Accommodation*, 2nd ed. (Berkeley: University of California Press, 1975); Martin O. Heisler with Robert B. Kvavik, "Patterns of European Politics: The 'European Polity' Model," in *Politics in Europe: Structures and Processes in Some Postindustrial Societies*, Martin Heisler, ed. (New York: David McKay, 1974), pp. 27–89; Jan Van Putten, "Policy Styles in the Netherlands: Negotiation and Conflict," in Richardson, *Policy Styles*, pp. 168–96.

54. Gerth and Mills, *From Max Weber.*

55. Diamant argues, however, that only routine decisions get made and that few significant innovations are made. Alfred Diamant, "Tradition and Innovation in French Administration," *Comparative Political Studies* 1 (July 1963): 251–74.

56. See, for example, Richard Rose, *Governing Without Consensus: An Irish Perspective* (London: Faber, 1971).

57. See chapter 3.

58. See, for example, John T. Dorsey, "A Communication Model for Administration," *Administrative Science Quarterly* 2, no. 3 (December 1957): 307–24. See also Prottas, *People Processing;* Michael K. Brown, *Working the Streets: Police Discretion and Dilemmas of Reform* (New York: Russell Sage, 1981).

59. Sjoberg, Bremer, and Faris, "Bureaucracy and the Lower Class," p. 325.

60. Almond and Verba, *Civic Culture*, p. 213.

61. Laurence Wylie, "Social Change at the Grassroots," in Stanley Hoffmann et al., *In Search of France* (New York: Harper & Row, 1963), p. 203.

62. See chapter 5.

63. Almond and Verba, *Civic Culture*, p. 270.

64. SOFRES, *Sondages* 25, no. 2 (1963).

65. Nils Elvander, *Intresseorganisationera i dagens Sverige* (Lund: CWK Gleer-ups, 1966); Lars Madsen, *Interressorganisationerne og det offentlige* (Copen-hagen: Handelshøjskolen, 1969); Johan P. Olsen, *Organized Democracy* (Ber-gen: Universitetsforlaget, 1983).

66. Again, relatively fewer studies have focused upon trust in administration than upon trust in more political institutions. See pp. 44–46.

67. Almond and Verba, *Civic Culture*, p. 142.

68. Paul R. Abramson and Ronald Inglehart, "The Development of Systemic Support in Four Western Democracies," *Comparative Political Studies* 2, no. 4 (January 1970): 419–42.

69. Arend Lijphart, *Politics of Accommodation;* Dankwart A. Rustow, *The Poli-tics of Compromise* (Princeton: Princeton University Press, 1955); Eckstein, *Division and Cohesion.*

70. "Opinion Roundup," *Public Opinion* 1 (July/August 1978): 31.

71. "Opinion Roundup," *Public Opinion* 2 (October/November 1979): 28.

72. Ibid., p. 30.

73. For some contrary evidence, see Richard Rose, *The Problem of Party Govern-ment* (London: Macmillan, 1974).

74. Eric Nordlinger, *The Working Class Tories* (Berkeley: University of Califor-nia Press, 1967).

75. Colin Crouch, *The Politics of Industrial Relations* (Manchester: Manchester University Press, 1979).

76. Sloman and Young, *No, Minister;* Kellner and Crowther-Hunt, *The Civil Service;* Maurice Wright, "Ministers and Civil Servants: Relations and Re-sponsibilities," *Parliamentary Affairs* 33 (1980): 293–313.

77. Effective "democratic" political institutions might be a more appropriate term. See Cynthia Enloe, *Ethnic Conflict and Political Development* (Boston: Little, Brown, 1973).

78. A good review is provided in Henry W. Ehrmann, *Politics in France*, 3rd ed. (Boston: Little, Brown, 1976), pp. 181–214; Joseph LaPalombara, *Interest Groups in Italian Politics* (Princeton: Princeton University Press, 1965); Jack Hayward, "France: The Dual Policy Style," in Richardson, *Policy Styles in Western Europe*, pp. 111–40.

79. Michel Crozier, *The Stalled Society* (New York: Vintage, 1973).

80. See, for example, Victor Olorunsola, *The Politics of Cultural Sub-Nationalism in Africa* (Garden City, N.Y.: Doubleday, 1972).

81. This role has generally been exercised by the army rather than the bureau-cracy. An interesting case study is Robert M. Price, "Military Officers and Political Leadership," *Comparative Politics* 3, no. 3 (April 1971): 361–80.

82. Lucian W. Pye, "Armies in the Process of Political Modernization," in

The Role of the Military in Underdeveloped Countries, J. J. Johnson, ed. (Princeton: Princeton University Press, 1962), pp. 77–80.

83. Arend Lijphart, "Consociational Democracy," *World Politics* 21 (January 1969): 207–25.

84. Val R. Lorwin, "Belgium," in Robert Dahl, *Political Oppositions in Western Democracies* (New Haven: Yale University Press, 1966), p. 174.

85. Val R. Lorwin, "Segmental Pluralism: Ideological Cleavages and Political Cohesion in the Smaller European Democracies," *Comparative Politics* 3 (January 1971): 141–75; Hans Daalder, "The Netherlands," in Dahl, *Political Opposition*, chap. 6. But see Hans Daalder, *Politisering en lijdelijkheid in de Nederlandse politick* (Assen: Van Coreum, 1974), as cited in Jean Van Putten, "Policy Styles in the Netherlands," in Richardson, *Policy Styles in Western Europe*, p. 172.

86. Arend Lijphart, *Politics of Accommodation*.

87. The impact of these views is well illustrated in Anthony King, "Ideas, Institutions and Policies of Government: A Comparative Analysis," *British Journal of Political Science* 3, nos. 3 and 4 (July and October 1973): 291–314, 409–24.

88. See chapter 5 on clientele groups.

89. Almond and Verba, *The Civic Culture*, pp. 70–75.

90. Richard Rose, "Government against Sub-government: A European Perspective on Washington," in Richard Rose and Ezra N. Suleiman, eds., *Presidents and Prime Ministers* (Washington, D.C.: American Enterprise Institute, 1980), pp. 284–347.

91. Gerth and Mills, *From Max Weber*, pp. 295 ff.

92. Ibid.

93. Herbert A. Simon, *Administrative Behavior* (New York: Free Press, 1957), pp. 124–28.

94. Victor Thompson, *Modern Organizations* (New York: Knopf, 1961).

95. This was especially true of the British rule in Africa. See L. Rubin and B. Weinstein, *Introduction to African Politics* (New York: Praeger, 1974), pp. 34–41.

96. Riggs, *Administration in Developing Countries*, pp. 182–84.

97. Lucian W. Pye, *Politics, Personality and Nation Building: Burma's Search for Identity* (New Haven: Yale University Press, 1962).

98. Colin Campbell and George J. Szablowski, *The Super Bureaucrats: Structure and Behavior in Central Agencies* (Toronto: Macmillan of Canada, 1979).

99. Gerth and Mills, *From Max Weber*, pp. 199–202.

100. Richard H. Tawney, *Religion and the Rise of Capitalism* (New York: Harcourt, Brace & World, 1926); Max Weber, *The Protestant Ethic and the Spirit of Capitalism* (London: George Allen & Unwin, 1930).

101. Harold Wilensky, *Organizational Intelligence* (New York: Basic Books, 1967), chap. 2.

102. Gerth and Mills, *From Max Weber*.

103. See, for example, the articles by White and Sjoberg, Capps, Hancock, and Elvander in Hancock and Sjoberg, *Politics in Post-Welfare Society*.

104. Perhaps the most thorough study of this type is G. Gurin, J. Veroff, and

S. Feld, *Americans View Their Mental Health* (New York: Basic Books, 1960).

105. See the discussion in Andrew Dunshire, *Implementation in a Bureaucracy* (New York: St. Martin's, 1978), pp. 16–38.
106. Kennedy, *Industrial Relations in Europe.*
107. For a more complete discussion of motivations in hiring and retention for the civil service, see chapter 3.
108. David J. Elkins and Richard E. B. Simeon, "A Cause in Search of an Effect: Or What Does Elite Culture Explain?", *Comparative Politics* 11 (1979): 117–46.

THE RECRUITMENT OF PUBLIC ADMINISTRATORS

Before anyone can make much progress toward administering a public program, the political system must enlist and train a group of public administrators. This is common sense, but it is used simply to point to the importance of recruitment in a study of public administration. In order to be able to say what a public agency will do, we must first have some idea of who will do it and for what purposes—public or personal. Unlike earlier assumptions concerning organizational management, such as Weber's ideal conceptualization of the bureaucrat or the Taylors' scientific-management school, the individuals who occupy organizational positions are not interchangeable parts.[1] This is widely understood for partisan political leaders—presidents, prime ministers, etc.—but the same ideological and personality characteristics assumed to affect political leadership are not assumed to influence bureaucrats. Bureaucrats bring with them to their jobs a host of values, predispositions, and operating routines that will greatly affect the quality of their performance in a bureaucratic setting.[2] Again we must emphasize that public administrators, even those at relatively low levels in the organizational hierarchy, are indeed decision-makers. The proverbial story of the judge having burned toast for breakfast and then sentencing the defendant to death may be as true, albeit in less extreme situations, of thousands of administrators passing on thousands of requests or demands for services from government. This chapter examines the way in which governments select administrators, and thereby the ways in which they narrow the range of possible outcomes of the policy-making process.

MERIT VERSUS PATRONAGE

Several somewhat conflicting themes have dominated the discussion of administrative recruitment. The first of these has been the search for efficiency through merit recruitment. One of the defining characteristics of Weber's model of bureaucracy was that the bureaucrats should be selected on the basis of merit rather than the ascriptive criteria of caste, race, class, or language. Heclo refers to this as selection by "neutral competence."[3] The assumption underlying merit selection is that bureaucracy must be able to recruit the best possible personnel, and merit recruitment is the logical means of filling the available positions with the most qualified personnel.

In developmental terms, a second impetus for the adoption of merit recruitment was the desire to remove the appointment of administrative positions from political patronage and to require merit qualifications.[4] Thus, in addition to removing the inequalities and possible inefficiencies of ascriptive recruitment, the merit reforms of civil service were intended to remove the inefficiencies and favoritism of political appointment.

As desirable as the idea of employing the best person possible for each job in the public service may be from the point of view of enforcing the achievement norms of a modern society, and perhaps of achieving new goals of social equality in a developing society, some important inefficiencies may result from merit recruitment. These may be especially noticeable when contrasted to the alternative: political appointment. Merit recruitment appears to imply the more mechanistic conception of the administrator or bureaucrat as the value-free administrator of programs who will administer public policies regardless of their intentions or impacts on society. It is assumed that sufficient technical criteria will guide their choices and that commitment to a program or rejection of it will have little influence on behavior. This conception of the administrator simply does not conform to the realities. Individuals were at least more disposed toward the programs of the political party in power than the supposedly neutral appointees of a merit system who may, in fact, be hostile to that program.[5] This requires that political appointees be selected for some combination of political disposition and administrative talent, however, and not for political predisposition alone.

This discussion of political versus merit appointment is, of course, one of degree. Virtually all political systems have some level at which appointments are quite clearly political—frequently referred to as "policy-making" positions— and they also have jobs for which appointment is made on a relatively routine basis on some sort of merit system. The question, then, is how far up the ladder of the administrative hierarchy merit, or at least not overtly political appointment, is intended to go; and conversely, what are the limits of political appointment? The differences between the United States and the United Kingdom illustrate the range that may exist. A president in the United States has the ability to appoint almost two thousand people to office, and four or even five echelons of political appointees may stand between a career civil servant and the cabinet secretary.[6] In the United Kingdom each ministry will have only a few political appointments other than the minister or secretary of state in charge—the largest number now is in the Treasury with seven appointments. But even then, the major interface between political and administrative leaders occurs between the minister and a single career civil servant, the permanent secretary.

What accounts for the differences among countries in the extent to which political appointments are employed as a means of attempting to ensure compliance within an organization? One argument is that bureaucratic structures simply have evolved over history and no one has seen any real reason to alter them. A more rationalist hypothesis would be that the more fragmented the decision-making structures of a government, the more likely it is to provide its ministers with a number of political appointees to provide some integration of political intentions and actual administration. The relative integration of the political elite and policy system in the United Kingdom, contrasted with that of the United States, could be taken to argue that the United Kingdom simply does not need so many political appointees on top to create compliance within the machinery of government.

We have been using the United States as the example of a country with a large number of political appointees, but several continental European countries could be used equally well. In those cases, however, the political appointees, rather than being inserted directly into the structure of the departments or ministries, are linked directly to the minister and his or her private office.[7] This removes some of the direct authority that the appointees might have, but it provides the minister with both advice and a group of people whom he can use anywhere within the ministry.

REPRESENTATIVE BUREAUCRACY

A second dominant theme in a discussion of recruitment into public administrative positions is the question of equality of opportunity and representativeness of the public bureaucracy.[8] Since Kingsley coined the term "representative bureaucracy," there has been concern over the extent to which the bureaucracy does, or should, represent the characteristics of the population in whose name it administers policy. Thus, just as some scholars have emphasized the necessity of merit in the recruitment of public administrators, others have stressed the importance of producing a set of administrators whose social and economic characteristics are similar to the people with whom they will be working. The arguments are twofold. The first is that narrow recruitment from any social stratum will tend to bias programs and policies. This is especially important in social programs because there is a higher probability that these personnel will be working with members of minority communities and may tend to impose dominant group values. Studies of teachers, social workers, the police, and other types of public employees indicate a tendency to reward those clients who correspond to accepted dominant values and punish those who do not.[9] This difference in value structures may not only impair the personal interaction of client and administrator, but will also tend to prevent a number of qualified individuals from receiving services.

The second argument in favor of greater representativeness is that the ability of the public bureaucracy to hire personnel should be used as a positive means to alter the social and economic structure of the society. Thus, hiring minority community members can serve not only to attack any prejudices within the society but also to provide a means of economic advancement for members of the minority community. In the United States this has taken the form of "affirmative action" programs in which employers (especially government) were pledged to make positive efforts to hire members of racial minorities and women.[10] In ethnically plural societies in which the differences between the communities are not necessarily those of dominance or submission, or in which the ethnic cleavage is rather intensely politicized, this argument is generally altered to say that representative recruitment can be used to *preserve* the social structure and the rights of each of the ethnic communities in administering policy.[11] In both versions of this argument, however, is the underlying premise that bureaucracies should be representative not simply because it is democratic for them to be so, but because the pattern of recruitment will have a fundamental effect on the shape of the social structure and social stratification across time.

Before one goes too far with the idea of representative bureaucracy, however, several important caveats must be advanced. The first is that research on representative bureaucracy has consistently found an overrepresentation of middle-class (broadly interpreted) backgrounds among civil servants. This is to be expected. The civil service is in itself a middle-class occupation, and the sons and daughters of the middle class tend to have a much higher probability of attaining middle-class occupations than do the sons and daughters of the working class. This is in part due to the nature of educational recruitment which, even in modern "welfare states," tends substantially to overrepresent the middle class, and in part due to the nature of the motivations and incentives inculcated in middle-class households.[12] In either case, the number of middle-class offspring in the civil service is not a particularly damning finding for the nature of the bureaucracy but is rather reflective of more general patterns of social stratification and mobility in the society. Interestingly, this pattern persists in societies that have sought to eliminate class barriers in public life, for example, the Soviet Union. Such evidence as we have would indicate that those occupying positions in the upper echelons of the Soviet civil service tend to come from families of fathers who also held "middle-class" occupations.

A second caveat is that the advocacy of representative bureaucracy assumes that the social class of parents will tend to determine behavior. This is an underlying assumption in a large amount of elite research, but the empirical research attempting to link background with behavior provides quite disappointing results.[13] Socialization is a lifelong process, and as administrators from working-class backgrounds will have attained middle-class status, they will tend to adopt the values of that class rather than their class of origin,[14] Further, although members of minority groups may not be able to change their status quite so readily, those who are in posts (especially senior posts) in the public bureaucracy will tend to support the values of the dominant community at a higher rate than other members of the minority group. This produces something of a paradox. Regardless of the degree of representativeness in the recruitment of civil servants, there will tend to be homogeneity of values.

Finally, we must realize that there may not of necessity be as broad a gap between merit recruitment and programs of "affirmative action" as there might appear to be at first glance. To some degree, the possession of certain ascriptive criteria may be an important qualification for the efficient administration of public programs, especially at the client-contact level of the bureaucracy. Language, race, or class differences may prevent the adequate administration of public programs; to prevent those differences from becoming too significant in administration, some attention to ethnic balancing of personnel must be given. Thus, to some degree, defining the person best able to carry out a job can depend upon ethnic characteristics just as it can depend upon formal education and the possession of certain skills.

PUBLIC VERSUS PRIVATE EMPLOYMENT

A final general question about the recruitment and retention of civil servants is the relationship between the advantages of public and private employment in terms of salaries, benefits, and working conditions. Most citizens want an efficient and well-qualified civil service, but many do not want that civil service to compete excessively with the private sector for the best personnel. The attractiveness of public jobs is especially great in times of recession because of the relative security of a government job. The argument against making civil service employment too attractive is that through taxation, employers are actually coerced into supporting their competition in the labor market; further, the public sector lacks any effective means of pricing most of its products. Therefore, governments can, to a point, drive up the price of labor to an unreasonable level from the viewpoint of actual productivity of personnel if employed in the market economy. This diseconomy may be especially evident when public personnel are allowed to unionize.[15] Thus, we come down to a rather simple question of the relative demand for public and private goods and the consequent willingness to pay for each type of goods. The evidence would appear to argue that there is considerably less demand for publicly produced goods—especially as they take on the characteristics of public goods—compared to the demand for private goods.[16] This may accentuate the diseconomies of public hiring. There may be no ready solution for this problem, but it is one that must be considered when discussing the extent and type of recruitment into the public bureaucracy.

METHODS OF RECRUITMENT

As well as the rather broad questions concerning recruitment outlined above, several questions deal with the more specific methods of recruitment and the judging of qualifications for positions. These questions are, of course, greatly simplified if political patronage or other sorts of nonachievement criteria are used, for then only simple appointment by the appropriate political official is required.

Education and Training

The first question is the type of training required for a position, and associated with it, the type of testing employed. Here we are interested primarily in the recruitment of the upper echelons of the bureaucracy rather than the clerical positions for which relatively uniform skill requirements can be established. In general, recruitment to policy-making positions requires some sort of postsecondary education, with the major question becoming the degree of specialization of that education. This brings us to the now standard argument between the advocates of generalists and specialists in the public bureaucracy.[17] The generalist school, as typified by practice in the United Kingdom, selects individuals for the top roles in the civil service largely on the basis of general abilities and performance in postsecondary education. The Northcote-Trevelyan Report of 1854 not only called for the establishment of a merit-based civil service in the United Kingdom but also noted that training in the classics was the best preparation for a future administrator.[18] The assumption was, and largely still is, that general intelligence is all that is required to master the job of sifting information and preparing advice for ministers.

The tradition of the talented amateur has persisted in Britain despite the increasing technological content of government work, and despite attacks on the policy by the Fulton Report (1968) and other public and private bodies.[19] As shown in Table 3.1, there are somewhat fewer arts and humanities graduates as a percentage of all entrants to the senior civil service, but that percentage remains well over half. Certainly those entering the higher civil service in Britain are extremely talented intellectually and will be able to master much of the required material while on the job, but they start at a severe disadvantage when dealing with technical (including economic) materials.

Recruitment to the civil service in the majority of continental European countries represents a different form of generalist education. In the majority

TABLE 3.1

UNIVERSITY MAJORS OF RECRUITS TO THE
HIGHER CIVIL SERVICE IN THE UNITED KINGDOM (IN PERCENTAGE)

	Arts and Humanities	Social Sciences	Natural Sciences and Applied Science	Other
1961–1967[a]	62	24	11	3
1975[b]	54	28	17	1

[a] Direct entrants to the administrative class; percentage of total concentrations mentioned.
[b] Recruits for Administrative Trainee positions.

SOURCES:
  A. H. Halsey and I. M. Crewe, "Social Survey of the Civil Service," *The Civil Service* (London: HMSO, 1968), vol. 3, pt. 1, p. 93.
  House of Commons, Expenditure Committee, 11th Report, 1976–77, *The Civil Service* (London: HMSO, 25 July, 1977).

of those countries the role of the administrator is quite similar to that of the jurist, and a law degree is a requirement for almost all senior positions. For example, in one study 66 percent of the senior civil service (*Beamte*) in the Federal Republic of Germany have legal degrees.[20] As with British civil servants, some training in technical matters will take place on the job, although it is much more common for German and other continental civil servants to take advanced degrees in a more technical subject, especially economics.

    The United States and France represent two different forms of specialist training for civil service careers. In the United States people are recruited to the civil service on the basis of having some particular educational qualifications prior to entry. For example, if an individual is seeking a job with the Department of Agriculture he or she might be expected to have training in agronomy or agricultural engineering, or some other relevant specialty. As a consequence of that pattern of recruitment, 35 percent of higher civil servants in the federal government of the United States have scientific or professional training of some type.[21]

    In France, the specialized training needed to become a top civil servant is provided by government itself. The principal source of entry into the higher civil service is the École Nationale d'Administration (ENA), which provides instruction in finance, management, and law. The engineers and technical staff needed by government are trained in the several *grands écoles*, such as the École Polytechnique. Lower-level administrators are trained in the Instituts Regionaux d'Administration (IRA). In total, the French government runs seventy-seven different types of schools for the training of civil servants.[22] In this system the government can prepare its future employees in exactly the manner it wants, either as administrators (ENA and IRA) or as technical and scientific staff.

Underdeveloped countries are in a more difficult position when deciding between generalist and specialist recruitment strategies. In the first place, they are frequently left with a civil service trained by the former colonial power and thereby trained according to the traditions of that European country.[23] Further, underdeveloped countries generally lack technical talent and must opt for a more generalist stance in recruitment into new positions. Some countries have attempted to replace an indigenous technical force with one drawn from Western countries—usually the former colonial power—but the demands of national pride and the need for jobs for their own people frequently require that jobs be given to less technically qualified individuals from the new nation.[24] At the same time that the administrative system may be somewhat deficient in specialized talent from an absolute point of view, it may have a relative monopoly on such talent within the country. A principal characteristic of many developing countries is that the political system is forced into the position of becoming the major directive force in social and economic reform. As one commentator put it:

> While there is no uniform pattern, the experience of many newly indepen-
> dent countries shows a growing emphasis on centralized planning, direction,
> and implementation of development programs. Thus, the government relies
> more on the bureaucracy than the private sector to carry out the task of
> nation and state building, economic growth, and social reforms—activities
> which are preeminent in the consciousness of the rulers and the ruled.[25]

The Western model of development—speaking broadly, as the Western economic and social systems evolved by several significantly different paths— assumed a long time span and the absence of developmental pressures from mass publics and organized segments of the society.[26] The developing countries today are faced with producing change within the context of widely disseminated information on the glories of development and consumerism. Their leaders face demands for increased production of consumer goods at the same time that they know the need for investment in capital projects, which will bear greater productive benefits in the long run but which require a short-term retreat from a consumer-oriented economy toward a more state-directed economy. Given these problems, it is rather apparent that these societies have a pressing need for specialized administrators capable of proposing some solutions to these problems and a large number of skilled personnel actually to manage economic enterprises that may be run directly by the state.

The above description of administration and administrative functions, if in the undeveloped countries taken to its logical extreme, might be a relatively accurate description of administrative functions in the Soviet Union and, to a lesser extent, other communist countries.[27] As the state becomes not only an economic planner, regulator, and adviser, but also the chief entrepreneur, the need for specialized talent tends to increase. Thus the average Soviet administrator, even if not administering a highly technical project, tends to have scientific or social science training. For example, by the 1960s over 80 percent of all politburo members and regional elites had technical training.[28] Interestingly, the more generalist talents of ideological argument and broad knowledge of the intended purpose of the Soviet state appear to be devalued by this set of upper-level administrators, who may differ little in this respect from administrators in other societies.[29] They have the same—if not greater—demands for production and efficiency that face other managers, and are often confronted with highly technical problems that only someone with a technical background may fully understand.

The above discussion has dealt with the recruitment of the higher civil service. At some point in the civil service hierarchy almost all recruitment is done on the basis of narrow, specific criteria. Typists, for example, are hired because of their ability to type. In terms of sheer numbers, therefore, most civil service recruitment is performed on the basis of specialized criteria.

Job Placement

Related to the type of training a prospective civil servant is expected to have is the question of the means through which the applicant and the position are expected to find each other. Again, there are two principal answers: centralized personnel organizations, or recruitment by each individual agency seeking employees. Centralized placement is practiced by the United States, the United Kingdom, France, Belgium, Italy, and the majority of Third World countries. The last set of countries has used centralized placement in large part as a function of inherited systems of administration. In the centralized pattern of recruitment there is a central civil service organization of some sort that is responsible for advertising new positions, testing applicants, and selecting some smaller set of applicants for final selection by the agency seeking the employee. The usual procedure is that the agency notifies the personnel organization of the position, a competitive examination is held, and then the agency seeking the person is sent a list of three or more names from which to select the new employee. The selection may be made on the basis of personal interviews or simply by taking the individual with the highest score on the examination or by any other rational or irrational criteria. This means of recruitment obviously meets the requirements of merit recruitment. Competitive tests are used to fill the position; these tests are centrally administered to prevent bias, and the hiring organization accepts only those deemed qualified on the basis of the examination. In practice, there may be ways around the merit system, especially for those who have professional qualifications, for example, physicians, lawyers, librarians, and the like. They may be qualified simply on the basis of their degrees and certificates and require no further examination.

The second means of hiring and recruitment is used primarily by the northern European countries, Spain, and many Latin American countries. In these systems there is no central personnel organization; rather, each agency is responsible for hiring its own personnel. The most common procedure is for the agency to publish notice of a vacancy and accept applications from prospective employees. These applications are generally judged on the basis of appropriate minimum qualifications for the job—especially legal training in the Scandinavian countries (Sweden, Denmark, Norway), West Germany, and Austria. After the individual is deemed minimally qualified, selection may be made on the basis of less achievement-based criteria. This system of decentralized recruitment obviously allows considerable latitude for the use of partisan and ascriptive criteria in hiring public officials, who can become tenured in office and virtually impossible for subsequent regimes to remove. Charges of partisanship are indeed made in these systems, even in Sweden and Denmark with their long histories of civil service independence and prestige.[30] For example, there were some concerns expressed as to whether a bureaucracy recruited under thirty-five years of Social Democratic government could serve the bourgeois coalition elected in Sweden in 1976. It is a simple matter to hire partisans when there are no formal restrictions to prevent it, and the parties in power would be extremely foolish if they did not try to provide employment for their own supporters and employ administrators likely to be favorably disposed toward the programs they will be administering. As with many administrative practices, this is not a simple case of recruitment by merit or by patronage, but rather something of an intermediate means of recruitment that combines some features of both ideal-type methods. There is the potential for substantial patronage, but these opportunities are restrained in practice by the norms, procedures, and pride of the administrators. In each country in Europe in which the recruitment of administrators by agency is practiced—with the possible exception of Spain—the civil service is a sufficiently respected profession that few practitioners would seek to demean it by an excessive or blatant use of the power they find themselves possessing.

The nature of recruitment by agency is made more complex when federalism is introduced as another variable. In Germany and Switzerland recruitment to public administrative positions is done not only by the individual agencies, but also by separate and in some cases highly independent subnational political units, which are in turn responsible for the administration of national programs.[31] This is further complicated by Swiss bureaucracy's need to preserve some balance among regional, linguistic, and religious subpopulations within the civil service. In general, the use of subnational bodies to perform the recruitment function may provide even greater possibilities for the use of nonmerit criteria in recruitment. Nevertheless, in Germany and Switzerland we find again that the norms of the bureaucratic system are sufficiently ingrained so that merit criteria are strenuously enforced. Those who are hired will have the necessary qualifications for the position—legal training and prior legal experience—and they will be made to undergo some sort of post-entry training in the work of administration before they are granted permanent positions as administrators.[32] There is an attempt, and actually a rather thorough attempt, to employ people who are formally qualified according to the requirements of the law. Thus, in this case as in others, although the rigidity of bureaucracies is often an impediment to innovation, it can also serve as an important protective device for the society in preventing illegal or immoral actions on the part of government.

Career Distinctiveness

A third question concerning recruitment is the extent to which the public service is a distinct career, one for which the individual may prepare specially and which is regarded as a separate career hierarchy from the rest of the economy. It is interesting to note that movement back and forth between public and private employment—especially in policy-making positions—has been used as an indicator of two rather different relationships between society and the political systems. On the one hand, such movement is frequently taken to indicate a healthy congruence between the value structures of polity and society, a means of ensuring the representativeness of the bureaucratic structures, and even a means through which "typical" citizens can exert some influence on public policy. On the other hand, such movement can also be taken to indicate the colonization of the society by bureaucrats or, conversely, the colonization of the public service by representatives of certain vested interests in the society. The former of these negative perceptions is best illustrated by the concern of the French over the *pantouflage*, or "parachuting," of upper-echelon civil servants into important and lucrative positions in the private economy.[33] This is taken as an indication of the attempt on the part of *fonctionnaires* and technocrats to manage the whole of society and not just the governmental apparatus. It also means that a great deal of executive talent developed at public expense is exported to the private sector free of charge. The second negative conception of lateral movement between public and private management is more representative of thought in the United States where, at times, the feeling is voiced that too much of the government is being run by administrators currently on leave from major corporations, major unions, and other significant interests in the society.[34] Consequently, there is a belief that much of government is run for the benefit of those interests rather than for the benefit of the public at large.

The degree of concern over, or distrust of, lateral movements between public and private sectors would appear to be a function of several normative concerns of the society, especially as they relate to the administrative roles of government. One concern is the perception of the values, job, and norms of the public bureaucracy as distinct from those of the private sector. In the French case, the *fonctionnaires* are perceived as a special set of the population. This perception contains some positive and some negative elements, but the most common is that *pantouflage* is a means through which they may seek to impose their conception of society onto the society. In other societies that seek as much as possible to distinguish bureaucratic careers from private careers, it is rather clear that employment as a public administrator is *supposed* to carry with it a rather distinct set of values and decisional premises. For example, in Germany and Sweden the public administrator has been traditionally conceived of in a modified legal role. It is assumed that he or she will act much as would a judge in impartially administering programs *pro bono publico* and in accordance with the letter of the law. This may be too much to expect from a mere human, but this separation and idealization of administrator and career patterns has been useful in justifying decisions made by administrators in societies that rely heavily on administration in the conduct of public business.

A second and related normative concern is the extent to which the society fears bureaucracy and therefore seeks to prevent the development of a large and inflexible bureaucratic structure atop society. There are a number of means of controlling the development of such a bureaucracy, and lateral entry at the upper echelons is certainly one of them.[35] This is perhaps the logical extension of the idea of the amateur in administration, but it is one way in which general social values can be injected into the conduct of government and administration, recognizing all the while that this will likely reduce the efficiency of organizations already attacked as being inefficient.

Civil service systems differ markedly in the extent to which their members have experience outside government. At one end of the dimension is the United Kingdom, where civil servants rarely have experience outside government and tend to stay in government for their entire working lifetime. For example, in one study of careers in the British civil service, it was found that only 29 percent of senior civil servants had any working experience outside central government. Of that 29 percent, 8 percent had experience in some other type of government and 12 percent had experience in teaching. Only 7 percent had worked in private sector firms.[36]

There are three patterns of greater civil service involvement in the economy and society. One is the American revolving door, or the "government of strangers" described by Heclo.[37] In this system there is a great deal of movement back and forth between the public and private sector, with most people staying in government only a few years. The majority of these posts would be political appointments, but they would be positions normally occupied by civil servants in other countries.

A second pattern is that in which individuals leave government at a certain stage in their careers and go to work for the private sector. In the United States this has been a move primarily of retired military officers who go to work for defense manufacturers, but it is more common in France and Japan. It is a normal step in the career pattern in Japan, for example, for top civil servants from MITI—the Ministry of Trade and Industry—to take lucrative posts in the private sector after retiring early from government.[38]

Finally, there are the interesting cases in which being a civil servant is not considered incompatible with a political career. This is most evident in West Germany, where the individual, once granted the status of *Beamte*, retains that status for life. The civil servant can leave government temporarily while pursuing a political career and then return. In 1975, 49 percent of the Bundestag were also civil servants.[39] Of course, in the Soviet Union and other communist countries the connection between administrative and political careers is necessary.[40]

Incentives and Motivation

We have already mentioned the question of incentives when discussing one of the more general aspects of recruitment in public bureaucracies. We now discuss more of the methods available to public administration to recruit and maintain their personnel. In a general overview of organizations and membership in organizations, Clark and Wilson developed a classification of the types of incentives that an organization can offer members; the three types mentioned were material, purposive, and solidary.[41] Material incentives are pay, benefits, and direct financial rewards. Purposive incentives are related to the ability of the individual within the organization to have some influence over the shape of public policy adopted and implemented by government, or simply to get something done on the job. Finally, solidary incentives derive from the social aspects of employment and group membership, which in the case of public employment may at times involve belonging to one of the more prestigious organizations in society.

Any organization will potentially provide some of each of these incentives to employees. However, there are cross-national differences in the extent to which each of the three is perceived as an effective means of motivation by current and potential administrators. Some evidence of this type can be gained by survey data, although such data are available for only a limited number of systems, largely from Western nations. As shown in Table 3.2, there are some differences in response patterns even in this relatively homogeneous set of countries. In the first place, it is interesting to note that purposive incentives, which might have been thought to be the most significant means of influencing people to join the bureaucracy, are not that important. In the cases for which we have data, one of the other incentives, most usually solidary, is mentioned by a larger percentage of the respondents.

It might be thought that the relative undervaluing of purposive incentives was a function of the subgroup within the civil service about which we have information. This is composed largely of administrators near the top of the administrative hierarchy; they have been in office for some time and may therefore be expected to have developed greater identification with the organization than with the *purposes* of the organization. In other words, they have become conservers.[42] The limited evidence reported from an Australian survey seems to dispute this, however, and the reasons reported for joining the civil service are less purposive than those reported for remaining in the service.

TABLE 3.2
INCENTIVES IN RECRUITMENT AND
RETENTION OF ADMINISTRATORS (IN PERCENT)

Incentives	United Kingdom (1967)[a]	France (1969)[b]	New Zealand (1966)[c]	Spain (1967)[d]	Italy (1978)[e]	Turkey (1965)[f]
Material	20	24	36	21	47.5	25.3
Purposive	19	32	27	39	10.9	12.1
Solidary	56	34	21	30	35.8	56.7
Other	6	10	16	10	5.8	5.9
	101*	100	100	100	100	100

* due to rounding.

Incentives	Australia (1975)[g] Join	Australia (1975)[g] Stay In	India[h] (1968)
Material	34.0	29.5	38.4
Purposive	12.7	27.3	6.2
Solidary	26.0	15.2	29.2
Other	—	—	26.2
Total	72.7	72.0	100.0

SOURCES:

[a] Brian Chapman, "Profile of a Profession: The Administrative Class of the Civil Service," in *The Civil Service* (Fulton Report) (London: HMSO, 1968), vol. 3, pt. 2, p. 12.

[b] Ezra N. Suleiman, *Politics, Power and Bureaucracy in France* (Princeton: Princeton University Press, 1974), p. 120.

[c] R. L. Green, M. R. Palmer, and T. J. Sanger, "Why They Leave," *New Zealand Journal of Public Administration* 30, no. 1 (Summer 1967): 27.

[d] Manuel Gomez-Reino and Francisco Andres Orizo, "Burocracias Publica y Privida," in Anales de Moral Social y Economica, *Sociologica de la Administración Publica Española* (Madrid: Raycar, 1968), p. 267.

[e] Franco Ferraresi, *Burocrazia e politica in Italia* (Milan: Il Mulino, 1980), pp. 120–121.

[f] Leslie L. Roos and Noralou P. Roos, *Managers of Modernization: Organizations and Elites in Turkey* (Cambridge, Mass.: Harvard University Press, 1971), p. 123.

[g] Royal Commission on Australian Government Administration, *Report*, Appendix 3 (Canberra: Australian Government Publishing Service, 1976). Percentage listing each type of incentive as "important" and "very important."

[h] Richard P. Taub, *Bureaucrats Under Stress* (Berkeley, Calif.: University of California Press, 1969).

The differences between the several sets of administrators for which we have data are not particularly striking, but we can note three rather interesting points. The first is the extremely high percentage of administrators in the United Kingdom who gave answers in terms of solidary incentives when questioned about their jobs. This would appear to conform nicely with the stereotype of British administration as a set of "old boys" who conduct administration in a collegial, gentlemanly fashion and whose role as amateurs may prevent any effective policy initiative from arising from the bureaucracy. Of course, numerous recent studies of the administrative apparatus of the United Kingdom indicate that although they may not be experts in any particular technical specialty, many administrators discharge quite significant roles in the formation of policy—in fact, that has been known by the practitioners themselves for quite a long time.[43] Still, it is interesting to note the extent to which the practitioners give more social reasons for either joining or staying in their positions. Of the countries on which we have data, the French upper-echelon administrators reported the highest levels of purposive incentives. This too conforms to the prevailing conception of the French bureaucracy as the *groupe diregante* of the society.[44] Traditionally, the way of getting things done in French government has been through administration, and we may expect that administrators would perceive a relatively great ability to accomplish things through their jobs. Finally, the Italian administrators gave a very high proportion of material answers, indicating the often cited tendency to use the bureaucracy as a means of personal advancement rather than as a force for policy change.

If the evidence on incentive structures for Western administrative systems is rather spotty, then the information on non-Western administrative systems appears virtually nonexistent. The data for a sample of Turkish administrators, however, show a close similarity to Western nations. Further, from a number of more descriptive studies, we can rather quickly develop the hypothesis that the major incentives for joining bureaucratic systems in non-Western societies are solidary and material rather than purposive. In the first place, given the colonial backgrounds of most of these societies, the pattern of goal achievement through administration was not well ingrained into these systems at the time of independence. Moreover, in the Latin American systems, which have been independent longer, the administrators are not always protected by merit systems and tenure, so that any attempt to use administration to alter the existing social and economic arrangements often meets with a prompt dismissal from office.[45]

There are also more positive aspects to the attraction of the bureaucracy for many prospective employees. The public bureaucracy is a stable and relatively remunerative institution of the society, and compared with opportunities that may exist in the private economy, the opportunity to work in the public bureaucracy is frequently an extremely attractive economic option.[46] The operation of the solidary incentives are perhaps less obvious. One of the social and cultural bases of many underdeveloped countries has been an emphasis on status and rank in defining social behavior. Also, in most of these societies the public bureaucracy has been able to establish itself as a high-status occupation. This may be in part related to the relatively brief separation in time from the period in which recruitment to these governmental positions—the authorities—was determined almost entirely by ascriptive criteria, and in fact the best families frequently chose to send their sons into the public service. As Kearney and Harris said when speaking of Ceylon:

> The great prestige enjoyed by the public servant has, however, probably contributed at least as much as material advantage or employment security to the attractiveness of a bureaucratic career. The social prestige of the modern bureaucrat is in large measure a heritage of Ceylon's feudal and colonial past.[47]

These authors go on to point out that the "social exclusiveness and supreme confidence" of colonial administrators tended to reinforce the impression that administrative positions were to be equated with superior social position.[48] Further, in societies that value social position above the more achievement-based criteria usually associated with Western societies, one may expect a high level of solidary incentives among those joining the bureaucracy.

The incentives of administrators joining the bureaucracy in the underdeveloped world are obviously different from the types of incentives that we would expect to characterize bureaucrats charged with bringing about important social and economic changes. Already noted is the load being placed upon administration in these transformations, and we find here a great disparity between the requirements of social change and the motivation of the people being recruited.[49] This cannot, of course, provide an optimistic outlook for the future of administered change.

To conclude this discussion of incentives, it is possible to make some highly conjectural statements about the nature of the bureaucracy in the Soviet Union and other communist countries. On the basis of descriptive accounts and descriptions of prior administrative systems, one can hypothesize that the incentive structures of these bureaucrats will be rather similar to those found for administrators in Western societies, for example, a balance of material, purposive, and solidary. The purposive incentives are rather obvious, given that the Soviet Union, like most Western societies, has become a heavily administration-oriented political system. It might be expected that people would feel the ability to accomplish certain goals through working in the administrative structures. The material incentives may appear rather odd in a supposedly classless society, but we know well that there are, if not classes, at least groups for which there are differential economic rewards.[50] The public bureaucracy is one such group; being a member of the "apparatus" of the state will generally pay off not only directly, but also indirectly through access to scarce consumer goods. Finally, one traditional description of Russian administration was as a set of small and closely knit primary groups operating within the context of a larger governmental structure.[51] We may hypothesize that this same sort of small group is still operating in the Soviet bureaucracy, so that there will be a high level of solidary motivation for the worker within such a group. Of course, these are only conjectures about the motivations of these administrators, but there is evidence that each of the incentives is likely to be effective. What is not known is the relative strength of these motivations and incentives.

Pay in the Public Sector

It has been established that money may not be the only, or even the best, means of motivating potential employees to accept government careers, or to continue in those careers once they have been employed. But pay is an important issue in the public sector, not least because many citizens believe that government employees receive large salaries for little work. In addition, it is not only the pay received during the working lifetime of the employees that produces resentment, but also the variety of benefits received by civil servants, not least of which is an inflation-proofed pension. The comparability of compensation in the public sector with that of the private sector is an important consideration in determining the satisfaction of government workers with their jobs, and for determining the satisfaction of citizens with their public servants.

Determining appropriate levels of compensation for government employees is not as simple a task as it may appear. It is true that many public sector jobs are directly comparable to jobs in the private sector; the tasks of a secretary in government are almost identical to those of a secretary in the private sector. However, some jobs in government have no private sector counterparts, and many jobs that appear comparable may not be. Being a policeman is different from any private sector job, even that of a private security guard. And although the job of a government executive may resemble that of a private sector manager of a similar-size firm, the private sector manager is spared the political responsibility, media exposure, and managerial difficulties (for example, civil service rules) of a manager in government. In addition, determining the value of an index-linked pension, or of the relative security of public employment, involves a number of assumptions about the future rates of inflation, future rates of unemployment, and the preferences of workers for future-versus-current income.[52]

Most studies of pay comparability between the public and private sectors find that government employees at the lower echelons are better paid than their private sector counterparts.[53] This is especially true of workers in unskilled or semiskilled positions, for example, sanitation workers or bus drivers. This relative advantage of public sector workers derives at least in part from the ability of these workers to exert pressure on political leaders by real or threatened strikes. However, as responsibilities increase, government employees are paid less well than workers in the private sector. Those working at the very top of public organizations frequently earn only a fraction of what they would be earning with similar responsibilities in the private sector.[54]

There are some significant exceptions to the above generalization. In societies with traditions of strong and prestigious government, senior civil servants are often well paid. For example, in the United Kingdom, the very top officials of the civil service (the "open structure") are well paid in comparison to the majority of like executives in the economy, although their pay has been falling behind since the late 1970s. These civil servants lack some of the perquisites of private sector employees, for example, a car, but do have an index-linked pension to look forward to after retirement. Also, in societies dominated by government, for instance, the Soviet Union or many Third World countries, government is by far the most rewarding place to be employed.

Pay determination in the public sector is more than a question of personnel management. It is also a crucial element in economic management. As government now employs a very large proportion of the total labor force (18 percent in the United States, 31 percent in the United Kingdom, and 42 percent in Sweden), pay determination in the public sector influences economic conditions for the economy as a whole; and when there is an attempt to implement an incomes policy, public sector wages serve as guidelines for the remainder of the economy.[55] Further, when governments come into conflict with labor unions over wages, the settlement reached can be used as an indicator of the power and resolve of the government, for example, Conservative governments in the United Kingdom in 1974 and in 1982.

Pay for public sector employees is determined in a number of ways. One is to link pay directly to changes in the private sector, or to consumer prices. For example, in the Netherlands civil service pay has been adjusted biennially to take into account changes in private sector wages, while in Australia pay is adjusted annually on the basis of changes in prices.[56] Pay for civil servants in the United States is nominally based upon comparability with the private sector, although the president and Congress make independent judgments about appropriate levels of compensation. For example, in 1981, Congress authorized a pay increase of 4.8 percent, rejecting the 15 percent figure proposed on the basis of comparability studies.[57]

Negotiation with unions is the other major means of setting public sector pay. In Denmark this bargaining occurs as a part of negotiations for wages throughout the economy, whereas in Italy, Canada, and a number of other countries the negotiation is independent of other negotiations. In all negotiations, however, comparability is at least an implicit part of the bargaining process. West Germany has a modified version of unionized pay setting in which the salaries of ordinary civil servants (*Angestelle*) are set by negotiations with unions, and then pay for the top civil servants (*Beamte*) is determined by the Parliament. The proposed new pay system for the civil service in the United Kingdom would depend upon interquartile bargaining, in which the civil service would expect to be paid more than the lowest quartile but less than the upper quartile for workers in similar jobs. Bargaining between the unions and government would occur within those ranges.[58]

Despite differences in the manner in which pay is determined, several generalities can be made. First, a balance must be struck between fiscal con-

straints and the need to attract qualified personnel. This is obviously more of
a problem at the upper levels of government than at the bottom but may
become a problem for skilled tradesmen as well as executives. Secondly, in
times of economic constraint, public sector pay makes a convenient target for
those who want to control the costs of government. This is true despite the
fact that personnel costs generally constitute a relatively small percentage of
total government costs, for example, 10 percent for the federal government
in the United States and 7 percent in Sweden. Third, public sector employees,
by virtue of their central positions in the economy and society (public transportation workers, firemen, defense, etc.) and their increasing levels of unionization,
are in powerful positions to influence their levels of pay. Finally, pay itself is
only a part of the total compensation package; to fully understand the benefits
of public employment, factors such as index-linked pensions must also be taken
into account.

PATTERNS OF RECRUITMENT

We have been discussing the methods by which administrators are chosen
and some of the issues involved in the choice of methods. This section examines
the effects of these choices by scrutinizing the actual patterns of recruitment
of administrators. Again, we are somewhat constrained by the lack of availability
of data for administrative systems, especially those of the less-developed countries. Despite these constraints, it is possible to find substantial recruitment
information on the administrative systems of twenty-five countries on several
dimensions of social background, preparation, and representativeness that can
give important information about how administrators are chosen. However,
some important caveats exist. This information was gathered by different individuals, at different times, and on somewhat different segments of the bureaucratic
population. The majority concentrates on upper-echelon administrators, but
in some cases definitions are broader. Therefore, care must be exercised in
the interpretation of differences among these countries, but the data serve an
important function of illustrating the general directions of recruitment in each
country. In each case, the source, year, and definition of the administrative
population (if different from "top" administrators) are noted.

The first dimension upon which there is data is the socio-economic background of the administrators. Given that the administration is essentially a
middle-class occupation, the major variance here is in the occupation of the
fathers—or the class of origin—of these administrators. We see from Tables
3.3 and 3.4 that not only is administration a middle-class occupation, but the
origins of the administrators are also primarily middle class. The definition of
class origin here is somewhat fuzzy, especially the difference between upper
class and middle class, but the largest single class of origin in each case is
middle class. This is even more striking when the categories are collapsed into

working class and bourgeois (by adding together middle and upper classes).
In each case, few if any children of workers ever make it into the ranks of
upper administration, with the most open system apparently being that of the
United States, where almost one-quarter of the federal executives came from
working-class backgrounds. Despite the elitist image, the French civil service
also had a relatively large percentage of inductees from the working class.[59]
West Germany would appear to be the most unrepresentative of the civil services,
for in the sample taken by Zapf of upper administrators, none came from
working-class backgrounds.[60] Somewhat different samples used by Aberbach,
Putnam, and Rockman show France to have fewer civil servants from working-
class backgrounds than does Germany.[61] Lest we become too critical of the
bureaucratic systems, we should note that this pattern of elitist recruitment is
far from entirely the fault of these institutions. The bureaucracies are at the
mercy of the educational system, and despite attempts to make postsecondary
education more available, it still remains a sanctuary of the upper and middle
classes. Given the job requirements for the vast majority of higher administrative
positions, be they for specialists or generalists, a postsecondary education is a
virtual necessity, and in most countries few working-class children are provided
that opportunity. This educational nexus is, in fact, the probable reason for
the rather positive showing of the United States. Postsecondary education is
more available in the United States than elsewhere, so the pool of potential
applicants is that much larger.

We should not, on the other hand, be too quick to absolve the bureaucracies of all guilt in their rather unrepresentative nature. All organizations tend
to replicate themselves, and there is a definite tendency to recruit people like
those already in the positions. This type of organizational bias is especially
strong during the personal interviews generally required for appointment to
upper-echelon positions.[62] Bureaucracies also use formal rules, such as the requirement for degrees or the difficulties in moving from one class of civil servant
to another (for example, the administrative and executive classes in the British
civil service prior to Fulton), as a means of maintaining their recruitment patterns
even in the face of democratization of the society and cultures of most Western
societies. This tendency to preserve a more elitist recruitment pattern may
not even be conscious, and those doing the recruiting may simply be functioning
with a mental picture of a good candidate that eliminates good working-class
talent.

Education

We now have some inkling that education may be an important characteristic in describing public administrators, and again especially those at the upper
levels of the hierarchy. Again, there is less than comprehensive data, but we
can get the same sort of impression about the educational levels that differ

TABLE 3.3
SOCIAL CLASS BACKGROUND OF
SENIOR CIVIL SERVICE PERSONNEL (IN PERCENTAGES)

Social-class Origin	United Kingdom (1968)[a]	United States (1959)[b]	France (1971–75)[c]	West Germany (1955)[d]	Denmark (1945)[e]	Sweden (1947)[f]	Switzerland (1969)[g]
Upper	21	19	40	13	38.3	9.1	—
Middle	56	44	30	68	48.9	81.9	85
Working	19	21	14	0	4.3	3.0	15
Other	5	16	16	0	8.5	6.0	—
Total	101	100	100	81*	100	100	100

* 19% did not answer.

Social-class Origin	Italy (1965)[h]	Canada (1957)[i]	India (1947–63)[j]	Turkey (1962)[k]	Republic of Korea (1962)[l]	Spain (1967)[m]	Pakistan (nd)[n]
Upper	17.4	18.1	29.2	29.0	13.2	—	22.4
Middle	65.4	68.7	66.1	61.5	70.3	96	76.1
Working	4.7	13.2	—	1.0	6.8	4	1.5
Other	12.5	—	4.7	8.5	—	—	—
Total	100	100	100	100	90.3*	100	100

* 9.7% did not answer.

Social-class Origin	Zambia (1969)[o]	Netherlands (1973)[p]	Australia (1970)[q]	Belgium (1973)[r]	Norway (1976)[s]
Upper	5	59	78	13	71
Middle	43	26	22	59	14
Working	23	15	—	11	15
Other	27	—	—	17	
Total	98	100	100	100	100

SOURCES:

a A. H. Halsey and I. M. Crewe, *Social Survey of the Civil Service*, vol. 3, pt. 1 of *The Civil Service* (The Fulton Report) (London: HMSO, 1968), p. 19.

b W. L. Warner, et al., *The American Federal Executive* (New Haven: Yale University Press, 1963), p. 29.

c Pierre Racine, "L'origine sociale des enarques," *La Fonction Publique, Cahiers Francais* (Paris: La Documentation Française, 1980).

d Wolfgang Zapf, *Wandlungen der Deutschen Elite* (Munich: Piper, 1966), p. 180.

e Henry Stjernquist, "Centraladministrationens Embedsmaend 1848–1946," in *Centraladministrationen 1848–1946* (Copenhagen: Ministerialforenigen, 1948), p. 282.

f Sten-Stuve Landstrom, *Svenska Ämbetsmans Sociala Ursprung* (Uppsale: Almqvist och Wiksell, 1954), p. 42.

g Ulrich Kloti, "Die chefbeamten der Schweizerischen Bundesverwaltuing: Ein Forschungsbericht," in *Annuairre Suisse de Science Politique* (1971) 2:57.

h Paolo Ammassari, "L'Estrazione Sociale dei funzionari dello Stato e degli enti locali," in Ammassari et al., *Il Burocrate di Fronto Alle Burocrazia* (Milan: Giuffre, 1969), p. 21.

i John Porter, *The Vertical Mosaic* (Toronto: University of Toronto Press, 1965), pp. 445–46.

j V. Subramanian, *Social Background of India's Administrators* (New Delhi: Ministry of Information, 1971), p. 145.

k C.H. Dodd, "The Social and Educational Backgrounds of Turkish Officials," *Middle Eastern Studies* 1 (1964): 271.

l Dong Suh Bark, "Korean Higher Civil Servants: Their Social Background and Morale" in Byung Chul Koh, *Aspects of Administrative Development in South Korea* (Kalamazoo, Mich.: Korea Research Publication, 1967), p. 27.

m Juan J. Linz and Amando de Miguel, "La Elite Funcionarial Española Ante La Reforma Administrativa," in Anales de Moral Social y Economica, *Sociologica de la Administracion Publica Española* (Madrid: Raycar, 1968), pp. 208–9.

n Ralph Braibanti, "The Higher Bureaucracy of Pakistan," in *Asian Bureaucratic Systems Emergent From the British Imperial Tradition*, ed. R. Braibanti (Durham, N.C.: Duke University Press, 1966), p. 271.

o Dennis L. Dresang, "Ethnic Politics, Representative Bureaucracy and Development Administration: The Zambian Case," *American Political Science Review* 68, no. 4 (December 1974): 1609.

p Samuel Eldersveld, Sonja Hubée-Boonzaaijer, and Jan Kooiman, "Elite Perceptions of the Political Process in the Netherlands Looked at in Comparative Perspective," in *The Mandarins of Western Europe*, ed. M. Dogan (New York: Halsted, 1975), p. 136.

q S. Encel, *Equality and Authority* (Melbourne: Chesein, 1970).

r Andre Molitor, *L'Administration de la Belgique* (Brussels: Centre de recherche et d'information socio-politique, 1974).

s Per Laegreid and Johan P. Olsen, *Byråkrati og Beslutningar* (Bergen: Universitetsforlaget, 1978).

93

TABLE 3.4
SOCIAL CLASS BACKGROUNDS OF
SAMPLES OF SENIOR CIVIL SERVANTS

	United Kingdom	France	Germany	Italy	Netherlands	United States	Average
Higher Management	51	66	46	46	37	39	48
Lower Management	17	30	21	36	23	30	26
Skilled Nonmanual	16	3	19	16	26	11	15
Lower Nonmanual	5	0	2	0	11	7	4
Skilled Manual	5	1	11	3	0	7	4
Semiskilled or Unskilled	8	0	1	0	4	7	3
Total	102	100	100	101	101	101	100

SOURCE:
Joel D. Aberbach, Robert D. Putnam, and Bert A. Rockman, *Bureaucrats and Politicians in Western Democracies* (Cambridge, Mass.: Harvard University Press, 1981), p. 55.

across cultures and educational systems. As much as possible, we have attempted to group the data into categories that would be meaningful to American readers. This may lose something in precision, but it should be compensated by an increased comparability of the data.

The previous discussion of the relationship of education and class in the selection of administrative personnel should have led us to expect a well-educated group of people serving as upper-echelon administrators. This expectation is well justified by the data. Almost universally, administrative personnel tend to have some form of postsecondary education, with the majority having completed the equivalent of a bachelor's degree. In some cases, this education may be within the confines of a specialized administrative college, but there is nonetheless a definite postsecondary phase of education for most administrators. The data taken from Aberbach, Putnam, and Rockman indicate that civil servants tend to be more educated than employees in similar types of positions in the rest of the economy.[63] This is to be expected in many cases simply because such education is a requirement for appointment. Interesting here is that the United States and Canada, which are frequently cited as having more "democratic" political cultures, tend to have larger percentages of their upper civil services lacking any postsecondary education.[64] Israel has by far the most open administrative structures, in part because of the newness of the country and in part because of the relatively poor pay levels.

As well as having completed college or its equivalent, these administrators have frequently attended the more prestigious colleges. Studies of the British civil service, for example, show over two-thirds of the senior civil service having gone to Oxford or Cambridge. The civil service appears to have declining appeal for "Oxbridge" graduates, however.[65] In his study of the backgrounds of Indian administrators, Subramanian reported that "the majority of recruits come from the six older and better known [universities]. . . . The significance of education in the right college is unmistakable."[66] Suleiman also reports that the majority— and in fact over three-fourths—of the entrants to the ENA had had their university education in Paris.[67] Forty-two percent of these entrants have had their entire education in Paris. A later study shows over half of all ENA students having all their education in Paris, with another quarter having had their higher education in Paris.[68] Thus, in these cases, the importance of not only attending college but also the right college is indeed unmistakable. Here again, the American experience is somewhat different from the other systems reported. The analysis by Warner et al. of the college attendance of American career executives shows a rather strong influence of large state-supported universities in the education of administrators.[69] If foreign-service executives are excluded, none of the Ivy League schools is among the top ten in terms of number of degrees held, and only three are in the top thirty. Among foreign-service executives, however, three of the Ivy League are in the top ten, and all eight schools are in the top thirty. This evidence would appear to offer some support for the conception of American society and its administrative system as being somewhat more

TABLE 3.5
EDUCATIONAL LEVELS OF SENIOR CIVIL SERVANTS (IN PERCENTAGES)

	United Kingdom (1967)[a]	United States (1959)[b]	France[c]	West Germany (1955)[d]	Sweden (1947)[e]
High School	2	5	0	0	23
Some College	27	14	7	23	
College Graduate	52	57	93	77	77
College +	19	24	0	0	
Total	100	100	100	100	100

	Switzerland (1969)[f]	Canada (1957)[g]	USSR (1950–66)[h]	Japan (1949–59)[i]	Republic of Korea (1962)[j]
High School	7	17	10	1.2	10.1
Some College		4	50		8.7
College Graduate	82 }	79 }	40	98.8	54.3
College +					26.9
Total	89*	100	100	100	100

* 11% did not answer.

	Turkey (1962)[k]	Pakistan (1948–64)[l]	Burma (1962)[m]	Israel (1969)[n]	Netherlands (1973)[o]
High School or Less	1.5	0		49.4	15
Some College		35.2	23.8	28.2	
College Graduate	98.5	64.8	76.2	22.4	85
College +					
Total	100	100	100	100	100

	Finland (1977)[p]	Belgium (1973)[q]	Italy (1961)[r]	Spain (1976)[s]
High School	} 71.9	} 19	17.8	45.0
Some College				38.3
College Grad	} 20.6	} 81	82.2	} 16.7
College +	7.5			
Total	100.0	100	100	100

SOURCES:

[a] A. H. Halsey and I. M. Crewe, *Social Survey of the Civil Service*, vol. 3, pt. 1 of *The Civil Service* (The Fulton Report) (London: HMSO, 1968), p. 64.

[b] W. L. Warner et al., *The American Federal Executive* (New Haven: Yale University Press, 1963).

[c] Ezra N. Suleiman, *Politics, Power and Bureaucracy in France* (Princeton: Princeton University Press, 1974), p. 67.

[d] Wolfgang Zapf, *Wandlungen der Deutschen Elite* (Munich: Piper, 1966), p. 178.

[e] Sten-Stuve Landstrom, *Svenska Ämbetsmans Sociala Ursprung* (Uppsala: Almqvist och Wiksell, 1954), p. 129.

[f] Ulrich Kloti, "Die Chefbeamten der Schweizerischen, Bundesverwaltung: Ein Forschungsbericht," in *Annuaire Suisse de Science Politique* (1971) 2:59.

[g] John Porter, *The Vertical Mosaic* (Toronto: University of Toronto Press, 1965), pp. 433–34.

[h] Philip D. Stewart, *Political Power in the Soviet Union* (Indianapolis: Bobbs-Merrill, 1968), p. 142. This is a sample of Obkom First Secretaries who hold politico-administrative posts.

[i] Akira Kubota, *Higher Civil Servants in Postwar Japan* (Princeton: Princeton University Press, 1969), p. 69.

[j] Dong Suh Bark, "Korean Higher Civil Servants: Their Social Backgrounds and Morale," in Byung Chul Koh, *Aspects of Administrative Development in South Korea* (Kalamazoo, Mich.: Korean Research Publication, 1967), p. 29.

[k] C. H. Dodd, "The Social and Educational Background of Turkish Officials," *Middle Eastern Studies* 1, no. 2 (1964): 273.

[l] Ralph Braibanti, "The Higher Bureaucracy of Pakistan," in *Asian Bureaucratics Systems Emergent From the British Imperial Tradition*, ed. Ralph Braibanti (Durham, N.C.: Duke University Press, 1966), pp. 279–81.

[m] James F. Guyot, "Bureaucratic Transformation in Burma," in ibid., p. 425.

[n] Nimrod Raphaeli, "The Senior Civil Service in Israel: Notes on Some Characteristics," *Public Administration* (London) 48, no. 2 (Summer 1970): 174.

[o] Samuel Eldersveld, Sonja Hubée-Boonzaaijer, and Jan Kooiman, "Elite Perceptions of the Political Process in the Netherlands Looked at in Comparative Perspective," in *The Mandarins of Western Europe*, ed. M. Dogan (New York: Halsted, 1975), p. 136.

[p] Charles Debbasch, ed., *La Fonction publique en Europe* (Paris: CNRS, 1981) (Total civil service).

[q] Andre Molitor, *L'Administration de la Belgique* (Brussels: Centre de recherche et d'information socio-politique, 1974).

[r] Franco Ferraresi, *Burocrazia e Politica in Italia* (Milan: Il Mulino, 1980).

[s] Debbasch (Total Civil service).

TABLE 3.6
COLLEGE MAJORS OF SENIOR CIVIL SERVANTS
(FOR THOSE WITH COLLEGE BACKGROUNDS)

Major	United Kingdom (1967)[a]	United States (1959)[b]	West Germany (1955)[c]	Japan (1949–59)[d]
Natural Science	13	42.9		14.3
Social Science	28	16.9	31	
Humanities	71	10.7		0.8
Economics and Business	—	7.8		5.5
Law	—	13.6	69	69.3
Other	2	8.1		10.1
Total	114*	100	100	100

* Greater than 100% because of dual majors.

Major	Republic of Korea (1962)[e]	Turkey (1963)[f]	India (1947–63)[g]	Sweden (1947)[h]	Sweden (1967)[i]
Natural Science	29.9	34.2	32.5	19.2	
Social Science	11.7	6.2	9.4	1.2	72
Humanities	—	13.1	20.9	17.7	
Economics and Business	12.0	15.8	36.4	9.7	
Law	25.3	17.5	—	52.3	28
Other	21.1	13.2	0.8	—	
Total	100	100	100	100.1	100

Major	Netherlands (1973)[j]	Belgium (1970)[k]	Italy (1961)[l]
Natural Science	25	44	27.2
Social Science	28	20	19.1
Humanities	—	5	4.7
Law	45	30	49.0
Other	2	1	0.0
Total	100	100	100.0

SOURCES:

[a] A. H. Halsey and I. M. Crewe, *Social Survey of the Civil Service*, vol. 3, pt. 1, *The Civil Service* (The Fulton Report) (London: HMSO, 1968), p. 91.

[b] W. L. Warner et al., *The American Federal Executive* (New Haven: Yale University Press, 1963), p. 363.

[c] Wolfgang Zapf, *Wandlungen der Deutschen Elite* (Munich: Piper, 1966), p. 178.

[d] Akira Kubota, *Higher Civil Servants in Postwar Japan* (Princeton: Princeton University Press, 1969), p. 79.

open than most. It further supports the contention that the public service in the United States has become an important means of social mobility.

The last question to be asked concerning the educational backgrounds of these administrators is the type of degree obtained. Here we are interested in the degree of technical or functional expertise that the administrators are likely to be carrying into their work as a function of their college education. We have already reported some data of this type for the United Kingdom, and they are reproduced in Table 3.5 and Table 3.6 along with data for such other countries as were available. There is considerably more variance in the *types* of education received than in the *level* of education, and apparently three rather distinct groups of educational degree types in this nonrandom sampling of administrative systems. The first is represented by the United Kingdom, with a great emphasis on general education, the arts and humanities, and consequently less emphasis on technical ability. As noted, this is indicative of the generalist conception of administration in the United Kingdom. A second type is typified by West Germany and Sweden. These systems place heavy emphasis on legal training, and consequently about two-thirds of their administrators have legal backgrounds. Many of the remainder also possess some form of professional qualification, such as engineering, medical, or educational degrees. France is somewhat similar but goes a step further by providing most of the upper-echelon legal and financial training through ENA. The final pattern of educational backgrounds is typified by the United States and several underdeveloped countries. The principal characteristic of these countries is the large percentage of natural science (including engineering) backgrounds in the civil service. As noted above, the United States tends to hire people with specialized backgrounds to do specialized jobs rather than hiring generally qualified personnel. In the Third World countries, there is a need to concentrate the available

e Dong Suh Bark, "Korean Higher Civil Servants: Their Social Backgrounds and Morale," in Byung Chul Koh, *Aspects of Administrative Development in South Korea* (Kalamazoo, Mich.: Korean Research Publication, 1967), p. 11.

f Republic of Turkey, Office of the Prime Minister, State Institute of Statistics, *The Government Personnel Census* 1 (Ankara: State Institute of Statistics, 1965), pp. 32–39.

g V. Subramanian, *Social Background of India's Administrators* (New Delhi: Ministry of Information, 1971), p. 155.

h Sten-Stuve Landstrom, *Svenska Ämbetsmans Sociala Ursprung* (Uppsala: Almqvist och Wiksell, 1954), p. 130.

i Thomas J. Anton, *Administered Politics: Elite Political Culture in Sweden* (Boston: Martinus Nijhoff, 1980), p. 28.

j Samuel Eldersveld, Sonja Hubée-Boonzaaijer and Jan Kooiman, "Elite Perceptions of the Political Process in the Netherlands Looked at in Comparative Perspective," in *The Mandarins of Western Europe*, ed. M. Dogan (New York: Halsted, 1975), p. 136.

k Andre Molitor, *L'Administration de la Belgique* (Brussels: Centre de recherche et d'information socio-politique, 1974), p. 73.

l Charles Debbasch, ed. *La Fonction publique en Europe* (Paris: CNRS, 1981).

technical talent in the country and to make the greatest use of this scarce resource. One way of doing this is to hire as much talent as possible in government and then use the government as a means of allocating resources. Moreover, given the relatively underdeveloped state of the economies of many of these countries, there may in fact be little option for the trained person but to work for government. Many political considerations may prevent the public bureaucracy in underdeveloped countries from fulfilling their potential for administering programs of social and economic change, but it would appear from these data that many of the countries have the raw material, in terms of personnel within bureaucracies, that might make those reforms successful.

Ethnic Representativeness

Another question to be looked at in the presentation of background data on civil services is the ethnic representativeness of the bureaucracies. Just as there is some cause for concern over the representativeness of public bureaucracies according to social class, so is there concern over their equality in recruitment of various minorities within the society. We may expect the same sort of pattern as was found with respect to class, with the dominant community having a disproportionate share of the members of the civil service, especially in elite positions. As the data in Table 3.7 show, these suspicions are confirmed. In most cases, there is a distinct overrepresentation of the dominant racial, language, or religious group. As with class, this may not be the result of overt discrimination but the result of the application of the usual educational criteria, which may more subtly discriminate.

Two special points should be made with respect to ethnic representation. The first is that these data are for upper-echelon personnel; as we go farther down the bureaucracy, the importance of the representativeness of the organization should increase rather than decrease. We have noted the importance of the client-contact personnel of agencies for the success of the agency in serving its clients. Such limited information as does exist on lower echelons of public agencies does indicate that they are more representative than are upper-management positions.[70] They may therefore be expected to be more successful in dealing with their clientele than would top management. Also, they may not be perceived as being as unrepresentative as they are, simply because the clients may deal only with the relatively more representative lower echelons.

The second point about ethnicity and representativeness is that this is frequently a point of bargaining in societies attempting to manage severe internal ethnic divisions. In some societies, most noticeably Belgium, this has gone to the extent of dividing several ministries by ethnicity (in this case, language) and actually providing two ethnically homogeneous units instead of one integrated unit that might tend to advantage one group or another.[71] Another variant of the same pattern is the Austrian method of carefully dividing the

TABLE 3.7
ETHNIC REPRESENTATIVENESS OF
PUBLIC BUREAUCRACIES (IN PERCENTAGES)

Ethnic Group	United States (1980)[a]		Canada (1978)[b]	
	Total	*Higher*	*Total*	*Higher*
Dominant	78.0	94.6	72.8	79.0
Minority	22.0	5.4	27.2	21.0
Total	100	100	100	100

Ethnic Group	Israel (1967)[c]	Malaysia (1960)[d]	India (1971)[e]	Zambia (1975)[f]	
				Total	*Higher*
Dominant	70.6	67	87.7	72.4	27.4
Minority	6.6	33	12.3	27.6	72.6
Total	77.2	100	100	100	100

Ethnic Group	Lebanon (1955)[g]	Switzerland (1969)[h]			
		Language		*Religion*	
Maronite	40.0	French	27.0		aa bb
Sunni	27.0	German	69.6	Catholic	12 42
Shi'ite	3.6	Italian	3.4	Protestant	88 58
Greek Orthodox	11.7	Romansh	—	Total	100 100
Greek Catholic	9.0	Total	100		
Druze	7.2				
Total	98.5				

SOURCES:

[a] U.S. Bureau of the Census, *Statistical Abstract of the United States, 1981* (Washington, D.C.: Government Printing Office, 1982). Minority—nonwhite.

[b] P. K. Kuruvilla, "Public Sector Recruitment in Canada," *Indian Journal of Public Administration* 26 (1980): 86. Minority—francophone.

[c] Nimrod Raphaeli, "The Absorption of Orientals into Israeli Bureaucracy," *Mid East Studies* 8, no. 1 (January 1972): 55–91. Dominant—European; minority—Oriental.

[d] Robert O. Tilman, "Public Service Commissions in the Federation of Malaya," *Journal of Asian Studies* 20 (February 1961): 194. Minority—non-Malay Asians and British.

[e] V. Subramanian, *Social Backgrounds of India's Administrators* (New Delhi: Ministry of Information, 1971), p. 146. Minority—non-Hindus.

[f] Dennis L. Dresang, *The Zambia Civil Service* (Nairobi, 1975). Minority—non-Zambian.

[g] Ralph E. Crow, "Confessionalism, Public Administration and Efficiency in Lebanon," in *Politics in Lebanon,* ed. Leonard Binder (New York: John Wiley, 1966), p. 172.

[h] Ulrich Kloti, "Die Chefbeamten Der Schweizerischen Bundesverwaltung: Ein Forschungsbericht," *Annuairre Suisse de Science Politique* 2 (1971): 58. The religious representation varies by ministry. Ministry (aa)—Volkswirtschaft—is heavily Protestant, while ministry (bb)—PTT—approaches proportionality.

posts in each ministry according to ethnicity or, more exactly in this case, religious or nonreligious preferences.[72] Similarly, the division of posts in the Lebanese administrative system between the numerous religious groups in that society was an important part of the bargain holding that otherwise tenuous union together prior to 1975.[73] Thus, there is no necessity for having unrepresentative bureaucracies in ethnically plural societies, but the equalization of the service often requires explicit bargaining and a recognition of the role of the bureaucracy in institutionalizing ethnic cleavage.

A final point to be made about the ethnic representativeness of the civil service is that the civil service has served as a means of social advancement for minority groups in part because of its reliance upon relatively objective criteria for recruitment. For example, while blacks and Hispanics constitute a rather small percentage of the civil service in the United States, they actually comprise a higher percentage there than in total employment in the economy.[74] Likewise, the civil service has served as a means of advancement for Italians from the poorer southern region; in 1978, 56 percent of the Italian civil service came from the southern part of the peninsula and Sicily.[75] Only 33 percent of the population lives in these regions.

Sexual Equality

A final dimension of representativeness is sex. The issue of equal treatment of women has become increasingly important in all phases of life, and the public bureaucracy is no different. The issue in the civil service is in general not about the total number of women employed; most governments already employ large numbers of women. The issue centers primarily on the types of positions in which women are employed. The majority of women in the civil service of almost every country are employed in lower-level jobs, such as clerks and typists, rather than in the higher civil service.

Table 3.8 clearly shows the disparity between the total number of women employed in the civil service and the number employed in the upper echelons. Although in some cases over half of total civil service employment is comprised of women, in no case does the higher civil service have more than 15 percent women. Further, that 15 percent figure, in Norway, is much higher than any other figure reported; the average is only 4.8 percent women in the higher civil service.

As with the cases of class and ethnic representativeness, we must consider whether these observed patterns are the result of overt discrimination or reflect other social or historical factors. It would be difficult to dispute that there has been discrimination against women in recruitment to senior posts in government, but historically there have been relatively few women putting themselves forward for the positions. As the more overt discrimination lessens, it will still

TABLE 3.8
EMPLOYMENT OF WOMEN IN
CIVIL SERVICE (IN PERCENTAGE)

Country	Total Civil Service	Higher Civil Service
Australia	34.9	1.8
Belgium	27.8	7.2
Canada	33.9	2.9
Finland	39.9	?
Greece	31.1	?
Hong Kong	?	6.5
Italy	35.4	3.9
Netherlands	18.9	2.3
Norway	?	15.0
Spain	13.5	?
Sweden	31.1	4.8
Switzerland	13.5	0.8
United Kingdom	55.3	3.5
United States	37.7	4.2

SOURCES:

Charles Debbasch, ed., *La Fonction publique en Europe* (Paris: CNRS, 1981).

Andre Molitor, *L'Administration de la Belgique* (Brussels: Centre de recherche et d'information socio-politique, 1974).

Per Laegreid and Johan P. Olsen, *Byråkrati og Beslutningar* (Bergen: Universitetforlaget, 1978).

John P. Burns, "The Changing Pattern of Bureaucratic Representation: The Case of the Hong Kong Civil Service," *Indian Journal of Public Administration* 27 (1981): 398–429.

Royal Commission on Australian Government Administration, *Report*, Appendix 3 (Canberra: Australian Government Publishing Service, 1976).

P. K. Kuruvilla, "Public Sector Recruitment in Canada: Some Perspectives and Problems," *Indian Journal of Public Administration* 26 (1980): 62–90.

require time for larger numbers of women to be recruited into entry-level positions for the higher civil service and to work their way up the career ladder.

SUMMARY

Noted here are several more general points about the composition and the representativeness of public bureaucracies. The first is that although these may be highly unrepresentative institutions, they are generally less unrepresentative than other public elites in the same countries. Parris notes, for example, that in Britain the membership of the House of Commons is at least as unrepresentative, if not more so, than the administrative class of the civil service.

If there are an excessive proportion of Oxbridge graduates in the Administrative Class, so is there in the House of Commons. The electorate ought to be blamed for making the wrong choice just as much as the Civil Service Commissioners. If too few civil servants have scientific and technological backgrounds, the same criticism can be made of industrial managers.[76]

The simple point is that elites are unrepresentative by the very function of their being elites. Success in society is related to social background, educational opportunities, and interests, and the elite that a society may choose to govern will differ only at the margins in most cases from an elite appointed to govern— at least in terms of social and educational backgrounds. The dangers of elitism and unrepresentativeness in public life are therefore general and confined simply to the public bureaucracy. They are only more apparent in the bureaucracy where the emphasis on merit criteria and open recruitment makes it a more ostensibly democratic institution in its selection. But, as Weber pointed out:

Democracy takes an ambivalent attitude toward the system of examinations for expertise. On the one hand the system of examination means, or at least appears to mean, selection of the qualified from all social strata in place of rule by the notables. But on the other, democracy fears that examinations and patents of education will create a privilege "caste" and for that reason opposes such a system.[77]

These words should not be taken as an exoneration of bureaucracies for their often elitist practices, but rather as a means of placing the problem of representative and unrepresentative bureaucracy in more perspective.

The second point is that all the furor over social class and ethnic background of administrators, especially top administrators, may be a somewhat misplaced attack on the institutions. Much analysis has shown that social background tends to have a rather slight effect on behavior in public office. This is true of legislators, judges, and administrators. A more important determinant of behavior would appear to be the nature of the organization and the goal of the agency. Again, this may be especially true at upper echelons; there may need to be greater representativeness at lower levels simply to be able to cope adequately with the clientele that an agency may serve. This is not to say that this need be simply a cosmetic gesture on the part of the agency; rather, it is a real need to be effective in interacting with and serving the clientele. But the more general point remains that in order to change the policy outcomes from the public bureaucracy, one may have to do more than simply gradually replace administrators drawn from one social class with administrators recruited more broadly from society. The operating routines of agencies, the tendency toward conservatism in organizations in general, and the process of organizational socialization all tend to reduce the variability of individuals in the organization regardless of their social background. Thus, changing policy may be a considerably more complex topic, and it is one that will be probed extensively during the remainder of this volume.

Policy does involve a human element. This chapter opened with a discussion of the failure of traditional models of bureaucracy to take into account human differences and variability. The differences, however, may be more in values, motives, and goals than in social background. We touched on this briefly when discussing the incentive structures of public bureaucracies, and also when discussing the administrative cultures of society. Thus, studies of recruitment need to delve somewhat into the nature of the personnel recruited to administrative careers, to determine not only where they came from, but more importantly where they think they (and the society) are going.

NOTES

1. Max Weber, "Bureaucracy," in H. H. Gerth and C. Wright Mills, *From Max Weber: Essays in Sociology* (New York: Oxford University Press, 1946), pp. 196–244; Frederick W. Taylor, *Principles and Methods of Scientific Management* (New York: Harper, 1911).

2. Some direct cross-cultural evidence of this is given in Robert Putnam, "The Political Attitudes of Senior Civil Servants in Western Europe," *British Journal of Political Science* 3 (1973): 257–90; Joel D. Aberbach, Robert D. Putnam, and Bert A. Rockman, *Bureaucrats and Politicians in Western Democracies* (Cambridge, Mass.: Harvard University Press, 1981).

3. Weber, "Bureaucracy," pp. 198–203.

4. Ari Hoogenboom, *Outlawing the Spoils* (Urbana: University of Illinois Press, 1968).

5. Two clear examples of this possibility are first the concern of some Britons that the civil service, generally recruited from the middle and upper classes and possessing generally conservative political views, might balk at administering the program of the Labour party after that party gained office in 1945. These fears proved to be groundless. A second example is the concern of many people in the developing areas that the public bureaucracies, many of which were recruited during colonialism, are not committed to the ideas of reform and may actually be slowing down the process of social changes. See K. Mathur, "A Committed Bureaucracy for India: Notes Toward a Theory," *Political Science Review* 10, no. 2 (July 1971): 113–23. See also Jackton B. Ojwang, "Kenya and the Concept of Civil Service Political Neutrality: A Case of Silent but Determined Politicization," *Indian Journal of Public Administration* 24 (1978): 430–40.

6. Richard Neustadt, "White House and Whitehall," *The Public Interest* 2 (1966): 55–69.

7. The president currently has appointment powers over 1,800 administrative positions.

8. J. Donald Kingsley, *Representative Bureaucracy* (Yellow Springs, Ohio: Antioch Press, 1944); V. Subramanian, "Representative Bureaucracy: A Reassessment," *American Political Science Review* 61 (1967): 1010–19; Samuel Krislov

and David H. Rosenbloom, *Representative Bureaucracy and the American Political System* (New York: Praeger, 1981).

9. See Peter Rose, Stanley Rothman, and William J. Wilson, *Through Different Eyes* (New York: Oxford University Press, 1972). Conflict between clients and administrator, despite its recent vogue, has been a subject of research for some time. See Gabriel Almond and Harold Lasswell, "Aggressive Behavior by Clients toward Public Relief Administrators," *American Political Science Review* 28 (1934): 643–54; Peter M. Blau, "Orientation Toward Clients in a Public Welfare Agency," *Administrative Science Quarterly* 5 (1960).

10. Lloyd G. Nigro, ed., "Mini-symposium on Affirmative Action in Public Employment," *Public Administration Review* 34 (1973).

11. See Martin O. Heisler, "Patterns of European Politics: The European Polity Model," in *Politics in Europe,* ed. Martin Heisler (New York: David McKay, 1974), pp. 27–89. Recruitment of administrative personnel in supranational bodies is another obvious example of this type of representativeness. See also L. Dubois, "La politique de choix des fonctionnaires dans les Communautés Européennes," in Charles Debbasch, ed., *La politique de choix des fonctionnaires dans les pays Européens* (Paris: CNRS, 1981), pp. 261–83.

12. OECD, *Social Objectives in Educational Planning* (Paris: OECD, 1967); Richard F. Tomasson, "From Elitism to Egalitarianism in Swedish Education," *Sociology of Education* 38 (1965): 203–23; Robert D. Putnam, *The Comparative Study of Political Elites* (Englewood Cliffs, N.J.: Prentice-Hall, 1976), pp. 205–14.

13. See Lewis J. Edinger and Donald D. Searing, "Social Background in Elite Analysis," *American Political Science Review* 61 (1967): 428–45.

14. Orville G. Brim, "Socialization Through the Life Cycle," in Orville G. Brim and Staunton Wheeler, eds., *Socialization after Childhood* (New York: Wiley, 1966).

15. This problem of "administrative pricing" is felt to contribute to many of the problems of public bureaucracy and the alleged inefficiencies of public bureaucracies. See William Niskanen, *Bureaucracy and Representative Government* (Chicago: Aldine, 1971). See also Samuel P. Huntington, "Postindustrial Politics: How Benign Will It Be?" *Comparative Politics* 6, no. 2 (January 1974): 179–82.

16. Albert Breton, "A Theory of the Demand for Public Goods," *Canadian Journal of Economics and Political Science* 32 (November 1966): 455–67; Anthony Downs, "Why the Government Budget Is Too Small in a Democracy," *World Politics* 12 (July 1960): 541–63.

17. See F. F. Ridley, *Specialists and Generalists: A Comparative Study of the Professional Civil Service at Home and Abroad* (London: Routledge & Kegan Paul, 1968).

18. E. N. Gladden, *The Civil Services of the United Kingdom 1855–1970* (London: Frank Cass, 1967), pp. 18–21.

19. Brian Chapman, one of the leading commentators and critics of British administration, once referred to the "luxuriant amateurism and voluntary exclusion of talent" in British administration. The Fulton report on reform suggested that specialized training be given more weight in recruitment, but that recom-

mendation was ignored. See Brian Chapman, *British Government Observed* (London: Allen & Unwin, 1963).

20. Aberbach, Putnam, and Rockman, *Bureaucrats and Politicians*, p. 52.

21. U.S. Office of Personnel Management, *Occupations of White Collar Employees* (Washington, D.C.: Government Printing Office, annual).

22. Serge Salon, "Recrutement et formation," in *La Fonction Publique*, vol. 2 (Paris: Les Cahiers Francais, No. 197, 1980), pp. 2–7.

23. At one extreme see M. Hanson, "Organizational Bureaucracy in Latin America and the Legacy of Spanish Colonialism," *Journal of Inter-American Studies* 16 (1974): 199–219.

24. See, for example, L. G. C. Wallis, "Nigerianization of the Public Services in Western Nigeria," *Journal of African Administration* 12, no. 3 (July 1960): 144–46; Krislov, *Representative Bureaucracy*, pp. 88–92; J. Donald Kingsley, "Bureaucracy and Political Development, with Special Reference to Nigeria," in *Bureaucracy and Political Development*, ed. Joseph LaPalombara (Princeton: Princeton University Press, 1963), pp. 301–17.

25. Fred A. Clemente, "Philippine Bureaucratic Behavior," *Philippine Journal of Public Administration* 15, no. 2 (April 1971): 119–47.

26. For a discussion of these several paths and the relationship of administration to development in Europe, see John A. Armstrong, *The European Administrative Elite* (Princeton: Princeton University Press, 1974); Fritz Morstein Marx, "The Higher Civil Service as an Action Group in Western Political Development," in LaPalombara, *Bureaucracy*, pp. 62–95.

27. Allen Kassof, "The Administered Society: Totalitarianism without Terror," *World Politics* 16 (1964): 558–75; Jerry Hough and Merle Fainsod, *How the Soviet Union Is Governed* (Cambridge, Mass.: Harvard University Press, 1979).

28. T. H. Rigby, "The Soviet Politburo: A Comparative Profile, 1951–1971," *Soviet Studies* 24 (1972): 11–12; Robert E. Blackwell, "Elite Recruitment and Functional Change: An Analysis of the Soviet Obkom Elite, 1950–1968," *Journal of Politics* 34 (1972): 135–7.

29. Jerry F. Hough, *The Soviet Prefects* (Cambridge, Mass.: Harvard University Press, 1969), pp. 292–305.

30. The recruitment by agencies is, in fact, governed by statutes requiring certain qualifications, etc. See Poul Meyer, "The Administrative Aspects of the Constitutions of the Northern Countries," *Nordisk Administrativ Tidskrift* (1960), pp. 254–65.

31. Brian Chapman, *The Profession of Government* (London: Allen & Unwin, 1959), pp. 82–85; Fritz W. Scharpf, ed., *Politikverflechtung: Theorie und Emperie des Kooperativen Föderalismus in der Bundesrepublik* (Kronberg: Scriptor, 1976).

32. Wolfgang Pippke, *Karrieredeterminaten in der öffentlichen Verwaltung* (Baden-Baden: Nomos, 1975).

33. Vincent Wright, *Government and Politics of France* (London: Hutchinson, 1978), pp. 90–91.

34. See G. Calvin Mackenzie, *The Politics of Presidential Appointments* (New York: Free Press, 1981).

35. Peta E. Sheriff, "Outsiders in a Closed Career: The Example of the British Civil Service," *Public Administration* 50 (1972): 397–418.
36. Peta E. Sheriff, *Career Patterns in the Higher Civil Service*, Civil Service Studies (London: HMSO, 1976), p. 59. See also William Plowden, "Whate'er is best administered," *New Society* (9 April 1981): 53–54.
37. Hugh Heclo, *A Government of Strangers* (Washington, D.C.: The Brookings Institution, 1977).
38. Chalmers Johnson, *MITI and the Japanese Miracle: The Growth of Industrial Policy, 1925–1975* (Stanford: Stanford University Press, 1982).
39. Adalbert Hess, "Statistische Daten und Trends zur Verbeamtung der Parlamente in Bund und Länder," *Zeitschrift fur Parlamentsfragen* 7 (1976): 34–42.
40. Rolf H. W. Theen, "Party and Bureaucracy," in Gordon B. Smith, ed., *Public Policy and Administration in the Soviet Union* (New York: Praeger, 1980), pp. 18–52.
41. Peter B. Clark and James Q. Wilson, "Incentive Systems: A Theory of Organizations," *Administrative Science Quarterly* 6 (1961): 129–66.
42. Anthony Downs, *Inside Bureaucracy*, pp. 96–101.
43. Most notably, Heclo and Wildavsky, *The Private Government*; Michael R. Gordon, "Civil Servants, Politicians and Parties: Shortcomings in the British Policy Process," *Comparative Politics* 4, no. 1 (October 1971): 29–58.
44. B. Gournay, "Une groupe dirigente de la societé française: les grandes fonctionnaires," *Revue française de science politique* 31, no. 2 (April 1964): 215–42. Anne Stevens, "The Higher Civil Service and Economic Policy-Making," in Philip G. Cerny and Martin A. Schain, eds., *French Politics and Public Policy* (London: Pinter, 1980), pp. 79–100.
45. J. L. Weaver, "Expectativas de los functionarios latinoamericanes en relacion con la administracion publica," *Aportes* 25 (July 1972): 119–45.
46. See, for example, James F. Guyot, "Bureaucratic Transformation in Burma," in Braibanti, *Asian Bureaucratic Systems*, pp. 382–84.
47. Robert N. Kearney and Richard L. Harris, "Bureaucracy and Environment in Ceylon," *Journal of Commonwealth Political Studies* 2, no. 3 (November 1964): 254–55.
48. Ibid., p. 255.
49. J. R. Nellis, "Is Bureaucracy Development? Political Considerations in Development Administration," *African Studies Review* 11 (1971): 390–401; John D. Montgomery, "The Populist Front in Rural Development: or Shall We Eliminate the Bureaucrats and Get on with the Job?" *Public Administration Review* 39 (1979): 58–65.
50. Mervyn Matthews, *Privilege in the Soviet Union* (London: George Allen and Unwin, 1978).
51. Michel Crozier, *The Bureaucratic Phenomenon* (Chicago: University of Chicago Press, 1964), pp. 228–9.
52. *Inquiry into the Value of Pensions*, Cmnd. 8147 (London: HMSO, 1981).
53. Sharon P. Smith, *Equal Pay in the Public Sector: Fact or Fantasy?* Research Report no. 112 (Princeton, N.J.: Princeton University, Industrial Relations Section, 1977); Siv Gustafsson, *Lönebildning och lönestruktur inom den stätliga sektorn* (Stockholm: Almqvist and Wicksell, 1972); R. Lazard, A. Marin,

and A. Zabalza, "Trends in Civil Service Pay Relative to the Private Sector," *Inquiry into Civil Service Pay* (The Megaw Report), Cmnd. 8590, vol. 2 (London: HMSO, 1982), pp. 95–129.

54. Employees in grade GS-15 were estimated to be paid on average $16,234 less than their private sector counterparts in October 1982. The underpayment for grades GS-16 through GS-18 is undoubtedly much more. Advisory Commission on Federal Pay, *Report on the Fiscal 1983 Pay Increase* (Washington, D.C.: Advisory Commission on Federal Pay, 1982), Table 1.

55. J. L. Fallick and R. F. Elliott, *Incomes Policies, Inflation and Relative Pay* (London: George Allen and Unwin, 1981).

56. For a summary see *Inquiry into Civil Service Pay*, pp. 122–124.

57. Advisory Commission on Federal Pay, *Report on the Fiscal 1982 Pay Increase* (Washington, D.C.: Advisory Commission on Federal Pay, 1981).

58. *Inquiry into Civil Service Pay.*

59. The development of the second *concours* as a means of entry into the ENA was intended as a means of widening the social basis of recruitment. As noted by Suleiman, this effort has been far from entirely successful. See Suleiman, *Politics, Power*, p. 59; J. L. Bodiguel, "Nouveaux concours, nouveaux enarques," *La revue administrative* 186 (1978): 610–18.

60. Wolfgang Zapf, *Wandlungen der Deutschen Elite* (Munich: Piper, 1966), pp. 180–82.

61. Aberbach, Putnam, and Rockman, *Bureaucrats and Politicians*, p. 55.

62. R. K. Kelsall, *Higher Civil Servants in Britain* (London: Routledge & Kegan Paul, 1955), pp. 70–71, provides a good description of the effects of interviews on recruitment in Britain. For a balanced view see F. F. Ridley, "The British Civil Service," Report for Roundtable of the Association Internationale de la Fonction Publique (Avignon, 1983), p. 11.

63. Aberbach, Putnam, and Rockman, pp. 48–49.

64. Seymour Martin Lipset, *The First New Nation* (New York: Basic Books, 1963), pp. 226–31; John Porter, *The Vertical Mosaic* (Toronto: University of Toronto Press, 1965), presents a different picture of Canadian society. Robert Presthus shows that the Canadian bureaucracy has higher rates of social mobility than other institutions in the society. See Robert V. Presthus, *Elite Accommodation in Canadian Politics* (Cambridge, England: Cambridge University Press, 1973), p. 277.

65. Peter Kellner, "A Failure to Reform?" *The Sunday Times*, 19 March 1978.

66. V. Subramanian, *The Social Backgrounds of India's Administrators* (New Delhi: Ministry of Information and Broadcasting, 1971), p. 39.

67. Ezra Suleiman, *Politics, Power*, p. 67.

68. "De l'origine sociale et géographique des élèves de l'École nationale d'Administration," *Promotions*, No. 100 (Paris: Cahiers Francais, 1976).

69. W. Lloyd Warner, *The American Federal Executive* (New Haven: Yale University Press, 1963), p. 372.

70. Pierre Escoube, "Les Hommes dans l'Administration," in École Practique des Hautes Études, *Traite de Science Administrative* (Paris: Mouton, 1966), pp. 359–72; Krislov, *Representative Bureaucracy*, pp. 112–14; Republic of Turkey, Office of the Prime Minister, *The Government Personnel Census*, vol. 1 (Ankara: N.P., 1965); Kenneth John Meier, "Representative Bureau-

cracy: An Empirical Assessment," *American Political Science Review* 69 (1975): 526–42.

71. Martin O. Heisler, "Institutionalizing Societal Cleavages in a Cooptive Polity: The Growing Importance of the Output Side in Belgium," in Heisler, *Politics in Europe*, pp. 212–15; Andre Molitor, *L'Administration de la Belgique* (Brussels: Centre de recherche et d'information socio-politique, 1974).

72. See Kurt Steiner, *Politics in Austria* (Boston: Little, Brown, 1972), pp. 390–97.

73. Ralph E. Crow, "Confessionalism, Public Administration and Efficiency in Lebanon," in *Politics in Lebanon*, Leonard Binder, ed. (New York: John Wiley, 1966), pp. 71ff.

74. B. Guy Peters, "Public Employment in the United States," in Richard Rose, ed., *Public Employment in Western Societies* (Cambridge: Cambridge University Press, forthcoming).

75. Franco Ferraresi, *Burocrazia e Politica in Italia* (Milan: Il Mulino, 1980), pp. 114–7.

76. Henry Parris, *Constitutional Bureaucracy* (London: Allen & Unwin, 1969), p. 315.

77. Gerth and Mills, *From Max Weber*, p. 240.

CHAPTER 4

PROBLEMS OF ADMINISTRATIVE STRUCTURE

Concern over the structure and design of organizations has traditionally dominated the study of public administration. This may have resulted from the lack of any readily quantifiable measures of organization—such as profit—in public organizations, so that greater attention was placed on theoretical questions of organizational design. Moreover, the responsibility of public organizations to external political forces and the general opprobrium associated with the word "bureaucracy" also placed pressure on public administrators to design the perfect organization. For whatever reason, public administration has been almost obsessed with constructing the best organizational structures for implementing public programs.[1] This tendency reached its height with the theories of administration, dismissed by Simon as the "proverbs of administration," based on concepts such as unity of command, span of control, and POSDCORB management.[2]

In addition, the structure of the public sector depends very significantly upon history and economic and social conditions, as well as ideas about the purposes of government. No reform of government, however well informed by organization theory, is likely to be able to overcome all the inherited traditions embodied within the machinery of government. Unless that macro-level of organizational constraint is understood, any attempt to alter the character of the internal functioning of the organization is doomed to failure.

This chapter has two objectives. The first is to describe in a brief fashion four major administrative systems, representing a range of variation along a number of dimensions. This should provide the reader some basic information about how administrative systems are structured. Second, the chapter will examine some of the points concerning governmental structures that are raised by organizational theory and assess the responses made by governments. The range of these answers can be used to gain some idea of the relationship of organizational structure to the functioning of the public sector.

WEST GERMANY

West Germany is the heir to a long tradition of administrative development, beginning with the Prussian reforms of 1807–1811. This development has produced a highly professionalized civil service, based upon a merit system of recruitment and possessing a high degree of commitment to the service of the State. The nature of the civil service has been altered very little by the numerous political changes that have taken place in Germany since the days of the Hohenzollern empire.

The contemporary structure of administration is highly decentralized in some ways, although some aspects of administration remain centralized. A relatively small percentage of the total number of civil servants in West Germany are employed directly by the central (*Bund*) government. The central ministries of the *Bund* government are small planning organizations that develop policies to be implemented by the state (*Land*) governments.[3] The major exceptions to this generalization are the military, the post office, and certain nationalized industries such as the state railways. Of the 3.7 million public employees in West Germany, only 38 percent are employees of the central government. However, despite the decentralization of the implementation structures, the procedures and standards of administration are centralized. All public employees must meet the same standards for employment, and for the particular positions for which they are employed, and they are subject to the same legal strictures. Likewise, their training after entry into the public service is centralized and conducted by the central government. And, unlike the majority of other nations, the same requirements and procedures apply to many of the employees of the nationalized industries.

The German civil service is divided into several classifications, with admission to one or the other being dependent upon educational qualifications. The highest level—the *Beamte*—requires university education and passing an examination administered by a board composed of practicing civil servants and professors (actually in Germany professors *are* civil servants). The *Beamte* are roughly equivalent to the "supergrades" in the United States, or the old Administrative Class in the British civil service. They occupy the principal decision-making posts in the bureaucracy and consequently can substantially influence the outcomes of policy making. Below the *Beamte* are the *Angestellen Dienst*, who constitute the major body of clerical and other lower-level white-collar employees. Finally, there are the *Arbeiters* (workers), who constitute the blue-collar work force both in the nationalized industries and in conventional governmental functions, for example, sanitation.

Almost invariably, those who are permitted to become *Beamte* will have a degree in law (*Justiemonopol*), indicating the highly legalistic conception of administration in Germany. Public administration is seen as the application of public law to particular situations, rather than policy making. This is, of course, a mechanistic conception of the inherently political process of administration, but it is one that has persisted long after Weber wrote about administration in such terms.[4]

Contrary to practice in most Anglo-Saxon countries, once the individual obtains the status of civil servant, it remains with him or her. Thus, the status is vested in the individual, not in the position that the individual occupies at any particular time. This allows civil servants to become involved in private activities without losing their status as civil servants. Perhaps even more importantly, they may engage in political activity and still retain their status.[5] As important as the status of civil servant is, however, it may be more subject to influence by political leaders than would be true in many other countries. The political leaders have the power to pension off any members of the higher civil service (those positions being defined as political despite their legalistic trappings) and to appoint anyone to fill the resulting vacancy. Up to one-third of the senior administrative posts in the West German government are filled by individuals appointed from outside the bureaucratic career structure.

A special case of the connection between politics and administration in West Germany is the attempt to prevent students who have been involved in radical political activity from becoming civil servants (the *Berufsverbot*). This was especially important during the period of student activism in the late 1960s and early 1970s but continues as a means of ensuring that those employed by government are favorably disposed toward the continuance of the democratic political institutions established in postwar Germany, a policy perhaps supported by a fear of the fragility of those institutions.

Thus, the administrative structures of West Germany present an internal contradiction. On the one hand, the role of the public servant is considered to be highly legalistic, and the definition of the activities attached is strictly defined by statutes. On the other hand, there is considerable involvement in politics by administrators, and some political involvement in administration. The legalistic, Weberian definition of administration simply does not apply to a complex political system administering a wide variety of politically sensitive programs, but there is a desire to maintain some of the high status and quasi-judicial trappings of the civil servant. This mixture need not be dysfunctional, for the legalism and high status of the *Beamte* can be used as a means of making what are patently political decisions more acceptable to the public.

THE UNITED KINGDOM

Attempting to capture the complexity of British administration in a few pages is a difficult task. Unlike many of the other countries under discussion, British administration has evolved over centuries with few attempts (and even fewer successful ones) to rationalize and reorganize the machinery of government. Further, unlike the continental countries, bureaucracy and administration did not play a prominent role in British thinking about government. As a consequence of both of those factors, British administration has developed by accretion with relatively little planning and arguably without a central organizational format that would make the system more comprehensible.

To gain some understanding of this complexity of administration, it is first necessary to sort out the major organizations in British government. There are four major types, each of which stands in a different relationship to the political authority of Parliament and Cabinet. The executive departments, for example, the Department of Health and Social Security, are most closely connected to that authority. These are typically staffed by civil servants (in the restrictive sense of the term), headed by a politician sitting in Cabinet, and have somewhat similar forms of organization. However, despite their importance and their familiarity, these organizations employ a relatively small proportion of total public employees in the United Kingdom (6 percent).[6]

The second form of organization is local government. The United Kingdom is a unitary government, so that the number and functions of local authorities are controlled by the central government, and much of the cost of local government is borne by the central government. Despite this centralization, local authorities have some freedom in the way in which they structure their own organizations, and to some degree in the qualifications they impose on their employees. They have almost as much latitude as the subnational governments in federal West Germany. Local authorities are organized on a two-tier scheme, with regional governments and district governments, in addition to the Greater London Council, which serves as an umbrella government for the London area.

The third major group of public employees comprises the health services. These employees stand in a variety of relationships to government, depending upon how they are employed and what functions they perform. In general, the employees of the National Health Service are definitely public employees, but they are not civil servants. Consequently, many of the benefits—and restrictions—of civil service employment do not apply to them. Hospital physicians (consultants) and all other employees of hospitals are salaried public employees, although they are employees of the National Health Service and not of government *per se*. General practitioners, on the other hand, are paid on the basis of the number of patients on their register, as well as for performing certain services to their patients, and function under a contract with the National Health Service.

Finally, there are a number of nondepartmental bodies in the structure of British government. These are in turn divisible into two groups. One consists of the nationalized industries, such as British Railways, British Steel, the National Coal Board, etc. These industries have a sponsoring department, and, although their employees are definitely public employees, they also lack the status of civil servants. An attempt is made to keep these industries at least partially removed from government, to provide as much market discipline for their activities as possible. In addition to the employees of nationalized industries there are some 138 thousand industrial civil servants, with full civil service status, who are employed primarily in government-owned enterprises supplying the Ministry of Defense.

In addition to the nationalized industries, there are a number of nondepartmental bodies, now commonly referred to as "quangos," (quasi-nongovernmental organizations), which in fact represent a large number of different types of organizations standing in various relationships to the government.[7] Some are simply sections of executive departments that have been "hived off" for some reason or another, for example, the Manpower Services Commission, and may still be staffed by civil servants. These would be quite similar to independent executive agencies in the United States. The universities represent another set of nondepartmental bodies that, while clearly in the public sector, are kept at arm's length from government for reasons of academic freedom. And finally, there are the true quangos, organizations that are private, or partially private, but that spend public money and exercise the authority of government. Also, there are a number of advisory bodies for ministries included among quangos. These bodies at the fringe of government represent great difficulties in administrative accountability and control, and have been subject to a round of "quango-bashing" during the Thatcher government.

The types of public employees staffing these institutions are almost as varied as the institutions themselves, and in our discussion we will concentrate on the civil service, and particularly the top civil service. The British civil service made its first major movement toward modernization as a result of the Northcote-Trevelyan Report of 1854, which stressed the value of a highly qualified civil service recruited on the basis of merit.[8] Also, the qualifications stressed by this report were of an abstract, intellectual variety, rather than the more specific and practical qualifications traditionally employed in the United States. This report and its sequels resulted in a civil service dominated by an administrative class composed almost entirely of honors graduates in the humanities (especially classics), who, though intelligent, did not have the training in the economic and technological issues that they increasingly were called upon to administer. The careers of this administrative class were varied, with frequent changes among positions and even among departments; these civil servants did not specialize in the work of any particular department until rather late in their career. The administrative class was a closed career; if someone was not selected initially for this bracket in administration, the opportunity to work one's way up was extremely limited. Also, lateral entry from the private sector was virtually unknown. All in all, this system produced a civil service composed of "talented amateurs."

The British civil service came under frequent attacks on the basis of these characteristics. The most comprehensive of these attacks was the Fulton Report, published in 1968, which recommended abolishing the existing internal divisions by class within the civil service, and putting into place a series of grades, similar to the general schedule in the United States, from the top to the bottom of the nonindustrial civil service, with promotion up this schedule being based upon merit.[9] In addition, the Fulton Report advocated abolishing the separation of a number of technical and professional services from the remainder of the civil service—a system that kept the technical personnel "on tap, never on top," even in departments whose subject matter was highly technical. And Fulton recommended that the civil service become less of a closed profession, that it be opened for lateral entry from the private sector at almost any point in the career structure.

As might have been predicted, the response to Fulton by those already in positions in the civil service was less than joyous. A number of weaknesses, some semantic, were pointed out in the document. After a process of negotiation and bargaining, some of the report's proposals for reform were adopted. The divisions between the Administrative Class, the Executive, and the Clerical Classes were formally abolished, with an Administrative Group being substituted. However, if an individual did not enter the Administrative Group at one of the points designated for future leaders, for example, the administrative trainee (AT) positions, the probability of reaching any significant position in the civil service was still extremely remote. Further, socially and in terms of training, the composition of the AT group remains quite similar to that of the prior administrative class. And the separation between the technical and professional groups and the rest of the civil service has largely been maintained, as has the isolation of the civil service from lateral entry. In short, with cosmetic changes, the system of the "talented amateur"—the rallying cry of the defenders of the system against the Fulton reforms—has been to a great degree maintained.

Another of the important characteristics of the British civil service is its political neutrality. It is assumed that a civil servant can serve any political master, be it a Conservative, Labour, or other government in power. This principle has come under recent attack as well. One group of critics, in particular Sir John Hoskyns, has argued that Britain needs a civil service committed to the program that it is administering, and as a consequence more posts—especially senior posts—should be obtained by political screening and appointment.[10] On the other hand, a number of people have argued that the civil service is in fact far from uncommitted.[11] Its members are perceived to be committed to policy goals, especially the preservation of the status quo in their own departments. This view has it that the civil service may be neutral politically, but it is far from neutral in policy terms.

FRANCE

France has had a long tradition of centralized and strong government, going back at least to the days of Louis XIV. Many of the institutions developed by Napoleon as emperor to govern France are still maintained, and the principal direction for all government activity in France continues to emanate from Paris. French government has been, if not dominated by bureaucracy, at least highly bureaucratic. It has been argued that because of the numerous changes in regimes in France, and the instability of cabinets in the Third and Fourth Republics, if France was to be governed, it would have to be governed by the central bureaucracy. This view may be overstated, but the bureaucracy continues to play a very significant role in French government and politics.[12]

Although it is centralized, the French bureaucracy also has a number of internal divisions. First, there are the vertical divisions between classes of administration (A, B, C, and D), which roughly represent educational qualifications needed for positions: A being administrative and technical posts requiring at least a university-level education, B requiring secondary education, C requiring some secondary education, and D having no formal educational qualifications.[13] As with the older conception of the administrative, executive, and clerical classes in the British civil service, movement between these classes is rare. Further, within each of these classes there are divisions based upon the nature of the position, specialty of the individual occupying the post, etc. Attempts at forming a unified civil service in 1946 were to prove hopeless, given the long tradition of these divisions in French public administration.

Perhaps the most important of all the divisions is the separation of class A into the *grands corps*, as well as some members who do not belong to any of the corps. The *grands corps* constitutes a vestige of Napoleonic administration and has been copied in other administrative systems influenced by the Napoleonic system—Spain, Italy, and some Latin American countries. The *corps* represent organizations within the civil service and have some of the attributes of fraternal organizations.[14] When an individual becomes a member of a *corps*, he or she remains a member for the duration of his or her career. There are two principal technical corps—*Mines* and *Ponts et Chausses*—and five major administrative corps—*Inspection des Finances, Conseil d'État, Cour des Comptes*, the diplomatic corps, and the prefectoral corps. The names attached to these *corps* reflect certain functional considerations, but an individual remains a member of his or her corps regardless of whether that function is being performed. Further, the individual remains a member of the corps even if working in the private sector, and indeed the contacts between public and private sectors are increased (perhaps to detrimental levels) by the number of civil servants who have "parachuted" into the private sector. The *corps* represent a government within government, as the informal contacts among members constitute a means of doing business even if formal channels are blocked.

An individual becomes a member of one of the *corps* on the basis of performance at one of the two major schools channeling people into the civil service. One of the schools, which provides personnel for the technical *corps* is the *École Polytechnique*, established by Napoleon to provide the engineers he required to modernize France and to modernize its army. The other school is the *École Nationale d'Administration* (ENA), which supplies recruits for the administrative corps. ENA was established in 1946 as the training ground for future public servants.[15] Its curriculum stresses law, administration, and, to a lesser extent, finance, emphasizing the legalistic conception of administration in France—not very dissimilar to the conception held in West Germany. Entry to the ENA depends upon passing a national competitive examination, although in practice those who have attended certain schools in Paris in preparation for the examination have by far the best chances of passing.

The members of the *grands corps*, and indeed any French civil servant, may become involved in politics. The members of the *grands corps* are particularly valued as political contacts because of their ties with the powerful membership of their organizations. They are particularly visible as members of the *cabinets* of individual ministers.[16] These *cabinets* are bodies of advisers for the minister of a government department, and it is considered essential to have a member of a *corps*, such as the *Inspection des Finances*, in these *cabinets*. Of course, when a civil servant joins such a body, he or she makes a political commitment and may become *persona non grata* for future governments. In that case there are always opportunities outside government for the members of the *grands corps*.

As in the other European countries under discussion, a large percentage of French public employees are not civil servants but, rather, work for nationalized industries or parastatal organizations. The employees of public enterprises are clearly public employees but do not necessarily have the same civil service perquisites of other government employees. There is an attempt to impose as much market discipline on these organizations as possible, and to do so their employees are not tenured (except by arrangement with unions), and their salaries are not so tightly controlled by the *grille* as those of civil servants. Some public enterprises, notably *Postes, Telegraphes et Telephones* (PTT), are components of the government, and their employees are civil servants.

Local governments in France have limited independence from the central government. The criteria for employment in local and regional governments are prescribed nationally. In addition, the major function of local government— education—is a national function, and the employees of local schools are actually direct employees of the Ministry of Education in Paris. Likewise, many local public works are controlled centrally by the technical *grands corps*, so that the latitude available to local governments is limited.

The latitude of local governments is limited even further by the prefectoral system.[17] France is divided into ninety-five *départements*, each named after a particular geographical feature. These divisions are also a Napoleonic device, designed to eliminate the traditional provinces in France, for example, Burgundy, Normandy, which limited loyalty to the nation. The *préfet*, also a Napoleonic invention, was designed to ensure that each of the *départements* was governed in the manner desired by the central government in Paris. Each *département* has a *préfet*, who is responsible to the Ministry of the Interior for the administration of government policy in his or her area. The *préfet* is responsible for the supervision of local government; prior to the reforms in the 1960s and 1970s, almost any little thing a local government wished to do, for example, repair a local street, might have to be approved in Paris through the *préfet*. The *préfets* do continue to exercise a great deal of control over local government, as well as check on the administration of policies by the field staffs of other ministries. The Ministry of the Interior and its *préfets* constitute a powerful centralizing force in French administration, although there is some evidence that the *préfets* may at times come to defend their regions against Paris, rather than simply imposing central directives.

In summary, French administration is a vast and contradictory institution. It is a major weapon of a centralizing national government, but it is itself deeply divided and internally fractious. It is highly legalistic in its own definitions and its behavior with clients, but at the same time it is deeply involved in politics. Individuals derive great status from their connections with administration in the *grands corps* but may spend the greatest portion of their careers in the private sector without losing that status. The system has managed to govern France when there was little alternative available from politicians, but it is not entirely clear that it can govern itself.

SWEDEN

Although it did not industrialize until much later, Sweden developed a skilled central bureaucracy quite early in its history. This development began during the reign of Gustavus Adolphus, whose entry into the Thirty Years War required the development of a competent bureaucracy if tiny Sweden was to be governed at home. Sweden had more civil servants per capita than did most countries during the eighteenth and nineteenth centuries, and the civil service that developed had an image of competence and honesty.[18]

Although its total numbers have been greatly expanded by the programs of the contemporary welfare state, much the same could be said of the modern Swedish civil service. The public bureaucracy is large relative to that of other countries and is also generally quite competent. In addition to its competence, the bureaucracy is also one of the most stringently controlled in the world, so that the opportunities for bureaucratic excesses are more limited than in other countries.

The organization of Swedish government is a combination of centralized and decentralized features. This characterization applies both to the structure of government and to the practices within government. First, although Sweden is technically a unitary government, there is a long tradition of communal liberty, and both the lowest tier of government (the communes) and the intermediate tier (the *lan*) have a number of powers, including control of taxation, which they can exercise independently. The *lan* governments, for example, are very heavily involved in providing hospital care and appear to compete among themselves over quality of facilities and services.

In addition to the division between levels of government, there are also a number of nationalized industries, as well as public participation in a number of joint-stock companies. In these ventures the dividing line between public and private sectors becomes extremely vague, although in general the employees of the joint-stock companies are not in any way considered to have civil service jobs, whereas those in the fully nationalized industries—especially the traditional ones such as forestry—do tend to have that status.

The formal structures for carrying out public business also have something of a decentralized character, even in the central government. The central ministries in Sweden are relatively small organizations, charged primarily with planning and policy formulation. The major task of implementing policy falls to the boards (*styrelsen* or *verk*), which are largely independent from the ministries supervising their work, except for the all-important budgetary process. The boards are governed in one of three ways. A few continue in the traditional pattern of a collegial management by top officials on the board, almost in the manner of a multimember court. Another group is controlled directly by a director general, an appointee of the crown (in practice, the government). The largest—and still growing—number of boards is managed by a lay board convened by the director general but containing a variety of representatives of important interests in the particular policy area. In all these instances, however, the boards are the major employers of public employees, and it is they who do the day-to-day work of administering Swedish government.[19]

The selection of personnel in Swedish administration also presents certain internal contradictions. On the one hand, recruitment is extremely decentralized. There is no central personnel office—for example, the Office of Personnel Management in the United States—which evaluates candidates for positions and channels them to openings in agencies. Recruitment is done by the ministries and boards themselves. On the other hand, this apparent latitude is tightly circumscribed by the legal statutes on the qualifications of civil servants, and the majority of those placed in the upper civil service continue to have degrees in law. Likewise, educational qualifications apply to other posts in the public sector, so that although there is latitude to select individuals, the individual selected must meet the necessary requirements and the field from which the choice can be made may be limited.

There are also internal divisions within the civil service, much as has been noted in French, German, and British administrations. Further, although Sweden is frequently cited as a prototype of a socialist society (a description in many ways patently untrue), these distinctions are as institutionalized in Sweden as in any of the other countries. Members of the civil service at different levels are not only on different pay plans, they are in different unions. Those with a university education belong to SACO, the union that represents only graduates, while those in white-collar positions but who lack a university education belong to TCO.[20] Finally, those in blue-collar jobs belong to LO, the principal labor federation.[21] Further, those in the top positions, the *tjänsteman*, have a status similar to that of the *Beamte* in West Germany, although the position does not have the quasi-judicial trappings found in West Germany.

Another of the apparent internal contradictions in Swedish administration is the emphasis on efficiency in a government that is (relatively) one of the largest in the world and was controlled from 1935 to 1976 by the Social Democratic party, a party of the moderate left. Sweden has had one of the most active programs of managerial improvement of all industrialized countries.[22]

THE STRUCTURE OF ADMINISTRATION

One of the most general questions of administrative structure concerns the basis of organization for the administrative apparatus as a whole. How will the entire public service be structured to achieve its tasks? Rather early in the formal study of public administration, Luther Gulick proposed that the organization of public administration could be founded on four alternative principles: purpose served, processes employed, types of persons or things dealt with, or geographical area covered.[23] Examples of these forms of organization are readily apparent. The purposes served are clearly the most frequent basis of organization, as departments or ministries of defense, education, and health would indicate. Organization by process is more commonly found at subministerial levels, with divisions or bureaus of accounting, legal services, engineering, and the like. Types of persons or things dealt with would include organizations such as the Veterans Administration in the United States, similar organizations in other countries, the Bureau of Indian Affairs, and various boards and commissions for (or against) foreign workers in European countries. Finally, the area served is frequently used as an organizational principle at the subdepartmental level, as in the use of regional offices, but may also be institutionalized at the departmental level, as in the Scottish and Welsh Offices in the United Kingdom.[24]

Each of these modes of organization has some assets and some liabilities, which have been rather thoroughly discussed by Gulick and others working on the problem. There is no need to engage in an extensive discussion of that literature here. Rather, let us begin to examine how these four categories of organization can be used to analyze differences in administrative systems cross-nationally, and what the implications of these differences are for administration. The bulk of our analysis is on modes of organization other than by purpose, since that mode is the most common and the one with the fewest comparative differences.

Organization by Area Served

Area provides the most interesting comparative differences across cultures. These differences in administration are largely related to broader organizational questions for the entire political system, especially the degree of centralization to be imposed upon the country by the central government. In fact, the two most important variants of areal administration emanate from quite different solutions to this problem. One solution is for the central government to attempt to control and supervise closely the execution of its policies throughout the nation. One of the most powerful means to ensure such uniformity is the use of prefectoral officers in localities. In a general sense, prefects are officers of the central government responsible for the execution of national programs at the subnational level. Each ministry may have its own field service, but these are coordinated and to some degree supervised by the prefect. In France, the prefect has also been responsible traditionally for the conduct of local government and has had veto power over most local programs and finances.[25] There are differences in the precise ways in which prefectoral systems operate, but the common thread running through such systems—as in France, Italy, and Japan—is that one officer will coordinate and be responsible for public policies in one subnational area.[26]

Prefectoral systems often operate quite differently from the formal model of central control. As well as serving as representatives of the national government to the locality, prefects also represent their locality—and themselves—to the center. That is, prefects may frequently be coopted by their localities and will support claims for local variances in national programs. Worms notes four points of convergence between the interests of the prefect and interests of local politicians.[27] The prefect, in practice, is often the man in the middle, linking the demands of the local constituency for special treatment and rapid action to the demands of the central government for uniformity. He also must think of his own career, so that it may benefit him to cooperate with the locality in order to obtain smooth and successful execution of the tasks of the local authorities.[28]

At the other end of the spectrum are several schemes for administrative devolution and administrative federalism. These either transfer control of administration downward to a subnational unit or provide deconcentrated control of the administration. Probably the most extreme version of this form of organization is found in West Germany, where the functions of the national bureaucracy are confined primarily to program development in the ministries in Bonn and the running of the state railroad, post office, and several nationalized industries. The majority of the work of administering public policies is done at the level of the *Länder*.[29] Although the federal ministers must assure that the programs of their ministry are administered properly and uniformly throughout the country, in practice they have few means of enforcing such uniformity. The system allows for considerable autonomy in the *Länder* with respect not only to the organization of their own civil service systems, but also to the manner of executing public policies. The logic behind such a system—from the administrative rather than political point of view—is that different local conditions and problems may require marginally different solutions.[30] Further, different local historical factors and differences in the religious composition of the *Länder* may require variations in the internal procedures of administration. Such a system raises a number of important problems concerning public accountability for policy, and, associated with that, public control of policy and administration. The centralized system may be inflexible and possibly autocratic, but at least responsibility for policy is clear. Thus, as with the internal management of organizations, the conflict between centralization and its associated responsibility for decision, and decentralization and its associated flexibility, rages at the broader level of the organization as a whole.

The decentralization of administration in West Germany is somewhat extreme, but virtually all central governments use their subnational governments to administer national policy. For example, in the United States, the majority of federal social programs—Medicaid, Aid to Families with Dependent Children, etc.—are administered by state and local governments. The central governments of Canada and Australia, two other federal governments, also depend upon their state governments to administer large shares of social and economic policy.[31] Even in more centralized governments local authorities administer central government programs. In the United Kingdom there is some decentralization of decision making to the Scottish and Welsh offices, and there are differences in the administration of the law (and in some cases the law itself) in these parts of the country. In addition, local (regional and district) governments administer policies such as housing, criminal justice, and education for the central government.[32] There can be conflicts between local governments and the central government over the manner in which the policies are implemented, for example, the Lambeth council refusing to implement controls on public expenditure for health. In other more centralized governments, for example, Belgium and Spain, there have been movements to decentralize administration to ethnic and linguistic areas that have demands for special considerations.[33]

Related to the decentralization of decision making is a second areal question of the size of administrative units, or the size of local governments themselves. There has been a consistent tendency among governments to reorganize

TABLE 4.1
REDUCTION IN THE SIZE OF
LOCAL GOVERNMENT UNITS

Country (Basic Unit)	Number of units		Population per unit
	1951	*1982*	*1982*
France (commune)	37,983	36,391	1,500
United States			
(all general purpose)	41,029	38,732	6,700
Germany (gemeinden)	24,500	8,510	7,200
Norway (municipalities)	746	454	9,000
Belgium (commune)	2,670	596	16,700
Netherlands (municipalities)	1,014	820	17,000
Sweden (commune)	2,500	279	29,800
United Kingdom (districts)	c. 1,500	484	115,100

SOURCES:
Richard Rose, *Understanding Big Government* (London: Sage, forthcoming).
U.S. Bureau of the Census, *Statistical Abstract of the United States* (Washington,
D.C.: Government Printing Office, annual).

administration and local government (the two may be synonymous) into larger
and larger units. As Table 4.1 indicates, Sweden, for example, reorganized over
2,500 local governments into 279, with similar changes occurring in other Scandinavian countries, the United Kingdom, and West Germany. These reforms
have generally been justified by economies of scale in the production of public
goods and services and by the ability of the larger units to provide a broader
array of public services.[34] There is, however, little systematic evidence that
these presumed benefits actually materialize. First, as the size of governmental
units increases, there is a tendency for overhead expenditures to increase as a
proportion of total expenditures; after some point, gains from the economies
of scale are absorbed by increases in overhead.[35] Further, each service has a
different-size unit at which it is most efficiently produced. Refuse collection
appears to be very efficient at a very large scale, while policing can be argued
to be more efficient for smaller units. Unless very complex systems with multiple
single-purpose governments are to be created, no single-size government will
be most efficient for all services.[36]

Leaving aside economics, as the size of the unit increases, there may be
a decrease in satisfaction with the services. This is perhaps a function of the
perceived cost of government in relation to the services actually provided. On
the other hand, as Fesler points out, as the size of government increases so
does the perception of its remoteness, and consequently so does the alienation
of the population.[37] This alienation is one of the causes of the increase in
neighborhood government and organization in large cities. Thus, the argument

can be made for the retention of small and "inefficient" administrative divisions, even in the face of demands for greater efficiencies and increased services.

Organization by Process

Government can be organized by process, or by the communality of the processes employed by the members of the organization and the communality of their professional skills, rather than by purpose of the organization. Taken to an extreme this principle might mean, for example, that all accounting or purchasing activities for government would be concentrated in single agencies, or that all engineers or lawyers would be concentrated in bureaus of engineering or law, and their services provided to other agencies as required.

The above examples may appear inefficient—and they probably are— but such options do exist for the organization of government. They can be justified as a means of concentrating skilled individuals, as a means of imposing relatively uniform professional practices, and as a means of streamlining the operations of other organizations. The most common process distinction is between "line" and "staff" agencies. Initially, the concept of staff was reserved for personal advisers to an executive—the Bakers, Deavers, and Meeses directly advising the executive. As the tasks of the political executive have broadened, however, so has the definition of staff. Executives have found that their own staffs expanded to the point where they could no longer be personally supervised, and differentiated organizations performing staff functions have been developed. For example, the Executive Office of the President in the United States, currently employing 1,700 people, is perhaps the largest staff organization in the world.

We have been employing the term "staff functions" rather glibly. Just what are the functions that a staff person or agency is expected to undertake? Personnel from line or operating agencies might be tempted to say that their principal function is to prevent those actually providing a public service from having access to the executive. This is hardly their real function, but it points to a potential conflict between staff and line agencies. The ostensible purpose of staff agencies is to do those things that line agencies have neither the time, the power, nor the competence to do. Perhaps the most important of these tasks is coordinating the programs of line agencies. Line agencies, having a limited scope of operations and consequently narrow perspectives on the tasks of government, are not really in a position to attempt to coordinate their own programs. In fact, their incentives—if we assume that agency growth is a prime bureaucratic goal—are to attempt to spread their services into policy areas already occupied by other agencies and thereby to provide, if not duplicate services, at least competing services.[38] Thus, the executive and his staff (here interpreted broadly as either personal staff or staff agencies) must intervene in order to prevent unnecessary duplication.

The "central agencies" of government are primarily responsible for controlling duplication and enforcing coordination in government.[39] These agencies include the central financial and budgetary organizations, such as the Office of Management and Budget in the United States or the Treasury in the United Kingdom. They also include central personnel organizations, such as the Office of Personnel Management in the United States or the Civil Service Commission in Canada. Planning is also an important aspect of coordination and budgeting. Line agencies tend to be so heavily involved in their ongoing work that they frequently lack the time for nonessential things such as planning what to do in the future, and any sort of comprehensive planning may involve a wider viewpoint than that of a single agency. Planning agencies tend to be directly attached to the executive and to provide a broader overview of the future.

Several differences appear in the use of staff agencies. Self provides an interesting discussion of staff functions in the United States and Great Britain. He notes that staff functions have not been institutionalized in Britain as they have in the United States, in part as a function of the differences in the forms of government. Specifically, in British Cabinet government, problems of coordination are in the main horizontal rather than vertical, with a number of (allegedly) equal departments competing for funds and programs.[40] As the heads of these departments are all members of the Cabinet, the problem of coordination becomes one of imposing collective decision, rather than analysis and coordination by executive decree. Further, rather than being performed by an isolated presidential agency such as the Office of Management and Budget, most coordination in Britain is done by one of the departments—the Treasury—whose leader is among the members of the Cabinet.[41] There was an experiment with coordination of personnel through a civil service department, but that function was returned to the Treasury after 13 years. As Self and others point out, such a system of coordination could not work in an administrative system less homogeneous and less well integrated than that of Britain.[42] Self further notes that, with the exception of Treasury control, there is virtually no formal means of coordination within government. Attempts to achieve coordination have included the creation of very large departments; any potentially duplicating or competitive services can be included within the confines of a single department and be subject to hierarchical coordination by a single minister.[43] Likewise, there have been attempts to impose "overlords," or superministries, on the existing Cabinet structure to ensure effective policy control. In practice, it would appear that as the size of the ministries is increased, the old administrative "proverb" of span of control would be increasingly violated, so that in practice one might actually get less coordination, or at least the need for more extensive staff work within the department.[44]

We have at several points intimated conflict between line and staff agencies. Conflicts are almost inherent in this system of organization. The line agencies tend to regard the other side as ivory-tower planners far removed from the day-to-day problems of program administration but still able to sell themselves as experts with more access to decision making than the operating agencies. The staff agencies are also seen as formidable obstacles to bureaucratic growth.[45] On the other side of the conflict, staff agencies often become highly suspicious of the motives of line agencies in resisting attempts to coordinate and "rationalize" public services and may resent the ability of the line agencies to mobilize political support for their programs outside the bureaucracy. Staff may come to regard the line agencies as spendthrifts, raiders on the public purse. Thus, one of the inherent limitations that organization by process, especially in terms of line and staff, may have is the tendency for intraorganizational conflict and resistance to coordination and streamlining of services.

The problem of line and staff occurs not only at the level of the whole government, but also at the level of each individual department. Just as national executives require staff services to do things that their operating agencies cannot do, executives of operating agencies have the same need. At the departmental level, these staff services are also concerned with coordination of programs and activities. One of the more notable examples of staff services within a department is the ministerial *cabinet* in France and Belgium. Each minister in the French government has the opportunity to appoint a *cabinet* consisting of up to ten members to provide a variety of staff services such as policy advice, press relations, control of potentially recalcitrant civil servants, communications, and planning.[46] Although appointments to these *cabinets* are ostensibly at the will of the minister, in practice they involve extensive political considerations in addition to concerns over the quality and political reliability of the staff work produced.[47] Especially important in terms of the actual direction of policy is the job of the *conseilleur technique*, who serves as a political appointee linking the formal organization of the ministry to the politically appointed *cabinet*.

The use of ministerial *cabinets* is even more extensive in Belgium, to the point that they have been termed "counteradministrations."[48] The divisions of Belgian society along several dimensions make it necessary to employ *cabinets* staffed by people known to be reliable, as opposed to civil servants who are highly politicized and consequently may not be politically loyal to the minister. Again, some contrast with British and American practice may be in order. One might argue the need for the ministerial *cabinets* in large part because of the relative inability or unwillingness of French and Belgian ministers to rely on their civil servants. This in turn necessitates the use of political appointees to drive the control of the minister farther down into the organization than would otherwise be possible and provides more of a check on the execution of ministerial directives within the organization. In the United States, the existence of several layers of political appointees between the cabinet officer and the upper echelons of the career civil service is one type of "staff" organization, although the appointees may actually hold positions in "line" agencies to ensure political control over presumably independent-minded civil servants. Britain is unique in the apparent willingness of political ministers to accept advice by career civil servants and the willingness of the ministers to allow those civil servants to control most day-to-day business within the ministry.[49]

One interesting variant of organization by staff and line, or more generally organization by process, occurs in Sweden. Here the two usual functions of the public bureaucracy—the development and the execution of public policy—are organizationally divided into two separate organizations. First, the ministries are charged with the development of public policy. The ministries are small, and their work is confined to staff-type work—planning, coordination, and program development.[50] The actual execution of public programs is left to a set of administrative boards. The boards are independent of the ministries, although linked through the budgetary process and a number of other ways, and perform "line" functions of actually implementing programs. This method of organization points to the extent to which organization by line and staff corresponds to the old adage about the separation of politics and administration.[51] Staff functions can be equated with the political functions of advocating programs and formulating policy, and assuring that the independent civil servants do what their political masters intended. Line functions are more normally associated with the execution of policy in a rather routine fashion. As we have pointed out—and will deal with more extensively later— the dichotomy between politics and administration is largely a false one, but it is important to note the extent to which it has been incorporated into public administration.

A final possibility for organization by process is organization by corps, or by some other internally homogeneous administrative bodies. The corps system is best developed in France but has been copied by a number of other countries, especially those derivative from a French or Napoleonic administrative tradition. The concept of the corps is a body of administrators with similar educational backgrounds and similar professional skills. Each of the grands corps is, in theory, specialized by function; in practice they have a pervasive influence on French administration and have adopted somewhat broader roles. Suleiman notes that it is virtually obligatory to have a member of the Inspectorate of Finances as a member of a ministerial cabinet or for directeur, if for no other reason than to have a ready avenue for appeal or consultation on the budget.[52] Members of the other corps are also included in a number of cabinets. These corps are specialized by function but together provide a high level of leadership within the public service, which might be lacking without the corps structure and the esprit de corps that such a system engenders. Moreover, the isolation of the grands corps from a number of the usual administrative pressures, their prestige, and their individual abilities allow them to enforce standards of uniformity throughout the administration, so that this form of organization by function contributes to the maintenance of centralized government in France.[53]

Several functions have been found to be amenable to organization by corps or process. Engineering has been one, and any number of countries have specialized engineering corps within their national civil services or militaries, for example, the Army Corps of Engineers in the United States.[54] If we look at administration broadly, the military officer corps and the diplomatic services could be considered as specialized corps, and as rather obvious cases of organization by function or process. Also, as with the Inspectorate of Finances in France, financial inspectors are frequently organized as a separate branch of administration, to ensure their impartiality in auditing public accounts. This goes so far, in the United States, as to isolate them almost entirely from the rest of the public service (in the General Accounting Office). Thus, we can say that those functions that tend to be organized by process tend to be those that require: (1) technical training or highly professional skills, or (2) a high degree of internal commitment and *esprit de corps*, or (3) impartiality and isolation from other portions of the bureaucracy and from political pressures.

In summary, organization by process can make some useful distinctions between the tasks of various civil servants and agencies, but as a general organizing principle it appears to be unwieldy. Even in its limited form, it tends to engender political conflicts between those who (at least from their own perspective) do the work of the civil service, and those who merely (?) plan, coordinate, and control. Likewise, organization by corps as a special example of organization by process can engender similar political conflicts and rivalries directed against an elite group with broadly defined competencies who appear all too ubiquitous in the exercise of their tasks and all too close to those who are responsible for decision. Thus, as will be said again, the organization of the public service, as well as being a problem for the administrative scientist, is a problem for the politician as well. Both must attempt to provide smooth and efficient government, and both must try to protect their own interests through organizational devices.

Organization by Clientele

The third possible basis for organization is the clientele to be served by the agency. Clientele groups presumed to have special needs or whose lifestyles, situations, or other characteristics are considered sufficiently distinctive may justify an organization for them and their interests. There have been two apparent reasons for developing clientele-based organizations: (1) to be able to provide better services for a special set of clients (especially those with political clout), for example, veterans, urban dwellers, farmers; or (2) conversely, to at once assist and *control* segments of the population lacking such clout, for example, Indians, foreign workers, aliens. The important fact about both these justifications is that they result in an organization that is an obvious avenue for influence by the clientele on government. That is, organization by clientele, even when undertaken for the purpose of regulation, generally results in more direct group influence on administration than might be found in other forms of organization. The reasons for this are perhaps obvious; they will be developed more in discussion of the politics of administration.[55] But we should point out here that in client-based organizations, a process of exchange and mutuality almost inherently results. The clientele group needs the access to government decision making provided by the public organization, and the agency in turn requires popular support from its clientele in political conflicts. Further, those public organizations may owe their existence to the activities of particular clientele groups and must therefore cater to the demands of those groups more than might be thought by others to be in the "public interest."

Perhaps the most important manifestation of this tendency toward cooptation and symbiosis between clientele and administration occurs in so-called independent regulatory boards. The underlying conception of these boards, as they are constituted in the United States and elsewhere, is that they should serve as administrative *qua* judicial bodies controlling the activities of some portion of the economy or society. The boards are made independent to prevent excessive partisan influence from being exerted over their decisions. They are intended to regulate in the public interest and without regard for political considerations.

No matter how commendable these ideas may be in theory, they are almost certainly doomed to failure in practice. Many of the activities that these boards were intended to regulate are among the most sensitive and societally important, including transportation, energy, and communication.[56] But, by being isolated from political demands in their tasks of regulating these industries, the boards are isolated from political supports as well. They essentially lack any strong and direct connection with the executive and cannot therefore easily appeal for assistance in financing, staffing, and general support for their regulatory functions. Any such executive interference might be regarded as antithetical to the depoliticized and nonpartisan conception of these boards. Thus, the independent regulatory boards must seek other sources of political support, with the most likely source being the very interests they were designed to regulate. The point of this argument, then, is that organization *by* clientele may rapidly change into organization *for* clientele.

Organization by client may also be made at the subdepartmental level, and may have many of the same consequences although they may be manifested primarily through intraorganizational conflict rather than through isolation and subversion of the public purpose. As a department or agency develops bureaus devoted to assisting or even regulating a particular client group, those bureaus frequently become captives of that group and become spokesmen for them in policy-related matters. As with the organization of departments by client, the subdepartmental agencies may also need political support for political conflicts. Their clientele can provide such support, but the price of that support is favorable treatment or regulation.

It is often difficult to distinguish client-based organizations from area-based organizations. Many of the same problems of organizations being captured arise with either basis of organization. Two interesting and countervailing examples of the interaction of organizations with clients groups are those of the forest rangers and the engineering corps. In these examples, local communities, or more specifically local business interests, operate as clients. In the case of the Forest Service, the organization attempts to counteract possible local influences on regulation. One task of a forest ranger is to regulate the use of national forests for commercial purposes such as lumbering and grazing. The Forest Service uses as a general guideline that no ranger should remain in the same community for more than two years. This is to prevent him from becoming too closely integrated into the local community and therefore too sympathetic to pleas from local businessmen for excessive use of the forests.[57] Civil engineering corps in both France and the United States—and probably elsewhere—get a significant portion of their political support by integrating themselves into local communities and at times providing special treatment for the localities. This provides a huge reservoir of political support should the executive or legislature seek to curtail the autonomy of the corps.[58] The first of these examples shows an attempt to prevent clientele organization from subverting the formal goals of the organization; the second shows a use of client organization to enable the agency to succeed in its political conflicts.

Organization by clientele is at times difficult to avoid. There are powerful political pressures to organize to benefit certain groups, and there is a certain logic to such organization when the needs of a clientele are distinctive. On the other hand, this form of organization has a number of possible dangers. It is difficult for the public agency to remain at all detached from its clientele and to be able to administer programs objectively and in the "public interest."

Organization by Purpose

The final possibility for organizing administration is the principal purpose, or goal, of the organization. This mode of organization is not always clearly distinguishable from the others already discussed. For example, is a Department of Agriculture organized on the basis of its major purpose—the promotion of agriculture—or is it organized around a ready-made clientele group—farmers? Organization by purpose, perhaps more than the others mentioned, points up the lack of exclusiveness of this set of categories.

There are, however, more important topics to be discussed with respect to organization by purpose. The first is, where do organizational goals and purposes come from? Presumably, the legislation establishing an organization will specify the tasks to be performed by that organization. In most cases, however, these tasks are put forth in only the barest outline, allowing substantial latitude for future elaboration and interpretation. In theory, the elaboration of these organizational goals will be primarily a political process involving the imposition of externally developed goals by politically selected leaders. However, given the barriers facing those political masters, the impact of external leaders on organizational goals is less than would be thought by listening to the formal discussions of the roles of civil servants and politicians.[59]

If the purposes of the organization do not come from the outside, as previously thought, where do they come from? The most obvious answer then is that they are generated internally. If that is true, we come to one of the most commonly noted pathologies of formal organizations: the displacement of goals.[60] There is a tendency in organizations gradually and almost imperceptibly to shift from what might be called public goals to what may be termed private goals. Even though the organization was established to fulfill some need in society, over time organizational survival and possibly organizational development may supersede that societal goal. Downs discusses this in terms of the tendencies of individuals within organizations to shift from zealot to conserver roles.[61] When young, they seek to achieve societal goals through their actions in the public service, but over time, because of a natural aging process, the growth of personal responsibilities, and perhaps cynicism about the possibility of social change, they become less interested in producing change but more interested in personal gain and security. Their major goals in office become: (1) to continue the existence of the agency, (2) possibly to expand its role and budget, and (3) finally to do something for the society. Similarly, Mohr speaks of the difference between transitive goals of organizations and reflexive goals. The transitive goals are those directed at some outside target, such as a client, while the reflexive goals are those directed at internal maintenance.[62]

Even if we do not accept the cynical view that after some (unspecified) point in time agencies become self-serving, we must understand that over time the goals pursued by an agency generally come to mean what the incumbents of the roles want them to mean. In other words, departments develop ideologies concerning the tasks that lay before them and the means of completing those tasks. Further, by controlling selection, socialization, and to some degree retention of members, they tend to preserve this ideology even when confronted with new members.[63] The organizational conception of goals and the means of achieving those goals are often functions of the period of political and organizational socialization of the incumbents to the leadership positions within the organization.

For example, most social-service agencies in the United States were developed or expanded dramatically during the New Deal era. The basic philosophy of social improvement was to throw money at the problem, and to some extent the imposition of middle-class values on clients of the agency.[64] These organizations were not particularly receptive to innovative or client-centered approaches to social problems, and so new organizations had to be created outside the existing framework to take new initiatives in social policy. In the same way, the foreign offices of many Western nations are still heavily influenced by a "Munich mentality," which dictates that any attempt at compromise with an enemy is a sign of weakness and a prelude to further threats and demands.

As a final example, one might cite the essentially conservative and elitist civil services inherited by many Third World countries from their former colonial masters. These civil services were not organized or staffed to undertake the massive programs of economic and social development that they faced, and some were opposed to them ideologically. Thus, there have been frequent expressions of hostility from the political leaders of these countries toward these seemingly recalcitrant civil servants who were impeding programs of rapid social change.[65] The major point to be made in this discussion of goal setting is that the purpose of a public agency is not necessarily the one outlined in the enabling legislation or in official policy statements. Setting goals is a political process, and very often it is an intraorganizational political process hidden from public scrutiny and public control.

Following the question of origin of goals is the question of what the agency does when it runs out of things to do. There are a number of rather amusing examples of agencies that have long outlived their stated purposes and have become essentially sinecures for the remaining employees. Our concern is not with blatant inefficiency and redundancy, but rather with the problem of the succession of goals in an organization. That is, how can an agency shift its principal concerns and orientations from one objective to another? Given the discussion above, we must first assume that this would be a difficult task, but we do know that organizations undergo such shifts in order to survive. There are a number of examples of this type of goal succession in private organizations; two commonly cited examples are the March of Dimes and the YMCA. The examples from public organizations are perhaps less clear, but they exist. One of the most common in European nations of late has been the transformation of agencies formerly concerned with the management of colonial territories into offices of overseas development and aid to underdeveloped countries. While still dealing with essentially the same clienteles geographically, the goals, operations, and politics of these agencies have been greatly changed. Similarly, the restructuring of American aid programs has necessitated a rather massive shakeup within the Agency for International Development, necessitating retraining of almost all the field staff. We can see that agencies can and do shift goals, but it requires some strong impetus to do so, with the loss or decline of agency support—both from the budgetary process and the public—being the most important impetus in public organizations.

Summary

We have discussed four broad methods of organizing government and public administration. As noted, the lines between these categories are not always clear. What is clear is that none of them offers the perfect solution to the problem of organizing public services, and each has its advantages and disadvantages. The decisions to use one or the other should be dependent upon two factors. One is the nature of the service to be delivered. Some services, such as police and fire protection, require dispersion by area, while others work very well with a highly centralized structure. Some services, for example, accounting, appear to function better when all the experts are concentrated, while others function better when expertise is dispersed. The architect of the public service must be clear that he or she understands the nature of the service to be provided by any organization being created.

The second factor that must be understood is the nature of the political system in which our architect is functioning. For example, a political system that is deeply divided by language, or race, or other primordial sentiment will—everything else being equal—function better with as many functions as possible organized by area or client. On the other hand, a society that values expertise and control will—again, everything else being equal—function better with as many organizations as possible organized by purpose. The nature of public organizations must conform not only to the wishes of organizational theorists, but also to the political realities of the nation.

INTERNAL ORGANIZATION

To this point we have been largely examining the problems of organizing the public service at the national level, with some attention to problems within agencies that are analogous to those at macroscopic levels. We turn now to a brief discussion of internal organization and management, particularly problems of hierarchical control and communication within agencies.

Hierarchical control, or the chain of command, and the associated need to communicate information and decision form a central core of the study of formal organizations.[66] Those who draw neat, pyramidal organization charts assume that the individuals on the top of the hierarchy are responsible for making decisions and that their decisions are binding for all members of the organization. Likewise, it is assumed that it is the task of subordinates to communicate all relevant information upward, so that the right decisions can be made by those at the top. Unfortunately for those who would like to see organizations function this way, such orderly management of organizations is rarely encountered in practice. In fact, many argue that the best way to understand organizations is not as a system of hierarchy but as a system of cooperation and bargaining.[67] In such an approach to organizations, all levels of the organization are seen as having resources and power.[68] Consequently, management involves building coalitions rather than issuing commands.

The nonhierarchical approach to organizations may be especially applicable to the public sector. In the first place, public sector organizations lack clear definitions of success or failure; they have no analogue of profit in the business world.[69] Managers therefore can be less certain about the orders that should be given and the relative effectiveness of employees. Also, the employees of most public sector organizations are permanent—or almost permanent—civil servants. This makes it difficult to employ many of the threats and incentives that would be available in private sector organizations. Finally, because of the mixture of political and civil service personnel in most public organizations, there are often differences in the long-term commitments of individuals to the organization, different motivations, and different perceptions of the time in which change should be brought about.[70] All these factors make the effective management of public organizations a particularly trying task.

The major purpose of hierarchical control is to create uniformity of action by subordinates within the organization. One of the hallmarks and presumed benefits of bureaucratic organization is the elimination of personal discretion and caprice from the decisions taken by the organization. Unfortunately for those attempting to manage organizations, individuals like discretion and power, not so much to be able to deal capriciously with their clients as to have the opportunity to exercise some personal initiative. Further, they enjoy being able to establish personal relationships—for example, those not strictly governed by the rules of the organization—with both superiors and subordinates. Many formal organizations tend to deny these opportunities to their members, with any number of adverse consequences both for individuals and for goal attainment within the organization. Leaving aside the consequences for individuals, let us look at the consequences for the organization.

One of the most important consequences is the isolation of strata within the organization.[71] Superior-subordinate relationships tend to become rigidified, with little opportunity for other than formal communication across strata. Each stratum becomes socially isolated from others, and each tends to develop its own norms of compliance with the directives of superiors. These norms are rarely in violation of the formal norms of the organization; in fact, there is a tendency to comply ritualistically with rules and directives while possibly subverting the real purposes of the organization. Thus, complaints about bureaucratic red tape and inefficiency may largely result from the need of lower echelons in the organization to protect themselves from their superiors by complying with the letter of regulations and refusing to take any personal initiative outside those regulations that might subject them later to punishment. Their compliance is real, but, paradoxically, by complying with the rules they may reduce the effectiveness and efficiency of the organization. This is another aspect of goal displacement, in that the rules become an end in themselves rather than a means to accomplish the goals of the agency.

Associated with the isolation of strata is a tendency for organizations to develop faulty communication patterns. Within organizations, information is conceptualized as flowing upward, just as authority is conceptualized as flowing downward. There is a tendency, however, because of the power of superiors over subordinates, for each stratum within the organization to be somewhat less than candid when it communicates with its superiors.[72] In fact, there is a tendency systematically to distort the information passed upward to place the best possible construction on events, especially in light of what subordinates think their superiors want to hear. This is in part a function of the general organizational problem of each level having to synthesize and pass on only the relevant information to superiors, in order to prevent an overload of information as one goes up the organizational ladder. Many characteristics of formal bureaucratic structures tend to exacerbate this problem by the introduction of systematic distortion of information. Interestingly, superiors (having reached their position, one would hope, because of some cleverness) tend to attempt to take into account the systematic distortion they believe has been introduced by subordinates, and to read reports skeptically and with an eye to what has been omitted or altered.[73] Unless the superior is cleverer than he or she has any right to be, this attempt to counteract bias will only introduce more distortion. As this compounded distortion proceeds upward through several levels of the organization, the possibilities of superiors knowing what is actually going on becomes very slight.

The distortion of information as it passes through hierarchies is especially important in modern public bureaucracies when we consider the types of individuals who tend to occupy positions at each level of the hierarchy. As Thompson argued some years ago, one characteristic of modern organizations is the concentration of technical expertise at the bottom of the hierarchy and the concentration of decision at the top.[74] In other words, we can expect the information passed up to decision-makers to be systematically distorted; further, the decision-makers might not have the ability to comprehend the technical content of the information even if it were passed on undistorted. The concentration of generalists in decision making in most public bureaucracies tends to exacerbate problems of hierarchical information flow, since they have little ability to absorb or develop information on their own.[75] Thus, if one were to make the most extreme case, one might say that decisions were being taken by people with inadequate and distorted information and that those individuals probably could not fruitfully utilize the proper information even if they had it. Even with a less extreme view, one can easily say that it is entirely possible that organizations have extreme difficulties in effectively processing information, especially information with technical content, and consequently may lose the ability to "steer" themselves in policy formulation.

Given these problems of hierarchy and communication, what are the possibilities of creating effective organizations, especially effective public organizations? There is no simple answer, but there have been a number of suggestions for change. Some have involved altering the personalities of individuals—at least in their organizational roles—and modifying the dynamics of groups.[76] Others have concentrated on changing the approach of managers to the task of management. One of the most innovative approaches to change is Landau's argument that it is essentially rational to be redundant and that the development of redundant channels of communication and control can be beneficial to an organization.[77] Redundancy was a tactic adopted by Franklin Roosevelt as president to prevent the existing bureaus from sabotaging or delaying his New Deal programs. The existence of dual hierarchies in Soviet administrative practice is perhaps an extreme version of redundancy intended to assure that there is a check on information and performance at all stages of the administrative process. To some degree the existence of ministerial *cabinets* in France and Belgium is a further use of redundant structures to check on the performance of administration. Downs further mentions the possibility of building in overlapping and redundant structures as a means of ensuring the flow of relatively unbiased information.[78] Likewise, Niskanen and others—adopting an economic approach to the study of public bureaucracy—have argued that redundancy and competition could improve the efficiency of government and reduce its total cost.[79] Interestingly, all these schemes involve the construction of organizations quite at odds with those that might be advocated by traditional students of management and public administration, for whom unity of command and the lack of overlapping functions were seen as two of the prime elements of proper organization.

VARIATIONS IN INTERNAL ORGANIZATION

The problems of internal organization are general, and we should expect variation by both nation-state and the characteristics of the particular policy area being administered. Differences occur between those two broad categories of Western and non-Western systems, or developed and underdeveloped countries.[80] Despite their own variations, Western cultures are more accepting of impersonality, hierarchy, and bureaucracy than are non-Western cultures. Thus, we might expect the dysfunctions of bureaucracy outlined above to be more evident in non-Western cultures if attempts were made to enforce such a system. Attempts to depersonalize administration and policy through rules and procedure have been shown in a number of instances to be rather ineffective as a means of achieving ends in those systems.[81] The formal structures of most bureaucracies in the non-Western world conform quite closely with those of Western administration, in part as a function of colonial inheritance and in part because of the need to comply with certain formalities in order to receive aid from developed nations and international organizations. However, the actual operations of these structures tend to be quite different from the form, with nonbureaucratic criteria tending to supersede the rules, procedures, and hierarchy of the formal structure. Some of the bureaucratic dysfunctions related to communication may be overcome by a reliance on communalism and nonbureaucratic criteria in recruitment, as may in fact some problems of rigidity with clients. What is given up is the entire justification for having bureaucratic structures in the first place, namely, a high level of uniform behavior and client treatment. The latter values are by no means perfectly attained in Western bureaucratic systems, but an attempt is made.

Western nations appear to show substantial variation in their prospects for effective bureaucracy. These have been discussed to some extent when discussing the "administrative cultures" of these countries.[82] What is important is the extent to which cultural differences tend to ease or exacerbate dysfunction in bureaucracy. One of the tendencies noted by Crozier in discussing these problems is the influence of general conceptions of authority and equality on the bureaucratic structure of organizations.[83] For example, he noted that perhaps as a function of generalized patterns of deference and acceptance of authority, the organizational structure of British ships tended to be substantially less complex and less dependent upon impersonal rules than those of American ships.[84] American crewmen, apparently socialized in more individualistic mores, were less willing to accept the personal authority of a superior, and formalized rules had to be devised to take the personal element out of rule enforcement. At the other end of the spectrum, societies in which authority is both accepted and revered, and where those in authoritative positions tend to view their roles somewhat paternalistically, can function with simple organizational structures and a relative absence of bureaucratic rules and still obtain high levels of uniformity in behavior. In their study of managerial attitudes cross-nationally, Haire, Ghiselli, and Porter found that there were several distinct blocs of Western nations in terms of their conceptions of the management role: Nordic, Anglo-American, and Latin-European.[85] The differences among these groups were rather subtle but pointed to important differences in attitudes toward managerial practice and authority even among Western nations.

There are also differences between types of organizations depending on the tasks they are intended to perform. Etzioni has provided one useful set of broad categories.[86] He classifies organizations according to the type of power that the organization seeks to use over its members and the type of compliance of the members. He classifies power as either coercive, remunerative, or normative. The compliance of organizational members may be alternative, calculative, or moral. Although there may be mixed organizations, the three model types of organizations in this typology are coercive-alienative, remunerative-calculative, and normative-moral. Rather obviously, a normative-moral organization such as a church or even a highly committed public bureau is able to do its job effectively with a simpler organizational structure, fewer impersonal rules, and less dysfunctional activity than would other types of organization. On the other hand, such an organization would have more difficulty in modifying its goals and retaining its personnel than would an organization relying on remunerative power. Some public organizations of all three types exist, and managers, although they may not conceptualize it in exactly these terms, have to know how to employ the appropriate incentives with each type of organization.

Other schemes for classifying organizations depend more on the services provided by the organization. Blau and Scott use a classification of organizations based upon the criterion of *cui bono*, or who benefits.[87] Most public organizations fall into their category of commonweal organizations in that the public at large is the prime beneficiary. Other public organizations would be service organizations in that the prime beneficiaries are the clients, for example, social-service agencies. Again we can see that the dynamics of organizations whose intention it is to provide a service to the public at large, generally free and with no exclusion, will have different organizational problems than an organization whose intention is to serve only a limited number of individuals, based upon the particular needs of those individuals.[88] Moreover, the clients (consumers of services) for the commonweal organization tend to be considerably less dependent upon those organizations than clients of service agents, so that for service organizations most conflicts emerge with the political representatives of the public at large over expense and responsibility.

Perrow, along with Thompson and Tuden, attempts to relate the characteristics of the problem of policy area to the type of decision making that is likely to occur.[89] Although both schemes (see Figure 4.1) were intended to have universal applicability, they also have relevance to problems of public administrative agencies. In Thompson and Tuden's scheme, the same types of variation in the agreement on ends and the agreement on means occur among public agencies as they do more generally. The examples in Figure 4.1 may not be universally agreed upon, but they should point out that, first, there is such variation, and second, that it will have consequences for public organizations. Likewise, the Perrow scheme, based largely on the characteristics of technology and raw materials, has also been given examples from among public

FIGURE 4.1

TYPOLOGY OF POLICY PROBLEMS
FOR ADMINISTRATION

		Preferences	
		Agreement	Disagreement
Perception of Causation	Agreement	Programmed Decisions (public health)	Bargaining (incomes policy)
	Disagreement	Pragmatic (comprehensive education reform)	Inspiration (research and development)

SOURCES: Derived from James D. Thompson and Arthur Tuden, "Strategy, Structure, and Process of Organizational Decision," in *Comparative Studies in Administration* (Pittsburgh: University of Pittsburgh Administrative Science Center, 1959); Charles Perrow, *Organizational Analysis* (Belmont, Calif.: Wadsworth, 1970), pp. 80–91.

organizations, and the assumption is that organizations dealing with a stable (or stabilized) raw material, for example, prisons, will have a vastly different type of organizational structure than will those dealing with essentially unknown materials, for example, research and development agencies.[90] Of course, the characteristics of the individuals likely to be employed in such agencies and the tasks set out for them will also have an impact, but it does appear useful to look at the correspondence between organizations and the raw materials—most commonly human—with which they must deal.

SUMMARY

This chapter has provided a brief overview of the complex topic of the structure of public organizations. As such, it has been largely an introduction to the problems and questions that arise, rather than a set of definitive answers to those questions. Nevertheless, it should be clear that the design of administration is not an entirely technical exercise. There are a number of rather broad questions concerning the nature of the establishment as a whole that must be answered by political leaders or constitution writers rather than by the civil service. These answers may in turn greatly influence the overall effectiveness of the public establishment as well as the satisfaction of the public with that establishment. Beyond these questions, there are any number of problems with the internal organization of agencies and with the managing of an ongoing public enterprise. These must be considered in the light of the particular nation in question and the characteristics of the task involved. The basic task of organizational analysis, however, is to design organizations that enable their officials to have at least the possibility of providing effective services to the population. No organization chart or diagram of responsibilities can ensure this, so the task of the manager is largely to make it possible and perhaps even probable. The ultimate success or failure of the agency will remain with the individuals who inhabit it.

NOTES

1. See, for example, Dwight Waldo, "Public Administration," in *International Encyclopedia of the Social Sciences*, Edward Shils, ed. (New York: Macmillan, 1968), pp. 145–56.
2. Herbert Simon, *Administrative Behavior* (New York: Macmillan, 1957), pp. 35–44.
3. Walther Fürst et al., *Beamtenrecht des Bundes und der Länder* (Berlin: Schmidt, 1973).
4. But see Kenneth Dyson, *Party, State and Bureaucracy* (Beverly Hills, Calif.: Sage, 1977).
5. Renate Mayntz, "German Federal Bureaucrats: A Functional Elite Between

Politics and Administration" (Paper presented to Conference on the Role of Higher Civil Servants, Centro de Investigaciones Sociologicas, Madrid, Spain, 1980).

6. Richard Parry, "United Kingdom Public Employment, Patterns of Change, 1951–1976," *Studies in Public Policy*, No. 62 (Glasgow, Scotland: Centre for the Study of Public Policy, University of Strathclyde, 1980).

7. Anthony Barker, *Quangos in Britain* (London: Macmillan, 1982).

8. E. N. Gladden, *The Civil Service of the United Kingdom, 1855–1970* (London: Frank Cass, 1967).

9. *The Civil Service* (The Fulton Report), Cmnd. 3638 (London: HMSO, 1968).

10. Sir John Hoskyns, "Whitehall and Westminster: An Outsider's View," *Fiscal Studies* 3 (1982): 162–72.

11. Hugo Young and Anne Sloman, *No, Minister: An Inquiry into the Civil Service* (London: BBC, 1982).

12. Alfred Diamant, "Tradition and Innovation in French Administration," *Comparative Political Studies* 1 (1968): 252–74.

13. Serge Salon, "La politique de choix des fonctionnaires en France," *L'Annuaire Européen d'Administration Publique, 1979* (Paris: CNRS, 1980), pp. 73–110.

14. Ezra N. Suleiman, *Elites in French Society* (Princeton, N.J.: Princeton University Press, 1977); Jean-Claude Theonig, *L'Ere des technocrats: le cas de Ponts et Chausses* (Paris: Les Editions d'organisation, 1973).

15. Marie-Christine Kessler, "L'École nationale d'administration," *La Fonction Publique*, vol. 2, *Cahiers Francais* (Paris: La Documentation Francaise, 1980), pp. 8–11.

16. Pierre Escoube, "Les grands corps administratif," *La Fonction Publique*, vol. 2, pp. 29–30.

17. Howard Machin, *The Prefect in French Public Administration* (London: Croom-Helm, 1977).

18. Daniel Tarschys, *Den Öffentliga Revolutionen* (Stockholm: Prisma, 1978), Table 3.

19. Thomas J. Anton, *Administered Politics: Elite Political Culture in Sweden* (Boston: Martinus Nijhoff, 1980).

20. SACO: Sveriges Akademikers Centralorganisationen, the Swedish Academics Central Organization; TCO: Tjänstemannens Centralorganizationen, the Officials Central Organization.

21. LO–Landsorganisationen, the Federation of Trade Unions.

22. Rune Premfors, "Sweden" in *Efficiency and Effectiveness in the Civil Service* (House of Commons, Treasury and Civil Service Committee, 8 March 1982).

23. Luther Gulick, "Notes on the Theory of Organization," in *Papers on the Science of Administration*, Luther Gulick and L. F. Urwick, eds. (New York: Institute of Public Administration, 1937), pp. 3–50; Schuyler Wallace, *Federal Departmentalism* (New York: Columbia University Press, 1941); George C. S. Benson, "Internal Administrative Organization," *Public Administration Review* 1, no. 4 (1941): 473–86.

24. See for example, James Kellas, *The Scottish Political System*, 2nd. ed. (Cambridge: Cambridge University Press, 1975), pp. 25–60.

25. Brian Chapman, *The Prefects and Provincial France* (London: Allen & Unwin, 1955), is now somewhat dated but still provides a useful description.

26. Robert Fried, *The Italian Prefects* (New Haven: Yale University Press, 1967).
27. Jean-Pierre Worms, "Le Préfet et ses notables," *Sociologie du Travail* 12, no. 3 (1966): 249–75.
28. Ibid., pp. 261 ff.
29. Some increase in the centralization of the system does appear to be occurring. See Kenneth Hanf, "Administrative Developments in East and West Germany: Stirrings of Reform," *Political Studies* 21, no. 1 (1973): 35–44.
30. Part of the political logic is, of course, to prevent the formation of a highly centralized political system, which might in turn be dominated by extremists. Herbert Jacob, *German Administration Since Bismark* (New Haven: Yale University Press, 1963).
31. Kenneth W. Wiltshire, *Administrative Federalism* (St. Lucia, Queensland: University of Queensland Press, 1977).
32. Brian W. Hogwood and Michael Keating, *Regional Government in England* (London: Oxford University Press, 1982).
33. Pierre Sulna de Bieusses, "Constitutional Norms and Central Administration," in David S. Bell, ed., *Democratic Politics in Spain* (London: Pinter, 1983), pp. 78–97.
34. See J. Westerståhl, *Ett forskningsprogram: Den Kommunale Självstyrelsen* (Stockholm: Almqvist & Wiksell, 1971).
35. See for example, Elinor Ostrom, Roger B. Parks, and W. E. Oates, "Do We Really Want to Consolidate Urban Police Forces," *Public Administration Review* 30 (1973): 423–33. See D. P. Bradford, R. A. Mott, and W. E. Oates, "The Rising Cost of Local Public Services: Some Evidence and Reflections," *National Tax Journal* 22, no. 2 (1969): 185–202; Kenneth Newton, "Is Small Really So Beautiful?; Is Big Really So Ugly?" *Studies in Public Policy*, no. 18 (Glasgow, Scotland: Centre for the Study of Public Policy, University of Strathclyde, 1977).
36. See Kirkpatrick Sale, "The Polis Perplexity: An Inquiry into the Size of Cities," *Working Papers for a New Society* (January/February 1978): 64–77.
37. Fesler, *Area and Administration*, p. 25.
38. Anthony Downs, *Inside Bureaucracy* (Boston: Little, Brown, 1967), pp. 211 ff.
39. Colin Campbell and George J. Szablowski, *The Super-Bureaucrats: Structure and Behavior in Central Agencies* (Toronto: Macmillan of Canada, 1979).
40. Peter Self, *Administrative Theories and Politics* (London: Allen & Unwin, 1972), p. 128.
41. Of course, the chancellor of the exchequer as head of the Treasury is somewhat more than just another minister, despite the alleged equality of the Cabinet. On the role of the Treasury in policy, see Hugh Heclo and Aaron Wildavsky, *The Private Government of Public Money* (Berkeley: University of California Press, 1974).
42. Self, *Administrative Theories*, pp. 133–34.
43. Ibid., p. 130; Sir Richard Clarke, "The Number and Size of Government Departments," *Political Quarterly* 43, no. 2 (1972): 169–86.
44. For an analysis of the concept, see William H. Starbuck, "Organizational Growth and Development," in *Handbook of Organizations*, James G. March, ed. (Chicago: Rand McNally, 1965), pp. 496–98.

45. The job of some staff agencies is explicitly to impose some central control on line agencies, especially with regard to funding. This is especially true of a growing number of staff agencies engaged in cost-benefit analysis and program budgeting. See chapter 6. See also Aaron Wildavsky, "The Political Economy of Efficiency," *Public Administration Review* 26, no. 4 (1966): 292–310.

46. See Jeanne Siwek-Pouydesseau, "French Ministerial Staffs," in *The Mandarins of Western Europe*, Mattei Dogan, ed. (New York: John Wiley, 1975), pp. 196–209.

47. Ezra Suleiman, *Power, Politics, and Bureaucracy in France* (Princeton: Princeton University Press, 1974), pp. 202–4.

48. Leo Moulin, "The Politicization of Administration in Belgium," in Dogan, *Mandarins*, pp. 163–84.

49. But see F. F. Ridley, "The British Civil Service and Politics: Principles and Traditions in Flux," *Parliamentary Affairs* 36 (1983): 28–49.

50. Pierre Vinde, *Hur sveriges styres* (Stockholm: Prisma, 1968); Thomas J. Anton, *Administered Politics.*

51. Vinde, *Hur sveriges styres; The Swedish Civil Service* (Stockholm: Ministry of Finance, 1967), pp. 18–21.

52. Suleiman, *Power, Politics,* pp. 263–64.

53. Ibid., p. 271.

54. See for example, Arthur Maas, *Muddy Waters: The Army Corps of Engineers and the Nation's Rivers* (Cambridge, Mass.: Harvard University Press, 1951); Elizabeth B. Drew, "Dam Outrage: The Story of the Army Engineers," *Atlantic* 225 (1970): 51–62; D. A. Mazmanian and J. Nienaber, *Can Organizations Change?: Environmental Protection, Citizen Participation, and The Army Corps of Engineers* (Washington, D.C.: The Brookings Institution, 1979); Theonig, *L'Ere des technocrates.*

55. See chapter 5.

56. Henry J. Friendly, *The Federal Administrative Agencies* (Cambridge, Mass.: Harvard University Press, 1962); Theodore J. Lowi, *The End of Liberalism,* 2nd. ed. (New York: Norton, 1979); James Q. Wilson, *The Politics of Regulation* (New York: Basic Books, 1980).

57. Herbert Kaufman, *The Forest Ranger: A Study in Administrative Behavior* (Baltimore: Johns Hopkins University Press, 1967), pp. 176–83. This rapid transfer scheme also has the organizational benefit of building the concept of the service as a distinct organization and career.

58. Jean-Claude Theonig and E. Friedberg, *La creation des directions departmentales de l'equipment: phenomenes de corps et reforme administrative* (Paris: CNRS, 1970), pp. 39 ff.; Grant McConnell, *Private Power and American Democracy* (New York: Knopf, 1970), pp. 216–19. This seems to imply an acceptance of the dichotomy between politics and administration. This is to reflect the formal-legal dichotomy concerning the development of legislation and the political responsibility for policy.

59. See Richard Rose, *The Problem of Party Government* (London: Macmillan, 1974), pp. 417–21.

60. The classic statement of this pathology is Robert K. Merton, "The Unanticipated Consequences of Purposive Social Action," *American Sociological Re-*

view 1, no. 4 (1936): 894–904; "Bureaucratic Structure and Personality," *Social Forces* 18, no. 4 (1940): 560–68.

61. Downs, *Inside Bureaucracy*, pp. 98–99.

62. Lawrence B. Mohr, "The Concept of Organizational Goal," *American Political Science Review* 67 (1973): 470–81.

63. Robert Presthus provides a thorough study of organizational socialization in private organizations in *The Organizational Society* (New York: Knopf, 1962); see also Sidney Baldwin, *Politics and Poverty* (Chapel Hill, N.C.: University of North Carolina Press, 1968).

64. See, for example, Gilbert Steiner, *The State of Welfare* (Washington, D.C.: Brookings Institution, 1971), pp. 75–121; Frances Fox Piven and Richard A. Cloward, *Regulating the Poor* (London: Tavistock, 1972).

65. See, for example, D. B. Abernathy, "Bureaucracy and Economic Development in Africa," *Africa Review* 1, no. 1 (March 1971): 93–107; Merilee S. Grindle, ed., *Politics and Policy Implementation in the Third World* (Princeton, N.J.: Princeton University Press, 1980).

66. See Dorwin Cartwright, "Influence, Leadership, Control," in *Handbook of Organizations*, James G. March, ed. (Chicago: Rand McNally, 1965), pp. 1–47; Andrew Dunshire, *Control in a Bureaucracy* (New York: St. Martin's, 1978).

67. The classic statement of this position is Chester Barnard, *The Functions of the Executive* (Cambridge, Mass.: Harvard University Press, 1960).

68. Crozier, *The Bureaucratic Phenomenon*.

69. William Spangar Pierce, *Bureaucratic Failure and Public Expenditure* (New York: Academic Press, 1981), pp. 33–7; Tribe points out that in some instances a few indicators may be worse than none. Laurence H. Tribe, "Policy Science: Analysis or Ideology," *Philosophy and Public Affairs* 2 (1972): 66–110.

70. See Hugh Heclo, *A Government of Strangers* (Washington, D.C.: The Brookings Institution, 1977), pp. 103–109.

71. Crozier's work on bureaucracy relies heavily on the concept of strata isolation. See Michel Crozier, *The Bureaucratic Phenomenon* (Chicago: University of Chicago Press, 1964), pp. 190–208.

72. See Gordon Tullock, *The Politics of Bureaucracy* (Washington, D.C.: Public Affairs Press, 1965), pp. 137–42; Downs, *Inside Bureaucracy*, pp. 112–31; Harold Wilensky, *Organizational Intelligence* (New York: Basic Books, 1967).

73. B. Guy Peters and Brian W. Hogwood, *The Pathology of Policy*, forthcoming.

74. Victor Thompson, *Modern Organizations* (New York: Knopf, 1961).

75. Modern civil services, despite their important differences, tend to have a concentration of "generalists" at the top of the hierarchy.

76. Daniel Katz and Robert L. Kahn, *The Social Psychology of Organizations*, 2nd. ed. (New York: John Wiley, 1978), pp. 702–717.

77. Martin Landau, "On the Concept of the Self-Correcting Organization," *Public Administration Review* 33, no. 6 (1973): 533–42; "The Rationality of Redundancy," *Public Administration Review* 29 (1969): 346–58.

78. Downs, *Inside Bureaucracy*, pp. 119–20.

79. William A. Niskanen, *Bureaucracy and Representative Government* (Chicago: Aldine/Atherton, 1971); Peter M. Jackson, *The Political Economy of Bureaucracy* (Oxford: Philip Allan, 1982), pp. 123–35.

80. Mason Haire, Edwin E. Ghiselli, and Lyman W. Porter, *Managerial Thinking: An International Study* (New York: John Wiley, 1966).

81. See, for example, the articles in Joseph LaPalombara, ed., *Bureaucracy and Political Development* (Princeton: Princeton University Press, 1963).

82. See chapter 2.

83. Crozier, *Bureaucratic Phenomenon*, pp. 231–36.

84. Stephen Richardson, "Organizational Contrasts in British and American Ships," *Administrative Science Quarterly* 1, no. 2 (1956): 189–207.

85. Haire, Ghiselli, and Porter, *Managerial Thinking*; A. W. Clarke and S. McCabe, "Leadership Beliefs of Australian Managers," *Journal of Applied Psychology* 54, no. 1 (1970): 1–6; L. L. Cummings and Stuart M. Schmidt, "Managerial Attitudes of Greeks: The Role of Culture and Industrialization," *Administrative Science Quarterly* 17, no. 2 (1972): 265–72.

86. Amitai Etzioni, *A Comparative Analysis of Complex Organizations* (New York: Free Press, 1961), pp. 3–21.

87. Peter M. Blau and Richard M. Scott, *Formal Organizations* (San Francisco: Chandler, 1963), pp. 45–57.

88. For a discussion of incentives of bureaucrats in commonwealth agencies, see Timothy M. Hennessey and B. Guy Peters, "Postindustrialism and Public Policy" (Paper delivered at annual meeting of American Political Science Association, San Francisco, California, September 1975.)

89. Charles Perrow, *Organizational Analysis: A Sociological View* (Belmont, Calif.: Wadsworth, 1970), pp. 80–91; James D. Thompson and Arthur Tuden, "Strategy, Structure, and Process of Organizational Decision," in *Comparative Studies in Administration* (Pittsburgh: University of Pittsburgh Administrative Science Center, 1959).

90. One of the classic studies of the organization of research remains Donald C. Pelz, "Some Social Factors Related to the Performance in a Research Organization," *Administrative Science Quarterly* 1, no. 3 (1956): 310–25.

CHAPTER 5

POLITICS AND PUBLIC ADMINISTRATION

The preceding chapters were, in essence, the foundation for this and the following two chapters. We have by now discussed the relationship of public administration to its environment through an elaboration of the social and economic surroundings of administration, the cultural milieu in which administration functions, attempts of administration to recruit personnel from that environment, and the patterns of bureaucratic structure. In this chapter we begin to examine the relationship of politics to the conduct of administration and to the policy decisions made by administrators. The interaction of administration with both formal and informal political actors in the society obviously has an impact on the behavior of administrators and on their decisions. The extent of this influence, and the manner in which it is exerted, are the subjects of investigation in this chapter and those that follow.

Perhaps the best place to begin this discussion is by again noting the survival of the ancient administrative proverb that politics and administration are separate enterprises and that such a separation is valid both in the analysis of the institutions and behaviors of government and in the actual conduct of public business.[1] Although any number of authors have attempted to lay this proverb to rest, it has displayed amazing powers of survival and reappears in any number of settings in any number of political systems.[2] We must therefore assume that this proverb, if not entirely or even partially valid from an analytic perspective, serves some purpose for administrators and politicians. What does the artificial separation of these functions do that makes its survival so desirable for both actors? For administrators, this presumed separation of administration and politics allows them to engage in politics without the bother of being held accountable politically for the outcomes of their actions. Further, they can engage in policy making—presumably using technical or legal criteria for decision—without the interference of political actors who might otherwise recognize political or ideological influences on policies and make demands upon them for the modification of those policies.[3] Thus, the actions of administrators may be regarded by politicians, the public, and even themselves as the result of the simple application of rational, legal, or technical criteria to questions of policy, which may make otherwise unacceptable decisions more palatable to the public.[4]

The separation of politics and administration also allows a certain latitude to politicians, which they might otherwise lack. In essence, the separation of these two types of institutional choices allows many of the difficult decisions of modern government to be made by individuals who will not have to face the public at a subsequent election.[5] Thus, it may allow politics to shape or at least influence an important decision that will be announced by a "nonpolitical" institution that will not be held publicly accountable. Further, this conception that political and technical decision making can be separated in public life has allowed political reformers to remove many important public decisions as far as possible from the realm of "politics"—meaning largely corrupt machine politics and other pejorative aspects of political life. This results in many important governmental functions being transferred from partisan political control to independent agencies, bureaucracies, and technocratic elites.[6] It is obviously assumed that the administrators who make decisions in these settings are in fact insulated from political pressures, and are able to make decisions *pro bono publico* because of that insulation. As we will show, however, these artificial separations of the political and administrative functions, instead of removing decisions from political influence, may actually subject them to different and more invidious types of political influences. These influences are believed to be more invidious because, having already been defined out of existence, they are difficult for the citizenry to identify and even more difficult to control.

Having still not completely exorcised the demon of the separation of political and administrative choice, we are now at least in a position to understand why the actors in the policy process may be willing to accept such a doctrine and why scholars may come to believe them. We will therefore go on to discuss the political environment of administrative decision as well as the political influences on those decisions. In so doing it is useful to distinguish several basic dimensions of the political activity of administrators. The first such dimension may be labeled "internal-external," or perhaps more appropriately "policy-survival." On this dimension we are attempting to distinguish between political activity within the agency, which seeks to take a variety of inputs from pressure groups, partisans, the political executive, and any number of other sources and develop a policy, from political activity directed toward the maintenance and

FIGURE 5.1
TYPES OF BUREAUCRATIC POLITICS

		Policy-Survival	
		Internal	External
Formality	Formal	Administrator-Minister Relationship	Budgeting; Accountability
	Informal	Administrative Lobbying	Public Support

growth of the organization. These two forms of politics are rarely so neatly separated in real life, and each contributes to the successful accomplishment of other goals. However, we can usefully distinguish these two for analytic purposes and discuss the types of influences likely to be brought and the major loci of political conflict for each.

The second dimension of administrative politics is one of officialdom, or formality. Administrators interact both with other governmental officials (legislators, the political executive, other administrators, representatives of subnational governments) and with unofficial political actors (largely the representatives of pressure groups). Again, these interactions are not always clearly separable, for officials often carry with them a continuing commitment to the cause of particular interests, and pressure groups may function in quasi-official capacities. However, it is useful to make such a distinction for analytic reasons because the style of the interaction, its legitimacy, and its probable influences on policy will vary as a function of the type of actor involved as well as a function of the type of agency activity involved.

The two dimensions of political activity by public administration, along with examples of each category of activity, are presented in Figure 5.1. We show four categories based upon a cross-classification of the two dimensions. Thus, we will be looking at administrative politicized actions that have a characteristic of being both formal and informal, and directed more toward policy formation or survival. Our example of internal (policy)-formal administrative politics is the relationship between an upper-echelon civil servant and the cabinet minister he or she is designated to serve.[7] Increasingly, the ministers charged with extensive political chores in addition to managing a large bureaucratic organization cannot be reasonably expected to have a sufficient grasp of the issues involved or of the information available for many policy decisions; such decisions will therefore be produced through either consultation with, or delegation to, the senior administrative officials.[8] Consequently, interactions of this type have become one of the dominant features of the policy-making process and must be better understood in order to predict the outcomes of the policy process in contemporary political systems.

External-formal administrative politics are perhaps best seen in two ways. The first is the process of public budgeting in which administrative agencies have to seek their continued and expanded funding from other institutions of government.[9] A number of authors note that this is perhaps the most crucial locus of administrative politics because of its pivotal role in the future programs of the agency.[10] It is certainly a political activity that is the focus of an enormous amount of effort on the part of the agencies and one that has received considerable attention in the popular and scholarly literature. It involves the mobilization of considerable political support for the agency, if it expects to be successful in obtaining its desired funding, and consequently is an activity that will involve considerable informal politics as well. The second important type of external-formal politics is the politics of public accountability through which other formal bodies may seek to curb the autonomy of the public bureaucracy. Given the importance of these two types of politics in contemporary politics, they will be discussed in chapters of their own.[11]

Internal-informal administrative politics is probably best characterized by the relationship of pressure groups and administration in the formation of policy. In virtually all political systems, attempts are made by interest (or pressure) groups to influence public decisions.[12] The openness of the administration to these influences and the success of groups in obtaining the policies they seek are again a function of a number of institutional, political, and cultural factors that require further discussion and elaboration. However, except in the most totalitarian society, there is generally considerable opportunity for group action and for group influence on the process of policy formulation in bureaucracy.

Finally, external-informal administrative politics is best characterized by relationships between interest groups, the public at large, and public bureaucrats attempting to develop support for their programs and for the continued success of the agency in the budgetary process. Those bureaucrats have several means of trying to influence even the inattentive public, including advertising and the promotion of a positive image among the public, for example, "The Marine Corps needs a few good men."[13] As noted, this type of activity is inextricably bound to the ability of pressure groups to influence policy and the ability of agencies to survive in a competitive environment.

Now that we have some general picture of the scope and variety of administrative politics, we begin our more intensive discussion of the politics of administration by examining the informal side of these interactions—that is, the relationship between administration and pressure groups, political parties, and other unofficial political groups seeking to influence the course of public policy or whom the administrators rely upon in justifying their future programs and funding. Our discussion of the relationships of political parties to administration is substantially briefer than that of pressure groups. This is in large part due to the fact that the major influence of party appears to be manifested through official mechanisms, as when members of the party occupy formal positions of leadership. Since, almost by definition, political parties are principally motivated by the opportunity to hold public office rather than the opportunity to influence policy through lobbying activities, it makes more sense to look at the official rather than the unofficial side of partisan activities.

BUREAUCRACY AND PRESSURE GROUPS

We must suppose that the conflict between the demands of pressure groups and the role of bureaucracy in decision making is, in most societies, one of the most basic in government. On the one hand there is an institution of government, representing the authority of the state, impartiality, and even a judicial temperament. On the other side of the conflict are groups that by their very nature represent only specialized narrow interests seeking some preferential treatment from government. This type of division of the role of the state and the role of interests is perceived differently in different political cultures. The conflict may not be as intense in Norway as in, say, France, but interestingly, this conflict has been sufficiently ameliorated in most societies so that the two sets of organization—administration and pressure groups—are able not only to coexist but even to cooperate effectively.[14] Further, it is especially interesting that societies that have tended to have the most positive conception of the public bureaucracy—Germany, the Netherlands, and the Scandinavian countries—have been more successful in accommodating to the roles of pressure groups in policy making than have political systems that have a less exalted conception of their civil servants.[15] In fact, a relatively positive evaluation of the civil service may be required to allow the civil servants latitude in dealing with the pressure groups and in making accommodations to their demands.[16]

Given the apparent conflict in the roles of these two sets of political actors and institutions, how are they able to cooperate so well, and so often, in making policy? In the first place, the stereotypical descriptions of the policy roles of these two sets of actors obscure some of the reality of their interaction. The civil service rarely speaks or acts as a unified entity. Rather, it is divided into organizations with narrow interests that happen to correspond to the interests of certain pressure groups. And pressure groups in most Western countries have found that acting in a less blatantly self-interested manner may produce more benefits for them in the long run.

Second, both sets of actors need each other to be successful. Administrators need the political support and influence of pressure groups in their external relationships with other political institutions, and they also need the information supplied by pressure groups for making and defending policies. Likewise, the

FIGURE 5.2
TYPES OF INTERACTION BETWEEN
PRESSURE GROUPS AND BUREAUCRACY
Characteristics

Types	Scope	Influence	Style	Impact
Legitimate	Broad	Great	Bargaining	Redistribution/Self-regulation
Clientela	Narrow	Moderate	Symbiosis	Self-regulation/Distribution
Parantela	Narrow	Moderate	Kinship	Regulation/Distribution
Illegitimate	Variable	None/Great	Confrontation	None/Redistribution

pressure groups need access to the political process and influence over the decisions that are taken. This mutual need, given the fragmentation of decision making in modern governments, is the basic dynamic explaining the frequent cooperation between public bureaucracies and pressure groups.[17] We are now left with the more formidable task of describing how the two partners in this exchange interact, and what the effects are of differing patterns of interaction.

Following is a classification of types of interactions between pressure groups and bureaucracies, along with the presumed characteristics and effects of each type, as illustrated in Figure 5.2. This classificatory scheme places the interaction between bureaucrats and pressure groups into four broad categories. This constitutes an informal continuum from situations in which pressure-group influence on policy is regarded as illegitimate to those where it is regarded as legitimate and necessary. These four categories are themselves rather broad and may contain substantial variation, but it is still useful to use such a classificatory scheme to begin to understand the broad differences in relationships between these actors.

Legitimate Interactions

The first category of interactions between bureaucrats and pressure group actions is labeled "legitimate." This denotes that in some political systems, not only are pressure groups an accepted fact of political life, but they are also legally and officially involved in the process of making and administering public policy. The major examples of this type are found in West Germany, the Low Countries, and Scandinavia, but a number of other countries have adopted legitimate roles for pressure groups in more limited forms.

Corporatism and Public Administration One variant of the legitimate relationship between interest groups and government has been described as "corporatism" or "neo-corporatism."[18] This is actually a rather extreme version of the legitimate relationship in that it tends to restrict the number of interest groups involved in the policy process and, to some extent, to incorporate that limited number into the state apparatus. Schmitter defines corporatism as an arrangement characterized by a ". . . limited number of singular, compulsory, noncompetitive, hierarchically ordered and functionally differentiated . . ." groups that are given a virtual license to represent their particular area of competence.[19] He further differentiates *societal corporatism*, in which the associations dominate the state in policy making, from *state corporatism*, in which the state is dominant.[20] This definition of corporatist arrangements implies a monopolistic relationship of interest groups in a particular policy area and sanctioning of this relationship by some state organization. This is in contrast to the more open, bargaining arrangements thought to characterize pluralistic interest group systems. Lehmbruch, however, discusses a somewhat less restrictive version of corporatism, in which the relationship between interest groups and government is less formalized and there is greater bargaining among the groups themselves. This variant, which is more reminiscent of pluralism, is termed "liberal corporatism."[21]

As initially formulated, neither of these two approaches to the relationship between groups and government had a great deal of say concerning the relationship of the groups and public bureaucracy. The major policy area discussed by the theorists of corporatism was the setting of national economic policy, as in "Harpsund Democracy" in Sweden or *Konzertierte Aktion* in the Federal Republic of Germany. These meetings of the major peak organizations of labor and management with the government involved negotiations about the future course of wages, prices, and profits. This was "high politics," directly involving top government officials, rather than the more mundane politics of policy making by bureaucracy.[22]

But corporatism does have some relevance for this more ordinary type of policy making. One of the major effects, similar to those that will be pointed out for the *clientela* relationships between interest groups and the bureaucracy, is to restrict advice and ideas coming into the bureaucracy.[23] If the strict corporatist definitions laid out by Schmitter do indeed apply, then there will be a one-on-one relationship between interest group and agency. In such an arrangement only the position of the official interest groups will be heard through this channel. Similarly, this form of relationship will likely produce even greater incoherence in government than might exist otherwise. If agriculture groups are talking to agriculture officials (be they political or administrative), labor groups to labor officials, etc., then governmental priorities and decision making will tend to be highly fragmented. This is especially so if there is also a fragmentation in the political executive, for example, through cabinet committees able to transmit this individualized priority setting into the highest reaches of government. A corporatist arrangement would not be without benefits, however; the presence of a captive interest group to assist in legitimating actions and in implementing them would certainly aid a governmental agency. Further, as the relationships between peak interest groups and their members are deemed to be hierarchical, there could be reasonably high levels of control exercised over pressure groups that may present potential challenges to the legitimacy of policies.

In general, corporatism may be of limited importance for understanding how government manages its relationships with interest groups. The entire pattern of relationships appears to be under threat now, as the pressures that almost all developed economies confront have made interest groups less cooperative with government and less willing to be coopted.[24] In addition, even at its high point, corporatism describes only a relatively small portion of the activities of interest groups—even those accorded some legitimate rights of participation in government—as they deal with government. The two means of interaction described below, although they involve some elements of corporatism, are more generic and affect a much wider range of behavior.

Required Consultation   The required-consultation mechanism for legitimating pressure group involvement in policy making is, as the name implies, the result of a variety of rules that require administrative bodies preparing new regulations to consult with the relevant pressure groups for their opinions and to solicit advice and information from them. In some cases this is done in the preparation of legislation to be sent to a legislative body for enactment; in other cases it is used for regulations that the administrative body can issue as a result of delegated legislative authority. In either case, required consultation permits an interest group direct access to the making of administrative policies.

One method of assuring such input is through the use of *remiss petitions* in Sweden and Norway. In both these countries, when policy modifications are being considered, the administrative agencies are required to ask for *remiss* from interest groups. These documents state the views of the group as well as some of the information that the group considers relevant to the case. Originally, the device was used only for pressure groups directly affected by the new set of regulations (for example, agricultural groups affected by new regulations from an agricultural marketing board). More recently, the system has been extended to include virtually any organized group that wishes to submit an opinion.[25] While such a system provides no guarantee that the advice of the group will be heeded, it does ensure access to the relevant decision-makers. Further, since it is customary for the *remisser* to be passed on with any proposed legislation, the system also provides some assurance that those who must finally pass legislation are also informed of interest group opinion. In West Germany, public agencies seeking to write new legislation or regulations are required by law to seek advice from interested pressure groups. In Germany, the array of pressure groups consulted on any one issue is not generally so wide as in the Scandinavian countries, but the mechanism does allow direct and legitimate input of information and opinions.[26]

While the *remiss* system relies on formal written communications for pressure groups to make their views known, other methods of required consultation employ more personal approaches. Most notable in this regard is the use of advisory committees in Scandinavian administrations.[27] The majority of public committees in these countries will include representatives of some organized interests. For example, in a study of Danish committees, Johansen and Kristensen found that functional interest groups were represented on the majority of committees, and that local interests and institutional interests within government itself were also frequently represented.[28] In Norway each committee will contain a variety of administrative and interest group personnel charged with advising the respective administrative body on the proper course of public policy. These committees then provide a forum for the interest group to present their evidence and make a case for their particular views. Interestingly, however, most representatives on these committees do not view their role as that of an advocate of a particular position, but rather as more of a technical expert and manager.[29] This role conception is obviously useful in facilitating compromise on even difficult questions of policy. Similarly, in West Germany interest groups are represented on advisory boards for the ministries as a matter of legal right. While these advisory boards exist in a number of political systems—France is said to have some 1,400 of them, and Switzerland rapidly creates and dissolves them—what distinguishes West Germany and Scandinavia is the official sanction given to the role of the groups in the process of making policy.[30] As Kvavik notes, these systems move the role of pressure group influence from that of input to that of withinput; that is, in non-Eastonian language, the political system recognizes pressure groups as an integral part of the decision-making process and therefore accords them some of the same status accorded to other official participants in the policy process.[31] In Germany this may be viewed as a continuation of some of the traditional corporate conceptions of the state, but in all systems this type of influence provides an important alternative to the usual liberal means of representation through elections and legislatures.[32] Moreover, with the rapid growth of administrative policy making, it may soon surpass the liberal means in its impact on public policy.

Implementation The second major form of legitimate interest group involvement in administration is the use of the groups as agents of implementation for public policies. Interest groups serve as quasi-official arms of the political system in implementing some programs about which they are assumed to have expert knowledge and skills. Again, this means of group involvement is particularly apparent in Scandinavia and also frequently occurs in the Low Countries.[33] One of the most common areas in which administration of this type occurs is agriculture, where either commodity groups or local farmers' organizations administer regulations or acreage allotments or contractual relationships with the government. In Sweden the implementation of many portions of the labor law is left to the individual groups most affected by the law.[34] Similarly, in the Netherlands much of that country's complex system of economic regulation is administered by boards composed largely of interest group representatives charged with the "self-policing" of a particular industry in order to maintain the delicate economic balance within the country.[35] In each case, the government essentially allows interest groups to engage in activities in the name of the public with only indirect "political" control over their actions. They tend to be somewhat restrained by having competing interests represented on the same administrative boards, but this is obviously a manner in which interest groups can have a quite direct impact on the shape of public policy and its execution.

Institutional pressure groups would appear to constitute a special class of legitimate pressure groups. By definition, these are members of an important social or political institution, or that institution itself, acting in the capacity of a pressure group seeking to influence the shape of public policy.[36] Some rather obvious examples are the church, the army, and the bureaucracy itself. Local governments, even in unitary regimes, may also act as institutional groups. These groups seek to obtain benefits for themselves or their members, and their actions are legitimated through the prestige of the institution or perhaps the threat of extreme actions in the case of the army in some societies. Johansen and Kristensen point out that these groups are increasing more rapidly than functional interest groups in their representation on public committees in Denmark.[37] Even in countries that tend toward legitimate patterns of interaction between interest groups and bureaucracy, institutional interest groups may actually be better conceptualized as a special class of *clientela* groups in that they have legitimate access when a number of competing groups may not, and tend to seek more special interest outputs than tends to be true in legitimate pressure group systems.[38]

Figure 5.2 presents a variety of the characteristics of the interactions of administrators and pressure groups. As noted, the scope of interaction between pressure groups and administration in "legitimate" situations tends to be quite broad. A single pressure group may be consulted on a variety of policies, and virtually all policy areas may be the subject of inputs from interested parties. Also, the influence of the groups on policy may be expected to be great relative to other types of interaction patterns. The legitimacy of the groups, their frequency of interaction with administrators, and their official or quasi-official status all make it possible for groups to have an impact that they would not have elsewhere. In part this is a function of not having to expend organizational resources simply to gain access, and in part a function of the roles adopted by the interest group participants in the process. These perceived roles contribute to the bargaining style of their interactions. As noted by Kvavik, the dominant-role type in these negotiations is the expert who supplies information and opinion but who does not serve merely as an advocate of his particularistic viewpoint.[39] This bargaining activity is described by Rokkan as follows:

> The crucial decisions on economic policy are rarely taken in the parties or Parliament: the central area is the bargaining table where the government authorities meet directly with the trade union leaders, the representatives of the farmers, the smallholders, and the fishermen, and the delegates of the Employers' Association. These yearly rounds of negotiations have in

fact come to mean more in the lives of rank-and-file citizens than have formal elections. In these processes of intensive interaction the parliamentary notions of one member, one vote and majority rule make little sense. Decisions are not made through the counting of heads, but through complex considerations of short-term and long-term advantages in alternative lines of compromise.[40]

When the influence of pressure groups must be more covert, this important bargaining mode of interaction is of necessity lost in the politics of gaining access, necessitating that few groups rather than many will be involved in any one decision. This characterization does not hold true, of course, in the corporatist arrangements described above, in which there is a one-on-one relationship between pressure group and government. The relationship may not be as particularized as in *clientela* relationships described below, but it lacks the broad bargaining style associated with most legitimate patterns of interaction.

Finally, the policy consequences of this interaction between pressure groups and administrators are generally confined to two types (phrased in terms of the Salisbury-Heinz typology): redistribution and self-regulation.[41] That is, in situations in which administrators are capable of imposing the choices made by groups through a bargaining and negotiation process, the decisions taken are likely to take from one group and give to another. This means of policy making is, however, a relatively safe manner in which to adopt redistributive policy, since it ensures the participation of both winners and losers as well as assuring the application of technical knowledge to the choice. These two characteristics—the technical knowledge of the participants and the presence of all competing sides—were in fact the criteria selected by respondents in Kvavik's sample as most important in legitimating their decisions.[42] Elvander likewise notes that in Sweden the inclusion of all competing groups is important for the smooth implementation of policies adopted by pressure group representatives cooperating with the government.[43] In addition, Heisler and Kvavik point out that continued access to policy making may be sufficient motivation in itself to produce compliance with the decisions taken, even in the face of adverse decisions in the short run.[44] In situations in which the elite may lack the cohesion and consensus necessary to implement a redistributive decision, these legitimate interactions between interest groups and administrators may result in policies of self-regulation.[45] In these cases organizations are allowed generally to manage their own affairs and thereby essentially manage a sector of public policy for the government. One example of this type of policy outcome is in the area of agriculture, where the conflict within the sector is relatively slight so that there may be little need for directly redistributive decisions, and where some policies—such as the allocation of acreage allotments—may have little effect on other groups.[46] Even here there is potential conflict, however, between agricultural groups wanting high subsidies and therefore high food prices and labor groups wanting low prices and therefore lower subsidies. The choice between redistributive and self-regulative policies may depend on the breadth of groups involved in any one decision as well as the integration of the elites making and enforcing the decisions. In other policy areas, one group may have such a monopoly of information and expertise that it is given the responsibility of self-regulation on the basis of that expertise. This has been especially true of medical and legal groups in the United States and is a prevalent finding for similar groups in a variety of other political systems.[47]

Clientela Relationships

The second type of interaction between interest groups and administration is one of the two major types discussed by LaPalombara. A *clientela* relationship is said to exist when

> an interest group, for whatever reasons, succeeds in becoming, in the eyes of a given administrative agency, the natural expression and representative of a given social sector which, in turn, constitutes the natural target or reference point for the activity of the administrative agency.[48]

This type of interaction is characterized by a perceived legitimacy on the part of administrators of one group rather than a formal statement of the legitimacy of all or virtually all groups. The consequences of this difference are, however, quite important. In the first place, the scope of interaction of pressure groups and administration tends to be rather severely constrained. Each agency tends to select a single pressure group as *the* legitimate representative of its particular social sector and to avoid most other groups seeking to present information and advice. Thus, whereas in the "legitimate" arrangement mentioned previously the agency might be able or required to consult a broad range of groups, in a *clientela* relationship it will entertain a quite narrow range of information and advice. This narrowing is especially evident when two or more groups seek to organize a single sector of the society but only one is accorded regular access to decision making. This tends to skew the sources of information, generally in the direction toward which the administrators tended in the first place. Suleiman, for example, notes that in France—and certainly elsewhere—legitimate groups tend to be those whose economic strength is undeniable and whose demands are in general accord with government policy.[49]

The second consequence of this form of interaction is that while the influence of one group may be increased, the overall influence of pressure groups on public policy will be lessened. Not having legitimacy in any formal sense obviously reduces the acceptability of special interest influence on policy for the general public, and the ability of the bureaucracy to accept advice is also limited. Further, each pressure group must expand relatively more of its organizational resources on the pursuit of access, so that less is available for the information and influence functions. Moreover, in this process of seeking access any conception of the "public interest"—even as an aggregate of pressure group interests—tends to be lost and replaced with a set of private interests, each represented in government by a single agency.[50] Associated with the above is a need to keep the negotiations and interactions of interest groups and administrators private and informal, thereby removing them even further from public scrutiny and accountability. All these characteristics of the scope and manner of interaction indicate that the pressure group universe will tend to be less broadly influential over policies, with virtually any influence that does occur having something of a taint of illegality among the general public.

The description of the interactions of interest groups and administration in *clientela* politics leads to the characterization of these relationships as symbiotic. As in biological symbiosis, this relationship implies a mutual dependence of the two participants. The administrative agency depends upon the pressure group for information, advice, prior clearance of policy decisions, and, most importantly, for political support in its competition with other agencies for the scarce resources within government. The pressure groups, on the other hand, depend upon the agency for access to decision making and ultimately for favorable decisions on certain policy choices. For both sides the existence of a *clientela* relationship serves to regularize the political environment and to develop friendships in what might otherwise be a hostile political world. This form of pressure group relationship with administration, noted by LaPalombara in Italy, has been used by several authors as a means of describing much of the politics of policy in the United States, and would seem to be prevalent in a number of other political systems that have strong interest groups but where the interactions of these groups and the government is at the margin of acceptability.[51] Heclo and others have argued, however, that this clientelist pattern is now less descriptive of the United States than it once was, and a much broader array of interests has come to be represented in Washington.[52] On the other hand, the by-now standard lament on the impact of "single issue politics" on American government may lead one to continue to accept the clientelist description.[53]

Finally, the policy consequences of the *clientela* arrangement produce essentially self-regulative and distributive outcomes. LaPalombara notes that regulation is one of the defining characteristics of a *clientela* relationship but goes on to note that the regulative activities undertaken are not necessarily those that would promote the "public interest."[54] Rather, they are activities that quite directly promote the interests of the regulated. This pattern of regulation, as noted, has been referred to as "self-regulation." Again, this tendency toward self-regulation appears endemic to administrative agencies and especially independent regulatory commissions in the United States. Lowi has argued that "interest group liberalism," or the appropriation of the power of the state for private ends, is in fact the dominant characteristic of contemporary public policy in the United States.[55] McConnell observes that the "outstanding political fact about independent regulatory commissions is that they have in general become the protectors and promoters of the industries they have been established to regulate."[56] Evidence from other political systems, however, is that this phenomenon is not confined to the United States but is a more general feature of industrial societies. In a variety of settings the need for political support is sufficient to necessitate the replacement of regulation with clientelism and self-regulation. Administrators may lack the resources and the central political support to enforce programs of regulation in the face of opposition of powerful and well-organized groups, so that in essence they must gain support from those groups. However, as with Heclo's analysis of *clientela* politics in the United States, there is an interpretation that regulatory capture is less prevalent in the United States than it once was, especially for the "new social regulation," in which the regulatory bodies have jurisdictions that cut across a variety of industries.[57]

As well as self-regulation, *clientela* relationships also tend to be associated with distributional outcomes, which may be merely more tangible types of self-regulative programs.[58] In distributional politics, however, instead of being allowed to make its own regulations, a group is granted continuing benefits. In Lowi's terminology, distributional politics "create privilege, and it is a type of privilege which is particularly hard to bear or combat because it is touched with the symbolism of the state."[59] The close relationship between the interest group and the government agency can ensure that the clients continue to receive something of value from government, and that questions of redistribution and the need for adjustment of the relative benefits are rarely subjects of discussion.

This form of policy making is in part a function of the peculiar politics and economics of public bureaucracies. Despite the arguments that regard bureaucracy and bureaucrats as integrated and homogeneous, seeking to take control of the political system (at a minimum), many bureaucratic systems are highly fragmented institutions. By being so fragmented, they may be forced into competition simply because there is rarely an effective central means of allocating resources according to the merits of programs or the needs of society.[60] Bureaucratic competition can easily be overstated, as in much of the "public choice" literature on bureaucracy, and much of what does exist is a function of sincere commitments to programs rather than of a desire to maximize budgets. But fragmentation contributes to the development of *clientela* politics.

The budgetary process then tends to force public bureaucracies to seek public support and make distributive accommodations in order to gain that support. This outcome is further magnified by the division among the other actors in the budgetary process and their needs for other types of benefits and accommodations. The clientelism that extends between the pressure group and the administration may extend to a type of clientelism between legislative committees and the administrative agencies they are ostensibly overseeing.[61] This is in part a function of the stability of the actors involved in the process, as in the United States Congress, but more generally is related to the joint need of administrators and legislators to serve a constituency. For example, legislators interested in agricultural matters tend to come from predominantly agricultural districts; any attempt to curtail the activities of an agricultural agency would not be well received in their constituencies, thereby threatening their chances for reelection.[62]

One particularly important type of *clientela* interest group is the institutional interest group. In industrialized societies these are local-government groups, as well as interest groups within government itself.[63] In less-developed countries, these groups might include the church, the military, or the bureaucracy itself. These groups all have claims upon government that are difficult or impossible to deny, and, like other *clientela* groups, these special claims are pressed for special privileges.

We find, then, that there will often be a tight intermeshing of interest groups, administration, and legislators, all of whom have something to gain by certain expenditures, producing patterns of policy similar to those predicted by Salisbury and Heinz in such situations: the parceling out of goods and services available through the public budget in a manner that will provide each organized sector with some portion of the benefits.[64]

Parantela Relationships

This is the second type of administrative pressure group relationship mentioned by LaPalombara in his discussion of Italian interest groups. A *parantela* relationship describes a situation of "kinship" or close fraternal ties between a pressure group and the government or dominant political party.[65] These relationships have been held to be most characteristic of preindustrial societies, but our discussion will show them occurring in a number of political systems in which there is a single dominant party or faction, and in which pressure groups must gain access and legitimacy through their attachment to that particular party rather than through their ability effectively to represent a sector of the society.

Parantela relationships between pressure groups and bureaucracies involve an indirect linkage between those actors rather than the direct linkage discussed in the *clientela* relationship. The important added linkage is the political party—most commonly a hegemonic party—with which the pressure group must develop some feeling of consanguinity. In these cases, the pressure groups obtain access to administrative decision making through the willingness of the party to intercede in its behalf with the bureaucracy and therefore in essence to control bureaucratic policy making.

There must, therefore, be a domination of policy making by a political party, which is not usually associated with Western democratic systems but which is still present in those systems. LaPalombara, for example, found relationships of this type existing in Italy with the Christian Democratic party.[66] In

France the Gaullists interceded with the notoriously aloof French bureaucracy in order to favor one pressure group over another in policy disputes. Williams and Harrison, for example, report an instance in which Debré (as premier) forced one minister of agriculture to resign and had him replaced with a more vigorous minister in order to counteract the slowness of the bureaucracy in implementing the program of one agricultural interest group—the CNJA.[67] While this issue was complicated by many issues internal to agricultural politics in France, the fundamental point of the imposition of party control over administration in order to favor one group is clear. This type of interaction does occur in Western political systems, but it is more typical of a number of political systems—the Soviet nations, a majority of African single-party states, and many Latin American countries—in which one party or coalition is dominant. As in the case of France, it is found also where partisan competition may exist but where there has been a tendency for one party to dominate government— France for much of the Fifth Republic, Italy, India, and Mexico. It is also common in more competitive political systems in the relationship that exists between organized-labor unions and political parties, for example, the relationship between the Trades Union Congress and the Labour party in the United Kingdom.

Another type of *parantela* interest group that has frequently existed in democratic societies represents an attempt on the part of government to organize some aspect of society traditionally difficult to organize. For example, in the United States, urban renewal and model cities programs required the development of organizations in the affected neighborhoods that would represent the interests of the residents. Such organizations have rarely been successful in that role and more often have been coopted by government as a means of social control in the neighborhoods.[68] Also, in several Western European countries, government has taken an active part in organizing consumers' groups— also traditionally difficult to organize—and these groups have frequently been criticized for being too subject to government influence.[69]

The effects of *parantela* relationships tend to be quite pervasive. It is, in fact, one tendency of these political systems that the hegemonic party will seek to impose its control over as much of the society and economy as is possible. One principal means of effecting this is the fostering of *parantela* relationships in a number of social sectors through the cooptation of existing interest groups or through the creation of new groups directly allied with the party. The above example from France is an example of the party taking the side of an existing interest group in its struggle with other groups seeking to represent the same social interests, while the previous Spanish regime's organization of the workers into official or semiofficial syndicates is an example of a party creating its own interest group structure.[70] In either case, this is an effective means through which the party can extend its scope downward into the society to control the nature of the inputs being generated and regularize the behavior of that social sector in accordance with the dictates of the party. It also serves as a means of checking bureaucratic autonomy within that particular policy area.

The above would seem to imply that pressure groups involved in a *parantela* relationship are little more than the pawns of a dominant political party, and such an interpretation would be justifiable in many instances. Weiner, for example, describing the relationship of the Congress party in India and its affiliated labor union, writes:

> The Indian National Trade Union Congress—in reality the labor wing of the Congress Party—is organized along these principles of political responsibility and supports the basic program of the present government. Its leaders proudly declare that their demands are in the national interest, not in behalf of sectional interests. Their first loyalties are to the Congress Party, then to the present government, to the nation, and last of all to the workers who belong to the union.[71]

While the Indian case is illustrative of many *parantela* relationships, it is by no means an entirely general finding. Even in the case of predemocratic Spain, Anderson can write:

> the conventional picture of unrepresentativeness and ineffectiveness of the syndicates can be greatly overdrawn. The government and the syndicates did not speak with one voice on public policy. The syndical leaders were expected by the system itself to play the role of militant spokesmen for labor. . . . In their language and style of militancy many of the syndical leaders were not unlike their counterparts in other Western nations. They were brokers, and they bargained for their clients, though in the last analysis they accepted the judgment of the constituted authorities.[72]

The behavior of militant members of the Trades Union Congress in the United Kingdom with respect to the policies of Labour governments represents the logical extremes of independence of *parantela* partners.[73] The pressure groups in these arrangements are frequently capable of exerting substantial influence over the course of public policy, and for many of the same reasons that motivate *clientela* pressure groups. The symbiosis between a hegemonic party and a pressure group is certainly not as important as that between the *clientela* partners, but it is present. The pressure groups can be expected to have some impact on bureaucratic choice because of their special relationship with the dominant party. Further, both the party and the bureaucracy gain the benefit of the specialized knowledge of the group, thereby reducing their own direct costs for policy development and planning. Moreover, the party's direct costs of social control may be reduced by developing subsidiary organizations to perform functions that might otherwise have to be performed centrally.[74] The above-mentioned example of the relationship between the syndicates and the government in Spain is one example of this type of control, as is the relationship between Communist parties and their unions in hegemonic and competitive situations.

The influences of *parantela* relationships are likely to be broad and pervasive, simply because the hegemonic parties will seek to spread their influence as widely as possible in the society, using the relationship with interest groups as one means. For example, the Convention People's Party in Ghana was sufficiently divided internally to preclude its being an effective instrument for social mobilization. As a consequence, Nkrumah placed emphasis on affiliated groups such as labor unions and cooperatives as a means of bringing about the types of economic and social changes his regime desired, including greater supervision of local administration.[75] Similar patterns could be found in other less-developed societies with strong parties having mobilization or developmental goals.[76]

To some degree the policies adopted by the participants in *parantela* relationships are a function of the ideology and program of the hegemonic party and as such may vary from programs of the far left to the far right. In general, however, there is a tendency toward distributive programs. This means there is a tendency toward distributing various goods and services among the faithful and directing groups to develop claims on certain public goods and services as the appropriate representatives of certain social sectors. In this sense, the party is acting as something of a "canteen" for its adherents and for official groups by essentially subsidizing their existence in the marketplace of pressure groups—and thereby essentially depriving any competing, or potentially competing, groups.[77] Thus, in some ways, the *parantela* arrangements closely resemble the corporatist pattern of interest group relationships described above, especially the state corporatist model.[78] Individuals would receive benefits under such an arrangement as a function of their membership in the appropriate corporate entity, rather than as a matter of individual right. Moreover, *parantela* relationships tend to be antithetical to the conception of modern politics about the universalism of the distribution of economic, social, and political benefits. Such benefits—even the most basic political benefits of the rights of organization and participation—are in *parantela* systems most definitely the function of having the proper political affiliations, and the influence that any group may expect to have over the outcomes of the decision-making process will be a function of this consanguinity.

A second effect of *parantela* relationships is also obviously regulative. This is true not only of the attempts of the party to regulate the outputs of the bureaucracy through regulating the advice that it receives, but more broadly to regulate the society as a whole through the use of intermediary groups. These intermediary groups not only structure inputs but also may serve as means of implementing the programs of the regime. The *parantela* relationships then serve as two-way streets, and information—and to a lesser extent power—can flow in both directions. The extent to which power can flow upward is, however, ultimately determined by the willingness of the dominant political party to entertain modifications and challenges.

Illegitimate Group Processes

The final category of interactions between administrators and pressure groups is labeled "illegitimate." This denotes a variety of situations in which the interaction of pressure groups with bureaucracy may be defined as outside the pale of normal political actions, but these interactions occur anyway. This may be a function of the political system as a whole, which may attempt to suppress pluralism, or it may be a function of the nature of particular groups, which are defined as being illegitimate as representatives of the social sector that they purport to represent. In the first three types of interactions discussed, some or all pressure groups were accepted as legitimate spokesmen for some social sector or another. In the case of the illegitimate pressure groups, neither the system as a whole nor individual administrators are willing to accept the legitimacy of the inputs of certain interest groups.

As might be expected, influence from pressure groups of this type is not the normal pattern of policy making. Such influences tend to be indicative of some rather fundamental failures of the policy-making system in satisfying demands of one or more sectors of the society. Thus, these individuals feel constrained to go outside the bounds of "normal" politics to seek what they want from the political system. We may, therefore, be discussing in large part the behavior of "anomic" pressure groups in their attempts to exert influence through protest, demonstrations, and violence. It is not necessary, however, to confine this discussion entirely to violent groups, for there are a number of situations in which pressure groups declared as illegitimate in *parantela* or *clientela* arrangements may still seek influence and may occasionally actually exert some influence on policies. The latter instances are rare. As one of LaPalombara's respondents noted on this topic:

> I know of no policy within the Ministry of Industry and Commerce that says that there are certain groups in Italian society whose representatives will not at least be received. It is true that once this is done we will assign different importance or give varying weight to the proposals made to us by such groups, but they are free to approach us.[79]

Suleiman notes that in France groups defined as *groupes de pression* (in contrast to the acceptable "professional" groups) may be received by the administrators but are unlikely to be able to produce the results they desire.[80] The illegitimate groups continue, however, to play by the administrator's rules and politely present their petitions, often knowing that their probability of success is nearly zero. We may ask why these groups continue in these seemingly irrational behaviors. There is the odd chance that they may actually have an influence. More commonly, however, they persist simply because this is what their members expect them to do. This is the reason the members pay their dues or give their allegiance to the group, and the leaders must carry out a seemingly pointless exercise.[81]

The interaction between illegitimate pressure groups and administration tends to produce high levels of frustration and alienation for those groups. The rather arbitrary categorization of pressure takes place even in political systems generally receptive—if not partial—to group influences. For example, in the United States, with a long history of pressure group influence on agriculture policy, one group—the National Farmers' Organization—was for all practical purposes classified as illegitimate; members reacted by descending on Washington, D.C., with their tractors.[82] The level of frustration may be even greater in political systems that attempt to suppress—rather than simply ignore—the activities of interest groups declared to be illegitimate. The suppression of Solidarity by the Polish government is the example of this type of behavior which comes most readily to mind.

We can better understand the characterization of the influences of these groups as coming essentially from extralegal activities—through some sort of conflict with the system—and their influence as at best episodic. Likewise, the impacts of their activities on public policy are extremely difficult to predict, if they occur at all. Despite these limitations, it is important to understand that these influences may occasionally be productive of important changes. The French student movement of May 1968 and its associated activities have been used as an example of virtually every political phenomenon known to man, but that should not restrain us from pointing out that this is one example of an essentially illegitimate pressure group having a substantial impact on a regime and on the shape of future public policy.[83] The American students and the Vietnam War constitute another example, while in some Latin American countries the argument can be made that to accomplish almost any type of policy change requires the kind of fundamental challenge to the system that can be offered by illegitimate groups. Also, the early successes of Solidarity in Poland produced some liberalization in the regime, although the ultimate result was the imposition of martial law.

When illegitimate groups are successful, the impacts of their activities tend to be redistributive, if for no other reason than they may force the system to recognize a set of demands that it could previously declare as being outside its concern. Most illegitimate pressure groups seek to transform the existing political system and its output distribution in the direction of a redistribution of privilege, be it political, social, or economic.

In addition, there are other significant differences among these classes of interactions. First, the activities of illegitimate pressure groups are clearly the most distinctive. The other three patterns accord some legitimacy to the activities and influence of one or more groups, so that there are accepted patterns of interaction between the groups and the bureaucracy. In the case of illegitimate groups, such interaction—at least if it is to have any effect on policy outcomes—occurs almost by definition only in times of crisis. Thus, the three legitimate patterns imply a certain stability and institutionalization of influence, while the illegitimate pattern implies episodic influence or no influence at all.

Second, the legitimate pattern of interaction is the only one of the four in which there is little or no politics of access. In this arrangement, access exists for virtually any group that seeks it—even those that almost certainly would be declared illegitimate in other settings. By removing access from politics, such an interaction pattern may in fact make the pluralist's dream of a self-regulating universe of pressure groups formulating public policy a possibility, if not a reality.[84] As long as access remains a scarce and a regulated commodity, the possibility of finding the "public interest" among a set of conflicting pressure groups is remote, if not nonexistent. Having legitimate interactions of pressure groups with administration—and perhaps more importantly open interactions of pressure groups with each other in advising the administrators—by no means assures that such a mystical entity as the "public interest" will emerge, but it is more likely to appear when interests are forced to bargain than in a case in which each interest is able to capture its own portion of the administrative structure. This capture tends to convert public policy into private policy. Likewise, unless one considers the hegemonic political party as an accurate representation of the interests of the population, the control of pressure groups and bureaucracy by such a party is also likely to produce distortions of outputs from what would emerge from a bargaining table, especially when many interests may be defined out of existence by the dominant party. To put this in the terms of our original typology of interactions, serious distortions of policy from what would emerge from a simple bargaining process among competing groups are likely to occur when the politics of policy making cannot be removed from the politics of organizational survival.

We should also note that we have not been able to argue clearly that any particular pattern of interaction characterizes any one nation or another, although the examples tend to point to some important patterns. In the first place, political systems with hegemonic political parties, be they ostensibly democratic or not, tend toward *parantela* relationships between interest groups and administrators, if for no other reason than that the hegemonic party is able to use these relationships as one means of social control and regulation. Second, legitimate interactions tend to be characteristic of the Northern European countries, which have had long histories of the involvement of organized groups in social and political life, and whose leaders have perceived a need to manage potentially divisive conflicts within the society, either ethnic or socio-economic in origin. Third, *clientela* arrangements tend to be quite common in any number of societies, especially when there is a fragmentation of interests and a lack of overall coordinating mechanisms in the political system (for example, a dominant political party or institution) that can regulate the competition among interest groups or among the competing agencies within the bureaucracy. Finally, illegitimate interest groups may arise in virtually any setting but tend to be most important in settings where they are least likely, for example, societies that seek to suppress interest groups or at least a wide variety of interest groups. That is to say, these groups are most important in settings where they serve as a fundamental challenge to the regime. This means that their day-to-day interactions with administrators will be unfruitful if they occur at all, but that they may produce substantial transformations of a political system.

Just as there is little pattern as to type of interest group–bureaucratic interaction by political system, there is also little pattern by type of interest or policy area. There is some tendency for interest groups that can be clearly defined geographically to be able to establish clientele relationships with administration, perhaps because of the ability to mobilize political support easily. The most obvious example of this pattern is agriculture, which has been notoriously successful in clientele relationships in a number of political systems. Likewise, interest groups that may be vertically integrated with political parties—frequently labor unions and labor parties—may develop *parantela* relationships, even within the context of competitive political systems.[85] Finally, groups that may be regarded as outcasts in normal social affairs, or that are not regarded as having differentiated political viewpoints by the dominant community—racial minorities, students, women—may tend to act through illegitimate relationships with bureaucracies, if they are able to form any relationship at all.

BUREAUCRACY AND POLITICAL PARTIES

In most contemporary political systems, the direct impact of partisan concerns on bureaucracy has been consciously limited by a number of structural and procedural devices. The most important of these, of course, is the institutionalization of the merit system for appointment and retention of administrators so that parties can no longer force large-scale changes of administrative personnel when there is a change in governing parties. While patronage arrangements certainly do exist, they are generally regarded in Western countries as evidence of corruption and mismanagement. A number of non-Western countries, despite the tutelage of their former colonial countries, have continued or reinstituted nonmerit systems of appointment to administrative posts—even the most routine and trivial of posts. This is justified largely on the need for national unity and mobilization in the face of the difficulties of development. In such situations, loyalty to the nation—or more exactly to the current regime—is considered more important than the possession of certain scores on objective tests or the possession of requisite diplomas. This practice is by no means universal in the non-Western world, but a number of one-party regimes tend to recruit their bureaucracies in this fashion. As Nkrumah said in relationship to administration in Ghana:

> It is our intention to tighten up the regulations and to wipe out the disloyal elements of the civil service, even if by so doing we suffer some temporary dislocation of the service. For disloyal civil servants are no better than saboteurs.[86]

Also, in French-speaking Africa a number of one-party regimes have attempted to use partisan control to replace "selfish individualism" with "patriotic socialism."[87]

The most obvious example of the utilization of partisan control over the state bureaucracy occurs in communist countries. This is accomplished to a great extent through dual hierarchies—one party and one administrative—simultaneously to execute policies and to check for the political orthodoxy of personnel.[88] Such a system of duplication appears redundant and inefficient to many Western analysts of organizations, but it is deemed crucial in a system where political orthodoxy is so important. As with the non-Western systems of the underdeveloped world, partisan control and the use of the bureaucracy as a mechanism for fundamental social and economic change seem to go hand in hand. Where political neutrality is not really acceptable, much less valued, then many of the Western dogmas concerning nonpartisan merit appointment simply are not feasible as criteria in evaluating recruitment and executive actions of administrators.

SUMMARY

We have developed a means of classifying and analyzing the politics of bureaucracy. Beginning with the notion that it is not useful to separate the political from the administrative in either real life or analysis, we have attempted to provide some means of better understanding how administration becomes involved with politics and political actors. This chapter has dealt primarily with administrative involvement with pressure groups, showing the extent to which these two political actors depend upon each other in their attempts to shape public policy and to survive in what might otherwise be an extremely hostile political environment. In three of the four patterns of interaction discussed, some type of legitimating relationship was developed so that a stable pattern of interaction between group and bureaucracy could be used in policy formation—the internal aspect of bureaucratic politics. These relationships could, in turn, directly (through clientelism) or indirectly (through *parantela* and legitimate interactions) produce some support for the programs and the continued existence of the specific bureaucratic agency involved. These are then two political actors who need each other in order to carry out their respective purposes in as efficient a manner as possible. Both operate on the fringes of political respectability and need friends in their battles. The symbiosis that tends to develop between bureaucracy and pressure group is readily explicable in terms of these needs for legitimation and support. The major question that remains is whether this symbiotic relationship is to be accepted—as with the legitimate groups—or forced further into the gray areas of politics.

We turn now to bureaucratic politics, more directly concerned with power and policy rather than access. These are the politics of dealing with other formal institutions of government. Each of these actors has access to the arena of political conflict, and their position in that arena is more secure than that of the bureaucracy. Here, then, the bureaucracy must engage in substantially different types of political behaviors, both to preserve its autonomy as an organization and to have an impact on public policy.

NOTES

1. Woodrow Wilson is often given the credit—or blame—for propounding this doctrine of separation. See his "The Study of Administration," *Political Science Quarterly* 2 (June 1887): 209–13. This doctrine was elaborated by such writers as Willoughby and Pfiffner. The attack on the doctrine was led by Paul Appleby in *Policy and Administration* (University, Alabama: University of Alabama Press, 1949).
2. Several recent studies of administrative elites discuss the degree of politicization of the administrator. See Robert D. Putnam, "The Political Attitudes of Senior Civil Servants in Western Europe," *British Journal of Political Science* 3, no. 3 (July 1973): 257–90; Thomas J. Anton, Claes Linde, and Anders Mellbourn, "Bureaucrats in Politics: A Profile of the Swedish Administrative Elite," *Canadian Public Administration* 16, no. 4 (Winter 1973): 627–51; Ezra N. Suleiman, *Politics, Power and Bureaucracy in France* (Princeton: Princeton University Press, 1974); Samuel Eldersveld, Sonja Hubée-Boonzaaijer, and Jan Kooiman, "Elite Perceptions of the Political Process in the Netherlands, Looked at in Comparative Perspective," in *The Mandarins of Western Europe*, Mattei Dogan, ed. (New York: Halsted, 1975), pp. 129–61; Joel D. Aberbach, Robert D. Putnam, and Bert A. Rockman, *Bureaucrats and Politicians in Western Democracies* (Cambridge, Mass.: Harvard University Press, 1981); Thomas J. Anton, *Administered Politics: Elite Political Culture in Sweden* (Boston: Martinus Nijhoff, 1980).
3. Putnam refers to this conception as that of the "classical bureaucrat." See Putnam, "Senior Civil Servants," p. 259; Bärbel Steinkemper, *Klassische und politische Bürokraten in der Ministerialverwaltung der Bundesrepublik Deutschland* (Cologne: Carl Heymanns, 1977).
4. A discussion of this in the context of the value of cost-benefit analysis is supplied by Peter Self, *Econocrats and the Policy Process* (London: Macmillan, 1975).
5. These problems as they relate to the democratic theory are discussed in Emmette S. Redford, *Democracy in the Administrative State* (New York: Oxford University Press, 1969).
6. Karl Mannheim, *Ideology and Utopia* (New York: Harcourt, Brace and World, 1946), p. 105.
7. Bruce Headey, *British Cabinet Ministers* (London: Allen and Unwin, 1975); Hugo Young and Anne Sloman, *No, Minister* (London: BBC, 1982); B. Guy Peters, "The Problem of Bureaucratic Government," *Journal of Politics* 43 (1981): 56–82.
8. Geoffrey Hawker, *Who's Master, Who's Servant* (Sydney: George Allen and Unwin, 1981). For a discussion of the problems of cabinet ministers in Britain,

see Richard Rose, *The Problem of Party Government* (London: Macmillan, 1974), pp. 402–9; see also Ernest Marples, "A Dog's Life in the Ministry," in *Policy-Making in Britain*, Richard Rose, ed. (London: Macmillan, 1969), pp. 115–32; Headey, *British Cabinet Ministers*.

9. See the literature cited in chapter 7.

10. Aaron Wildavsky, *The Politics of the Budgetary Process* (2nd ed.; Boston: Little, Brown, 1974), pp. 1–5; William Niskanen, "Nonmarket Decision-Making: The Peculiar Economics of Bureaucracy," *American Economic Review* 58, no. 2 (May 1968): 293–305.

11. See chapters 6 and 7.

12. This is true even for political systems that attempt to limit the influence of interests. See Gordon Skilling and Franklyn Griffiths, eds., *Interest Groups in Soviet Politics* (Princeton: Princeton University Press, 1971); Paul Cocks et al., *The Dynamics of Soviet Politics* (Cambridge, Mass.: Harvard University Press, 1976).

13. These slogans are used not only to attempt to influence the environment of the organization but also to gain greater commitment on the part of the members of the organization.

14. Johan P. Olsen, *Organized Democracy* (Bergen: Universitetsforlaget, 1983).

15. See, for example, Olof Ruin, "Sweden in the 1970s: Police-making (sic) Becomes More Difficult," in Jeremy Richardson, ed., *Policy Styles in Western Europe* (London: George Allen and Unwin, 1982).

16. This is well demonstrated in Anton, Linde, and Mellbourn, "Bureaucrats in Politics."

17. See, for example, Martin O. Heisler, with Robert B. Kvavik, "Patterns of European Politics: The 'European Polity Model'" in Heisler, ed., *Politics in Europe* (New York: David McKay, 1974), pp. 63–70.

18. Phillipe C. Schmitter and Gerhard Lehmbruch, *Trends Toward Corporatist Intermediation* (London: Sage, 1982). See also Martin O. Heisler, "Corporate Pluralism Revisited: Where Is the Theory?," *Scandinavian Political Studies* 2 (1979): 277–97.

19. Phillipe C. Schmitter, "Still the Century of Corporatism?," *Review of Politics* 36 (1974): 93.

20. Ibid.

21. Gerhard Lehmbruch, "Liberal Corporatism and Party Government," *Comparative Political Studies* 10 (1977): 91–126.

22. H. Adam, *Die konzertierte Aktion in der Bundesrepublik* (Koln: Bund Verlag, 1972).

23. See pp. 157–160.

24. Birgitta Nedelman and Kurt G. Meier, "Theories of Contemporary Corporatism: Static or Dynamic?" in Schmitter and Lehmbruch, *Trends Toward Corporatist Intermediation*, pp. 63–118.

25. Nils Elvander, *Interesseorganisationerna i dagens Sverige* (Lund: CWK Gleerup, 1969); J. Moren, *Organisasjonere og forvaltningen* (Bergen: Norges Handelhøyskole, 1958); U. Swahn, "Interest Representation in Swedish Lawmaking, 1922–78; Remiss Circulation of Swedish Official Reports (SOU)" (Paper presented to meeting of European Consortium for Political Research, Florence, Italy, 1980).

26. Lewis Edinger, *Politics in Germany* (Boston: Little, Brown, 1968), pp. 208–9.

27. Robert B. Kvavik, *Interest Groups in Norwegian Politics* (Oslo: Universitetsforlaget, 1978); Neil Elder, Alastair H. Thomas, and David Arter, *The Consensual Democracies?* (Oxford: Martin Robertson, 1982), pp. 105–43.

28. Lars Nørby Johansen and Ole P. Kristensen, "Corporatist Traits in Denmark, 1946–76," in Gerhard Lehmbruch and Phillipe C. Schmitter, *Patterns of Corporatist Policy-Making* (Beverly Hills, Calif.: Sage, 1982), pp. 199–203.

29. Robert B. Kvavik, "Interest Groups in a Cooptive Political System: The Case of Norway," in Heisler, *Politics in Europe*, pp. 93–116.

30. Jack Hayward, "Mobilising Private Interests in the Service of Public Ambitions: The Salient Elements in the Dual French Policy Style," in Richardson, *Policy Styles*, pp. 111–40; Yves Weber, *L'Administration Consultative* (Paris: Librarie General du Droit et Jurisprudence, 1968), p. 3; G. Mignot and P. d'Orsay, *La Machine Administrative* (Paris: PUF, 1972).

31. Kvavik, "Interest Groups," pp. 102–5.

32. See, for example, James H. Wolfe, "Corporatism in German Political Life: Functional Representation in the GDR and Bavaria," in Heisler, *Politics in Europe*, pp. 323–40.

33. Heisler with Kvavik, "Patterns," pp. 63–70.

34. Frank G. Castles, "The Political Functions of Organized Groups: The Swedish Case," *Political Studies* 21, no. 1 (March 1973): 33; Bo Carlson, *Trade Unions in Sweden* (Stockholm: Tidens, 1969), pp. 125–28; L. Försebäck, *Industrial Relations and Employment in Sweden* (Stockholm: The Swedish Institute, 1980).

35. James Goodyear Abert, *Economic Policy and Planning in the Netherlands* (New Haven: Yale University Press, 1969), pp. 55–67; B. M. Teldersstichtung, *The Public Industrial Organization in the Netherlands* (The Hague: Martinus Nijhoff, 1957); Arthur F. P. Wassenberg, "Neo-Corporatism and the Quest for Control: The Cuckoo Game," in Lehmbruch and Schmitter, *Patterns of Corporatist Policy-Making*, pp. 83–108.

36. Gabriel A. Almond and G. Bingham Powell, *Comparative Politics: A Developmental Approach* (Boston: Little, Brown, 1966), pp. 77–78.

37. Johansen and Kristensen, "Corporatist Traits," pp. 200–203.

38. Scarrow, "Policy Pressures," pp. 15–19.

39. Kvavik, "Interest Groups," 111–12.

40. Stein Rokkan, "Norway: Numerical Democracy and Corporate Pluralism," in *Political Oppositions in Western Democracies*, Robert A. Dahl, ed. (New Haven: Yale University Press, 1966), p. 107.

41. Robert H. Salisbury and John Heinz, "The Analysis of Public Policy: A Search for Theories and Roles," in *Political Science and Public Policy*, Austin Ranney, ed. (Chicago: Markham, 1968), pp. 164–74; and John Heinz, "A Theory of Policy Analysis and Some Preliminary Applications," in *Policy Analysis in Political Science*, Ira Sharkansky, ed. (Chicago: Markham, 1970), pp. 39–60.

42. Kvavik, "Interest Groups," p. 113. See also Olsen, *Organized Democracy*, pp. 199–211.

43. Nils Elvander, *Interessorganisationerna;* Lars Foyer, "Former för Kontakt och

Samverken Mellan Staten och Organisationera," *Statens Offentliga Utredningar 1961* (Stockholm, 1961).

44. Heisler and Kvavik, "European Polity Model."
45. See L. J. Sharpe, "American Democracy Reconsidered," *British Journal of Political Science* 3 (January–April 1973): 1–28, 129–67, for a discussion in the American context.
46. A brief discussion is provided in Salisbury and Heinz, "Analysis of Public Policy," pp. 55–59.
47. See, for example, Theodore R. Marmor and David Thomas, "Doctors, Politics, and Pay Disputes," *British Journal of Political Science* 2 (1972): 426–37. See also Alan Maynard, *Health Care in the European Community* (London: Croom-Helm, 1975).
48. LaPalombara, *Interest Group Politics*, p. 262.
49. Suleiman, *Power, Politics*, pp. 338–39.
50. Theodore Lowi, *The End of Liberalism* (New York: Norton, 1969); Grant McConnell, *Private Power and American Democracy* (New York: Knopf, 1966).
51. See, for example, James B. Christoph, "Higher Civil Servants and the Politics of Consensualism," in Mattei Dogan, ed., *The Mandarins of Western Europe* (New York: Halsted, 1975), pp. 46–48.
52. Hugh Heclo, "Issue Networks and the Executive Establishment," in Anthony King, ed., *The New American Political System* (Washington, D.C.: American Enterprise Institute, 1978), pp. 87–124.
53. Grant Jordan, "Iron Triangles, Wooly Corporatism and Elastic Nets as Images of the Policy Process," *Journal of Public Policy* 1 (1981): 95–123.
54. LaPalombara, *Interest Group Politics*, pp. 272–74.
55. Lowi, *End of Liberalism*.
56. McConnell, *Private Power*, p. 287.
57. William Lilley III and James C. Miller III, "The New Social Regulation," *The Public Interest* 4 (1977): 49–61.
58. Salisbury, "Public Policy."
59. Theodore Lowi, "The Public Philosophy: Interest Group Liberalism," *American Political Science Review* 61, no. 1 (March 1967): 19.
60. D. H. Davis, "Consensus or Conflict: Alternative Strategies for Bureaucratic Bargainers," *Public Choice* 15 (1973): 21–9.
61. Within the context of American politics, Fenno finds that the Executive—both political and administrative—tends to have a significant influence on policy, and that clientele groups have little direct impact. See Richard F. Fenno, Jr., *Congressmen in Committee* (Boston: Little, Brown, 1973), pp. 43–45.
62. Richard F. Fenno, Jr., *The Power of the Purse* (Boston: Little, Brown, 1966), pp. 141–43, disagrees with this analysis.
63. Samuel H. Beer, "The Adoption of General Revenue Sharing: A Case Study in Public Sector Politics," *Public Policy* 24 (1976): 157–60.
64. Salisbury and Heinz, "Analysis of Public Policy," p. 48.
65. LaPalombara, *Interest Group Politics*, pp. 306–7.
66. Ibid., pp. 308–15.

67. Philip M. Williams and Martin Harrison, *Politics and Society in deGaulle's Republic* (Garden City, N.Y.: Doubleday, 1972), pp. 339–42.
68. Marilyn Gittel, *Limits of Citizen Participation: The Decline of Community Organizations* (Beverly Hills, Calif.: Sage, 1980).
69. Major exceptions would be *Burgerinitiatives* in West Germany.
70. Charles W. Anderson, *The Political Economy of Modern Spain* (Madison: University of Wisconsin Press, 1970), pp. 30–34.
71. Myron Weiner, *The Politics of Scarcity* (Chicago: University of Chicago Press, 1962), p. 78.
72. Anderson, *Political Economy of Modern Spain*, p. 69.
73. Colin Crouch, "The Peculiar Relationship: The Party and the Unions," in Dennis Kavanagh, ed., *The Politics of the Labour Party* (London: Allen and Unwin, 1982).
74. This then has many similarities to the legitimate pressure group system with its use of groups to implement policy.
75. David Apter, *Ghana in Transition* (Princeton: Princeton University Press, 1963), pp. 340–44.
76. E. Philip Morgan, *The Administration of Change in Africa* (New York: Dunellen, 1974); Harry Harding, *Organizing China* (Stanford, Calif.: Stanford University Press, 1981).
77. For the concept of the "canteen" in administrative behavior, see Fred Riggs, *Administration in Developing Countries: The Theory of Prismatic Society* (Boston: Houghton Mifflin, 1964), pp. 105–9.
78. Schmitter, "Still a Century of Corporatism?," p. 93.
79. LaPalombara, *Interest Group Politics*, p. 265.
80. Suleiman, *Power, Politics*, pp. 340–46.
81. This obviously conflicts with the ideas of Mancur Olson in *The Logic of Collective Action* (Cambridge, Mass.: Harvard University Press, 1968).
82. Don F. Hadwinger, "The Old, the New and the Emerging United States Department of Agriculture," *Public Administration Review* 36 (1976): 155–65.
83. Michelle Salvati, "May 1968 and the Hot Autumn of 1969: The Responses of Two Ruling Classes," in Suzanne Berger, ed., *Organizing Interests in Western Europe* (Cambridge: Cambridge University Press, 1981), pp. 329–63.
84. Sharpe, "American Democracy," especially pp. 21–23, 135–44.
85. The most obvious example is the special relationship between labor union federations and Labor or Social Democratic parties in Europe.
86. Kwame Nkrumah, *I Speak of Freedom: A Statement of African Ideology* (New York: Praeger, 1961), p. 173.
87. Aristide R. Zolberg, *Creating Political Order* (Chicago: Rand McNally, 1966), p. 121.
88. Rolf H. W. Theen, "Party and Bureaucracy," in Gordon B. Smith, ed., *Public Policy and Administration in the Soviet Union* (New York: Praeger, 1980), pp. 18–52.

CHAPTER 6

THE POLITICS
OF
BUREAUCRACY

The previous chapter discussed the political relationship of bureaucracy to "informal" political actors such as pressure groups and political parties. We now turn our attention to the political relationships of the bureaucracy to formal institutional actors in government. In these relationships—labeled "formal-internal" and "formal-external" in our typology—the relative legitimacy of the bureaucracy is changed. When dealing with pressure groups, the bureaucracy represents the majesty of the state; when dealing with legislatures, prime ministers, presidents, and the courts, the bureaucracy becomes an extraconstitutional interloper in the affairs of government. Thus, as with pressure groups in our previous analysis, the bureaucracy must either seek to have its actions legitimated formally or be capable of bargaining successfully for influence over decisions. It must also bargain for funds to continue its existence and operations. Without carrying the analogy too far, these options might correspond to the legitimate and *clientela* options available to pressure groups in their dealings with bureaucracy.[1]

The task of the bureaucracy in gaining access to decisions is rarely as taxing as that of the pressure groups; if anything, the tendency has been for the more representative and legitimate political institutions to throw power at the bureaucracy rather than resist its pleas for influence. These representative institutions are incapable of formally abdicating powers (even if they might want to), but they must bargain to get the assistance in policy making and implementation that only the bureaucracy can provide. This shifting of power

174

relationships involves a delicate political process and some attention to public opinion. The public still regards its elected officials in legislatures and executives as responsible for the conduct of public business, and these institutions must therefore continue the form if not the substance of policy making in their interactions with the public bureaucracy.[2] Both sides in this exchange of power, influence, and money have a great deal to lose by a clumsy handling of the process, and a political "game" of conflict and compromise results.

Two elements must be examined to better understand the role played by bureaucracy in modern government. The first is an analytical understanding of the requirements for governing, whether that governing be by the legitimate political institutions or by the bureaucracy. The second is a thorough review of the existing knowledge about the role of bureaucracy in policy making with that analytical picture firmly in mind.[3] We would not expect an abdication by political institutions of their rights to bureaucrats, nor do we expect a declaration of bureaucratic government to emanate from the depths of some office building in Foggy Bottom, Whitehall, or Karlavägen. Rather, we are interested in the degree to which, given the lack of leadership alleged to be besetting traditional institutions of government and the difficulties that even skilled leaders have in managing government departments, the bureaucracy is capable of providing needed direction and leadership. This has been largely assumed by theorists of postindustrial society; we now intend to provide some direction in conceptualization, measurement, and analysis.

BUREAUCRATIC GOVERNMENT

What must any group of actors in politics do to effectively govern a country? The root word for "government" implies control and steering; can any group really be said to be controlling the large and complex societies and economies of industrialized countries? Further, can anyone really control the equally complex societies of Third World countries, which are subject to immense external pressures?

Richard Rose has provided a set of criteria that a party must fulfill if it is to provide government after it has been elected.[4] If these criteria are modified to remove certain elements that apply strictly to political parties they can be stated as follows:

1. The group must formulate policy intentions for enactment in office.
2. These intentions must be supported by statements of "not unworkable" means to the ends.
3. There should be some competition over the allocation of resources.
4. The group should be in sufficient numerical strength in the most important positions in the regime.

5. Those given office must have the skills necessary to running a large bureaucratic organization.

6. High priority must be given to the implementation of goals.

As noted, these criteria are somewhat modified and condensed versions of those developed for political parties, but the damage done to the original intentions does not appear mortal. The basic idea that to govern it is necessary for individuals with ideas about policy to be able to implement those ideas through the existing structures of government comes through even in this modified version of the model. Let us now begin to examine these several criteria separately to assess the importance of each for the role of bureaucracy in governance.

Policy Intentions: The Agency Ideology

The first criterion for government is one that ordinarily might be regarded as the crucial shortcoming of public bureaucracy as a workable alternative to other forms of government. The bureaucracy has traditionally been regarded in most societies as lacking ideas about what to do with the machinery of government that it appears to control. However, bureaucratic organizations frequently have well-developed ideas about what government should do. These ideas are not general statements, such as might be found in a political party platform, but rather are confined to the narrow area of expertise of the agency. To understand these "agency ideologies" better, it is necessary to differentiate two types of ideologies, here labeled "soft" and "hard."

The "soft" version of the agency ideology is that the existing program itself is a set of ideas that are favored by the bureaucracy, out of familiarity if for no other reason. Stated more positively, we may regard the ongoing program of an agency to constitute something of an agency ideology. Political executives coming into nominal positions of power over bureaucratic structures have almost invariably reported overt or covert resistance by their civil servants and the existence of a "departmental view" about policy that limits the effectiveness of any political leader. For example, the British Foreign Office has commonly been regarded as being pro-Arab, and the Department of Education as being in favor of comprehensivization of schools, so that any minister coming into office with different policy views would have to overcome these preexisting biases of his or her "servants."[5] There are few commentators on bureaucracy or executive leadership in industrialized societies who have not commented on the existence of this "soft" version of a bureaucratic ideology, so that if we can accept this as a minimalist version of the existence of ideas about policy in a bureaucracy, then clearly such ideas do exist.

The "hard" version of the policy intention criterion is that the bureaucracy must be interested not only in the preservation of the existing policies of the agency, but it must also be interested in imposing a new set of policies. Given that, on average, civil servants remain in their positions longer than do politicians, theoretically they could over time alter policies in the way they saw fit, but the civil servants' conceptions of good policy are also subject to change over time.

First, bureaucrats and bureaucracies are increasingly interconnected via organizational and professional memberships, so that what they want in policy may change over time to correspond to "best practice" in their profession. Some organizations to which civil servants belong may be strictly "bureaucratic," or concerned entirely with public sector management, while others may be organizations of subject-matter specialists in health, education, sanitary engineering, etc. In either case the bureaucracy may, through its professional contacts, generate challenges to existing policies based upon new ideas or the diffusion of policy innovations.

In Europe, the existence of a number of transnational organizations facilitates such diffusion and also development of bureaucratic policy agendas, such as minimum standards for social services.[6] Worldwide, organizations like the United Nations, the International Labor Organization, and the World Bank are responsible for spreading ideas about what governments should do and in turn serve as sources of policy ideas for bureaucracies.[7]

Even without diffusion, however, bureaucrats do have policy ideas. These typically derive from increasing professional qualifications and training of members of the public bureaucracy.[8] Mosher dates the rise of the "professional state" from the mid-1950s.[9] This form of state organization is characterized by the dominance of specialized professional knowledge concentrated in bureaucratic agencies.[10] Mosher was speaking primarily of the United States; in other countries—for instance, France—such a form of state organization may have arisen earlier.[11] The professionals in the agencies become the source of new policies within their sphere of competence, having both expert knowledge and some interest in the expansion of their agencies. Those bureaucrats interested in changing policies may have to wait a number of years before implementing their ideas, so that sufficient popular and political support can be generated. The movement for Medicare and the development of community mental-health programs in the United States are examples of policy changes generated within the bureaucracy that required a very long time between formulation and implementation.[12]

Taking either conception of the bureaucratic role in the generation of policy ideas, we would expect significant cross-national differences in the role of bureaucracy. One source of these differences would be the relative independence of agencies from centralized political control. So, in the United States or Sweden where agencies (or *styrelsen*) have substantial independence, and where they must compete directly for funds, we would expect greater policy advocacy than in political systems with more centralized administrative systems, for example, those under Treasury control in the United Kingdom.[13] Likewise— although Diamant's arguments would appear to refute the contention—the absence of effective political leadership would appear to allow greater bureau-cratic discretion and policy advocacy than would a more stable and effective political executive.[14] Philip Williams writes that in France "long-range policies had been the work of officials rather than politicians in the Third Republic as well as the Fourth. This situation was a by-product of ministerial instability; however undesirable in theory, it was preferable to no long-range policies at all."[15] Much the same situation is alleged to have obtained during the latter days of the Nixon administration. In Third World countries problems of political instability and inadequate leadership have frequently placed a considerable burden of policy formulation upon the bureaucracy.[16] By way of contrast, the doctrinal emphasis on ministerial responsibility in the United Kingdom makes even ineffective political leaders powerful in theory, if not always in practice.

Thirdly, we would expect that bureaucratic personnel systems that allow individuals to remain within a single or limited number of agencies during a career would experience greater bureaucratic policy advocacy than would admin-istrative systems requiring more diverse career patterns. Thus, the Scandinavian countries in which civil servants are hired by individual agencies or ministries rather than through centralized personnel services, or the United States where careers tend to be confined to a single department, would be more likely to have stronger policy advocacy by bureaucratic agencies than would the United Kingdom or France where the senior civil service will have held a number of different types of posts, albeit within the context of the grands corps in France.[17] Also, the development of a senior executive service in the American federal bureaucracy will mean that very senior civil servants will have more varied careers.[18]

Finally, there are definite attitudinal configurations that appear related to policy advocacy by bureaucracy. Aberbach, Putnam, and Rockman discussed such attitudinal configurations in their samples of higher civil servants from six industrialized countries.[19] A number of less quantitative studies have also discussed the cultural and dispositional elements of an active public bureaucracy.[20] In some instances there will be as much variation within a country as there is across countries, but the attitudes that individuals have toward an active role for the civil service in policy making is important in determining that role.

The Availability of "Not Unworkable" Means

If politicians are generally considered the masters of policy ideas, then certainly the bureaucracy is considered the master of routine and techniques. Thus, there should be little question about the bureaucracy being able to present feasible means to carry out a program. In fact, the danger runs the opposite way—what is feasible is often translated into policy. Thus, as with Lindblom's idea of reconstructed preferences, bureaucrats are frequently capable of molding not only techniques but also policies by their definition of what is feasible.[21]

The ability to mold preferences by appeal to feasibility may make the agency as much a victim of its own procedures as the master. The bureaucracy may wish to be innovative but frequently is limited by a reliance on accepted procedures for a definition of what can—and should—be done. Feasibility may be defined in terms of the ability of the program to be administered through the standard operating procedures of the agency, as with Allison's concept of the organizational process model of policy making.[22] Thus, while agencies may indeed develop feasible means for implementing a program, these means may in turn blind both bureaucrats and politicians to the range of available policy alternatives. For example, the government of the United States and the governments of Western European nations are all involved in industrial policies of one sort or another. To a great extent the differences appear to be differences of what are considered feasible programs. In the United States programs of regulation, tax subsidy, and limited direct subsidies are the common approaches.[23] In the majority of European countries—even those with conservative governments—the common approach has been to nationalize industries or for the government otherwise to become directly involved.

Bureaucracies may clearly have procedures to implement any program they may wish to, but, rather than being an undivided asset, this may at times be a liability. Agencies may be able to implement a weak conception of program advocacy mentioned above but may be impeded in making any substantial changes in program because of accepted procedures and methodologies. Their agenda may be defined by how they are accustomed to doing business, rather than by what they would like to do. There is a tension, therefore, between the role of the bureaucracy as advocates of innovation in policies and their role as conservers of procedures.[24]

The role of bureaucracies as conservers of procedures is a variable, just as is their role as policy advocate. It varies in part as a function of tradition and culture, but is also related to more specific political and structural features. One of these is the legalistic emphasis given public administration in some countries. If the activity of government is inclined toward judicial activity, then procedures will almost inevitably come to dominate. A second important aspect is the extent to which there are external pressures for control that would make administrators wary of actions unjustifiable as part of the usual procedures. In all democratic—and some nondemocratic—countries there have been growing pressures for increased accountability of the public bureaucracy.[25] With such pressures, there is a natural tendency for civil servants to retreat behind a wall of procedures for protection, with a consequent loss of innovation and flexibility. As with so many situations dealing with public administration, there is an obvious trade-off between two important attributes here, and no firm basis upon which to make a decision.

Competition among Agencies

One criterion for governance usually associated with democratic and partisan government is competition among contenders for office. Bureaucrats already have office and are unlikely to lose it. What they do not have is money. Thus, while the currency of partisan competition is votes, the currency of bureaucratic competition is currency. The competition for budgets among agencies may provide many of the same benefits at an organizational level that partisan competition is assumed to provide in democratic politics. Just as partisan competition is presumed to allow voters to choose among alternative governments, which in turn are supposed to be related to alternative policies, bureaucratic competition allows political and administrative personnel to choose more directly among alternative policies.[26] This competition is frequently conducted without the direct involvement of elected officials, as with many spending decisions made within the British Treasury or the ministries of finance of most countries.

An entire chapter will be devoted to the budgetary process, but here we emphasize the strictly competitive and policy-choice aspects of the budgetary process. There is substantial disagreement among analysts of bureaucracy as to both the nature and efficacy of this competition among agencies. Some argue that the conflict is intense and pervasive, with the principal intention being to maximize the agency's budget.[27] Others have argued that the competition is less frequent and more restrained, seeking to preserve a "fair share" for the agency and even seeking cooperation in dividing the available budget pie.[28] Some would argue, in fact, that agencies will frequently avoid conflict and agency growth if that growth may threaten their basic purpose and perhaps expose weaknesses in their existing programs.[29] In addition, Downs among others has argued that competition among bureaucracies, just as with industries in the model of the free market economy, is a positive force encouraging policy innovation and also serving as a check on bureaucratic autonomy.[30] In any of the above conceptions, however, competition among agencies does have a place as a means of allocating resources among competing policies and thus allowing some to flourish and some to languish or, less frequently, to die.[31]

No matter what the stakes of bureaucratic competition may be, such competition will occur to a different degree in different bureaucratic systems. The structure of some governments, for example, the United States or Sweden, allows more latitude for bureaucratic competition and bargaining than is true in more centrally managed systems.[32] The existence of a large number of agencies with relatively little coordination except through the budgetary process—and the ability of those agencies to argue directly for their own appropriations and to mobilize political support—makes competition a more important part of the lives of the agencies and much more important for their survival. This means that these agencies will be more capable of providing an alternative source of governing—at least within a single policy area—than will agencies more constrained by central political and administrative control. Thus, bureaucratic competition appears to go hand in hand with the "hard" conception of policy advocacy, if for no other reason than that policy ideas provide one means by which the competition is conducted.

The nature of bureaucratic competition has two principal effects on politics and government. First, it may in part account for some of the massive growth of the size of government—as reflected in public spending—over the past several decades.[33] Old programs become institutionalized as commitments of governments—and entitlements for citizens—and the need to compete for increased funding produces new programs and new policies from the agencies.[34] Some authors have argued exactly the opposite—that in fact competition among agencies would decrease the size of government, but that analysis seems severely to underestimate both the persistence of agencies and their ability to limit the scope of competition to areas outside their "heartlands."[35] It does appear that competition for funding and for new policy initiatives are related to an expansion of public expenditure. The cause may not be entirely the desires of the bureaucracy, however, as politicians may also favor the expansion of government because it provides them more benefits to distribute among constituents and thus a better chance for reelection.[36] One study of the growth of American government, for example, argued that the major source of expansion had been congressmen seeking to use new programs to make names for themselves.[37]

The second major effect of bureaucratic competition is that it limits the internal consistency or coherence of governments. The bureaucracy does not act as an integrated tool of the public instrument, but rather as a set of subgovernments each serving a clientele group crucial in the political game of survival. Depending upon whether one adopts a more rigid "iron triangle" conception or the more flexible "issue network" perspective, such subgovernments are either immutable and totally self-centered or merely an important aspect of the professionalization and specialization of government.[38] But with highly competitive agencies, there may be bureaucratic governments but no bureaucratic government. As Natchez and Bupp put it, "Priority setting in the Federal bureaucracy resembles nineteenth-century capitalism; priorities are established by aggressive entrepreneurs at the operating levels of government."[39]

The Incumbency of Positions

Another necessary condition for the ability of a bureaucracy to provide an alternative source of governance is that officials must occupy the most important positions in policy making, and further, they must be in sufficient numbers to be able to make their decisions effective. The bureaucracy clearly satisfies the quantitative aspect of this criterion, even though it is never certain that those in the lower echelons of the bureaucracy will always comply with the directives of their superiors. However, the bureaucracy may not be able to fulfill the qualitative aspect. Politicians have been thought to be in the most important positions for policy making, and bureaucrats only in a position to implement decisions.

There are two points, however, that qualify the traditional assumption. First, the contact of the bureaucracy with the environment of the organization, as well as the concentration of technical expertise in the lower echelons of organizations, tends to give bureaucracies a substantial control over information and expertise crucial for policy making. Thompson's analysis of the separation of expertise and authority in modern organizations is most important here, and the ability to control information is a major influence over policy in the hands of the bureaucrat.[40] Further, to the extent to which information is passed through the bureaucratic hierarchy, it is selectively distorted. Thus, although there may be enough people in the bureaucracy—and perhaps a few extra— there may still be an imbalance between those making decisions at the top and those with the information for making the decisions at the bottom.[41]

Political institutions have been attempting to break the monopoly on information that the bureaucracy appears to hold by creating their own independent sources of information. These "counterbureaucracies" are most numerous in the United States—for example, the agencies of the Executive Office of the President, the Congressional Budget Office, and the growing committee staffs of Congress—but also exist in a number of other political systems.[42] Some have sought to provide this information through ministerial *cabinets*, while others have established research offices such as the Central Policy Review Staff in Britain.[43] Still others have tried unsuccessfully to use their political parties as instruments for policy research.[44] Despite these efforts, the bureaucracy retains a central role in the development and dissemination of policy-relevant information and thereby retains a powerful position in policy making.

A second factor vital to assessing the relative importance of bureaucratic and political positions in policy making is the weight assigned to implementation in defining policy. As already pointed out, it can be easily argued that "policy" is what happens, rather than what is stated in legislation.[45] Many public programs allow a substantial degree of latitude for the implementers of a policy, for example, in police work or in defining the eligibility of applicants for social programs, and the lower echelons of the bureaucracy may be as important as those in the nominal policy-making positions in defining the realities of a policy.

Finally, it should be emphasized again that the bureaucracy retains one principal advantage in a struggle over power and policy—it is simply so numerous. The sheer immensity of the task of controlling a large, complex, and knowledgeable public bureaucracy possessing substantial political support may defeat all but the hardiest politician. Even in the United States, where presidents have a very large number of political appointees compared to most other countries, the size of the bureaucracy and its relationship to important political forces make it difficult to control. As one presidential aide said, "Everybody believes in democracy until they come to the White House. . . ," meaning that presidents would like to have more control over government than they sometimes have.[46]

In summary, bureaucrats may occupy the most important positions in government simply because they occupy the most positions. In addition, they occupy positions that involve both the direct delivery of services and the definition of what the programs really signify for clients. This may mean that they will disagree with the political leadership of their organization, except perhaps on the crucial question of whether the organization should survive. Their ability to loosen up some of the fetters of political control, given their numbers and their expertise, may have some of the same results mentioned for competition among agencies. There is an increased ability for agencies and their personnel to go their own ways, with ever-increasing incoherence among government programs.

The Possession of Managerial Skills

Political leaders frequently lack the managerial skills necessary to manage a large, complex organization such as a government department.[47] It is assumed that the bureaucrats who occupy these organizations permanently do have the skills, if for no other reason than they appear to keep the organizations running on a day-to-day basis. So, just as they frequently find themselves boarding a policy train that has a great deal of momentum, politicians coming on board their departments find that the organizations of which they are nominally in charge tend to run on their own with little direction from above.

When compared to some absolute scale, rather than to the abilities of politicians, the skills of bureaucrats are not so overwhelming. In fact, many of the standard complaints about bureaucracy, and more specifically public bureaucracy, concern their internal managerial dysfunctions. Discussions of "red tape," displacement of goals, and general chronic inefficiency have filled the literature on bureaucracy.[48] Therefore we must be concerned whether these internal problems are not sufficiently great to limit the ability of bureaucracy to provide effective governance when conventional political institutions have proven themselves ineffective.

The "publicness" of the public bureaucracy and the lack of measurable outputs both contribute to the difficulties of managing public organizations. Being public, these organizations must be more concerned about the adherence to norms, procedures, etc. than private organizations. They are responsible for public money and act in the name of the people, and must therefore be held accountable to the people. Accountability, in turn, may force the bureaucrat to protect himself or herself against possible complaints, with the only protection being in the strict or even rigid adherence to rules and procedures.[49] This protection is as important when dealing with superiors as it is when dealing with clients, and policy leadership from the top of the organization may be thwarted by bureaucratic rigidities and procedures within the organization. The best-conceived policy innovation will fail if the administrators implementing it are more concerned with their own protection than the success of the program.

These general problems of control are exaggerated by the absence of measurable outputs for most public organizations. The major means of evaluating success in a public bureaucracy is consumption rather than production.[50] That is, the standard measure of success is a larger budget rather than more services rendered. Therefore, lacking a single measure such as profit, which would allow an assessment of effectiveness, public sector managers are forced to use rules, regulations, and hierarchical control more than would be true for other types of managers. What is attained more often than not is dysfunction rather than smooth operation.

The degree to which internal managerial dysfunctions beset public bureaucracy accumulates from many factors. Some are purely organizational, while others appear related to cross-national differences in conceptions of authority and hierarchical control.[51] Many of the dysfunctions are universal but are particularly apparent in some settings. For example, societies with a resistance to the imposition of impersonal authority are more likely to experience bureaucratic dysfunctions than others more accepting of authority.[52] Likewise, and somewhat paradoxically, the greater the extent to which individual public servants are likely to suffer as a result of an improper action, the more likely bureaucratic dysfunctions will be; the individual will retreat behind a wall of rules, regulations, and delay for protection.

Finally, it has become a truism to say that in modern government there is an increasing interdependence of the public and private sectors.[53] Not only does policy have to descend from above, but it must be cleared from below. This places bureaucrats in a strategic position to link the public and private sectors, but it also makes their jobs more difficult.[54] Not only must there be compliance within the organization, but there must also be compliance in the society, with many more built-in "clearance points."[55] These naturally make management more difficult and increase the probability of bureaucratic delay and failure.

A High Priority Given to Implementation of Policy

Some of the problems of internal management within public organizations have already been discussed. There are also numerous problems with communication that inhibit the flow of information upward and internal rigidities that block the smooth flow of authority downward.[56] The sixth criterion for government is directly concerned with the translation of decisions made at the top of the organization into effective actions in the field. As noted, the "real" policy of a government is the policy as implemented, rather than the statements of legislatures, political executives, etc. A number of studies have documented the variety of pressures on field-workers that may limit their ability to take the program passed by the legislature and put it into effect.[57] This concern with lower-echelon administrators complying with the law as written may appear to conflict with our earlier concern about flexibility and the exercise of discretion. However, this concern with "red tape" focused on compliance with the procedures of the organization rather than with the substance of the policy.

A significant portion of this failure of implementation can be explained by political factors rather than organizational factors. As an administrator finds himself or herself farther and farther from the center of organizational power, there is a loss of political support and policy reinforcement. The administrator becomes more subject to political pressures from outside the organization, if for no other reason than that these pressures are more relevant and more immediate than those from the home office. Kaufman's now-classic study of the U.S. Forest Service is a case in point of local pressures on a field officer.[58] Pressman and Wildavsky's study of implementation illustrates this problem in an intergovernmental context, as do the problems of ensuring compliance in the decentralized administrative structure of West Germany.[59] Even the French *préfet* must negotiate and attempt to coopt local political forces in order to govern his territory successfully.[60] The necessity of mobilizing political support for policy, and its attendant need to bargain away some policy intentions of central government, may be fundamental to the political process when attempting to put legislation into effect. However, it is the one area of the policy process, as Pressman and Wildavsky point out, about which we have the least reliable information.[61]

Given the relative lack of information about the implementation process—a weakness that is being remedied rapidly—it is difficult to make reasonable hypotheses about the sources of variation in effective implementation. One obvious hypothesis is that in highly decentralized administrative systems, for example West Germany, there will be greater problems in ensuring implementation than in more centralized systems. Likewise, the degree of sectionalism and local autonomy would be related to failures of implementation, as would the abilities of political leaders with strong sectional bases to place pressures on the bureaucracy for special considerations.[62] Several studies in implementation in Third World countries have emphasized the importance of local power relationships and patron-client relationships in limiting effective implementation.[63] Also, the degree of vertical separation of the client-contact levels from the center of the organization may make it more likely—and more necessary— that lower-echelon workers bargain with local and client interests. Finally, the lack of political support for an organization, as with the independent regulatory commissions in the United States, may make it crucial for organizations to develop operative policies somewhat different from those intended in their enabling legislation.[64]

In addition to the pull of clients and geographical interests, there are other factors within public bureaucracies that limit effective implementation. These organizational factors have been documented in a number of studies.[65] More importantly, as outlined above in the discussion of agency ideologies, organizations may have goals of their own and consequently may not accept the goals of their nominal political superiors. Opposition to the policies of politicians is rarely overt, as this might violate the formal relationships between elective and permanent officials in government. More commonly, bureaucrats defeat politicians by obfuscation, delay, and the use of rules, regulations, and procedures.[66] Politicians, being short-term occupants of their positions, rarely understand either the procedural mechanisms or the substance of policy as well as their nominal servants and consequently are frequently at the mercy of civil servants. They are particularly at the mercy of their civil servants when the policy in question falls among several departments, so that the policy is the result of the ". . . groups of officials in the thousands of interdepartmental meetings, luncheons, and telephone calls that take place every day."[67] An interorganizational network exists in government, both among departments and among levels of government, and an individual needs substantial length of service in order to learn the network and how to get what he or she wants out of it.[68] Civil servants have that longevity, while politicians rarely do.

We should not count politicians out too readily, however, and politicians have developed a number of mechanisms to attempt to restore their control over the structures and policies of government, increasingly considered to be dominated by bureaucracy. We have already mentioned the use of ministerial *cabinets* in France and Belgium, as well as the role of the Central Policy Review Staff in the United Kingdom. Also, there is an increasing use of political appointees in positions in which they were previously infrequent. Mrs. Thatcher has placed several appointees into the Treasury, while in Sweden appointees have become more common in the central ministries.[69] In West Germany there has been a long tradition of patronage appointments at the local government level to ensure the responsiveness of bureaucracies to elected officials, and the development of "matrix organizations" in the *Bund* ministries has been, in part, an attempt to improve control within these organizations since it is so difficult to exercise control over *Land* administrations.[70]

Implementation is a central problem in contemporary political systems. Breakdowns of implementation represent a fundamental failure of those systems to translate political ideas into effective action. Bureaucracies are a central component of this failure, although usually not from malice but more from the rigidities built into the structure, or from sincere beliefs in the policies already being pursued or regarded as preferable.

While implementation is an important problem, it is not the only problem. At times there is a tendency to design programs for ease of implementation without asking whether that is really what governments want to do or should do. As in the earlier discussion about the domination of procedures over substance in bureaucracies, implementation considerations can come to dominate real policy considerations. Certainly the true meaning of the policy is the policy that is implemented, but there is little point in having it implemented if it is the wrong policy in the first place.

Summary

We have been exploring the question of the ability of bureaucracy to provide government—a set of coherent policy intentions and the implementation of those intentions—in contemporary political systems. The conclusion is that although bureaucracy may be able to go some distance in providing such leadership, it is also thwarted by many of the same problems that limit politicians seeking to exercise governance. Those whose primary concern is democratic politics and popular control of government may welcome this analysis initially but upon reflection may be chastened. What this analysis indicates is that there are difficulties in public management and government that are more basic than the short-term political and economic forces cited as the causes of most contemporary problems.

The problems—termed "overload" in much of the European literature—appear to be more fundamental and deep-seated.[71] They have to do with the loss of confidence of citizens, the decline of obedience and quiescence, the exhaustion of budgetary appeals to citizens by politicians, and—last but not least—the machinery of government itself. The sheer bulk and inertia of bureaucracy, combined with its needs for external political support from clientele groups, tends to fragment control and divert attention from problems of governance to problems of organizational survival. The political life and to some extent the values of bureaucratic agencies are tied up in questions of organizational survival.

Thus, government by bureaucracy is a problem. Bureaucracy may be capable of supplying government, but unlike political parties that supply government by "directionless consensus," government supplied by bureaucracy may be government by "non-consensual directions." The government supplied will not go in any single direction but in many, dependent upon the agency and its relationship to its clientele. For the same reason it will be nonconsensual and incoherent government. There would be no integrating ideology or philosophy, only a set of specific ideologies about specific policy problems. These ideologies, rather than integrating the activities of government, tend to fragment government and render it a set of competing, or at least not cooperating, fiefdoms.

STRATEGIES IN BUREAUCRATIC POLITICS

Even if we can agree that government by bureaucracy, meaning by an integrated and purposive elite, is not a likely occurrence, this does not mean that the struggle over power and influence over policy between elective officials and permanent officials will not go on.[72] In such a struggle each side has important weapons and important stratagems. This section will discuss some of these weapons and how they may be employed.

The Resources of Bureaucracy

The first, and perhaps most important, resource of the bureaucracy is *information and expertise*. To the extent that government has at its disposal information, this information is concentrated in bureaucratic agencies. Going along with that information is the technical expertise to understand and interpret it. This relative monopoly of information can be translated into power in several ways. The most blatant is the argument that since they (the agency) know more about the subject, they should be given control over it. In other words, they are likely to do a better job (technically) of making policy in a certain issue area than would the relatively ignorant political executive and legislature. If that argument fails, as it often does, and the politicians are sufficiently audacious to attempt to make policy themselves, then the major source of information for formulating those policies will still be the bureaucracy.[73] This means that the bureaucracy is in a situation in which it can at least implicitly trade information for influence over policy, and indeed information may be produced selectively to make one type of decision a virtual inevitability. In the same vein, Bartlett has referred to legislatures "subsidizing" bureaus in order to get information about their operations, that is, trading information for money.[74]

A second power at the disposal of the bureaucracy is their *power of decision*. Despite the "metaphysical pathos" about the red tape and inefficiency of bureaucracy (especially public bureaucracy), compared to many political institutions—especially legislative institutions—they seem a model of efficiency.[75] Having few procedural rules concerning free discussion, voting, and the like, bureaucracies are in a position to act more rapidly than legislatures on many issues. There are, of course, some procedural safeguards and delays for would-be bureaucratic rule-makers, for example, the Administrative Procedures Act in the United States, but relatively speaking the bureaucracy can act quickly.[76] They also do not have to be as sensitive to the political pressures that may be coming from constituents in making their decisions. Political executives may share the advantage of rapid decision in situations where they are independent of the legislature, for example, the French and American presidencies, but they are more commonly bound in democratic systems by a reliance on legislative action and approval.

Third, just as political institutions have their *political supporters*, so do bureaucratic institutions. In our previous chapter we discussed the relationship between bureaucracy and interest groups. In two of the four types of interactions there is a definite political linkage between an interest group and an agency. The bureaucracy has the ability to mobilize these political supporters in making claims for funding or for policy autonomy. The political support of other political institutions tends to be less policy specific than that of the agencies, and the agency can consequently mobilize a more interested and vocal group of supporters on an issue than would be likely for any legislative group that sought to oppose them.[77] This is especially true given the internal difficulties of decision within the legislature. This issue-specific political support can be of special importance because of the fragmented nature of decision making in many legislative bodies, with committees or other specialized bodies having a substantial influence over policy and funding. The agency is able to mobilize support before the appropriate committee, which may not have the interest or latitude to consider alternative uses for funds, and develop the case that indeed there is a large demand for the agency's services. The bargain struck with the client group, allowing access and influence, is generally consummated in front of a legislative committee.[78]

Having discussed the political powers of the bureaucracy, we now proceed to discuss the advantages they have by being *apolitical.* This may appear to be a contradiction, but it is an important means of understanding how bureaucracies are able to compete successfully for influence and power in decision making. Bureaucracies have the advantage of being formally divorced from partisan politics. Civil servants do not have to stand for election, are not faced with constituency pressures or pressures for conformity from their own party, and have been effectively neutered politically in most societies. This isolation from partisan politics allows them to argue that not only are they expert in what they do, but also that their decision will not be affected by the need to placate voters. This partisan impartiality goes hand in hand with the expertise of the bureaucracy to make a strong argument that their decisions will be superior on technical grounds to those that would be taken by political institutions.

As already mentioned, bureaucracies develop *agency ideologies* as a means of justifying their actions. These ideologies are important weapons in the struggle over influence, as they tend to be impervious to the argument and evidence of outside "nonexperts" and to be self-serving for the agency. One of the classic examples of such an agency ideology is the doctrine of strategic bombing held by the United States Air Force. This doctrine, stated simply, is that the best means (if not the *only* means) of bringing an enemy to its knees is through strategically bombing its means of war production. This is alleged to have brought about the demise of Germany and Japan in the Second World War, and these cases are cited as proof of the doctrine. Such evidence as does exist on the effects of the bombing, however, indicates that if anything, production of war matériel increased during the bombing rather than decreased.[79] The air force— for obvious reasons—persists in its claim that bombing is the answer to the problems of war.

There are a number of other examples of the rigidity of military bureaucracies to ideologies of this sort, but some of the same behavior can be found in social and economic bureaucracies as well. Even though most social agencies at least pay lip service to the idea that most social problems are multidimensional, they tend to see them and act on them largely in terms of their own expertise, to try to capture clients rather than sending them on to seek other types of help, and to argue for increased funding in terms of the ability to solve social problems through their particular program. The numerous problems of agency coordination in social services are one indication of the reliance on agency ideologies about policy and solutions to problems.[80]

To return to the central point of this discussion of bureaucratic ideologies, we can see that the existence of such an ideology is important for the success of the agency in dealing with political institutions. Political actors rarely have a ready reply to such policy-specific ideologies. They labor under a number of disadvantages in competing with the bureaucrats, not the least of which is a frequent lack of any specific policy ideas. Many political leaders, when put into a ministerial or cabinet role, simply don't have the background in the policy area to contribute much in the way of policy direction, and the demands of the job often prevent them from developing such a direction. The civil servants who work within the department—even the generalists at relatively high levels—rarely have such difficulties and are quite capable of providing a direction for the department's program.

Finally, the bureaucracy has the advantage of *permanence and stability*. It is difficult to fire a civil servant and may even be difficult to have one transferred. Civil servants can always adopt a strategy of waiting and delay. Ministers come and go, but the basic work of civil servants does not change simply because the ministers rarely have time to learn what has to be changed or to put such a program into effect.

The Resources of Political Institutions

Perhaps the ultimate weapon at the disposal of political institutions is their *legitimacy*. Associated with legitimacy is the formal and constitutional authority to do the things that government is intended to do. Few constitutions even mention bureaucracies, much less vest any formal powers of decision making in them. Therefore, whether by delegation, funding, or acquiescence, bureaucratic actions must be legitimated by constitutionally prescribed actors. More often than not this legitimation comes through inaction and acquiescence rather than through formal action, but it still involves a transfer of authority.

Almost as important as the formal power and authority to perform tasks is the wherewithal to do them: money. The second major power held by political institutions, then, is the *power of the purse*. In order to survive, prosper, and grow, agencies require money and must be able to influence political institutions to provide them that money. The budgetary process—or the politics of survival, as we referred to it earlier—is one of the crucial points of interaction in bureaucratic politics. The bureaucracy seeks money and the autonomy to spend it, while the political institutions seek control of their funds and also seek to ensure accountability as to how it will be spent. The importance of the budget for both sets of actors has led to the development of a number of techniques on both sides to attempt to counteract the powers of the other.

Third, and certainly related to the first two items, is something that we might call *latitude*, or *autonomy for the agency*. In general, agencies seek to acquire as much latitude as they can. This refers primarily to latitude to make policy; they might seek a blanket grant of authority in an area of policy. It also may refer to budgeting; they might seek some latitude in the way in which funds must be spent. On the other hand, the power to grant such latitude is a powerful weapon for the political institutions to gain concessions of information. It is their constitutional role to regulate policy and the implementation of policy. Moreover, they must be responsible politically for what happens to the country, and they want to control policy if they are to be held responsible for it. Thus, as well as bargaining over money, agencies and political institutions must also bargain over the degree of autonomy to be granted, the responsibility for funds and accounting, and the procedures for delegating authority.

The powers of political institutions mentioned to this point are largely formal and legal. These institutions have substantial political resources as well, if for no other reason than they are—to some degree—*representative of the public*. It may be argued exactly how representative the institutions are along several dimensions, but they are generally the most representative institutions available.[81] As such they are able to mobilize political strength through their relationship to the public, political parties, and interest groups. The public will rarely rise up as a mass in righteous anger, but the politicians are quite capable of making it seem that way.[82] By any number of means—investigation, publicity, electoral campaigns, speeches, debates, etc.—the political institutions may be capable of pitting the "people" against the bureaucrats. Given the nature of bureaucracy, there is little the people are capable of doing even in their aroused state, but the bureaucracy can ignore public opinion only for so long. Moreover, the arousal of public opinion may make it considerably easier for the political institutions to employ the formal powers at their disposal.

Bureaucratic Ploys

Having discussed the weapons available to both sides in the struggle over policy and money, we proceed to the dynamic ways in which those powers can be exercised. This is of necessity only a partial listing of all the ploys available but should provide an idea of the ways in which both bureaucrats and political leaders play the game of politics within formal organizations.

We begin with a set of devices, stratagems, and structures that greatly assist the bureaucracy in gaining its ends of control over policy and stable if not expanding budgetary commitments. In most cases these ploys are related to the ability of the bureaucracy to mobilize information and expertise, and secondarily to the ability to mobilize bias in the form of pressure group support for programs. These ploys largely involve the removal of policy from consideration by political officials and placing it in the hands of presumably neutral, expert, and objective administrators. As admirable as this may sound in theory—at least to those who advocate "rational" policy making in government—it represents a movement away from the ability of elected or even selected leaders to control government and supply the quality and quantity of goods and services demanded by the public.

Planning The first and perhaps most important of the strategies of expanding bureaucratic influence is public planning. This device began as a means of controlling the economy but has been extended to a variety of social and economic spheres such as land use, transportation, urban areas, and even social services.[83]

The need and justification for planning is obvious from a number of perspectives. In the first place, planning involves the systematic application of knowledge to important areas of human concern and allows some long-range manipulation of the state of the economy and society. Likewise, it can make the nature of the economy more amenable to the desires of the public and by removing many decisions from the marketplace allow for investment in areas that, while socially desirable, may not be particularly profitable in a private market. By removing to some extent macro-economic policy from the political agenda, the device may successfully defuse many important political conflicts, especially where politics is heavily influenced by segmental disputes within the society. As Abert says of economic planning in the Netherlands, ". . . the technical process of economic planning is accorded a position of major influence [because of] the lack of a political consensus that might resolve economic issues through the electoral process."[84] Thus, the tendency toward adopting planning as a means of making long-range policy tends to remove some aspect of public policy from the partisanship and divisiveness of politics and transport it to the rarefied atmosphere of "rational" decision making.

It should be clear that planning is an important weapon for the bureaucratic politician. It places the regulation of the national economy or some other aspect of national policy in his hands. If planning is accepted as the "proper" means of making policy for the nation, then the proper policy becomes the one that the planners advocate, and the burden of proof falls on those who advocate anything else. This may be especially true of policy areas other than the economy where the effects of the policy decisions are not as apparent through such factors as inflation and unemployment, and where the requirement of capital investment means that the effects will be years in the future.[85]

A second item in favor of bureaucracy planning, especially economic planning, is that it is difficult for the average layman—or politician—to understand. Much current economic planning is done using such devices as mathematically sophisticated econometric models processed by computer and dependent upon large quantities of economic theory. Few members of the political community have the skills, or are willing to invest the time required to acquire the skills, to understand fully the reasoning behind these planning methods or the assumptions on which they are built. The politicians are at the mercy of the planners in having the programs and their implications explained to them.[86] Some political systems have gone even farther in having the plan go into effect unless actively blocked by the political institutions.[87] Given that this would be a difficult and time-consuming activity with very little probable payoff to a politician, since his constituents probably wouldn't understand it anyway, this active blocking will rarely be undertaken.

A third item favoring the bureaucracy and the planners is the integration of the plan. Almost by definition, planning offers something of an integrated and comprehensive view of some aspect of social or economic life and an integrated set of policies for achieving certain ends in that policy area. As such, any attempt by political institutions to modify the plan can be opposed as upsetting the whole plan. As Shonfield put it:

> if parliament is to play an effective part in the business of national planning—and if it does not the outlook for the future of democracy is bleak—then members of parliament will also have to recognize some theoretical as well as practical limitations on the exercise of their collective sovereignty. These theoretical limitations apply to the whole procedure of introducing a parliamentary amendment to a set of planning proposals, whose merit is their intellectual coherence and self-consistency. If any significant element in them is changed, the whole structure must be adapted to accommodate the alteration.[88]

He goes on to argue that such adaptability is crucial on the part of the planners, but the presence of an integrated plan makes it difficult for any political organization to make the types of alterations and modifications at which they are perhaps most adept. The burden of proof would again appear to fall on those who want to change the plan rather than those who want to accept it.

Following from the above, it is difficult for political institutions to attack the efficacy of the planning process as a means of allocating resources. Certainly some plans are more successful than others, but with the exception of a few societies that approach being totally planned, there are always sufficient areas of independence so that plan failures can be blamed on those nonplanned sectors of the economy, or on oil prices, or on drought. This not only can be used as a means to argue for more public control of the marketplace but also prevents the public and its representatives from measuring bureaucratic or planning output in the same way they might measure the output of other governmental programs such as garbage collection or water supply. Planning is thus one of the public goods mentioned previously that often defy accurate pricing.

In this discussion we should be careful not to assume that planners and the rest of the bureaucratic establishment are necessarily homogeneous. In many cases, in fact, there is significant friction between the traditional bureaucracy and newer planning agencies.[89] As with the conflict between line and staff, the presence of planning agencies threatens line agencies, and planning tends to direct resources away from pet projects of line agencies. However, the planning process must be seen as directing political control and authority away from the "political" institutions and toward bureaucratic (especially when each agency or department does its own planning) or technocratic agencies.

Planning constitutes a major weapon in the hands of the bureaucracy, both at agency and societal levels. It provides a technical means of reinforcing and quantifying the positions of the bureaucracy and at the same time removes many important and sensitive matters from the hands of partisan decision-makers. Planners can argue that their decisions will be objectively superior to those reached by partisan institutions, that they can impose a longer time perspective on the problem than the politicians, and that they can prevent special-interest considerations from determining policy. Despite these to-some-degree commendable attributes of planning, the major effect that we must be concerned about here is to remove those decisions from the hands of politically responsible officials and place them into the hands of bureaucratic elites.

Budgeting An entire chapter is devoted to the role of budgeting in the life of public agencies, but some points should be made here briefly, as budgeting is such an important weapon for both bureaucrats and politicians. On the bureaucratic side, a number of highly sophisticated and technical approaches to the problem of allocating resources have been useful in mystifying the process of making budgets. This in turn has placed the more amateur political leaders at something of a disadvantage. These approaches to budgeting, such as PPBS (Planning-Programming-Budgeting System, or simply program budgeting) and ZBB (Zero-base Budgeting), were undertaken with the admirable intention of improving the objective quality of public decisions and of relating budgeting more directly to the final products of public programs. Interestingly, if anything, these reformed systems of budgeting were designed to break the stranglehold of the bureaucracy on the budget through incrementalism. Their effect, however, would appear to have been actually to strengthen the position of the agency in relationship to parliaments or political executives.

In the first place, program budgeting requires considerably more information about the activities of the agencies than is required for traditional line-item budgeting. Where is that information to come from? Clearly it must come from the agencies themselves. Assuming that the agencies do not directly fib about the operations of their agencies, this still gives them a substantial impact over the outcomes of budgeting. Program budgeting requires a considerable investment of time and money to be effective, so programs as well as agencies are selected for more intensive analysis in any one year. It has become the practice in several nations to allow agencies to select the programs to be reviewed with the effect that those programs with the greatest potential for growth are reviewed.[90] Frequently, centralized budget agencies—if they exist—lack sufficient staff to scrutinize the activities of agencies fully, or to collect independent information. The bureaucracy may therefore not be effectively restrained by this device in its search for secure funding.

A second point is that program budgeting forces some decentralization of control within the bureaucracy. One effect of the programming process is to allow each bureau chief considerably more latitude than would be allowed under a line-item budget. Instead of funds being allocated for items such as personnel, equipment, etc., they would be allocated for doing a job. The bureau chief would be allowed latitude in how he used the funds. For example, if he found that he could build roads more cheaply by using less sophisticated machinery and more hand labor, a bureau chief would be able to do so. While this may, and should, have the effect of producing better policy outputs at a lower or equal cost, the *political* effect is to make it more difficult to impose central control on the operations of the bureaus and agencies, although priorities will be determined centrally.

Third, few political bodies are likely to be willing or able to invest the time and money required to undertake their own program review of agencies. They rarely have the staff to compete with those of the agencies, so that the competition for control becomes a conflict between a "computer and slide rule."[91] Even if legislatures or political executives were to respond favorably to the imposition of such management techniques—and the evidence is largely that they have not—they might still be at a severe disadvantage in attempting to understand and alter the outputs of program budgeting by the agencies and centralized budgeting agencies.

Related to both planning and program budgeting is what we might call "technical budgeting." By this we refer to a tendency to assign the budgetary function to a special body having highly developed technical skills and little if any political responsibility. Another variant of budgeting with some of the same implications is a tendency to develop middle-range budgetary forecasting, with projected budgets made for five- to seven-year periods.[92] The formulation of the national budget in Norway is perhaps the best example of technical budgeting. The budget is formulated by a group of civil servants and technicians using a quite complex model of the Norwegian economy.[93] These "technocrats" develop a draft budget that is then scrutinized by a select committee of civil servants and the government, is reformulated, and is finally passed. This procedure gives to one set of civil servants rather obviously great powers over the formulation of the Norwegian budget. As Higley et al. argue:

> It is in the nature of the process that the choices of the civil servants who collect and analyze the mass of data from which the national budget is constructed are of fundamental importance to the outcome. It is so because the civil servants have a virtual monopoly of the technical knowledge necessary to the process and because the process gives the initiative to them throughout. . . . Moreover, many of the communications from the civil service to the government take the adversary form: civil servants tell the government how the national budget should be composed. Thus, not only are they in control of the general framework in which decisions are made, but they also define the important questions, influence the directions

of the politicians' attention, and argue for their proposed solutions with the help of esoteric knowledge that is difficult to refute.[94]

The authors point out that elected ministers can and do have an impact on the final shape of the budget, but the choices they make are likely to be small relative to the overall content of the budget, and these choices will tend to be within the general parameters already established. Planning the reformulation of one aspect of the budget will tend to require a reformulation of the entire document, and the substitutions of the judgment of ministers and politicians for that of experts. This is quite a burden for politicians to bear in attempting to retain control over policy.

Here again, as with the conflict between planners and line bureaucrats, we find that the "bureaucracy" as a whole rarely marches to the same drummer. There is an almost inherent conflict between the spending ministries and the financial ministry. They are all bureaucrats in the generic sense but show here a lack of any common interest that might make them a unified body controlling public policy. We might be better able to understand the outcome of what happens in budgeting in terms of the *conflicts* of these agencies. This would in fact be the conflict of differing types of expertise: one of policy areas and one of economic effects. In any case, despite who may win that conflict, the political institutions of legislatures and presidents may be excluded from it. The anticipated reactions of the actors may be influenced by the threat of the imposition of political authority, but in day-to-day operations, it is a bureaucratic war.

Advisory Bodies   Another useful device for the bureaucracy in gaining control over policy areas is the use of advisory bodies or committees in the formulation of policy. We have previously discussed bodies of this type that are attached to ministries, but they also provide a useful means of understanding something of the influence of administration on policy. It is, in fact, in part because of the pressure group connection that these bodies can become so successful in assisting bureaucratic power. In the societies where the use of advisory bodies is so important in making policy—principally Scandinavia and the Low Countries—the imprimateur of pressure groups is important in legitimating policy. Since these advisory boards are attached to the ministries and thereby interact largely with civil servants, there is the possibility of substantial reciprocal influence over policy. Further, many of the members of the advisory bodies are themselves members of the civil service. For example, in Norway, one study showed that in 1966, 272 civil servants held 623 positions in 351 (of 954) advisory committees.[95] In France, although the numerical membership of civil servants in ministerial advisory boards is generally not large, they tend to hold the more important positions of chairman and *rapporteur*, so that what the committee advises is at least interpreted by the civil service before dissemination.[96] Thus, the civil service can be expected to have a significant influence over the findings of ministerial advisory boards, and these boards often have a crucial role in determining the final outcome of policy. Board or committee findings tend to have the approval of both pressure groups and the civil service, have substantial informational backing, and therefore become quite difficult for anyone to oppose politically. Thus, the vertical integration of many pressure groups into the ministries and the general ability of the ministries to dominate one policy area make the formulation of much public policy in practice—if not officially—the product of negotiation between representatives of pressure groups and the civil service.[97]

A second type of advisory committee tends to be independent of any particular ministry, although it may be working on a problem clearly identified with the concerns of the ministry. Again, we have discussed bodies such as royal commissions, presidential task forces, and the like when discussing pressure group impact on policy.[98] These advisory bodies tend to have substantial bureaucratic input as well, and, if anything, the influence of the bureaucracy has been increasing in recent years.[99] This growing influence has been in part a function of the growing technical expertise of the bureaucracy in a variety of policy areas and in part a recognition of the need to obtain cooperation from the civil service if the program is to be effective once adopted.[100]

It should be obvious that, whoever benefits directly by the use of such advisory bodies, it is not the political actors who will be ultimately held responsible for their actions and policies. These political actors gain in the short run by having a sensitive issue defused, but in the long run the likely effects are to increase bureaucratic influence over the policy. Further, the issues likely to be sent to commissions of this type are the truly sensitive ones that cannot be resolved easily by political actors. Thus, if we are willing to admit that most routine decisions are largely determined administratively, and now we see that many extremely broad and sensitive decisions are increasingly influenced by bureaucracy, the roles of the political institutions are being diminished rather dramatically. They do not have the time or staff to handle most decisions, and they lack the consensus to handle most major decisions, leaving them with the task of setting broad policy guidelines on issues where there is already a certain amount of consensus. This may be an extreme statement, but the evidence to this point in the analysis would seem to support it.

The listing of the various ploys and strategies available to the bureaucracy, and in fact often unwittingly placed in their hands, gives some idea of the way in which their expertise, internal organization, and position in the structures of government can be translated into effective political power. The devices listed above have relied largely on the expertise and information available to the bureaucracy and consequently have assumed the lack of same on the part of the political institutions. In the next section we look at the ways in which the political institutions have sought to counterattack against growing bureaucratic influence on policy.

Politicians' Ploys

Given the imposing list of formal powers that the political institutions have been said to have, it may seem strange that they would need to search out new means of asserting their power and their control over policy and the budget. However, the skills and expertise of the bureaucracy (at least in relative terms) and the largely antiquated structure of many political institutions have made such a search necessary.

Special Budgetary Institutions   One of the first things that the political institutions must seek to recover is some effective control over the public budget. In order to do so, several forms of specialized budgetary institutions have been devised. The most common is something on the order of the Office of Management and Budget (OMB) in the United States.[101] The idea of these bodies is to develop an expert institution responsible directly to the political executive rather than to the bureaucracy. Most budgeting systems require a review of agency requests by other civil servants in a ministry of finance, treasury, or some other similar body, but few provide for an office so directly responsible to a political actor or institution. It is expected that the existence of such a body will allow the executive to be able to have an independent watchdog on expenditures and to have a policy staff directly concerned with expenditures and policy. A vigorous bureaucratic agency such as the British Treasury or the Swedish Ministry of Finance may be able to provide something of the same type of control, but the linkage to the chief political executive may not always be so clear. This lack of linkage will often result in deliberations between civil servants over policy rather than the imposition of executive guidelines.

Unfortunately, little is actually known about the ability of OMB to control expenditures effectively either in the aggregate or in an allocative sense. Such accounts of the ability of the agency to impose presidential goals are that the success is partial, and as is often true, the weakness tends to be rather far down the bureaucratic hierarchy. In this case it is with the individual budget examiners attached to the agency. Their job is to keep a close eye on the spending of the agency and to work with the agency in the preparation of expenditure requests for the coming fiscal year. It is often easy for a budget examiner to become a captive of the agency he is supposed to control.[102] He sees considerably more of the people whose budget he is supposed to watch than he does of those for whom he is ostensibly controlling it and may tend to adopt their view of policy priorities rather than that of the budget bureau. On the other hand, the informal norms concerning careers in OMB have been that it pays to cut budgets, and only those with records of cutting budgets successfully are likely to advance within the organization.

Although OMB may be far from totally successful in imposing its (and the president's) will on the budgetary process, it is at a distinct advantage compared to the task allotted to many chief executives in seeking to control their budgets. As noted, most countries use essentially a bureaucratic agency as a means of performing the budget-examining functions—the Treasury in Britain and the Ministry of Finance in most countries. Despite the norms of these organizations, they remain essentially civil service organizations and as such may not willingly accept the goals of an executive attempting to improve his political future. In addition, many parliamentary political systems tend to be apprehensive about a prime minister attempting to control the budget from his office rather than through the collectivity of the cabinet, so that the internal negotiations over the budget may become so difficult that bureaucratic domination is inevitable. Even in West Germany, where the chancellor is in a stronger position than most parliamentary executives, the chancellor's use of his position to impose priorities in budgeting is not well received, and much of the power devolves to the Ministry of Finance.[103] Thus, although independent executive budgeting agencies may be far from a perfect solution to controlling public expenditure and the powers of the bureaucracy, they are probably a better solution than has been found in many political systems.

Legislatures have also begun to evolve a number of specialized institutions for dealing with the problem of budgeting. The development of the Congressional Budget Office in the U.S. Congress, and its provision of a rather large and well-qualified staff, is one obvious example of a legislature attempting to regain some control over the level of public expenditure.[104] In this case, the conflict is obviously with both the bureaucracy and the presidency. In Britain there have been attempts to revive the Public Accounts Committee as an effective policy as well as financial instrument of Parliament. While these efforts are certainly steps in the proper direction from the point of view of the legislatures, they are as yet unproved, and the general direction is actually more that of giving the legislature less of a role in the budgetary process.

Organizational Differentiation   The formation of committees such as those noted above is a part of a general tendency toward organizational differentiation that is manifesting itself in many political institutions seeking to control public expenditure and public policy. In order to be able to counteract the specialization and differentiation of the bureaucracy, executives and legislatures have adopted some similar organizational tactics. In general, there has been a growth of the organization within the office of the chief executive, even in countries such as Britain where the individual power of the chief executive tends to be restricted by a number of conventions.[105] This tendency has been especially apparent in many single-party states faced with either opposition or a lack of enthusiasm in the bureaucracy. This has forced political leaders to develop their own means of monitoring the implementation of programs or of actually implementing them themselves.

The ability of many public organizations to differentiate is often limited by law, so the institutions will be at a severe disadvantage in attempting to compete with the bureaucracy. For example, in France, the National Assembly is constitutionally limited to six committees, which in turn greatly limits their ability to compete with a highly developed bureaucracy and political executive.

Further, congressional actions have limited the ability of the American president to reorganize his office and expand its staff; again, some limitation of the differentiation, undertaken for political reasons, will have the effect of limited ability to manage effectively.

Counterstaffs   One extremely important means which political leaders can employ in attempting to control the powers of the bureaucracy is the development of their own staffs and sources of information. This enables them to remove the bureaucratic bias in the information received. These independent sources of information may be institutionalized, as in the Executive Office of the President of the United States, or they may be the more casual use of outside consultants.[106] In either case, the stratagem involved is to break the hold that the bureaucracy has on expertise. It also enables the political leader to break the stranglehold that the bureaucracy often has on the initiation of policy.

The use of counterstaffs varies rather markedly across political systems and across policy areas. In the first place, there must be a source of counterinformation, and until recently, this has not existed in policy areas such as atomic energy, space technology, or defense. Also, in most underdeveloped countries, the available scientific and technical ability of the country tends to be concentrated in the public bureaucracy, so there may simply be no other source of internal information. It is also more likely that counterstaffs and information—often by the ton—will be available on highly politicized issues, those that involve well-developed professional organizations, and those in which pressure groups have a direct interest. However, most of these issues are ones on which the average politician is also likely to have information or a strong ideological commitment; consequently, much of this information may be redundant.

A principal reason for the use of counterstaffs is the problem of segmentalization and politicization in the society. In the first place, there may be conflict or, at a minimum, distrust between a minister who belongs to one segmental group in the society, for example, Catholic, francophone, or Ibo, and a civil servant of a competing segmental group. Politics itself may serve to generate segmental conflicts, and frequently political leaders of newer countries cannot trust their civil servants, who are either expatriates or were trained under the colonial regime. Even in more developed political systems, many incoming political leaders feel that they cannot trust the advice of civil servants left over from the previous cabinet. This is especially true for ministers from leftist political parties, who tend to regard the civil service—perhaps properly—as a conservative institution.[107] This is not to say that civil servants would purposefully obstruct or sabotage a program—there is little evidence of that—but rather that perhaps unwittingly their implementation of programs and their granting of proper advice would not be as energetic as it might be.

The second form of politicization that affects the use of existing staffs by political leaders is the level of institutional politicization or the perceived conflict between different political institutions for control of policy in government. For example, in the United States, one of the major reasons for the development of large executive staffs by the president, and for the development of relatively large staffs by Congress, is the perception that these two branches of government are in conflict over the control of the policy-making machinery. In countries with long histories of strong bureaucratic control of policy—or at least perceived bureaucratic control of policy—there will be a similar perception of conflict with the bureaucracy. So, in France, the ministerial *cabinets* constitute a counterstaff attempting to combat the influence of the bureaucracy.[108] On the other hand, a society that is more integrated politically in both segmental and institutional terms—such as Britain—will develop relatively few staff personnel directly accountable to politicians.[109] The norms that the civil service is sufficiently trustworthy and sufficiently devoid of any ideological dispositions allow politicians to accept their advice even after long periods in opposition. While there is little objective evidence of the impartiality of those civil servants, Britain is perhaps less well served in policy terms because of the belief. Although in comparison to most politicians, civil servants are experts, compared to the types of policy staffs developed in other countries, the British may remain "talented amateurs."[110] This results in much policy being determined by "muddling through" or by "directionless consensus."

Control of Staff One principal weapon available to the civil service in any attempt to gain control over policy is its permanence. Politicians may come and go; the bureaucracy remains. This not only presents several long-term strategies to administrators who are not pleased with their current political "master," but it also presents those political masters with some quite difficult problems of controlling their civil servants. Counterstaffs are one solution to this problem, but there may also be solutions within the context of the civil service and personnel policy.

The most obvious means of allowing political control over their civil servants is enabling them to select their own, at least those who will be their immediate subordinates and more importantly, their policy advisers. This can provide some of the advantages of the counterstaff without involving its redundancy and dual lines of authority. Given the limitations of most civil service systems, this means that the choice must come within the confines of the available civil servants, but some systems such as France allow the minister to select among the available personnel for his *directeurs*.[111] The system in the United States is similar in its effect, but the immediate subordinates of political executives are political appointees rather than civil servants. They are therefore not protected by any statutory guarantees of tenure and can be shuffled at will. Thus, in the United States political appointees fill policy-advisory and managerial posts that are filled by senior civil servants in other democratic political systems, allowing considerably more direct political supervision of implementation and more directly partisan policy advice.[112] Even in the United

Kingdom, where the civil service has been independent of political control, the Thatcher government has become more deeply involved in the selection and placement of senior personnel, most importantly Treasury officials.[113]

Most Latin American countries have not fully institutionalized the norms of civil service impartiality or tenure, so any changes in the government may also occasion changes in the civil service.[114] This may occur primarily at the upper echelons of the civil service, so the routine tasks of government continue to be performed much as they always have been, but this system does allow some flexibility for political leaders in seeking advice from civil servants. It is, of course, roundly condemned by advocates of "proper" public personnel procedures and may affect the behavior of bureaucrats who want to remain in office regardless of regime. However, for a political situation in which the policy differences are likely to be great, this sort of flexibility may be a crucial means of managing the senior civil service.

The Party Another powerful option available to some political leaders is the existence of a strong political party or movement that can be used to ensure the compliance and control of the civil service. This mechanism is available most notably in the communist countries and in single-party states in the Third World. In these situations the existence of the party and its associated ideology perform a dual service in controlling policy initiatives by the public bureaucracy. First, the party provides definite ideological and policy guidance, which an astute civil servant can either internalize or at least follow in making and advising on policy. Since the inception of an ideological regime is usually associated with a significant reshuffling of the civil service, most of those placed in positions of authority are likely to have internalized the ideology and program, but even in cases in which the existing civil service continues—often from the lack of any available alternative personnel—the existence of an ideology can provide them some ready guidance in what to propose and implement.

The second means through which the existence of a strong ideological party assists the ability of politicians to reduce bureaucratic initiative and dominance of policy making is that of providing a check on performance and usually a means of correcting unsuitable performance. In such political systems the party tends to be more involved in everyday life than in most democratic political systems, to check more thoroughly on bureaucratic actions, and to be more resentful of bureaucratic domination of policy than even democratic systems. Thus, for example, in the People's Republic of China, the party and ideology serve as a means of guiding and correcting bureaucratic policy, either through direct action or through self-criticism. In the Soviet Union and in Eastern European countries, although it may be difficult at times to distinguish political from administrative personnel, the dual hierarchy of party and bureaucracy serves as a mutual check on policy formulation at each level of government. This does not necessarily mean that policy making in the Soviet Union is any less bureaucratic than elsewhere—to the extent that we mean bureaucratic policies as those divorced from control by market forces or public opinion—

but only that the bureaucracy that does make policy is likely to be more sensitive to political cues than other bureaucracies. They will be generally more willing to comply with the demands of a political elite, and given the presence of an expressed ideology, they may also be more capable of finding what the leaders want to do. Thus, although the policies that ensue may be divorced from direct control by popular opinion, they may paradoxically be more responsive to some political forces than are policies made in democratic systems. The conflict between "Red" and "Expert" may not always be resolved in favor of "Red," but the divergence is rarely as great as occurs in less ideological regimes.

The Military   The military may constitute a special case of party or ideological governments. It is a special case largely because of the greater willingness to employ physical coercion to obtain its ends, among them the submission of the bureaucracy to the demands of politicians—in this case military politicians. As well as an ideology and a set of coordinating principles—or at times instead of them—the military may just have guns. It does not follow, however, that military governments must employ force to gain their ends in dealing with the bureaucracy. In the many cases in which the military and the bureaucracy are primarily conservative forces, they often willingly coalesce against forces of the left.[115] This pattern has been more common in Latin America, while the pattern of the military representing modernizing ideals in opposition to a conservative bureaucracy—frequently inherited from colonial days—has been more common in Africa.

SUMMARY

Have we come to the point where a new elite structure based on information, technical expertise, position, and policy ideas has come to determine who gets what, when, where, and why?

Our answer to this question is ambiguous and would depend in part on whether one thought in terms of an integrated bureaucratic elite producing policies, having common values, and essentially conspiring to remove authority from more responsible political decision-makers; or whether one thought in terms of a number of independent policy elites whose powers were confined to one specific policy area and who were frequently in conflict with other similarly placed elites. If we wish to speak about an integrated bureaucratic power elite— as some rather apprehensively have—running a nation from a computer-equipped ivory tower, then we believe that no such creature actually exists, and Rose's characterization of government emerging by "directionless consensus" may be appropriate. On the other hand, if we wish to talk about a cartel of bureaucratic elites, each responsible for a particular area and functioning with a virtual monopoly over information in that area, then there does seem to be some verisimilitude in the idea of "bureaucratic government." However, as pointed out, this would be government by "nonconsensual directions." One of the characteristics of contemporary government may be its increasing incoherence and the associated lack of true governance.

The conclusion that emerges from this analysis is that the public bureaucracy is in a quite strong position vis-à-vis other potential policy-making institutions. It has the expertise, the time, the stability, and the techniques required to be an effective policy-maker in a modern age. What is required, however, is legitimacy and popular control. The legitimacy can perhaps be gained in part through effectiveness, and if largely bureaucratic processes of decision making are capable of producing results valued by the population, then the institutions are likely to be accepted as appropriate decision-makers. They may lack formal legitimacy, but in terms of having operational legitimacy, they may become the appropriate collective allocators of values.

The question of popular control is perhaps more difficult. This has two possible interpretations. The first is the ability of the public to make its preferences known to the bureaucracy, through some yet unspecified means, and to have the bureaucracy make decisions consistent with those expressed preferences. If we extend the arguments presented in the chapter, then the general public must be seen as being in an even more difficult position in dealing with the bureaucracy than the political elite. The second possible meaning of popular control is the ability of the citizens to obtain redress of grievances for certain administrative actions that violate the rights—economic or civil—of individuals. This is more of an ex post facto control, for which a number of procedural devices have been developed and which have met with a variety of successes and failures. These problems of popular and democratic control will be addressed in chapter 8, where we will concentrate more on the application of broad policies, determined in the manner we have discussed here, to individual cases, and the remedies available when they are applied unfairly. However, before turning to that topic, we will discuss the budgetary process as another example of policy making within bureaucratic structures and perhaps the principal arena in which conflicts between political and bureaucratic elites are resolved.

NOTES

1. See chapter 5.
2. See chapter 2.
3. For an earlier version see B. Guy Peters, "The Problem of Bureaucratic Government," *Journal of Politics* 43 (1981): 56–82.
4. Richard Rose, *The Problem of Party Government* (London: Macmillan, 1974).
5. Joe Haines, *The Politics of Power* (London: Coronet, 1977); Maurice Kogan, *The Politics of Education* (London: Penguin, 1971).
6. Specifically, the "best practice" doctrine for social policies attempts to benefits in all European Community countries upgraded to those available in the most generous country.

7. This has been true of procedures, most notably program budgeting, as well as of substantive policies.

8. Frederick C. Mosher, *Democracy and the Public Service* (New York: Oxford University Press, 1968), pp. 105ff; "Professionals and the Public Service," *Public Administration Review* 38 (1978): 144–50.

9. Ibid.; Samuel H. Beer, "The Adoption of General Revenue Sharing: A Case Study of Public Sector Politics," *Public Policy* 24 (1976): 157–60.

10. Francis C. Rourke, "Bureaucratic Autonomy and the Public Interest," *American Behavioral Scientist* 22 (1979): 537–46.

11. It could well be argued that the initiation of the *grands écoles* and the *grands corps* under Napoleon laid the groundwork for such a system.

12. Theodore R. Marmor, *The Politics of Medicare* (Chicago: Aldine/Atherton, 1973); Henry A. Foley, *Community Mental Health Programs: The Formative Process* (Lexington, Mass.: D. C. Heath, 1975); Martha Derthick, *Policymaking for Social Security* (Washington, D.C.: The Brookings Institution, 1979), pp. 17–37.

13. Daniel Tarschys, *Petita* (Stockholm: Liber, 1975); Hugh Heclo and Aaron Wildavsky, *The Private Government of Public Money* (Berkeley, Calif.: University of California Press, 1974).

14. Alfred Diamant, "Tradition and Innovation in French Administration," *Comparative Political Studies* 1 (1968): 251–74; Ezra N. Suleiman, *Politics, Power and Bureaucracy in France* (Princeton: Princeton University Press, 1974), pp. 160–70.

15. Philip Williams, *Crisis and Compromise: Politics in the Fourth Republic* (New York: Doubleday Anchor, 1965), pp. 365–6; Laurence Scheinemann, *Atomic Energy Policy in the Fourth Republic* (Princeton: Princeton University Press, 1965).

16. See, for example, Merrilee Serrill Grindle, *Bureaucrats, Politicians and Peasants in Mexico* (Berkeley, Calif.: University of California Press, 1977).

17. See chapter 3.

18. Carolyn Ban, Edie Goldenberg, and Tony Marzotto, "Controlling the U.S. Federal Bureaucracy: Will SES Make a Difference?" in Gerald E. Caiden and Heinrich Siedentopf, *Strategies for Administrative Reform* (Lexington, Mass.: D. C. Heath, 1982), pp. 205–220.

19. Joel D. Aberbach, Robert D. Putnam, and Bert A. Rockman, *Bureaucrats and Politicians in Western Democracies* (Cambridge, Mass.: Harvard University Press, 1981).

20. Suleiman, *Politics, Power and Bureaucracy*; Thomas P. Murphy, Donald E. Nuechterlein, and Ronald J. Stupak, *Inside the Bureaucracy: The View from the Assistant Secretary's Desk* (Boulder, Colo.: Westview, 1978); Peter Kellner and Lord Crowther-Hunt, *The Civil Service* (London: Macdonald, 1980).

21. Charles E. Lindblom, *The Policy-Making Process* (Englewood Cliffs, N.J.: Prentice Hall, 1968), pp. 101–8.

22. Graham Allison, *The Essence of Decision* (Boston: Little, Brown, 1971).

23. See B. Guy Peters, "Comparative Public Policy" in Dan Jacobs, David Conradt, William Safran, and B. Guy Peters, *Comparative Politics: An Introduction* (Chatham, N.J.: Chatham House, 1983).

24. This tension is reflected in the "garbage can" model of decision making in which means seek ends, rather than vice versa. See Michael D. Cohen, James G. March, and Johan P. Olsen, "The Garbage Can Model of Organizational Choice," *Administrative Science Quarterly* 17 (1972): 1–25.
25. See chapter 8.
26. Breton speaks of this as moving the competition from a public to a private arena. Albert Breton, *The Economic Theory of Representative Government* (Chicago: Aldine, 1974), pp. 162–3.
27. Niskanen argues that such competition should be expanded to provide a quasi-market for services and (presumably) improve the performance of public bureaucracies. William A. Niskanen, "Competition among Government Agencies," *American Behavioral Scientist* 22 (1979): 517–24.
28. Robert E. Goodin, "The Logic of Bureaucratic Backscratching," *Public Choice* 24 (1975): 53–68.
29. Matthew Holden, "Imperialism and Bureaucracy," *American Political Science Review* 60 (1966): 943–51.
30. Downs, *Inside Bureaucracy*, pp. 198–9.
31. Kaufman argued that few do die. Herbert Kaufman, *Are Government Organizations Immortal?* (Washington, D.C.: The Brookings Institution, 1976). But see Brian W. Hogwood and B. Guy Peters, *Policy Dynamics* (New York: St. Martin's, 1983), table 4.1.
32. Tarschys, *Petita;* Harold Seidman, *Politics, Power and Position,* 3rd ed. (New York: Oxford University Press, 1980). This may be true even in more centralized political systems. See J. J. Richardson and A. G. Jordan, *Governing Under Pressure* (London: Martin Robertson, 1979), pp. 53–9.
33. Richard Rose and B. Guy Peters, *Can Government Go Bankrupt?* (New York: Basic Books, 1978).
34. Daniel Bell, "The Public Household: On 'Fiscal Sociology' and the Liberal Society," *The Public Interest* 37 (1974): 29–68.
35. Downs, *Inside Bureaucracy*, pp. 211–16.
36. Morris Fiorina, *Congress: Keystone of the Washington Establishment* (New Haven: Yale University Press, 1978); Douglas Arnold, *Congress and the Bureaucracy* (New Haven: Yale University Press, 1979).
37. Advisory Commission on Intergovernmental Relations, *The Federal Role in the Federal System: The Growth of Government in the United States* (Washington, D.C.: ACIR, 1980).
38. Hugh Heclo, "Issue Networks and the Executive Establishment," in Anthony King, ed., *The New American Political System* (Washington, D.C.: American Enterprise Institute, 1978), pp. 87–124.
39. Peter B. Natchez and Irving C. Bupp, "Policy and Priority in the Budgetary Process," *American Political Science Review* 67 (1973): 963.
40. Victor Thompson, *Modern Organizations* (New York: Knopf, 1961).
41. Gordon Tullock, *The Politics of Bureaucracy* (Washington, D.C.: Public Affairs Press, 1965), 137–141.
42. Thomas E. Cronin, "The Swelling of the Presidency," *Saturday Review of Society* 20 (January 1973): 30–36; Allen Schick, "The Battle of the Budget," in Henry C. Mansfield, Jr., *Congress Against the President* (New York: Praeger, 1975), 64–69; Michael J. Malbin and M. A. Scalley, "Our Unelected Representatives," *The Public Interest* 47 (Spring 1977): 16–48.

43. Suleiman, *Politics, Power and Bureaucracy*, pp. 201–238; Hugo Van Hassel, "Belgian Ministerial Cabinets," *Res Publica* 15 (1973): 357–369; "Belgian Civil Servants and Political Decision Making," in Dogan, *The Mandarins*, pp. 187–195; Heclo and Wildavsky, *The Private Government*, pp. 304–339.

44. See the speech by Shadow Industry Minister John Silkin, *The Guardian*, 5 December 1979.

45. See pp. 10–12.

46. Thomas E. Cronin, "Everybody Believes in Democracy Until He Gets to the White House," *Law and Contemporary Problems* 35 (1970): 573–625.

47. Richard Rose, *The Problem of Party Government;* Bruce Headey, *British Cabinet Ministers* (London: Allen and Unwin, 1975); B. Chenot, *Être Ministère* (Paris: Plon, 1967); Hugh Heclo, *A Government of Strangers*.

48. See, for example, Herbert Kaufman, *Red Tape* (Washington, D.C.: The Brookings Institution, 1977).

49. Michel Crozier, *The Bureaucratic Phenomenon* (Chicago: University of Chicago Press, 1964), pp. 213–20.

50. William Spangar Pierce, *Bureaucratic Failure and Public Expenditure* (New York: Academic Press, 1981), pp. 33–7.

51. Crozier, *The Bureaucratic Phenomenon*, pp. 210–64; *On ne change pas la societé par décret* (Paris: Grasset, 1979).

52. Crozier, *The Bureaucratic Phenomenon*, pp. 213–227.

53. Murray Weidenbaum, *Business, Government and the Public* (Englewood Cliffs, N.J.: Prentice-Hall, 1983).

54. See Johan P. Olsen, *Organized Democracy* (Bergen: Universitetsforlaget, 1983), 148–187.

55. Jeffrey L. Pressman and Aaron Wildavsky, *Implementation* (Berkeley: University of California Press, 1973). But see Elinor R. Bowen, "The Pressman-Wildavsky Paradox," *Journal of Public Policy* 2 (1982): 1–21.

56. See Dietrich Garlichs and Chris Hull, "Central Control and Information Dependence: Highway Planning in the Federal Republic of Germany," in Kenneth Hanf and Fritz W. Scharpf, *Interorganizational Policy Making* (London: Sage, 1978), pp. 143–66.

57. Chris Hood, *The Limits of Administration* (New York: Wiley, 1976).

58. Herbert Kaufman, *The Forest Ranger* (Baltimore: Johns Hopkins University Press, 1960), pp. 75–80.

59. Pressman and Wildavsky, *Implementation;* Garlichs and Hull, "Central Control"; Nevil Johnson, *Federalism and Decentralization in the Federal Republic of Germany* (London: HMSO, 1973).

60. Jean Pierre Worms, "Le Préfet et ses notablés," *Sociologie du Travail* 3 (1966): 149–75.

61. *Implementation*, pp. 166ff.

62. See Basil Chubb, "Going Around Persecuting Bureaucrats: The Role of the Irish Parliamentary Representative," *Political Studies* 11 (1963): 272–86; Allan Kornberg and William Mishler, *Influence in Parliament: Canada* (Durham, N.C.: Duke University Press, 1976), pp. 191ff.

63. Merilee Serrill Grindle, *Bureaucrats, Politicians and Peasants in Mexico* (Berkeley: University of California Press, 1977); Edward J. Schumacher, *Politics, Bureaucracy and Rural Development in Senegal* (Berkeley: University of California Press, 1975).

64. Theodore J. Lowi, "The Public Philosophy: Interest Group Liberalism," *American Political Science Review* 61 (1967): 5–24.
65. Hood, *The Limits of Administration.*
66. Leslie Chapman, *Your Disobedient Servant* (Harmondsworth, England: Penguin, 1978).
67. Dudley Sears, "The Structure of Power," in Hugh Thomas, ed., *Crisis in the Civil Service* (London: Anthony Blond, 1968).
68. See the work in Hanf and Scharpf, *Interorganizational Policy Making.*
69. As a parody on practice in the Soviet Union, these officials are referred to as *politruker.* See Neil Elder, "The Functions of the Modern State," in Jack Hayward and R. N. Berki, *State and Society in Contemporary Europe* (New York: St. Martin's, 1979), p. 66.
70. Renate Mayntz and Fritz W. Scharpf, *Policy-Making in the German Federal Bureaucracy* (Amsterdam: Elsevier, 1975), pp. 63–78; George Otte, "The Political Role of the German Municipal Bureaucracy" (paper presented at 1979 Annual Meeting of the American Political Science Association, Washington, D.C., September 1979).
71. Anthony King, "Overloaded Governments," *Political Studies* 23 (June/September 1975): 284–296; Todd LaPorte, *Organized Social Complexity* (Princeton: Princeton University Press, 1975); Fritz W. Scharpf, "Public Organization and the Waning of the Welfare State," *European Journal of Political Research* 5 (December 1977): 339–362; Erwin Scheuch, *Wird die Bundesrepublik Unregeirbar?* (Köln: Arbeitgeberverband der Metallindustrie, 1976).
72. See B. Guy Peters, "The Relationship Between Civil Servants and Political Executives: A Preliminary Comparative Examination" (Paper presented to the American Political Science Association Annual Meeting, September 1981).
73. See Guy Benvieniste, *The Politics of Expertise* (London: Croom Helm, 1973), pp. 123–26.
74. Randall Bartlett, *The Economic Foundations of Political Power* (New York: Free Press, 1973), pp. 63–64, 70–75.
75. Alvin W. Gouldner, "Metaphysical Pathos and the Theory of Bureaucracy," *American Political Science Review* 49 (1955): 496–507.
76. James O. Freedman, *Crisis and Legitimacy: The Administrative Process and Government* (New York: Cambridge University Press, 1981).
77. See chapter 5.
78. This relationship between interest group agency and committee has been referred to as the "iron triangle" in American policy making. It is especially important to note in this case that the committees are hardly impartial but tend to represent constituencies vitally concerned with the policy area. See Charles O. Jones, "The Role of the Congressional Subcommittee," *Midwest Journal of Political Science* 6 (1962): 327–44.
79. See Wilensky, *Organizational Intelligence,* pp. 24–34.
80. See James L. Sundquist, "Coordinating the War on Poverty," *Annals of the American Academy of Political and Social Sciences* 385 (1969): 41–49; Hugh Heclo, "The Frontiers of Social Policy," *Policy Studies.*
81. See chapter 3.
82. See Marilyn Gittel, *Limits of Citizen Participation: The Decline of Community Organizations* (Beverly Hills, Calif.: Sage, 1980).

83. Some idea of the breadth of modern planning is given in Jack Hayward and Michael Watson, eds., *Planning, Politics and Public Policy: The British, French and Italian Experience* (London: Cambridge University Press, 1975).

84. J. G. Abert, *Economic Policy and Planning in the Netherlands 1950–1965* (New Haven: Yale University Press, 1969), p. 39.

85. Even in the economy, planning can be a means of obscuring the relationship between political choice and economic outcomes. In areas such as transportation or social policy the relationship is quite obscured.

86. John Higley, Karl Erik Brofoss, and Knut Groholt, "Top Civil Servants and the National Budget in Norway," in Mattei Dogan, ed., *The Mandarins of Western Europe* (New York: Halsted, 1975), pp. 252–74.

87. In practice this is not so undemocratic as it may appear because the process of consultation going into the preparation of the plan requires that everyone's views are known and, to some degree, taken into account in the final shape of the plan.

88. Andrew Shonfield, *Modern Capitalism* (London: Oxford University Press, 1965), p. 235.

89. See Michael Watson, "Planning in the Liberal-Democratic State," in Hayward and Watson, *Planning, Politics and Public Policy*, pp. 464–77.

90. Heclo and Wildavsky, *Public Money*, p. 293; Bravo, "La R.C.B.," pp. 339–42.

91. Rudolf Klein, "The Politics of PPBS," *Political Quarterly* 43 (1972): 280–81.

92. Karl Heinrich Friauf, "Parliamentary Control of the Budget in the Federal Republic of Germany," in Coombes, *Power of the Purse*, pp. 74–77; Frieder Naschold, "Probleme der mehrjahrigen Finanzplannung des Bundes," in *Praxis*, V. Ronge and G. Schmieg, eds. (Munchen: Piper, 1971).

93. Higley, Brofoss, and Groholt, "Top Civil Servants."

94. Ibid., pp. 266–67.

95. Higley, Brofoss, and Groholt, "Top Civil Servants," pp. 262–3; Johan P. Olsen, *Organized Democracy* (Bergen: Universitetsforlaget, 1983).

96. Yves Weber, *L'Administration consultative* (Paris: Librarie General du Droit et Jurisprudence, 1968), p. 3.

97. See chapter 5.

98. Francis Toye, "Don't Take Decisions: Appoint an Inquiry," *The Sunday Times*, 10 April 1983.

99. See, for example, H. Meijer, "Bureaucracy and Policy Formation in Sweden," *Scandinavian Political Studies* 4 (1969): 103–16.

100. See Renate Mayntz and Fritz W. Scharpf, *Policy-Making in the German Federal Bureaucracy* (Amsterdam: Elsevier, 1975), pp. 92–93; Barbara Castle, "Mandarin Power," *Sunday Times*, 10 June 1973.

101. Thomas E. Cronin, *The State of the Presidency* (Boston: Little, Brown, 1975), pp. 129–30.

102. For a similar finding in a different context see Caiden and Wildavsky, *Planning and Budgeting*, p. 110; Wildavsky, *Politics of the Budgetary Process*, p. 39. See also Heclo and Wildavsky, *Public Money*, pp. 118–28. See also James W. Davis and Randall B. Ripley, "The Bureau of the Budget and Executive Branch Agencies: A Note on Their Interaction," *Journal of Politics* 29 (1967): 749–69.

103. Mayntz and Scharpf, *Policy-Making in Germany*, pp. 38–45. A good summary is provided in Malcolm E. Jewell and Samuel C. Patterson, *The Legislative Process in the United States* (2nd ed.; New York: Random House, 1973), pp. 249–77.
104. Allen Schick, *Congress and Money* (Washington, D.C.: The Urban Institute, 1980), pp. 131–165.
105. John W. Ellwood and James A. Thurber, "The Politics of the Congressional Budgetary Process Re-examined," in Lawrence C. Dodd and Bruce I. Oppenheimer, eds., *Congress Reconsidered* (Washington, D.C.: Congressional Quarterly Press, 1981), pp. 246–71; Allen Schick, *Congress and Money* (Washington, D.C.: Urban Institute, 1980).
106. See Thomas E. Cronin, "The Swelling of the Presidency," *Saturday Review of Society* 1 (February 1973): 30–36; Norman C. Thomas and Hans W. Baade, eds., *The Institutionalized Presidency* (Dobbs Ferry, N.Y.: Oceana Publications, 1972). In contrast see Peter Hennessey, "The Cabinet Office," *Times* (London), 8 March 1976.
107. James Petras, *Politics and Social Forces in Chilean Development* (Berkeley: University of California Press, 1969).
108. Sisson refers to the *Cabinet* as the political "dynamite" for the ministers within the administration. C. H. Sisson, *The Spirit of British Administration and Some European Comparisons* (London: Faber & Faber, 1959), p. 10.
109. Headey, *British Cabinet Ministers*, pp. 110–31; S. Brittan, "The Irregulars," *Crossbow* (October-December 1966).
110. A good discussion is provided in R. G. S. Brown, *The Administrative Process in Britain* (London: Methuen, 1971), pp. 38–63.
111. Ezra N. Suleiman, *Politics, Power and Bureaucracy in France* (Princeton: Princeton University Press, 1974), pp. 137–54. This choice may be circumscribed, but it is still there.
112. See Richard Neustadt, "White House and Whitehall," *Public Interest* 2 (1966): 55–69.
113. Peter Hennessey, "Unusual Ascent to Top Treasury Job," *The Times*, 5 April 1983.
114. F. Tannenbaum, "Politica y administracion publica en Latino-America," *Foro Internacional* 4 (1963): 243–59; J. C. Rey, "Burocracia y politica," *Revista de la Facultad de Derecho* (Caracas) 29 (1964): 83–100. The Sexenio in Mexico has many top bureaucrats leaving office at the same time, as presidents change every six years. Grindle, *Bureaucrats, Politicians and Peasants*.
115. Henry Bienen, "Public Order and the Military in Africa," in his *The Military Intervenes: Case Studies in Political Development* (New York: Russell Sage, 1968), pp. 35–69. In many cases the civil service and the officer corps are recruited from the same middle-class stratum and tend to represent the conservative values of that stratum.

CHAPTER 7

PAYING FOR GOVERNMENT: THE BUDGETARY PROCESS

Perhaps the most central political process affecting the public bureaucracy is the budgetary process. Clearly, if an administrative agency is to accomplish any or all of its mandated tasks it will require an adequate supply of money. And, in addition to the instrumental need for money, there is a more affective reason for desiring budgetary success. Money is one means for bureaucratic agencies to demonstrate their political "clout" and their importance to the remainder of the political system. On the other side of the green baize table, the budgetary process may be the arena in which political officials can demonstrate their power and their concern for the average taxpayer by limiting the amount of money allocated to the public sector, and especially to the less popular programs of government. With the increasing pressures on government both to provide services and to contain or reduce its costs, the budgetary process has become a crucial battleground determining not only the prospects of any single government agency, but also the prospects of many citizens for a high quality of life and for the success of the entire economy.

BASIC QUESTIONS

When the process of budgeting is considered cross-nationally, there are several basic questions that should be addressed. These questions arise in any political system, but the manner in which they are answered, or indeed can be answered, will vary according to a number of political, social, and economic characteristics of individual nations. Also, since each country in the world is facing many of the same budgetary constraints, the world can serve as a useful laboratory for understanding the possibilities of controlling public expenditure through innovative mechanisms and procedures.

Macro-allocation

Inherent in the process of budgeting is the problem of the allocation of resources, and the first form of allocation that must be considered is the allocation between the public and private sectors of the economy. Government must decide just how much it is willing—and able—to tax its citizens in order to provide benefits through public expenditure. In industrialized societies these decisions produce public sectors that range from 51 percent of Gross National Product (Sweden) to 24 percent of GNP (Japan).[1] Despite the importance of this decision for the economic management and the general nature of public programs in a country, there are several factors that limit the ability of governments to make definitive decisions about the "size" of government, and that must therefore be analyzed when attempting to understand how governments decide to spend money.

The first problem for a government attempting to control its public sector is that many forms of public expenditure are not as easy to control as is assumed by many critics of government expenditure. As of 1981, 76.4 percent of public expenditure at the federal level in the United States has been considered "uncontrollable" in any one budget year.[2] The programs that comprise this sum of $500 billion are entitlement programs, such as social security, unemployment compensation, and Medicare, which depend as much upon demographics and economic conditions to determine levels of expenditure as they do upon explicit political decisions. The majority of other industrialized countries would have even higher proportions of uncontrollable expenditures than the United States, given their larger-scale social programs and smaller defense budgets (an estimate for the United Kingdom would be 81 percent of the budget, while for Sweden it would be 84 percent).

Just as the numerator may not be controllable, so too the denominator is not readily controllable. Governments have taken upon themselves the control of the economy as a crucial function since at least the end of World War II, but, despite the successes in the 1950s and 1960s, governments do not now appear capable of producing the sustained economic growth they would desire. The best-made budgetary allocations and calculations can be overturned by fluctuations in the economy. Governments invest a good deal of time and effort in forecasting the future state of their economies but often fail miserably. This failure results in part from the time span over which the estimate must be made—sometimes the budgetary process is initiated eighteen months prior to the implementation of the budget—and results also from the still-inadequate knowledge of economic dynamics in industrialized economies.[3] Also, governments themselves have an interest in presenting overly optimistic forecasts to their citizens. Even in socialist economies, where control is assumed to exist over the major elements of the economy, there are still difficulties in forecasting the state of the economy for more than a few months in advance.[4]

Another factor limiting the efficiency of macro-allocations is the simple fact that there is almost invariably more than one level of government involved in deciding how much the public sector will spend. This is especially true of federal political systems in which subnational governments have a substantial degree of fiscal autonomy. State governments in the United States, for example, make their revenue and expenditure decisions almost entirely independently from the federal government, with the major impact of federal expenditure priorities caused by the stimulative effects of some matching grants.[5] Several central governments in federal systems have found this degree of fiscal autonomy unacceptable and have developed mechanisms to better coordinate spending at all levels of government (see page 230).

Finally, for the majority of actors involved in the budgetary process, the ratio of public expenditure to available economic resources is not the primary consideration in their budgetary behavior. For spending agencies, be they managing "uncontrollable" programs or not, the primary consideration is what they can extract from the central pool of resources.[6] In behavioral terms, this will mean that the spending agencies will tend to coalesce to oppose attempts at controlling expenditures by finance ministers and/or the principal executive. If their collective success in extracting resources means that the ratio of expenditures to GNP would increase, that becomes someone else's problem, and it is always the other agency's program that should be reduced or terminated.

Micro-allocation

The last point concerning macro-allocation brings us to the stage of budgetary process in which decisions must be made among the huge number of competing programs in government, each one considering itself especially worthy and each one competing with all other programs for limited funding. The separation of these decisions from the macro-allocative decisions may be artificial, since the constraints imposed upon the funding of any particular agency are at least in part a function of the desire of those controlling the economic management functions of government to bring the total budget in at a particular total. When that level of expenditure is low, compared to previous levels of expenditure and levels of inflation, then those programs with the fewest uncontrollables will be the targets for disproportionate cuts.

It is at the level of micro-allocation that most of the politics of budgeting occurs. It is at this level that the priorities of individual political leaders interact to produce an allocation of resources within government. Despite the enormity of the task of assembling the public budget in any modern society, there is a tendency to regard budgeting as a rational process that produces an allocation of resources to match the policy preferences of the public, or at least those of their elective officials.[7] But there are a number of barriers preventing the process from reaching such an optimal allocation.

One of the principal factors affecting the rationality of the allocation is the disaggregation of the budgetary process into isolated segments. Frequently separate committees or sections of budgetary review organizations perform the major analyses and make the major decisions about budget. For example, in the United States the most important decisions about the budget in Congress are made in subcommittees of the appropriations committees, and each of these subcommittees tends to have its own perception of national priorities. In Canada, the "envelope" system of budgeting (see pages 227–228) places considerable power in the priorities committees whose decisions tend to dominate the final determination of expenditures. Similarly, in Sweden, with the allocation of resources among the boards (*styrelsen*) under a ministry, there is a process that allocates predetermined blocks of expenditures rather than attempting to compare the marginal value of expenditure across a range of functions. It is only in a cabinet setting, where the entire budget is (at least in theory) open to determination, that any real detailed considerations of competing priorities can be made. And even in those settings the outcome may be determined by the deliberations of staffs, or by the personality of a few dominant members of the cabinet, so that the confrontation of all the alternative utilizations of public expenditures will not occur.

A second crucial factor affecting the range of consideration of budgetary alternatives is the status quo. The sheer magnitude of the budget in a modern government makes it difficult for a legislature—or for an expert budgetary analysis organization such as the Office of Management and Budget, the Treasury Board Secretariat, or a ministry of finance—to make any extensive analysis of the possible patterns of expenditures. As a consequence, there is a tendency to accept the previous year's allocation as a given and to examine primarily marginal changes in that allocation. This incremental result is, in fact, explicitly written into the French budgetary process, where items in the *services votés* are accepted unless there is an explicit challenge and only new items (*measures nouvelles*) are given detailed scrutiny.[8] There is also a tendency to regard not only the existing distribution of expenditures as acceptable, but also the rate at which the budget has been increasing. Evidence exists that agencies tend to retain the same rates of increase in their budgetary allocations from year to year. This rate of increase would not be the same across agencies—in some instances there might be significant differences—but for each agency there is an accepted rate of increase on top of the accepted base, which allows the budget to increase from year to year. Many of the innovations in the budgetary process (see pages

220–226) have been advanced for the explicit purpose of rectifying this incrementalism in budgeting.

Competing Bureaucracies

The above discussion of the processes of allocating spending authority has already indicated another of the important features of the budgetary process. This is that—more than in any other area of the policy process—budgeting forces a conflict between central staff agencies and line agencies.[9] These central agencies, such as the Office of Management and Budget in the United States, H. M. Treasury in the United Kingdom, or the ministry of finance in a number of other countries, have the task of preparing the budget and, in the process, develop a proprietary interest in protecting the public purse. But these agencies, despite their centrality and close relationship with the chief executive, are in the position of being "ganged up" against by the spending agencies.[10] This is especially true in cabinet government, where the spending ministers and the financial ministers must sit together in the same political body making budgetary decisions, and the financial minister may be supported only by the prime minister, if that.

In the political conflict between competing bureaucracies over the budget, each side has several important weapons at its disposal. The central agencies have the advantage of being closely connected to the chief executive. This association with political authority makes it more difficult for the spending agencies to oppose the decisions that may be made; in fact, the central agencies may be able to make some decisions by fiat. In addition, financial agencies in the center tend to be expert and are able to expend their full energies on budgetary matters. The spending agencies have other assignments, and although the budget is significant, it is but one of many important tasks.

On the other hand, the spending agencies have a political advantage in that they provide services directly to citizens and consequently have constituencies that would support them in the quest for more money. Also, the constituencies of the agencies are constituents of elective officials and, as a consequence, can make political appeals over the head of the central financial agencies, and perhaps even the chief executive. Finally, the administrative agencies control information and are capable of deceiving the central budgeters as to the true cost of producing certain services.[11] Central agencies may have to trade money for information, so that they can attempt to manage the national economy.[12] Thus, in this instance, the macro-management role may interfere with the micro-management role.

The relative success of the two sets of bureaucracies will depend upon situational factors as well as their own relative powers in the political process. One obvious factor is economics. Times of economic insecurity will obviously advantage the central financial managers, especially when they are backed by external agents such as the International Monetary Fund or foreign banks threatening to call in loans. On the other hand, the perception of specific needs for expenditures, for example, a perceived need to increase defense spending, will tend to favor the spending agency in question. Few spending ministers would be willing to sacrifice their own expenditures in order to finance another minister's expansion, and consequently the entire level of spending may increase. Finally, the introduction of any of a number of innovations in budgeting may provide financial agencies with a variety of weapons—one of them being the complexity and obscurity of the method itself—that can be used to exercise control of spending ministries. The power of these instruments may, however, be overstated frequently, and technique is a complement to politics, not a substitute for it.[13]

The Importance of Resources

One of the most important factors affecting the style of budgeting exercised by a country is the economic climate within which the budget is constructed. Wildavsky argued that two economic factors are crucial in determining the style of budgeting: wealth and predictability.[14] Wealth is self-explanatory, but the concept of predictability may require some explanation. We have already discussed the difficulties that even wealthy, industrialized countries have in predicting their revenues and expenditures. These difficulties are even greater for Third World countries whose economies are subject to huge fluctuations resulting from weather, changes in the international economy, and internal political and economic changes. The chief executive of an industrialized country may be upset when forecasts of revenues and expenditures are 5 or 10 percent inaccurate. The leaders of many Third World countries would be gleeful over such a level of accuracy. Without some degree of predictability about the major components of the budget, decision-makers are only guessing what they will receive as revenues and what they will spend, and must develop methods for compensating for that uncertainty.

Affluent nations with certain revenues and expenditures will tend to have incremental budgeting. This is indicative of a stable political process where government can fund its commitments with a minimal necessity of making difficult choices among competing expenditure priorities. At the other end of the budgetary spectrum, poor countries with uncertain revenues will engage in repetitive budgeting and will, of necessity, construct a succession of budgets during a fiscal year in order to adjust to changing conditions. Political systems that are relatively poor but that can predict their revenues accurately for a year will engage in "revenue budgeting." They will spend what they can collect—no more and no less—but lack the type of predictable, incremental patterns of change that would characterize more affluent political systems. Finally, wealthy but uncertain budgetary systems alternate between incremental and repetitive budgeting as a reflection of political instability, or their administrative incapacities will lead them to supplemental budgeting. In this latter form of budgeting, the basic budget document will remain in force, but supplements will be added throughout the fiscal year as the revenue and expenditure figures become clarified.

When Wildavsky originally presented this argument, it was assumed that industrialized countries, such as the United States and the United Kingdom, would have incremental budgetary processes. However, within one year of the publication of the book, economic conditions had forced the United Kingdom to issue three budgets in a single year, thus following the pattern of a poor and uncertain country.[15] The United States has also begun to engage in either repetitive or supplemental budgeting to an extent unheard of prior to the economic difficulties that began in the mid-1970s.

INCREMENTALISM IN THE BUDGETARY PROCESS

The Wildavsky typology hypothesizes that incrementalism is peculiar to the budgetary environment of relatively few affluent countries. But despite the special conditions in which incrementalism is argued to arise, it has become something of a prevailing description of the budgetary process for all countries. Even in countries clearly beyond the range of incrementalist nations in the Wildavsky typology, there are pressures for incrementalism in the preparation of budgets that may override the relative poverty or unpredictability of a particular budgetary environment. The process of budgeting itself appears to push toward incrementalist outcomes, even in an economic environment that would appear to call for "rational decrementalism."[16] This section will discuss some of the pressures toward incrementalism in budgeting, to be followed by a section discussing the variety of mechanisms by which political systems attempt to manage those pressures, with the goal of outcomes more objectively suited to changing social and economic conditions.

The Nature of Incrementalism

Incrementalism is both a descriptive and a prescriptive concept. Descriptively, it refers to observed patterns of change in budgets and other outcomes of the policy process in which those outputs increase in a stable and predictable fashion. For example, in a major empirical work on incrementalism, Davis, Dempster, and Wildavsky have analyzed changes in the appropriations of a number of agencies at the federal level in the United States.[17] They found that the majority of changes in appropriations can be described as a simple linear function of the preceding year's expenditures. There is a pronounced tendency in the data examined by these three scholars for Congress to appropriate the same percentage increases for an agency across time. Although there were significant differences in the percentage increases provided to different agencies, in each individual agency the increases tended to be stable. In short, this legislative body (as well as many others that have been studied) tends to allocate money on the basis of simple and stable decision rules.

Prescriptively, this stability and predictability in decisions is regarded positively by incrementalists. It makes planning simpler for the agencies and reduces the decision-making load on the legislative body. More importantly, it is argued that a more comprehensive (synoptic) approach to decision making would not of necessity produce better decisions, because of the absence of information about the future and about the social and economic processes being addressed through the budget.[18] In addition, major departures from the status quo may be irreversible without extreme expense. Therefore, the incrementalists would argue, the most rational approach to budgeting of other types of decision making is to make relatively minor departures from the status quo, monitor the effects of those new policies, and then adjust the policies in future decision making.

Critiques of Incrementalism

The critiques of incrementalism have also been directed at its descriptive and prescriptive features. The degree of incrementalism found in budgets appears to be a function of the level of aggregation at which the researcher looks: The larger the program or organization, the more incremental the outcomes will appear. There is a great deal of variation in the levels of program appropriations, as some are initiated and others are terminated.[19] Critics also point out that the incrementalist approach may be quite adequate to explain or describe changes in the majority of programs for the majority of years but provides no mechanism for explaining changes in the percentage increases that may be allowed an agency across time, or for explaining the differences in the percentage increases allotted each year to different agencies.

Prescriptively, it has been argued that the incrementalist approach to decision making tends to institutionalize the status quo and to curtail more creative thinking about the possible uses of scarce resources. This is especially true during a period in which "decrementalism" is more appropriate than incrementalism. Thus, the argument is that there is a need for a more comprehensively rational approach to the problems of allocating resources in government. In addition, critics point out that incremental decisions are not necessarily reversible, as a program expansion may well add clients who will expect to continue to receive benefits.[20] In fact, the more often incremental adjustments are made in a program, the more probable it is that the program will continue, as each small change may constitute a vote of confidence in the fundamental validity of the program.

Pressures toward Incrementalism

Two fundamental factors in the budgetary process tend to work in favor of incremental outcomes. The first is the sheer magnitude of the process itself. The typical public budget in industrialized countries involves making decisions that allocate almost one-half of the total goods and services in the economy. In the United States, where the federal budget accounts for "only" about 22 percent of the Gross National Product, this still involves the allocation of $725 billion among hundreds of programs. In addition, the decisions to spend all of this money must be made in a relatively short time period under substantial political pressure. Consequently, there is a tendency to accept the existing distribution of expenditures as a given, and therefore to concentrate time and attention on the relatively few deviations from existing patterns. The French budgetary process institutionalizes this distinction with *measures nouvelles* receiving extensive scrutiny, while *services votés* receive almost none. The budgetary process at the federal level in the United States, through its use of the Current Services Budget, also contains something of this distinction. Thus, as there is not the time and the analytic staff to completely rework the budget each year, legislators tend to accept the existing budget and to employ very simple rules of thumb when making deviations from that pattern, for example, the stability of the constant percentage changes.

The second feature of the budgetary process that helps to produce incremental solutions is the sequential and repetitive nature of budgeting. A new budget must be created each year, or even more often. Consequently, both administrators and legislators involved in the process tend to assume that errors made in one year can be corrected in subsequent years. Further, the actors involved in making the budget—bureaucrats, legislators, and analysts—tend to retain their positions for long periods. This is especially true where, unlike the United States, a change in government involves very few changes in those responsible for constructing the budget, or where a central agency with a permanent and expert staff tends to dominate the budgetary process, for example, the Treasury in the United Kingdom.[21] The long tenure in office of the principal actors in budgeting results in their having the opportunity to develop an accommodation among themselves and to shape the budget in the manner they find acceptable. Therefore, all they must do on an annual basis is to make marginal adjustments from the accepted pattern. Further, those wishing to make any significant departures from existing patterns have several strong incentives to adopt cautious strategies. They should be aware that they are involved in a long-term "game" and that slow adjustments are far more probable than sudden shifts in budgetary priorities. Further, all actors must play the "confidence game," and gain the trust and respect of others involved in the budgetary process to be effective in getting what they want.[22] This cautious and conservative behavior in budgeting produces considerable frustration for those who come into political office with new ideas and priorities, expecting to generate change overnight.

ALTERNATIVES TO INCREMENTALISM

The wealthy, predictable world so conducive to the development of incremental budgeting no longer exists in the majority of industrialized countries—and never existed for most other countries.[23] In response to the fiscal pressures faced by virtually all political systems in the 1970s and 1980s, a number of mechanisms have been devised to break the grip exerted by incremental solutions over resource allocation in government. These solutions demonstrate the creativity of politicians and civil servants when faced with genuine problems but have had varying degrees of success. Apparently none has, however, altered the fundamental pattern of slow, evolutionary change in budgets typical of incrementalism.

But it is not just the "fiscal crisis" that has produced the interest in alternative budgeting mechanisms. Even during periods of affluence, several more "rational" approaches to budgeting have been advocated, primarily because of their appeal to human rationality and their potential to break the cycle of incrementalism. The simple and apparently irrational decision rules involved in incrementalism have been an affront to those who believe that there must be better ways of making decisions in government. And even when resources are plentiful, there is no need to use them in a profligate manner. Government should, it is argued, get the most "bang for the buck" (or *frappe* for the franc) and should allocate resources so that a Pigovian optimum is obtained.[24] That is, the budget should be adjusted so that the marginal utility of the last dollar spent for each of the numerous functions of government is equal. Of course, in the real world such an optimal allocation of resources would almost certainly be unknowable and unattainable, but it is argued that we should still attempt to reach such a "perfect" allocation.

The following discussion will present budgetary mechanisms developed for the general problem of more efficient allocation, as well as those developed as specific responses to contemporary fiscal problems. In some instances this separation is artificial, but it may be useful in understanding how governments have attempted to respond to the most basic problems in governance: deciding how to decide what is important.

First discussed will be some of the more general methods advanced for the enhancement of rationality in budgeting. These have been popularized principally in the United States but have been exported to other countries.

Several have been developed outside the United States as responses to particular problems of a country and particular problems of governance in that country.

Program Budgeting

The most familiar of these approaches to budgeting is program budgeting, or PPBS (Planning, Programming, Budgeting System), as it was practiced in the United States. Although commonly associated with the Defense Department under Robert McNamara, PPBS actually came to Washington during World War II and was introduced into several domestic agencies, most notably the Department of Agriculture.[25] This approach to budgeting has been exported to several countries. For example, program budgeting has been one of several stages of budgetary reform in Canada, and France developed a system of program budgeting entitled *rationalization des choix budgetaires* (RCB).[26] Also, the United Nations adopted the concept of program budgeting for Third World countries, and for a period of time some of the countries of the world least capable of meeting the data and analytic requirements of PPBS were required to meet those standards in order to receive development aid from the United Nations.

Program budgeting is based most fundamentally upon a systems concept of government. In contrast to the usual organizational or programmatic basis of budgeting, program budgeting assumes that organizations are not sacrosanct or independent. Rather, it assumes that all programs are interconnected, and that there may be many means for attaining the same goals. PPBS attempts to address the questions of the goals of government, and how those goals can be best achieved. Program budgeting also depends heavily upon policy analysis and data in order to attempt to derive optimal solutions to budgetary problems. It requires that all those involved in budgeting identify alternative courses of action, along with the financial implications of those alternative courses, and justify the selection of one course over the others.

This approach to budgeting is obviously just as much a system of budgeting for wealthy countries as is incrementalism. It requires the luxury of a wealth of information and a wealth of analytic ability, as well as some predictability of the revenues and expenditures of government. Program budgeting is also a budgeting system for relatively centralized and elite-dominated political systems. It is almost inherently centralizing, as it requires the identification of goals at a very high level and the central authority to implement program-based decisions. Thus, a political system such as that of the United States, which is highly decentralized and depends upon the goal setting of relatively autonomous administrative agencies, is not likely to find program budgeting very compatible. On the other hand, a more centralized political system such as France or even Sweden might find the system more compatible.[27] Similarly, the importance of the legislature in the political system will affect the acceptability of program budgeting. Program budgeting, because it allocates resources to programs without the line-item designations so conducive to legislative control, tends not to be favored by legislatures. Also, strong legislatures like to be able to allocate resources to their favorite organizations and to protect those organizations in budgetary battles. Program budgeting does not lend itself to that degree of legislative involvement, but interestingly, in political systems dominated by a strong executive, for example, Fifth Republic France, program budgeting may make the criteria for allocation more subject to legislative scrutiny.[28]

Different policy areas also appear more amenable to program budgeting than do others. Defense has been the policy area to which program budgeting has most commonly been applied. This may be simply because of the absence of any means of verifying the validity of the data and scenarios used to defend the budget requests—short of a war. The sophistication of the methods used in these forecasts and the absence of alternative information make it difficult for others to oppose the results. On the other hand, areas such as social policy, which are more commonly understood and in which value assumptions are more clearly involved, are likely to produce more obvious conflicts in budgeting and a greater involvement of legislative and nongovernmental actors. Consequently, the technocratic and centralized decision making associated with program budgeting is less appealing in these areas.

Zero-Base Budgeting

A second form of "rational" budgeting, which has been confined almost exclusively to the United States, is Zero-base Budgeting. Incremental budgeting, either explicitly or implicitly, assumes that there is a budgetary base—the previous year's level of appropriation—that is guaranteed, and there is only a question of how much of an increment will be given. As pointed out above, however, this appears to be true at the level of the department or agency, but not true of individual programs. Even if it is not entirely true, it is a common perception about budgeting, and Zero-base Budgeting (ZBB) was designed to solve this perceived problem.[29] The most fundamental idea behind ZBB is that the agency should have to justify its entire budget from the ground up each year. This would be somewhat impractical, given the magnitude of the task for any national government budget. Therefore, ZBB forces each budget unit to develop contingencies for various levels of funding. The most basic level of appropriations would be the "survival package," which is the minimal level of funding needed for the organization to survive and to provide for its basic services. Agencies might also be asked what they would do in the face of 5 or 10 percent cuts in their budgets, and what they would require to maintain their current levels of services. Finally, a set of decision packages, reflecting various alternative packages of new programs, would be presented as the priorities of the organizations for expanding their programs. These decision packages are reviewed at successive levels in each organization to develop a set of "consolidated decision packages," reflecting the priorities of the executive department along with its various components.

This form of budgeting does not contain the complicated and threatening assumptions of program domination over organizations, but it does have a number of problems that have limited its political acceptability. Obviously, organizations do not like to allow outsiders to know on how little they could survive. And if there is an assumption that the survival level of funding for an organization is open to very fundamental challenges each year, political conflicts are perpetuated and old disputes opened annually.[30] This may be especially threatening to programs, such as some social programs, that lack broad popular support or a well-organized constituency group to defend them.

Management by Objectives

Although it is not strictly a budgeting system, Management by Objectives (MBO) does have implications for public expenditure and should be discussed briefly in this context.[31] Like Zero-based Budgeting, MBO is a transplant from the private sector. Also like ZBB, the idea behind MBO is deceptively simple and commonsensical. The basic idea is that managers should set objectives and develop plans for attaining those objectives, and individuals in the organization should be rewarded on the basis of their attainment of objectives. In the public sector, these seemingly simple ideas have some very serious complications.

One of the complications is that MBO can be very centralizing. A common feature of government is that there may be as many objectives as there are organizations, and if any agreed-upon list of objectives is to be conceived, it must be conceived by central political (or possibly administrative) officials.[32] Like program budgeting, this centralization of the process of goal determination did not conform to the usual patterns of American government, with its tradition of highly decentralized goal formulation. The Nixon administration was the primary advocate of MBO at the federal level in the United States; these centralizing tendencies may have been exacerbated by some of the individuals involved in that administration, but it is likely that similar problems would arise under any president. If government is to determine *the* priorities it will seek to attain, the central officials must be very heavily involved and ultimately determine those objectives.

A second problem that besets MBO, PPBS, or any system attempting to install "rational" policy analysis in government is that operational indicators of the attainment of objectives must be developed for the system of performance evaluation to be effective. Unfortunately, the search for such indicators rivals the search for the philosopher's stone in its apparent futility.[33] Many of the actions that government takes are taken in the public sector simply because they involve vague, ill-defined, possibly contradictory, and unmeasurable consequences. At best we can develop measures of the activities of government organizations, but in reality those activities may be inversely related to the attainment of the real objectives of government. For example, we can measure the number of people receiving welfare payments, but the ultimate purpose of the social service system is to make its recipients self-sufficient.

Finally, the personnel systems of government do not allow the flexibility-in-pay rewards assumed by the majority of advocates of MBO. Pay levels for the majority of public employees are determined by their length of service and their job classifications. Only a very few personnel systems, for example, the Senior Executive Service in the United States, allow more individualized determination of compensation, and then primarily in terms of bonuses for outstanding performance.[34] The central premise of public pay schedules appears to be equality within the classification, with the classification being determined as much by the job as by the individual, so that there is little opportunity to adequately reward more effective employees, or punish the less effective.

Thus, while MBO is an admirable idea that few would oppose at a theoretical level, it runs counter to many of the established practices of government. Perhaps most importantly, MBO forces decisions upward toward the chief executive and the top administrators. It forces those individuals to determine the goals of government, while government is composed of many organizations and individuals with conflicting objectives. Thus, the goals espoused may tend to be either so bland as to be meaningless or simply not accepted by many who may be charged with their implementation. This is especially true of countries with highly decentralized political systems, such as the United States, but may also be true of systems that are nominally more centralized.

The Public Expenditure Survey

In the United Kingdom, although there were certainly some elements of crisis management involved, the Public Expenditure Survey Committee (PESC) system was designed to make better expenditure decisions about the allocation of public expenditures, regardless of the degree of fiscal restraint required.[35] PESC had five processes that it was intended to perform in the management of public expenditure. The first was planning. One of the common shortcomings of the budgetary process is its failure to take into account the long-term implications of an expenditure decision made in one year. A program may be small at its inception, but if it has the ability to accept clients at will it may grow very quickly to have substantial expenditure. PESC involved forecasts of expenditure requirements for all programs, as well as medium-term forecasts of the balance of public expenditure with the rest of the economy.

PESC also involved allocation among the competing purposes of government. Suggestions for this allocation were by the committee, but those suggestions obviously had to be validated by the Treasury and the Cabinet. But as with any "rational" approach to policy making, the results of the PESC exercise carry a substantial degree of weight.

The PESC system is also charged with the execution of the budget. Another of the common problems of budgeting is ensuring that the actual expenditures match the projected expenditures. This is a legal problem of ensuring that all expenditures are made legally, but it is also an important economic problem for a modern government that attempts to use the budget as a means of controlling its economy. If expenditures are above or below the levels projected, there may be serious repercussions for the economy.

The PESC system was also involved in the evaluation of expenditures. As with program budgeting, there is an attempt to assess the cost-effectiveness of public expenditure and to propose alternative means of reaching policy goals. Until the demise of the Programme Analysis and Review (PAR) system, PESC was supplemented in these efforts by the more extensive policy-analytic capabilities of PAR.[36]

Finally, PESC was involved with accounting for the expenditures made by government. This function is an after-the-fact control on expenditure, whereas the control functions of PESC mentioned above constituted more continuous monitoring of expenditure levels throughout the year. The postaudit is a long-standing function in government, but continuous control has become more important as the size of the public budget has increased and the importance of that budget for the national economy has increased proportionately.[37]

When PESC was first introduced, in the 1972–73 fiscal year, the primary emphasis was on planning and the forward look. Relatively speaking, this was a period of affluence for Britain, and the major problem was perceived as making appropriate decisions about future public expenditure. But as there have been numerous shocks to the British economy since that time, the emphasis has been switched from planning to control.[38] But there is a fundamental emphasis on rational allocation in the program, even when the major concern is monitoring rather than forecasting the future. But, as observed below, the changes that have been made in PESC have altered it almost entirely, so that the assumptions of the PESC system exist in name only, and there is a substantially different system of expenditure control in effect.

Bulk Budgeting

Finally, New Zealand has experimented with what it calls "bulk budgeting."[39] The idea is quite simple. Instead of allocating an organization funds in the usual input categories such as personnel or equipment, organizations are allocated a lump sum of money and told to get on with the job. It is assumed that managers will use the input categories in the preparation of the budget request, but after the funds are allocated the manager is free to do anything legal with them in order to achieve the stated goals of the organization.

This is assumed to allow the manager greater flexibility in achieving the goals, and especially in responding to changing circumstances. In many ways, this form of budgeting resembles PPBS, but without all the intellectual apparatus and without the threats to the survival of organizations.

To implement bulk budgeting requires several elements not always available in government. One is a good information system that will allow managers to judge performance and the effects of their choice of instruments to achieve goals.[40] It also requires an effective and professional auditing organization to ensure that the money really is spent properly and perhaps to provide—as does the General Accounting Office in the United States—some independent advice on efficiency and effectiveness.[41] And it requires some flexibility with staff ceilings, a means by which the growth of government has been controlled in difficult economic times, as well as some flexibility in pay to provide incentives for managers to use their flexibility to the utmost. However, despite these difficulties and caveats, bulk budgeting offers an interesting opportunity to allow public sector managers to manage and to then be judged by the success of their efforts.

REACTIONS TO STRESS

The changes in PESC comprise but one of many reactions to the fiscal stress in Western political economies that have been manifested through the budgetary process. We will first discuss the changes in PESC and then go on to other alternative methods for allocating resources—through both the macro- and the micro-budgetary processes—that have been developed.

Cash Limits

One of the principal changes in PESC has been the introduction of cash limits. The calculations of expenditure forecasts were made in terms of constant (although the base was changed constantly) pounds. That is, PESC allocated resources according to the volume of services to be provided, rather than according to the costs of those services in the current monetary units.[42] In an inflationary period this meant that the cost of services in terms of the pounds or pence that the average citizens were paying as taxes might increase very rapidly, whereas the value in constant terms might not increase at all. This system made control by Parliament difficult since the calculations were in the form of "funny money," and additionally there was little constraint on the administrators who never quite knew how much they could—or should— spend until long after the time had passed. Because of the difficulties arising from this form of volume budgeting, cash limits were imposed in April 1976. These imposed an absolute expenditure limit in current pounds on approximately

75 percent of public expenditure. The limits applied only to year one of the five-year PESC exercise, but since that is the most important year—the year's budget actually being executed—it represents the domination of control over planning in response to the increasing financial crisis of British government. Associated with the introduction of cash limits was the use of the contingency reserve in public expenditure as a means of short-term control, rather than as a general "honey pot" that anyone who overspent could dip into.[43] Interestingly, after the introduction of cash limits, there was a tendency for government organizations to underspend and, indeed, to underspend significantly. While fiscal conservatives may regard that as a positive outcome, those attempting to manage the public budget in order to manage the economy—and the possible beneficiaries of the expenditures—did not regard the outcome so positively.

Interestingly, the British government has now abandoned the cash-limits system as it was implemented, in favor of a system involving cash limits in the present budgetary year with future budgets being expressed in terms of cash but with forecast price levels. One analyst has called this system "hiccup money," as it is a new kind of volume budgeting expressed in cash terms. The same analyst has argued that the major effect of this change will be increased confusion over the published budget figures.[44]

Envelope Budgeting

Another approach to the problems posed by economic deceleration during the 1970s and early 1980s is the system of envelope budgeting developed in Canada.[45] This approach to budgeting depends upon two levels of allocation. At the first level resources are allocated among eleven "envelopes," or policy areas, for example, defense, social affairs, etc. These envelopes are allocated their resources based in part upon tradition and in part on the basis of priorities developed by the Cabinet and by the Treasury Board Secretariat and the Ministry of Finance. Within each of these envelopes the ministers concerned meet together to allocate the scarce resources. Given that there is a fixed amount of money, increases in one area must be matched by reductions in others, and the ministers or their deputies are given the difficult task of making those decisions. Their decisions are still subject to review and confirmation by the plenary Cabinet and the Parliament but in general survive as the final allocation of resources.

This is an interesting approach to the problem of allocating scarce resources, first proposed by the short-lived Clark government in 1979. It involves the political leaders of the government directly in making the difficult choices in preparing a budget, rather than their only responding to the decisions reached by the Ministry of Finance or other expert organizations. But it may also be a somewhat impractical approach to the problem, given that there will always be special pleas that can be taken outside of the envelopes to plenary Cabinet, and also given that politicians do not appreciate being pinned with this type of decision.[46] In addition, the most important decisions—the allocation of resources among the envelopes—is beyond the purview of these committees, so that they are frequently in the position of facing the unenviable task of allocating a total that is less than they believe they need as a group. This method of budgeting involves the affected ministers in a more effective manner than most other methods but may, in a period of declining affluence, only involve spreading misery rather than making any significant changes in the priorities of government. This is especially true given that in periods of "cut" there is a tendency to adopt decision rules, such as equal proportional cuts, that attempt to prevent any alterations in the existing priorities. But the real virtue of the method may be that it coopts all members of the Cabinet in making the tough decisions and thereby prevents recalcitrant members from causing political trouble by attempting to oppose their own government's expenditure policies, as the "Wets" did with Mrs. Thatcher's budgets.

This "scrap and build" approach to controlling public expenditures is not confined to Canada. For example, as a part of its COPE system (Committee of Officials on Public Expenditure), since 1980 departments in New Zealand requesting new programs must specify how they can achieve commensurate savings from other of their programs.[47] There may still be room for new programs, but some attempt must be made to create room by cutting back on old programs. This approach differs from that in Canada by keeping the considerations strictly on a departmental basis, with the trade-offs between different agencies being achieved by COPE and by the Treasury, but again puts politicians in the position of balancing the importance of new and old programs.

Structural Budget Margin

Although macro-budgeting is a logical first step in the preparation of the budget, the final budget figures frequently reflect as much the aggregation of figures resulting from decisions about individual programs as they do the result of making decisions about the allocation of goods and services between the public and private sectors. The use of the structural budget margin is a mechanism for institutionalizing the macro-control over the amount of public expenditure. Further, it is based upon medium or long-term trends in the growth of the economy and therefore should lack the shorter-term political considerations that have tended to color a great deal of budgetary decision making. Structural budgeting works by setting a target figure for the size of the public sector relative to the total economy, and then setting public expenditure equal to that percentage based upon long-term trend projections of economic growth. As it was practiced in the Netherlands in the 1970s, the plan was to keep the public sector at about the same size as it was when the program began.[48] As it was practiced, the structural budgeting system of the Netherlands bore a strong resemblance to the ideas of the Brookings Institution concerning the "full employment budget."[49] The idea here was to calculate what the budget—both in terms of receipts and expenditures—would be if the economy were operating at full employment. Naturally, if it were operating at less than full employment, tax receipts would fall and expenditures for a variety of social programs would increase. This would create a "full employment deficit," which under this approach to budgeting would be justifiable as a means of bringing the economy back to full employment. However, any deficit beyond that level would not be economically justifiable but would be the product of politicians attempting to purchase votes through programs not paid for from taxes but rather paid for by borrowing.[50]

Structural budgeting is to some extent a decision about making decisions. It sets the limits on bargaining within the budgetary process by defining the maximum total increase. As such, the mechanism is particularly suited to the nature of Dutch politics.[51] The degree of partisan fragmentation and the linkage of interest groups to their respective ministries would make an attempt to develop budget control from the bottom up, as in PESC, rather difficult. By imposing a ceiling on expenditures, this method could not eliminate difficult political decisions about the competing uses of resources, but it could limit the outcomes in a manner perceived to advantage economic growth. It also made the consideration of these issues less short-term decisions that were made primarily on political grounds and more decisions based upon long-term growth and development. This has also arguably made the decisions more technocratic and has reduced political control over a crucial element of public policy.

The structural budget margin also illustrates the interdependence of budgeting and other aspects of economic policy. Given that a major component of the total costs of government is the wage bill of its employees (approximately 30 percent of the budget in the Netherlands in 1979), a policy of limiting the expansion of the budget could not work effectively without some coordination with wage and price policy.[52]

GENERAL PROBLEMS OF BUDGETING

The above are but three examples of a range of innovations that have been attempted in response to the "fiscal crisis" of Western governments and economies.[53] They illustrate, however, the types of problems that must be addressed, as there is a perception that government spending has gotten out of control. These methods are all to some degree perceived as short-term responses to short-term problems, although they may be reflective of more long-term considerations. There are, however, several other problems that have not been addressed in these programs, and these are problems that any government will have to face when deciding how much to spend, and how to spend it.

Intergovernmental Budget Control

A problem that is especially important in federal countries is the coordination of expenditure policies across levels of government.[54] And even in unitary governments, the subnational levels of government may have sufficient control over their own expenditures to prevent the development of a coordinated fiscal policy. The importance of coordination arises from the utilization of budget as a means of regulating the economy, requiring that the central government obtain the overall balance of revenues and expenditures, not just on its own accounts. If the central government should choose to adopt an expansionary policy and reduce taxes, the effects of that decision may be nullified by the actions of subnational governments increasing taxes. For example, some of the impact of the Kennedy administration's tax cut in 1963 were mitigated by increases in state and local taxes in the same and subsequent years.[55] And in the United Kingdom, a unitary regime, local authorities have at times opposed both the general nature of the government budget as well as its particulars. They have sometimes spent more or less than was desired by the central government, in part through their ability to raise revenues via local property taxes— the rates.[56]

West Germany has developed one mechanism for dealing with this problem. During "normal" years, state (*Land*) and local governments in West Germany can decide how much they choose to tax and spend (although revenues are closely tied to federal revenues). However, there are provisions whereby the federal government can impose its wishes on issues such as tax-rate changes, governmental credit provisions, and the use of contingency funds if there is an economic crisis.[57] These provisions would not direct the state governments as to how to spend their money and could only indirectly affect total expenditures. But this mechanism does provide greater opportunity for coordination, especially when combined with the consultative bodies of the economic council and the Financial Planning Council. This approach should improve the ability of the Bonn government to produce the types of economic outcomes it desires—a conclusion reinforced by the success of West Germany's economy relative to that of other industrialized countries. Other federal governments such as Canada and Australia have provisions for consultations on economic stabilization, but none has developed the degree of coordination present in West Germany.

Capital Budgeting

Most government budgeting is discussed in terms of the operating budget, but equally important are governmental decisions concerning the allocation of capital resources in the society.[58] This problem is especially pronounced when there are a large number of nationalized industries that depend upon the government for their capital requirements. Making capital decisions presents a number of significant questions to government. The most important is the decision of whether the available capital stock of the country could best be employed in the public or the private sector. This is to some degree the same choice imposed when constructing the operating budget, but capital budgeting may have even greater long-term implications. First, decisions to build in the public sector will create a "stock" of certain types of goods that may influence future policy making and limit future choices. The construction of a large amount of public housing in the United Kingdom means that any future housing policy is to some degree determined by this capital decision. Also, resources used to build or buy capital goods in the public sector will mean that fewer can be purchased in the private sector, with a resulting slowdown in economic growth. Finally, there has been a tendency to use public capital funds, especially when speaking of nationalized industries, to bail out losers rather than to subsidize winners.[59] That is, given the political importance of nationalized industries as providers of employment, any government will be under pressure to allocate capital to existing organizations already providing identifiable jobs to identifiable workers, rather than attempting to allocate the same funds to subsidize the development of new growth industries. In a similar fashion, even where parliamentary bodies exercise strong control over expenditures, they are on average less reluctant to spend on capital—especially for their own district—than they are on operating items. Capital expenditures create identifiable monuments for the legislators, who can thereby demonstrate to their constituents that they have been effective legislators. But finally, if legislators do wish to build monuments to themselves, they may be better advised to build statues rather than hospitals, schools, or defense establishments. Statues require only an occasional cleaning, while all the other forms of public capital investment involve ongoing maintenance and operating expenditures that soon surpass the initial capital costs.

It is difficult to discuss and evaluate the various forms of allocation developed for capital funds. Many different approaches have been adopted, few of which fit into neat theoretical niches, but several general points should be raised. One is that capital budgeting is frequently conducted in a highly deceptive fashion, although it is unclear who is fooling whom. That is, it is a common practice to allocate to nationalized industries, or other ailing industries, capital loans, although almost everyone with any understanding of the situation knows that these loans will never be repaid. It is simply more palatable to give a loan through the visible budget (and loans may in fact not be shown in the budget) and then later to write that debt off at a future, less visible moment. Likewise, some capital allocations can be made without the government directly spending a penny, as when governments guarantee private loans to industry.[60] Unless the firm fails to make its loan payments, this does not involve any direct expenditure from government but merely requires a signature that will back the loan with the taxing power of government. But the resources are diverted into the firm—for example, Lockheed or Chrysler in the United States—although those loans would not be economically justifiable. The final point to be made about capital budgeting is that it is the least incremental form of budgeting. Capital expenditures constitute the easiest type of expenditure to avoid, as they involve few—if any—ongoing commitments to individuals. There may be situations in which a previous capital expenditure requires some additional expenditures in order to lend it productivity, but even if those expenditures are not made, there will merely be a loss of potential benefits rather than the removal of benefits from an individual. Therefore, when governments are in a period of forced retrenchment, capital expenditures are among the first items to be cut. This may be penny-wise and pound-foolish, for capital expenditures are often related in the short run to operating savings in the long term, as in the installation of newer and less labor-intensive machinery or the construction of newer, energy-efficient buildings.

Coordination of Taxation and Expenditures

Another problem that besets those making budgets is the coordination of taxation and expenditures. These two elements of the public budget are closely interconnected; depending upon the perspective, available revenues stimulate expenditures or the pressures from increased expenditure demands require increased revenues. In either case, it is difficult to know how much to spend without knowing how much revenue will accrue, and it is difficult to tax without knowing the amount of spending intended. Despite the close connection of these two elements of the public budget, decisions are frequently made by quite independent processes, with the obvious possibilities of discrepancies. This is less likely in a country with a parliamentary government, which is able to exercise relatively close control over policies through the cabinet, than would be true in a presidential regime with greater legislative power. But even in a parliamentary regime, the revenue bills and expenditure bills are often voted upon at different times and may be developed by different institutions. In the thirty-two years from 1950 to 1981 the government of the United States passed twenty-eight unbalanced budgets, although this was a period of great economic growth. But the United States is by no means alone; in the same period the government of the United Kingdom passed thirty unbalanced budgets, and Italy had a deficit in every year. Even the fiscally prudent government of West Germany passed unbalanced budgets for twenty-six years.[61] Thus, it is not implied that economic necessities create fiscal deficits in governments; the very nature of decision making that separates revenue and expenditure may contribute to the outcomes.

If the process of coordinating taxation and expenditure is difficult in affluent, industrialized countries, it is even more difficult in Third World countries. The ability to predict either component of the budget is very limited, and the combination of the two errors makes budgeting a process of vague estimation and frequent adjustments. It also means that these countries must first attempt to shift their revenue sources toward those that may be less buoyant in times of economic growth but may be more predictable. It may also mean that these countries will become increasingly dependent upon the loans and grants of multinational financial institutions: the International Monetary Fund, the World Bank, the Inter-American Development Bank, and the like. When there is a budget surplus, there will be great political pressures to spend it, given the generally poor state of the economic and social conditions of less-developed countries. And when there is a deficit, there are few places to turn for support, other than these international bodies.

SUMMARY

Budgeting is a crucial process for both government and citizens. It determines to a great extent who will receive what from government, and who will pay for it. Our focus in this book is on administration and administrators, and the budget is obviously crucial for those whose livelihood comes from the public budget. There are also psychological and prestige elements associated with the budgetary process that may surpass the importance of minor differences in appropriations from year to year, or from agency to agency. Success in the budgetary process is a means of tabulating the winners and losers in political struggles, and budgetary outcomes may indicate tides in the interests and priorities of government.

Budgets have become even more crucial as citizens in a number of countries have come to question the desirability of many components of public expenditure, and to question particularly the desirability of paying the taxes to finance that expenditure. A number of procedural and institutional changes have been made to respond to these concerns. All have been well intentioned, but the common evaluation appears to be that if there is a real commitment to control expenditure, then the procedures are useless. Institutions and procedures are certainly important but cannot substitute for the determination and abilities of the inhabitants of these structures.

NOTES

1. Organization for Economic Cooperation and Development, *Revenue Statistics of Member Countries, 1965–1980* (Paris: OECD, 1982).
2. Office of Management and Budget, *Budget of the United States, 1981, Special Analyses* (Washington, D.C.: Government Printing Office, 1980).
3. D. J. and A. F. Ott, *Federal Budget Policy*, 3rd. ed. (Washington, D.C.: The Brookings Institution, 1977).
4. Alec Nove, *The Soviet Economic System* (London: George Allen and Unwin, 1977).

5. Edward Gramlich, "Intergovernmental Grants: A Review of the Literature," in Wallace E. Oates, ed., *The Political Economy of Fiscal Federalism* (Lexington, Mass.: D. C. Heath, 1977), pp. 219–239.

6. But see Robert E. Goodin, "Rational Politicians and Rational Bureaucrats in Washington and Whitehall," *Public Administration* (1982), pp. 23–41.

7. Much of the literature in economics on the growth of the public sector makes these types of assumptions. See Alan H. Meltzer and Scott F. Richard, "Why Government Grows (and Grows) in a Democracy," *The Public Interest* 52 (1978): 111–118.

8. Guy Lord, *The French Budgetary Process* (Berkeley: University of California Press, 1973); R. de la Geniere, *Le Budget* (Paris: Presse de la Fondation Nationale des Sciences Politiques, 1976).

9. For a discussion of the importance of central agencies see Colin Campbell and George J. Szablowski, *The Superbureaucrats* (Toronto: Macmillan of Canada, 1979).

10. Hugh Heclo and Aaron Wildavsky, *The Private Government of Public Money* (Berkeley: University of California Press, 1974), p. 160.

11. Peter S. Cleaves, *Bureaucratic Politics and Administration in Chile* (Berkeley: University of California Press, 1974).

12. William Niskanen, *Bureaucracy and Representative Government* (Chicago: Aldine/Atherton, 1971).

13. Cleaves, *Bureaucratic Politics*, pp. 316–317.

14. Aaron Wildavsky, *Budgeting: A Comparative Theory of the Budgetary Process* (Boston: Little, Brown, 1975).

15. Naomi Caiden and Aaron Wildavsky, *Planning and Budgeting in Poor Countries* (New York: Wiley, 1974).

16. Barry Bozeman and Jeffrey D. Straussman, "Shrinking Budgets and the Shrinkage of Budgetary Theory," *Public Administration Review* 42 (1982): 509–515; Daniel Tarschys, "Rational Decremental Budgeting," *Policy Sciences* 14 (1981): 49–58.

17. Otto A. Davis, M. A. H. Dempster, and Aaron Wildavsky, "Towards a Predictive Theory of Government Budgeting," *British Journal of Political Science* 4 (1974): 419–452.

18. William Ascher, *Forecasting: An Appraisal for Policy Makers and Planners* (Baltimore: Johns Hopkins University Press, 1978).

19. Peter B. Natchez and Irving C. Bupp, "Policy and Priority in the Budgetary Process," *American Political Science Review* 67 (1973): 951–963.

20. See Brian W. Hogwood and B. Guy Peters, *Policy Dynamics* (New York: St. Martin's, 1983).

21. Heclo and Wildavsky, *The Private Government*, pp. 37–75.

22. Ibid., pp. 14–21.

23. Richard Rose and B. Guy Peters, *Can Government Go Bankrupt?* (New York: Basic Books, 1978).

24. A. C. Pigou, *A Study in Public Finance* (London: Macmillan, 1928).

25. David Novick, "Origin and History of Program Budgeting," *Rand Corporation Paper*, No. P-3427 (October 1966).

26. Jacques Bravo, "La R. C. B. et le management de l'État," *Revue de science financière* 64 (1972): 289–356; Douglas Hartle, *The Expenditure Budget Pro-*

cess *in the Government of Canada* (Toronto: Canadian Tax Foundation, 1978).

27. Pierre Vinde, *Hur Sverige Styres* (Stockholm: Prisma, 1967).

28. Jean-Claude Ducros, "The Influence of RCB on Parliament's Role in Budgetary Affairs," in David Coombes et al., *The Power of the Purse* (London: George Allen and Unwin, 1976), pp. 148–162.

29. Peter A. Phyrr, "The Zero-Base Approach to Government Budgeting," *Public Administration Review* 37 (1977): 1–8.

30. Aaron Wildavsky, "A Budget for All Seasons: Why the Traditional Budget Lasts," *Public Administration Review* 38 (1978): 501–509.

31. Rodney H. Brady, "MBO Goes to Work in the Public Sector," *Harvard Business Review* (1973): 65–74.

32. Richard Rose, *Managing Presidential Objectives* (New York: Free Press, 1976).

33. I. C. R. Byatt, "Theoretical Issues in Expenditure Decisions," in Michael V. Posner, ed., *Public Expenditure: Allocation Between Competing Ends* (Cambridge: Cambridge University Press, 1977): 142–158.

34. Leonard Reed, "The Joys of SES," *Washington Monthly* (September 1980): 43–48.

35. Sir Richard Clarke, *Public Expenditure, Management and Control: The Development of PESC* (London: Macmillan, 1978).

36. Douglas E. Ashford, *Policymaking in Britain* (Philadelphia, Pa.: Temple University Press, 1981), pp. 97–134.

37. H. V. Kroeker, *Accountability and Control: The Government Expenditure Process* (Montreal: C. D. Howe, 1978); G. W. F. Pidgeon, *Financial Control in Developing Countries* (London: Longman, 1971).

38. Maurice Wright, "From Planning to Control: PESC in the 1970s" in Wright, *Public Spending Decisions: Growth and Restraint in the 1970s* (London: George Allen and Unwin, 1980).

39. Warren Skeats, "Bulk Budgeting: Its Impact," *Public Sector* 3 (1980): 10–11.

40. Andrew Likierman, "Management Information for Ministers: The MINIS System in the Department of the Environment," *Public Administration* 60 (1982): 127–142.

41. See chapter 8.

42. This is called "volume budgeting." See the comments by Wildavsky, "A Budget for All Seasons," pp. 505–506.

43. Sir Leo Pliatzky, *Getting and Spending: Public Expenditure Employment and Inflation* (Oxford: Blackwells, 1982).

44. Harold Copeman, "Analyzing Public Expenditure: (1) Planning, Control and Price," *Journal of Public Policy* 1 (1980): 289–306.

45. Privy Council Office, *The Policy and Expenditure Management System* (Ottawa: Privy Council Office, March 1981).

46. R. Van Loon, "Stop the Music: The Current Policy and Expenditure Management System in Ottawa," *Canadian Journal of Public Administration* 24 (1981): 175–199.

47. "New Zealand" (Seminar on Public Expenditure Control, Organization for Economic Cooperation and Development, Paris, May 1980).

48. J. Diamond, "The New Orthodoxy in Budgetary Planning: A Critical Review of the Dutch Experience," *Public Finance* 32 (1977): 56–76.

49. Alan S. Blinder and Robert M. Solow, "Analytical Foundations of Fiscal Policy," in Blinder et al., *The Economics of Public Finance* (Washington, D.C.: The Brookings Institution, 1974), pp. 3–14.

50. For a critical review see James Buchanan and Richard Wagner, *Democracy in Deficit: The Political Legacy of Lord Keynes* (New York: Academic Press, 1977).

51. Jan van Putten, "Policy Styles in the Netherlands: Negotiation and Conflict," in Jeremy Richardson, ed., *Policy Styles in Western Europe* (London: George Allen and Unwin, 1982), pp. 168–196.

52. See J. L. Fallick and R. F. Elliot, "Incomes Policy and the Public Sector," in Fallick and Elliot, eds., *Incomes Policies, Inflation and Relative Pay* (London: George Allen and Unwin, 1981).

53. See also Maurice Wright and Christopher Hood, *Big Government in Hard Times* (Oxford: Martin Robertson, 1981).

54. Oates, *The Political Economy of Fiscal Federalism.*

55. Federal income tax increased by only 2.5 percent from 1963 to 1965 and barely kept pace with inflation. State taxes increased by 12.9 percent. In the period of 1963 to 1965 one state added an income tax and ten increased their tax rates. U.S. Bureau of the Census, *Statistical Abstract of the United States* (Washington, D.C.: Government Printing Office, annual).

56. C. D. Foster, R. Jackman, and M. Perlman, *Local Government Finance in a Unitary State* (London: Allen and Unwin, 1980); G. W. Jones and J. D. Stewart, "The Treasury and Local Government," *Political Quarterly* 54 (1983): 5–15.

57. Jack H. Knott, "Stabilization Policy, Grants-in-Aid, and the Federal System in Western Germany," in Oates, *The Political Economy of Fiscal Federalism,* pp. 75–92; Albrecht Zunker, "Consequences of the Federal System for Parliamentary Control of the Budget in the Federal Republic of Germany," in Coombes, *The Power of the Purse,* pp. 46–65.

58. See Alberta M. Sbragia, "Capital Markets and Central Local Politics in Britain: The Double Game," *Studies in Public Policy,* No. 109 (Glasgow: Centre for the Study of Public Policy, University of Strathclyde, 1983).

59. Gunnar Eliasson and Bengt-Christer Ysander, "Picking Winners or Bailing out Losers," *Working Paper,* No. 37 (Stockholm: Industriens Utredningsinstitut, 1981).

60. Andrew S. Carron, "Fiscal Activities Outside the Budget," in Joseph A. Pechman, ed., *Setting National Priorities: The 1982 Budget* (Washington, D.C.: The Brookings Institution, 1981), pp. 261–269.

61. Organization for Economic Cooperation and Development, *National Accounts of OECD Member Countries* (Paris: OECD, annual).

CHAPTER 8

THE POLITICS OF ADMINISTRATIVE ACCOUNTABILITY

We have documented the growth of public administration and the increasing influence of administrative agencies on policy. These developments make the perennial political problem of the control of administration more important than ever. This problem may be phrased in terms of "control," "accountability," or "responsibility," but the basic problem remains: How do political leaders and the public persuade, cajole, or force administrative agencies to do their bidding?

Traditionally there have been two broad schools of thought regarding this question. The first has assumed that responsibility was "an inward sense of personal obligation"; the second assumed that personal obligation was not enough, and some external forces must be employed in order to enforce responsible behavior.[1] The first approach to the problem assumes that civil servants have ethical values and professional standards that will guide them in the performance of their tasks. The second assumes that these values are not sufficient; there must be a means of punishing behavior not in accordance with stated law and legislative intent.

This chapter dwells heavily on methods of enforcing responsibility, in large part because governments have spent so much time in trying to devise methods of control. However, throughout, it must be remembered that civil servants are probably no better or worse ethically than individuals who work in the private sector. The major difference is that they work for the government, and in democratic government it is assumed that they work at least indirectly for all of us. Even in liberal democracies the state has a number of presumptive claims on individuals (such as arrests, taxes, and conscription) that threaten abuse. Thus, the problem of accountability is more acute in public agencies, not because of the nature of the individuals employed and their lack of personal responsibility, but because of the nature of the jobs and the nature of the responsibilities vested in government.

Another factor that produces problems of control and responsibility is the vast growth of administrative involvement in government. Not only do public administrators execute the laws, but they consciously also make laws and even adjudicate laws. Much of the legislation coming out of the legislative organs of political systems these days is actually enabling legislation for the bureaucracy. It sets the broad outlines of policy but requires the bureaucracy to issue regulations to fill in the details.[2] If it were not for this, legislatures would be more bogged down than they already are. In the same way more adjudication is carried on in administrative tribunals than in the regular courts in many countries.[3] Although conducted by administrators, and often informally, these adjudications have the same impact as if heard in a regular court.[4] Thus the problems of controlling administration have grown from simply (?) controlling the execution of policy to the more complex tasks of also controlling policy formulation and adjudication.

DIMENSIONS OF RESPONSIBILITY

In a discussion of accountability and control, the basic dualism with which the man in the street—not to mention politicians and academic commentators—regards bureaucracy is apparent.[5] On the one hand, bureaucracy is characterized as a leviathan, a monolithic and virtually uncontrollable force eating away at personal liberties and economic resources. On the other hand, bureaucracy is a fool: a fragmented set of individuals so bound with red tape and rule books that they don't know what they are about at any one time, sending television sets to people who lack electricity and doing research on the optimal shape of toilet seats. It is truly remarkable the degree to which these apparently contradictory viewpoints about bureaucracy can coexist in the thoughts and writings of the same commentators. Leaving inconsistencies aside, it is also important to note the extent to which these two perspectives on the problems of bureaucracy in modern government point to different problems and different requirements for accountability and control.

On a more personal level, there is also a dualism in reactions to bureaucracy, although this is rarely expressed by the same individuals. On the one hand, there are frequent complaints about bureaucracy and bureaucrats operating *ultra vires*, beyond the scope of their authority. Complaints about police brutality, the role of the FBI and CIA in domestic surveillance in the United States, Swedish tax collectors breaking into homes, and Danish welfare workers removing children from their parents are all complaints about bureaucracy operating in an apparently illegal or arbitrary manner.[6] Bureaucrats have gone beyond the scope of their prescribed authority and are acting on the basis of personal values and "initiative." On the other hand, we frequently hear complaints from clients of public agencies concerning excessive adherence to rules and procedures. In these cases the clients—most commonly the clients of social service agencies— feel that they are denied the type of assistance they need, or indeed deserve, because of strict adherence to procedures. This is a case of adherence to rules with a vengeance, so much so that the initial intention of the program may be lost. These two forms of maladministration are reflected in one British minister's list of bureaucratic errors: ". . . bias, neglect, inattention, delay, incompetence, ineptitude, perversity, turpitude, arbitrariness and so on."[7]

The first two types of perceived problems with bureaucracy, the leviathan and the fool, are essentially institutional problems, involving the activities of the bureaucracy as an entity. The second set of problems is more commonly associated with the behavior of individuals occupying positions within the hierarchy—usually at the bottom.[8] Two of the problems involve the use of excessive power or the evasion of legal safeguards, or, conversely, the failure to go outside normal channels in seeking information, advice, or coordination. These four types of perceived problems of administrative accountability can be seen as the product of the interaction of two dimensions of control. One is the personal or institutional level at which the problem occurs, and the second is the degree of activity of the administrator in question (overactive or underactive). These two dimensions and the resulting four types of problems are shown in Figure 8.1.

Other than as an intellectual exercise, the cross-classification of these two dimensions of administrative complaints should enable us to conceptualize better the politics of administrative accountability. On one dimension—the institutional-personal—the politics are those of the institutional conflict of the bureaucracy with other political institutions such as the legislature or the execu-

FIGURE 8.1
A TYPOLOGY OF PERCEIVED
DIFFICULTIES WITH BUREAUCRACY

| | | ACTOR | |
		Institution	Individual
ACTION	Excessive	CIA Surveillance	Police Brutality
	Too Little	Red Tape	"Buck-passing"

tive, as opposed to the politics of influencing the behavior of individual administrators who interact with clients. The institutional control may involve large-scale political conflict often of a quite intense nature, while individual control may involve only altering the attitudes or behavior of one individual. Obviously, different solutions are needed for the two types of problems. However, we must be aware of the possibility of individual problems escalating to institutional crises, as illustrated by the role of the FBI and CIA in domestic surveillance and the relationship between actions of individual policemen and urban unrest in the last decade in the United States.

On the other dimension of accountability, the difference in politics appears to be the difference between institutionalizing and enforcing controls versus the politics of relaxing existing regulations. These actions are again somewhat contradictory, but both involve getting administrators to do what the public, the clients, and the political leaders want them to do. The former involves political action in writing legislation and, perhaps more importantly, political will in enforcing existing regulations. It may also involve the willingness on the part of individual citizens to invest large amounts of time and possibly money to combat what they consider to be injustices resulting from the administrative process.

The loosening of institutional rules of procedure is a more difficult process. To some degree it involves the legislation of discretionary powers for administrators, an action that clashes with the concern of control and accountability mentioned above, and also with many general constitutional statements concerning the responsibility of *political* actors for policy. Such an approach is now, however, strongly advocated as a solution to the problem of "regulatory unreasonableness."[9]

Another dimension in loosening the bonds of the proverbial red tape is more personal and involves training administrators for an understanding of clients and their problems. Finally, some changes may have to be made within the individual administrator—and within the culture of the agency—and would involve an increased willingness to take responsibility for actions and willingness to use rules for the benefit of client rather than the protection of the civil servant. Each of these, especially the latter, is more easily said than done.

Another factor that must be taken into account in this prologue to the study of administrative accountability is that much of the problem is a function of that often-mentioned desire to separate administration from politics.[10] In this case it is especially important that most Western societies and nations following their examples have sought to separate the tenure of administrators from political control, except in the most extreme cases, and even then only after a rather arduous process.[11] When there was a spoils system—not necessarily the good old days—many problems of administrative accountability we face today simply did not arise. The administrator was in office at the pleasure of a political official, and if the civil servant did not do what was expected, the civil servant was out of a job. This system did not assure any more accountability to the public, and its difficulties have been well documented by reformers.[12]

Few people would seriously advocate returning to a patronage system of allocating public jobs, but it is important to remember that the choice of a merit system for public management has a number of latent consequences for administrative accountability. The most important is the security, and to some degree the unresponsiveness, of the public employee. The goods and services produced by public service are not marketed, or if they are it is in a monopolistic situation. The failure to make a profit or break even isn't associated with the termination of public employment, so there is little to make the civil servant responsive to the wishes of markets, politicians, or the public. The job carries sufficient security so that after a suitable probationary period, the civil servant can be terminated only by a lengthy process proving positive malfeasance or nonfeasance. This discussion should not be taken to imply that public employees are inferior people morally, or that they are in their jobs only to make a secure living. Rather, it is to imply that the structure of incentives within most civil service systems places more emphasis on security than on project completion or public responsiveness.[13] Thus, in an attempt to insulate civil servants from political pressures, reforms in the public service have gone far to insulate the civil service from *all* pressures, thus creating significant problems of accountability and control.

There is, of course, a great deal of variation in the ability of political leaders to influence appointments under them. In the United States, the relatively large number of appointees who come and go with a change in the presidency helps to make the executive departments more accountable.[14] Likewise in Sweden, and to a lesser extent West Germany, political leaders can exercise considerable discretion in choosing their senior civil servants, while in France and Belgium the ability to appoint a *cabinet* gives the politician some control.[15] These countries may be contrasted with the United Kingdom, where until recently political leaders had little choice among the civil servants who were to serve them. Mrs. Thatcher's opportunity to be involved in the appointment of eight new permanent secretaries and her greater personal involvement in those choices represent a departure from past traditions.[16]

Now, with some idea of the dimensions of the problem of administrative accountability and control, it is time to look at the instruments by which accountability may be enforced. The instruments available to each actor seeking to exercise control will be described and an attempt made to evaluate these instruments within different contexts. In this discussion, these instruments and their effectiveness will be linked back to these basic dimensions and the particular types of control over problems already outlined.

INSTRUMENTS OF ACCOUNTABILITY

The list of procedures, institutions, and actors that have been devised to attempt to control administration is by now very long and equally varied. We cannot hope to discuss each of them in this chapter, not even in one book. Therefore, we shall concentrate on those that seem to offer the most promise of being effective—either to us or to significant portions of public opinion. The one common thread that binds all these proposed solutions together is that they depend upon implementation by someone, and this is the weak link in the chain of control. Most of the methods to be discussed could be effective, but all rely on human implementation. It is important, therefore, also to seek to determine which methods have the lowest political costs for the implementers and, consequently, which have the fewest disincentives.

Organizational Methods

The simplest means of policing public administration is to allow the civil servants to police themselves. One means is that suggested by Friedrich—relying on the internalized values of the civil servants—and we shall return to that option later.[17] What we are interested in here is the use of popular or legal sanctions within the organization to gain compliance. Thus, while each individual in the organization may not have accepted the standards proposed by Friedrich, are there still means by which the organization itself can control them? It should be pointed out that although ostensibly the simplest method of control, this may in fact involve the highest political costs simply because of the internal strife within the organization that it may create. And it may open up the agency to further attacks from other political institutions.

Publicity   Although it may be considered a method in itself, publicity is one organizational means of controlling the bureaucracy. It would tend to be particularly useful in dealing with individual actions both going beyond, or excessively adhering to, rules and procedures. The characterization of this method as organizational may strike the reader as a bit odd, but the point is that publicity carries little or no direct sanction but instead depends largely upon the organization to correct the errors brought to light. If the organization does not respond, then the legislative or legal methods can come into play. However, it is easier, cheaper, and quicker for the organization to respond. It reduces the external control on the organization and may preserve for it some latitude for future action. It is the hope of those advocating publicity as a means of control that this will indeed happen.

Perhaps the administrative system most notable for the use of publicity is Sweden. Swedish public officials have been described as working within a "goldfish bowl," in that their actions are almost entirely open to public inspection.[18] Whenever an official reaches a decision, this decision must be justified in writing, and the written justification is recorded as a part of the file to be made available to the citizen(s) upon request. In addition, many forms collected by the government that in most societies would be regarded as confidential—such as income tax returns—are made public in Sweden.[19] This system is intended to make the administrative system and the political system as a whole more responsive to the people for the simple reason that if people know what decisions have been reached and why, they are better able to contest them. Further, openness to the press enables even greater dissemination of information. This openness also must have a deterrent effect on administrators; they will not do anything that cannot be well justified. Of course, there are means of circumventing the system. An officer in each ministry decides which materials are private or confidential, and although there is an appeal from that decision, in most cases it is final. Likewise, information that is sensitive can be sent through private communication rather than through public channels. Finally, the press is frequently criticized for being insufficiently interested in pursuing matters that appear in the files.[20] Despite these problems, the system seems to be a step in the right direction for those wishing to control more fully the activities of the public bureaucracy.

The Swedish system is the most publicized of several systems relying upon information for control, but some steps have been taken in other systems to use information as a mechanism of control. Norway has adopted a system of publicity quite similar to that in Sweden. In the United States the excesses of Watergate and some general increase in distrust of government have led to the passage of the Freedom of Information Act at the federal level along with similar acts in at least thirty-nine states, and a number of "sunshine laws" at state and local government levels allowing public access to records and to meetings of administrative bodies, especially those functioning in a quasi-legislative or quasi-judicial manner.[21] Canadian administrative procedures have been modified to allow greater publicity of decisions and information. It is probably fair to say that a general increase in distrust of government and in political awareness of populations has been associated with increased pressure on government to open up its proceedings to the people and the press.

Publicity, as with many questions of administrative responsibility and accountability, is not a wholly positive value. While it is certainly important that the public have access to relevant information about administration, working in a goldfish bowl cannot be as efficient as working in private. Further, it tends to expose the activities of administrators to political pressures that might not be felt directly in a more closed system. The contrast with Great Britain comes to mind almost immediately. The tradition and practice of British administration has been that of almost total secrecy and privacy for administrators.[22] Although the press is tending to place pressure on this secrecy, as far as most of the public know—especially when it comes to policy decisions and advice— the bureaucrats are "faceless." Secrecy has been adopted quite simply to ensure that administrators as public servants will be isolated from short-term political pressures and be free to make decisions in what they consider to be the "public interest."[23] Decisions concerning the publication of the Crossman diaries, and other similar memoirs, and the institutionalization of a parliamentary ombudsman have opened even this system of administration to greater public scrutiny, but it remains very much more private than most. The point is that certain values can be maximized by a closed and private system of administration, just as certain benefits can be gained by having a very open system of administration. It is simply a matter of choice for the public and for political elites of what type of system they want and can have.

Internal Discipline　Internal discipline within public organizations is another potentially effective means of controlling administration without having to resort to the imposition of external political control. It is therefore a relatively "cheap" means of control in terms of time and total institutional energy. On the other hand, it assumes that there will be someone in a responsible position within the hierarchy who has values more in line with those assumed to be held by the public than those held by erring subordinates, or even erring superiors. Given our conception of the average public administrator as probably no better or no worse than the average citizen, the probabilities of finding such a person in the hierarchy are good. However, there are a number of impediments to any person exercising authority over subordinates guilty of other than the most obvious malfeasance in office.

First, the sanctions available within civil service systems are not particularly strong, especially if the person involved is not a "climber" seeking advancement.[24] These problems are especially apparent when the individual whom the superior would like to sanction is guilty only of being overzealous in the application of rules rather than in circumventing rules. Further, the application of such sanctions as do exist requires long and often complex administrative hearings, with the scales apparently weighted in favor of the civil servant.[25] Police review boards, for example, generally include mostly other policemen who, despite their intentions of maintaining the integrity of the force, also well understand the problems of the individual policeman faced with a dangerous or compromising situation. Finally, unionization of public employees—both industrial and nonindustrial—has added to the difficulties in implementing internal controls.[26] One official in the Carter administration, for example, abandoned attempting to discipline an employee because it would have taken up the rest of his time in office.[27] Thus, those sanctions that can be readily employed tend to be rather weak, and those with teeth are difficult to implement.

There are also powerful organizational reasons for failing to enforce sanctions against employees. As noted in earlier chapters, bureaucratic politics play a major if not paramount role for many public administrators and their agencies.[28] They must compete for money, employees, and legislative time with all other agencies, and there is not a quicker way to reduce their potential success in this conflict over resources than to have a scandal. Although the agency can try to make the best of it by saying they were "cleaning their own house," it may still produce considerable difficulty for the agency at the next budget time.[29] In these days of tight public funds, the firing of an employee may mean the loss of a position. It thus becomes difficult for any public administrator, no matter how committed to proper administrative practice, to impose discipline upon an employee, especially when word of such discipline will leak out to concerned politicians.

Related to the above point is that administrators (one hopes) want to get things done and consequently do not want to employ excessive amounts of time and energy in prosecuting members of their own organizations. And, they generally get rated themselves on their ability to get the job done, not on the internal discipline of their organization. Therefore, those who are themselves "climbers" will tend to expend more effort on program execution than on organizational control. For many agencies—social service agency or the police—this tendency is enhanced by the fact that the clients are neither of high status nor skilled politically, so their claims against the organization can be easily dismissed.

Another factor favoring nonenforcement of administrative regulations within an agency is that it is frequently necessary to circumvent regulations in order to achieve the stated goals of the organization. In the United States and other countries that have had recent major political scandals, this reasoning may sound dubious to many readers, but there are situations in which administrative rules and regulations are impediments to providing a service or getting a job done. Blau provides a classic example in the FBI agents who had to engage in an explicit violation of the rules requiring reporting an attempted bribe in order to perform their jobs well.[30] Many regulations associated with the granting of social services make it more difficult for the client to receive aid, and these must frequently be ignored by employees seeking to assist a client.

Finally, we must remember that the civil service constitutes a career just as does working in any other organization or profession. As such, there is a certain amount of camaraderie and *esprit de corps*, which makes strict adherence to internal discipline more difficult. Despite formal lines of authority, informal organizations may link individuals who are formally superior and subordinate as equals, thus making the imposition of discipline difficult. In situations where the civil service is regarded as a highly differentiated organization from the rest of society (France?), or within segments of the public bureaucracy that are themselves highly integrated (the police or the military), there is an unwillingness to bring discredit upon the service, so many internal matters may not be exposed.[31] Even in less differentiated positions there may well be a feeling that one should not criticize one's fellow civil servants unduly, if for no other reason than the tables may be turned.

A special case of internal controls on bureaucratic abuse is "whistle blowing."[32] This term refers to individuals taking actions to expose what they consider wrongdoing in their own agency, especially when that wrongdoing is by their superiors. The most familiar case of whistle blowing was the accountant in the Department of Defense who exposed the massive cost overruns on the C-5A airplane. This led to a great deal of embarrassment for the Department of Defense and the firing of the accountant.[33] Since that time greater protection for whistle-blowers has been built into the American federal bureaucracy, including inspectors general who serve as officials to whom such abuses can be reported with little fear of reprisal.[34]

Thus, administrative control depends not only on the existence of a set of institutions and procedures, but also on the willingness to employ those procedures. In the case of internal discipline, both are frequently lacking. The lack of will is rarely due to collusion or widespread immorality, but more commonly due simply to the politics of bureaucratic agencies and their need to survive. Likewise, the methods available are at best awkward and cumbersome, and at worst absolutely unworkable.

Group and Public Pressures

Another means of exercising control of administration without resort to formal conflicts between institutions is through pressure group activity and public opinion. We have already discussed something of the relationship between pressure groups and the bureaucracy, with the conclusion that pressure groups may frequently be the source of administrative failure to operate in the "public interest."[35] How can these same pressure groups also serve as a check on administration? In the first place, although pressure groups may not in fact serve the public interest broadly defined, they do certainly serve a narrow clientele, and it is frequently that clientele that is most affected by the activities of a certain agency. Thus, by informing their members of the activities of the agency, they can in turn exercise some effective popular control. Of course, the end result of this is frequently legislation or administrative action favoring the special interest, but even this constitutes *some* responsiveness on the part of the agency.

Second, one of the most important political developments in recent years has been the organization of so-called public interest pressure groups, organized and functioning much as any other pressure group but ostensibly representing no special interest. In the United States this movement has manifested itself through Common Cause and the whole consumer movement beginning with Ralph Nader.[36] Publicity and the publication of complaints against government are the weapons most frequently employed by these organizations, but they have also engaged in lobbying both legislators and administrative agencies. Finally, in the American context these organizations have been reasonably successful in the courts, while in the European nations the creation of a number of ministries and boards for consumer affairs has tended to absorb many complaints without resort to judicial means.[37]

Third, closely related to the development of consumer groups has been the formation of so-called "action groups" or *burgerinitiateven* in continental European countries. These are typically single-issue groups that come into being to protest a single decision or policy and then go out of existence after either their success or their frustration by government. These groups are frequently more oriented toward the decisions taken by political officials but also concern themselves with bureaucratic decisions.

Another especially interesting aspect of the use of organizations as a check on bureaucracy has been governmental fostering of organizations, almost to the extent of creating their own opposition. During the War on Poverty in the United States the doctrine of "maximum feasible participation" was designed to allow the residents of communities affected by these social programs to have some input into the making and implementation of policies.[38] The idea was to allow residents to gain political skills and simultaneously to prevent programs from becoming excessively bureaucratized and bound in red tape.[39] In Britain, one reorganization of the National Health Service has included the development of Community Health Councils designed to prevent domination of the service by specialist physicians and ensure greater regard for community wishes.[40] In many African countries undergoing political mobilization and social change, village councils or organizations have been developed, again with the intention of providing local input and serving as a check on bureaucratic excesses.[41] In all these cases, the governments have actively fostered organizations that would serve as oppositions to the government's own bureaucracy, an interesting if not always entirely successful approach to administrative accountability.

Another development has been the growth of client organizations for some public services. These have existed for some time for middle- and upper-class services, such as education, but the more interesting development is the growth of organizations of lower-status recipients of social benefits. These people had once been regarded by the community, and even by themselves, as having the right to express nothing but gratitude for receiving benefits. Now, however, they have become increasingly vocal in their demands for improved benefits and improved administration.[42] Also important in this regard has been the increasing political mobilization of the elderly, so that "gray power" can become effective in placing pressure on government for increased pensions and improved administration of pension programs. While these organizations clearly do not represent the broader public interest, they can be effective in placing pressures for improvements in social administration.

In evaluation, despite the obvious success of some groups, it is difficult to be very sanguine about their efficacy as a general solution to the problems of administrative control. Their effectiveness is limited by the same factors limiting the effectiveness of pressure groups more generally, mainly that they must work through second and third parties in order to have their suggestions or demands realized. Further, despite successes in the short run, many of the social groups that could benefit most by organizations of this type still have few of the political and organizational skills required for continued success. Finally, consumer groups and consumer agencies may, in the long run, prove to be little different from other types of agencies and other types of pressure groups. They may come to represent a special interest or, more appropriately, a special approach to consumer problems, requiring yet another set of controls to control the controllers.

Political Methods of Control

If the methods of publicity, organization, and internal discipline within the organization do not prove effective in controlling administration—as indeed they may not—then a second level of control will have to be introduced. This control is through political institutions. The logic is that political institutions rightly regard themselves as the representatives of the people, even when they have not been directly elected. They rightly regard themselves as the source of the delegated powers that the bureaucracy may currently exercise and as having the right to withdraw those powers if they are abused. The conflict between the political institutions and the bureaucracy over policy has already been discussed.[43] Many points made there apply to this discussion as well. Rather than arguing over the ability of these two sets of institutions to control policy in a broad sense, here we shall be looking at their respective abilities to control decisions in more specific cases, even if only in an ex post facto manner. Many powers of the several institutions are the same, but it is necessary to examine the ways in which those powers can be brought to bear on specific cases of administration or maladministration.[44]

The Legislature   Legislative institutions have come more to the forefront of the battle over administrative control in recent years. This is in part because the growing concern among voters has been translated into action by their elected representatives. Further, the sheer volume of administrative work now being performed has meant that there is more need for the legislature to exercise its oversight functions. This is especially true of the increasing volume of administrative rulings having the force of law and issued by powers delegated from the legislature. It is up to the legislature to try at least to keep track of these rulings, even if it is not always possible to control their content. Finally, executive dominance in policy making has left harassing administration one of the few remaining ways in which the individual legislator can acquire wide publicity and national stature.

1. *Funding*   Funding programs is a principal means through which the legislature is able to exercise control over administration. Some problems of exercising policy control through funding have already been discussed at length. However, although the power of the purse may be a blunt instrument in exercising broad policy control, it may be successful in dealing with a recalcitrant administrator or agency. Although we might hope that legislatures had something better to do with their collective time, the instances of committees and even whole legislatures spending substantial amounts of time on small problems of individual agencies, and even individual administrators, are legion, especially

within the United States. Few other political systems have allowed legislative bodies such freedom in budgeting to enable them to delve into the financial and administrative details of agencies. At the subnational level, again within the United States, legislative involvement in administration via the budget is even more evident, to the point of removing people from office simply by refusing to appropriate money for the positions they occupy. The punishment for improper administration is rarely so direct, but it does frequently occur by reducing the appropriations for the whole agency. These powers over budgeting give the American Congress and state legislatures significant controls over agencies that have been largely forfeited in parliamentary systems with stronger party discipline.[45]

Another aspect of the power of the purse in checking administration is a much blunter instrument. This is the ability to pass private legislation to compensate individuals for the actions of public administrators. Most political systems provide some means of passing "private bills" to afford such compensation, but these stipulate no penalties for the offending civil servant and require political leverage for the citizen who wants his grievances redressed.

The funding control of legislatures over administration is potentially a vital and powerful force, but as with many legislative weapons, it is a difficult one to employ effectively. By their very nature legislative bodies tend to be cumbersome, and detailed consideration of administrative actions can occur only in the sensational or highly politicized cases, even in systems such as that of the United States, which pride themselves on the ability to use the budget as a means of control. Also, the increasing importance of macro-economic policy has meant that substantial control over the budget has passed from legislatures to executives and central banks.[46] Budgets have become too important (economically and politically) to allow legislatures to use them to punish the wicked and reward the just.

2. *Investigation.* Probably the most frequently cited power of the legislature to control administration is through investigations. These may range from simple questions and interpolations in legislative sessions to full-scale committee investigations to the institutionalization of an officer to investigate for the legislature. All these devices rely in part upon publicity as a means of righting a wrong, but they can also be useful in writing new legislation and correcting defects in old legislation.

The simplest form of legislative investigation is the parliamentary question period. In virtually all parliamentary systems there is some means for legislators to ask questions of government ministers. While these may be about policy decisions made by the minister, they may also pertain to questions of administration within the ministry. This is especially true of systems in the British tradition, where the minister is considered responsible politically for all that goes on within the ministry, even down to the behavior of lowly clerks. The question hour can extract information, embarrass the government, and alert an "attentive public" to current problems of administration. Other than producing broader political debate on the topic, however, it can go no further. It depends upon the actions of the government, administrators, and the public to be effective in bringing about change.

Within the American context the most common form of legislative investigation is the congressional committee, generally operating through hearings.[47] The functional specialization of congressional committees and the further specialization into subcommittees, special committees, and select committees provide an extensive and well-qualified array of investigative bodies. This investigative role in Congress came into most prominence during the McCarthy period in the early 1950s and more recently has been prominent in investigations over the role of the CIA in internal affairs and the activities of the Food and Drug Administration. While these hearings have made headlines, they are overshadowed in volume by a large number of ongoing investigations into virtually every policy area. The ostensible purpose of these investigations is legislation, but in practice both the airing of information and the ability of the legislature to delve into the conduct of administration affect the behavior of the public bureaucracy.

Although the committee system of Congress and its investigations in the United States are most familiar, similar methods exist in other political systems. Germany has an extensive array of legislative committees specialized along functional lines and involved in legislative oversight of administration.[48] The United Kingdom has instituted a series of select committees of Parliament intended to monitor the work of Cabinet departments. There is also a select committee that monitors delegated legislation, a particularly difficult subject in a system predicated upon parliamentary responsibility for policy.[49]

We could go on enumerating slight differences in committee and investigatory arrangements, but the basic point is that legislatures investigate, they tend to do so through committees, and the investigations are generally related to exercising oversight within a specific policy field. These committees and their investigations have generally comprised a most effective legislative means of influencing the conduct of administration. The relationship between the committee and the agency tends to be an ongoing one, so the agency has a great deal to gain in the long run by cooperation. Further, the committees tend to be expert especially where members can and often do remain on the staff of the same committee for a long time. Nevertheless, there is a danger of the committee and the agency becoming too friendly, much in the way described in reference to pressure groups.[50]

The final method of legislative investigation might be discussed as a separate topic, given the amount of interest that has been expressed in it. This is the institution of the ombudsman or its equivalent.[51] Although often presented as a magical cure for what ails administration and society, this method of control generally relies upon the legislature as a means of implementation. Although there are variations between countries, the powers of the ombudsman generally do not include the ability to issue binding judgments on administrators or to effect restitution for an aggrieved citizen. In general, the ombudsman can investigate, negotiate with civil servants, report to the legislature, or perhaps introduce legislation. The legislature is then expected to carry the case onward if some reason for further action is found. Most commonly, this will involve simply providing some redress for the citizen, but several systems allow the ombudsman to introduce more general suggestions concerning procedures to prevent future problems.[52]

The ombudsman has been most commonly associated with Scandinavian countries, but the institution has now been adopted in the United Kingdom, New Zealand, Israel, Japan, in West Germany for military affairs, Yugoslavia, and in modified forms in Poland and the Soviet Union.[53] Also, several states in the United States have adopted the system.[54] Variations among systems are rather great, and little is to be gained from a detailed examination of those differences here. One major difference is the ability to act independently or not, with some officers such as the Parliamentary Commissioner in the United Kingdom requiring a request from a Member of Parliament before initiating action.[55] Another variation is the ability of the officer to initiate legislation or not, with the Finnish ombudsman, among others, having the ability to introduce legislation as a matter of right.[56] There is also the question of the coverage of policies, with some countries extending the system to cover prisoners and soldiers and others confining it to civil administration.[57]

On balance, the ombudsman system is difficult to evaluate. On the one hand, it provides a tribune for the people, with the advantage of being both inside and outside government. Being inside, or more properly being an officially sanctioned gadfly, allows the ombudsman access and requires that this person's findings and suggestions be taken seriously. On the other hand, being outside government makes the office appear to most people as one in which they have an advocate who is free of most bureaucratic impediments, and who will therefore freely speak for the "people."[58] At the same time that the office is symbolically well placed, its success requires a number of steps to be gone through. Most importantly, citizens who may be most in need of services are quite unlikely to be aware of the office. Success also depends upon the willingness of the legislature to follow through. This is in part dependent upon the stature of the individual holding the office, the degree of institutionalization of the office in the particular country, and legislative procedures in handling suggestions from the ombudsman.[59] It may also depend upon the type of results sought, whether compensation for individuals or punishment for administrators. The former may be easy to obtain, since sums of money sought are frequently minute or privileges rather minor. Actions against individual administrators may be more difficult to obtain, may have destructive effects on morale in the civil service, and may in fact accentuate problems of rigidity within the public bureaucracy. Thus, this system may be useful in redressing personal grievances but less successful as a means of bringing about significant procedural or policy changes within the public service.

3. *Constituency Service.* A third major means through which the legislature can influence the conduct of the civil service is what Americans refer to as "constituency service."[60] In Ireland it has been referred to as "going around persecuting civil servants."[61] The idea is the same. The average citizen frequently feels powerless in the face of bureaucracy and looks for some means of influencing that bureaucracy. One of the handiest such devices is the elected representative. After all, the citizen put this person in office, and the citizen should therefore be able to get the representative to do something for him. Thus, many legislators are expected to spend significant portions of their time solving problems that their constituents have encountered with the civil service. Perhaps the constituent did not get a pension check on time, or the veterans' death benefit is not paid as it should be, or a grant-in-aid for a local project is not approved. The legislator can become directly involved in attempting to find out what has happened, to get the problem corrected as quickly as possible. In practice, many legislators find this to be a significant portion of their jobs and an activity that is highly visible to constituents. While it may be a useful means of control, it often is also an inefficient means. It concentrates on particular cases, and the legislature may not have time to develop legislation to cover the more general problem. It also exhausts much of the credit that the legislators may have with the bureaucrats, by "persecuting" them over relatively petty issues. It is a method of control that is generally highly regarded by the recipients of its benefits, but that may in the long run perpetuate problems of control rather than solve them.

4. *Postaudit.* The final legislative power over administration to be discussed here is the postaudit of accounts.[62] Already noted are the powers of the legislature in the appropriations process; the legislature also exercises an oversight function after the funds have been spent. In virtually all political systems the postaudit function is a legislative function. In the United States the General Accounting Office is a creature of the Congress, responsible for reporting to the Congress on the improper expenditure of public money by administrative agencies.[63] The vast majority of auditing agencies, for example, the *Bundesrechnungshof* in West Germany and the Italian *Corte di Conti*, report to the legislature. Two significant exceptions are the French *Cours des Comptes* and the Controller and Auditor General in the United Kingdom. The *Cours des Comptes* is linked to the civil service through recruitment and staffing and to the president by formal organization. The office of Controller and Auditor General has, over time, changed in status from being a creature of Parliament to being more responsible to the Treasury and the government. Legislation introduced in the 1982–83 Parliament seeks to reverse the historical precedent, as well as to extend the authority of the Controller and Auditor General to nationalized industries.

The idea of the postaudit is fairly simple. The legislature appropriates money for specific purposes, and it must therefore be sure that the executive spends the money as appropriated. In some systems this is justified by the concept of the separation of powers, while in others it is simply to ensure that the public treasury is protected from undue demands. In either case, real spending is compared with authorized expenditure, and any discrepancies are noted. Depending on the system in question, individuals may be held personally responsible for any difference.[64]

The postaudit system of legislative control of administration made a great deal of sense when the bookkeeping of government was a bit like your father's old ledger in the desk upstairs. It is still a valuable means of checking on what has happened, but less so as the finances of government become more complex both in terms of variety of items purchased and complexity of financial arrangements. Government programs can no longer be readily calculated on the basis of annual appropriations; building a dam or an aircraft carrier simply takes much too long. So funds appropriated in any one year may be kept "in the pipeline" and quite legally spent some years later. Also, the exact purposes for which the funds were originally allocated may have become obsolete or the cost of performing a function may become (remarkably) cheaper, so that some of the funds in the pipeline may become almost discretionary. The Pentagon once calculated that, although Congress might cut off funds for the Vietnam War, it still had sufficient funds authorized in that proverbial pipeline to keep the conflict going for some months.[65] Not only does the pipeline present a problem to auditors, so do many reserve financial powers granted governments.

As noted, the budget is now a much too important part of economic policy and economic stability to allow it to be shackled entirely by decisions taken by the legislature some months in advance of execution. Therefore, many political systems allow the government considerable latitude in shifting not only the types of expenditure made, but even the aggregate total in order to attempt to overcome economic problems.[66] This is further affected by the uncontrollable nature of many expenditures dependent upon fluctuations in the economy (for example, unemployment benefits) and the greater latitude given public managers under reforms such as PPBS.[67] All in all, modern governmental finance makes the job of the auditor difficult and makes the job of the legislator in understanding the findings of the auditor equally difficult. Except in cases of *clear* misappropriation, the legislature must deal with a number of gray areas of law and policy, making control that much more difficult.

An even grayer area of control is the increasing interest in efficiency, or "value for money" audits.[68] Instead of being concerned solely with the legality of expenditures, auditing organizations such as the General Accounting Office have become increasingly interested in the efficiency with which outputs are produced for an input of money.[69] This has developed most significantly in Sweden, where not only do several organizations monitor efficiency, but new organizations have been created to develop procedures for more efficient government.[70] However, as well intentioned as these efforts are, the fundamental problems of defining outputs—and even defining inputs—makes the measurement of efficiency in government a very difficult problem.

5. *Summary.* The instruments of administrative control available to legislative bodies then, while important, suffer from many of the difficulties mentioned when discussing the relative strengths of the legislature and the bureaucracy in making public policy. These powers depend upon the concerted action of the legislature, which is not always forthcoming. Further, even if it is forthcoming, it is more likely to be far removed in time from the actual commission or omission of the offending administrative action. Likewise, it is increasingly difficult for legislatures to keep pace with the quantity of work required to be done in modern governments, making delegated legislative powers of the administrative agencies even more crucial to the conduct of government. Finally, the political power base of the legislator is not generally enhanced by performing the time-consuming, painstaking, and generally dull job of keeping track of agencies and their actions. Even if it were, the influence of partisan loyalty on decisions might prevent full exercise of oversight. Except for the occasional case that can be used to make publicity and political hay, much of this oversight work is unlikely to aid a legislator's career either with his constituents or his own party. There are, however, two major sources of legislative strength in exercising control. First, the major defense is an internal value structure within the legislature—possessed to some degree by certain committees in the American Congress and the German *Bundestag*—which places a high value on keeping track of the bureaucracy.[71] These norms are difficult to enforce and do little for the legislator who is not reelected, but they are crucial to effective control. Second, as policy-making powers pass to bureaucrats and to the political executive, the legislature's role may become increasingly that of watchdog. More time and energy may be available for the job of pursuing problems and persecuting the perpetrators.

The Executive In examining the organization chart of government, the political executive would appear to be in the best position to exercise control over the performance of the public bureaucracy. The lines of authority and control are all right there on the organizational chart; all that is required is the exercise of that authority. Or so it appears when we look solely at the formal structures. In practice, the operation of executive authority over the bureaucracy is substantially more difficult. The existence of the civil service system and other aspects of public personnel management frequently prevent political executives from obtaining the service and advice of the administrators that they might most like to employ. This is confounded by the feeling of many legislative bodies—perhaps quite accurate—that the best way of controlling an executive is to control the executive latitude in dealing with and leading the bureaucracy. Thus, the ability of the executive to control the bureaucracy—which frequently operates as an almost entirely separate branch of government—is seriously curtailed.

In the absence of the ability of the executive to hire, promote, move, and fire whomever he wants, a number of other less blatant controls come into play. Some of those operating through the budgetary process have already been mentioned, although more drastic executive fiscal powers such as impoundment may be used to place controls on the bureaucracy. These controls in many ways may constitute a meat ax rather than a scalpel and consequently cannot be readily employed. They offer little if any means of dealing with recalcitrant individuals or just plain rigidity in administration.

1. *Personnel Powers*. The powers of the executive in dealing with the bureaucracy are variable across political systems. The major variations come in the ability to appoint and remove officials, the ability to shuffle employees around among agencies and on and off personal staffs, and the ability to use executive authority to bring about reorganization of government. As for the ability to appoint, some variations have already been noted. The ability of an American president to appoint about two thousand people in the executive branch, to remove most of them without approval of the Senate, and to appoint his own personal staff are important powers even though restrained by many customs and procedural checks.[72] It becomes especially significant when compared with the British prime minister, whose appointment powers are virtually nonexistent and whose ministers have only a limited choice over the permanent secretary who will serve them in office. This may also be contrasted with the ability of the French, Belgian, and German ministers to select whomever they want as the *chef du direction* or its equivalent.[73] Attempts have been made, however, to more fully politicize the British civil service.[74] Likewise, many underdeveloped countries—especially those of Latin America—have developed the form without the substance of civil service arrangements, so that an incoming government has a fairly wide choice of its senior civil servants and advisers.[75] Totalitarian or authoritarian systems have more extensive controls over personnel; those who may be considered politically unreliable can be easily removed, demoted, or reappointed.[76]

2. *Investigation*. The executive also has the ability to conduct investigations of administrative activities. These investigations may be initiated by legislative actions, as when the results of a question in Parliament prove sufficiently embarrassing to provoke an executive response. Investigations are commonly done internally, and in fact many executive departments have their own divisions associated with continuous inspection and review. The military is perhaps most notable in this regard, with institutions such as the inspector general serving as an internal check on the administration and efficiency of the services. Likewise, the use of inspectorates is a quite common feature of the administrative system of France and of administrative systems derivative from the French tradition.[77] While their work is not entirely investigative, it certainly does involve some snooping into proper administration of the laws, especially financial laws. Finally, many political executives, meaning here mainly individuals at the ministerial or Cabinet level, may initiate their own investigations of problems and procedures simply because they are concerned about the functioning of their department.

However, just as was true for agencies, there are strong incentives for a "spending minister" to keep any irregularities in administration very quiet indeed.

Investigations of administration may also be initiated by higher executives—such as presidents and prime ministers—and will then frequently involve very broad perspectives on administration. In the American context, the Brownlow Commission and the two Hoover Commissions were examples of executive initiatives directed at thorough reviews of the structures and procedures of administration.[78] In the United Kingdom, commissions such as Fulton and Plowden have also involved extensive investigations into the basic structures and procedures of administration, with advocacy of sweeping reforms,[79] as did the Lambert Commission in Canada.[80] Other executive initiatives in investigating the work of public administration may be less sweeping and tend to be initiated by scandal or crisis. Even in societies with long histories of respect for the bureaucracy and of good administration, major scandals frequently generate large-scale investigations of administration.[81]

3. *Reorganization.* One important power granted to executives is the power to reorganize government. This power is not totally executive, with legislatures having at times equal or coordinate powers. While the legislature may help to change the shape of the organization chart and then go away to see what happens, the executive gets the opportunity to work with the new structure created. So an executive such as Franklin Roosevelt was able to effect extensive reorganizations and use those reorganizations for his own purposes in office.[82] At other times, the results of reorganization may not be those anticipated, as with the numerous reorganizations of the British government in the 1960s and 1970s.[83] However, the executive still gets the opportunity to try and make them work.

Reorganization can be used to place a mortmain on the activities of future executives and can therefore serve as a check on administration for some time in the future. Reorganizations—if that is not too weak a word—such as nationalization of industry make it difficult for any future executives to reverse the economic policies of one particular administration. It is simply too difficult to nationalize and reprivatize industry after every election, so once done, nationalization tends to persist. Mrs. Thatcher's widespread reprivatization is the exception that proves this rule, as is the Labour party's pledge to renationalize the next time they are elected. Likewise, when activities of government are "hived off" and depoliticized, it becomes difficult for subsequent executives, or, in many cases, incumbents of positions, to alter their structure without the appearance of being excessively partisan in handling policy.[84] Thus, "hiving off" may actually be "blanketing in."

Reorganization may also be important for establishing executive control. Many subnational governments, and some national governments, have gone to great lengths to depoliticize, hive off, and judicialize important political decisions. The existence of numerous appointive commissions, boards, institutes, etc., many of which are self-perpetuating or have sufficiently long tenures of office to prevent a political executive from having much real control over their composition, severely dilutes the ability of an executive to carry out control. He becomes, much as Neustadt's president, a bargainer but not a commander.[85] The justifications for the existence of independent bodies is well known, but the latent consequences must also be considered. As executives have come to be blamed, if not praised, for virtually everything that occurs within their governments, they want to be able to control what actually does happen and consequently would want to bring as many functions as possible under their purview. This does not ensure their success in exercising control, but it does give them a structural base with which to try. Even when agencies are under the control of the executive, reorganization can be used to attempt to make them conform more with the program of the executive, as the moving of the functions of the Office of Economic Opportunity under more conventional agencies can illustrate.[86] Again, there is no guarantee of success, but only of the opportunity.

4. *Fiscal Powers.* Finally, the executive may seek to control administration through fiscal powers. In most political systems the budget is an executive function and an executive document. Legislatures may certainly be involved in the final determination, but in a parliamentary system this is frequently little more than a rubber stamp. Thus, the executive has the opportunity to reward friends and punish enemies in a tangible fashion. On the other hand, the actual impact of many fiscal powers of the executive is often limited.

First, the fiscal powers are not often sensitive or flexible. It is difficult to punish one administrator, or at times even one agency, through the budget. This might involve reduction or elimination of appropriations of a larger administrative unit, which may be exactly the policy area in which the executive wanted more rather than less activity. Further, even if the powers were more sensitive, the political base of the agency may be such that the executive could not realistically afford to cut appropriations.

An executive is also limited in his ability to control many of the actors in the budgetary process. A prime minister in Britain, for example, may find it somewhat difficult to control the actions of the Treasury, just as it is difficult for other executives to control the actions of economic and fiscal planners or central banks.[87] In general, ministers of finance and their counterparts have gained substantial institutional powers over the budget, so that it may be difficult or impossible for a chief executive to intervene in the process personally, especially when this is seen to be politically motivated.[88] Further, the expertise of financial ministries may make such political imposition unwise. The chief executive may certainly have political influence over the actions of the finance minister, but frequently that cannot be translated into control of the budget, so the ability of a chief executive to use the fiscal powers will depend upon his ability to command the loyalty and obedience of the financial officer.

One fiscal power given to the president of the United States, but which is only implied in the majority of other political systems, is impoundment. Under the Congressional Budget and Impoundment Control Act of 1974 a president's power to reduce the appropriations of Congress is limited. If the president wishes to cancel that appropriation—a recision—he must obtain the agreement of both houses of Congress within forty-five days or the appropriation is continued. However, if the president only wants to delay the expenditure of money—a deferral—then unless one house of Congress disapproved, the wishes of the president would be implemented. These powers over expenditures, even with the possibility of congressional veto, give the president substantial independent control over expenditures and over the priorities of government.

5. *Summary.* The powers of the executive in dealing with the bureaucracy, despite the formal positions in the organizational chart of government, are somewhat constrained. Just as with internal discipline within administration, many tactics that would be useful in enforcing accountability would involve some political risk to the executive. Further, many reforms in the nineteenth and twentieth centuries have removed many of the options available to executives in controlling their organizations. Thus, the executive is left with a number of powers, but these are blunted by difficulty in distinguishing between whole agencies, individual administrators, and even effects on clients. The executive remains in a strong position to negotiate with the bureaucracy for compliance on policy and on procedure but is rarely in a position to command their obedience.

The Judiciary   The final set of institutional checks on the accountability of the civil service is the legal system. Virtually all political systems provide a means of citizens' challenging the actions of administrators and at times the policy choices made by government through administration. There are, however, a number of important variations in these judicial powers, which become important for an understanding of judicial control of administration.

The first major difference among Western and Western-derivative systems of law is between those systems having a separate system of administrative courts and those relying on the regular courts. This difference is not entirely clear-cut, however. Even systems of law using the regular courts for administrative matters (such as the United States, the United Kingdom, and many former British colonies) have large numbers of administrative hearings conducted in separate administrative tribunals within the administration itself.[89] These, in volume terms at least, greatly surpass the number of cases in the regular courts. Further, these systems tend to have separate bodies of administrative law, dealing with such matters as proper administrative procedure, the rights and duties of administrators, and the like even if these cases are adjudicated in the regular courts. Finally, even in countries using the regular courts, there may be some special courts that handle purely administrative matters, especially taxation. These three caveats aside, there is a difference between countries such as the United Kingdom, Denmark, and Norway, which use regular courts, and France, Germany, and Sweden (among others), which use administrative courts to handle administrative matters. To reach the regular courts, a case must generally have some importance as a matter of general law—in the United States it may frequently involve a constitutional question or denial of guaranteed rights such as due process or equal protection. This simply makes it more difficult to bring cases than in systems that are more used to dealing with strictly administrative malfeasance.

The general format of administrative courts is illustrated by the French mode, with a series of administrative courts roughly paralleling the organization of the regular courts. These end in the *section de contineaux* of the Conseil d'État.[90] The individuals serving as judges in these courts are generally themselves former administrators or at least trained as administrators in the ENA. As such, they bring special knowledge to their roles as adjudicators, which also raises the problem of their being potentially partial to the side of the administrator in a conflict. These courts have the right to both quash administrative actions and provide redress for individuals harmed by administrative actions— this redress may at times be recovered from the offending administrator. They can also provide punishment for the offending civil servant, even to the point of having him dismissed from service.

While the legal protections available in administrative law are certainly important, they too present a number of significant difficulties for the average citizen seeking to receive relief from what he considers an improper administrative act. The proceedings are legal, even in systems having separate administrative courts, and therefore involve specialized knowledge of procedure and form, which only a lawyer can provide. Thus, the expense of acquiring a lawyer— even if compensated later as it is in some systems if the citizen wins the case— can present an impediment to most citizens. Likewise, the need to have a justifiable complaint against the administrator, as opposed to simply a complaint about rudeness or delay that did not produce any real economic or personal harm, limits this as a device for control of mundane but still irritating aspects of maladministration.

Finally, administrative law operates as a check after the fact. It can generally only redress harm or quash actions; only rarely can it command the administration to perform actions. As such, it remains a negative check on bureaucracy. Thus, despite the general importance of the existence of administrative law as a control on administration, the check is limited by the complexity of most procedures, the slowness of the proceedings (the Conseil d'État currently has a backlog of several years), and the negative nature of the remedies available.

Normative Restraints

The final means of enforcing administrative accountability—that advocated by Friedrich—is normative control.[91] By this is meant the development of mechanisms within the bureaucracy and for individual bureaucrats that can serve as a guide to administration "in the public interest." This is certainly the cheapest form of control obtainable, and in the end the most efficient in that it can *prevent* grievances rather than merely correcting them ex post facto. Even if all the institutional mechanisms for control outlined were more effective than we tend to think they are, the lack of commitment to public service— or more properly an active commitment to private service—could prevent them from working just through the sheer magnitude of the problem. And if such a commitment to the public service is generally held—as indeed we believe it is—the need to employ institutional mechanisms would be rather slight, and any of them could do the job. The current state of administrative practice would seem to approximate more closely the latter situation than the former one of rampant bureaucratic malfeasance, even given the number of complaints that do arise against bureaucracy. If we look at the volume of complaints relative to the number of decisions and actions taken, it seems that most civil service systems on the average do a decent job. We still need institutional mechanisms for the deviant cases, but fortunately these remain the unusual rather than the typical.

It should be pointed out that all administrative systems need not have— nor do they have—the same values concerning the accountability of public officials. Ilchman speaks of the need for role congruence between the expectations of the population and the behavior of administrators.[92] The ideas of universalism and equality that are prized so highly in Western societies—and that form the basis of many complaints against bureaucracy—would find few supporters in non-Western countries. In fact, an administrator seeking to employ such values in decision making would encounter some of the same difficulties as an administrator in Western countries attempting to make decisions primarily on the basis of clan membership or race. In other words, the problems of accountability vary, just as do the cultures of administration, the basic consideration being that administrators do what is expected of them by the citizens.

Other than singing songs of praise to good administrative values, what can be done to promote accountability through normative constraints? In the short run probably very little. As noted, most political systems have a rather well-established conception of their bureaucracy, and in most systems this conception is not generally positive.[93] It is perhaps becoming less favorable due to increases in the size and cost of the public bureaucracy. Thus, the projection of good administrative values cannot come from the larger society, so it must be generated internally. This is relatively easy to do among the elite branches of the civil service, which have strong *esprit de corps*, a feeling of responsibility for the guidance of society, and already-favored positions in society.[94] It is considerably more difficult among the run-of-the-mill public employees, who have little to distinguish themselves from private employees upon whom great demands of public service and loyalty are not made. Again, we do not think that those who opt for public service are any better or worse than those who opt for private employment; the major difference is the demands and expectations of the job. If an employee of a private firm does not give the customer satisfaction, there is recourse to future consumer behavior. If a public employee fails to provide satisfaction, it may literally become a federal case.

The vast improvements in public salaries and benefits, condemned on many accounts, may also serve a useful function in terms of internalized controls in bureaucracy. The higher salary levels make the public service a safe and rewarding place of employment, and they also provide some tangible reward for the demands of the office. Higher salaries may also recruit more people of great talent to the public service, people who would have been deterred previously by the relatively low compensation.

The causal factor in some of the increases in public salaries—unions of public employees—may also play a valuable role in raising morale and standards in the public service. Unions can make the job of the civil servant more of a profession, just as higher salaries attract more qualified people. This is especially important in societies such as the United States or Australia, where the civil service has not been highly regarded and has not enjoyed the high status it commands in Western Europe.[95] One possible side effect, however, is to make the public service too much of a profession, and further isolate it from the society at large.

Normative control, then, is the ultimate control on bureaucracy. It is cheap, reliable, and operates before the grievance rather than simply providing compensation afterward. Most societies are indeed fortunate that they have such high levels of this form of control already in operation, so that the institutional mechanisms painfully outlined above have to be employed relatively infrequently.

THE LIMITS OF CONTROL

Aside from the average, garden-variety problems of administrative accountability and control, there are a number of more specialized problems and considerations that also deserve attention. In these cases, public control and accountability reach their limits and are often exceeded. Nevertheless, these problems are not that unusual any longer and require some extensive thought to be brought into line with normal thinking about responsible bureaucracy.

The Professions

One of the most commonly mentioned problems straining administrative control is the existence of professional employees within the public bureaucracy. Almost by definition, a professional has the type of internalized value structure concerning relationships with clients that were advocated earlier for civil servants. The problem is that these values often conflict with the values of the agency for which the professionals work. A common case is the scientist who works for a government research office. One norm of the scientific profession is the free flow of information and ideas.[96] Such free flow of ideas, during work for the government on secret materials, just would not be tolerated. In the same manner, a physician employed by a public agency continues to believe in his or her primary responsibility to the patient, which may come into conflict with record-keeping demands or requirements of standard treatment in the public organization. The list of similar conflicts could be extended, but the basic point is made. Professionals may have values that conflict fundamentally with the requirements of their public jobs. The public sector needs to employ professionals, so some accommodation of values must be made, perhaps on both sides. This is, however, one important instance in which the normal procedures of control and accountability may simply not be applicable.

Nationalized Industries

When government goes into business it also creates new problems of control and accountability.[97] In some ways public corporations appear to present fewer problems of control. After all, they have a statement of profit or loss (usually the latter), so that one can see at a glance just how well they are managed. In practice it is really not as easy as all that. In the first place, making a profit is but one goal, and perhaps not a very important goal, for a public corporation. If the function was profitable and profit was all we cared about, the industry might just as well have been left private. In the case of public transportation, the goals of providing cheap transportation and rapid transportation, reducing the numbers of automobiles on the roads, spreading out peak hours of traffic, redevelopment of declining areas, etc. may all conflict with the goal of making a profit. Thus, evaluation of the management of a public corporation may involve considerably more than simply looking at the balance sheet at the end of the year.

Second, there is almost invariably a difficulty in controlling public corporations that have been "hived off" from direct political control.[98] The most common structural arrangement for such corporations is to have an independent or semiindependent board of management. They are thus removed from direct lines of executive authority. While these lines of authority are no panacea for the problems of control, they at least provide a connection with government. A nationalized industry or public corporation is generally supposed to be independent of such control, presumably so that it can make economic rather than political judgments about its progress. This leaves the corporation in the position of obviously being a political entity but with only limited connection with political leadership and guidance. It is perhaps as awkward a position for the managers as it is for the public. It is also an awkward position for political leaders who may be held accountable for actions over which they have little or no control.

Unions

In addition to the positive benefits that unions of public employees can have for the public service, some problems of control are also engendered. As well as the protection afforded public employees by civil service regulations, many are now provided additional protection through unions. Likewise, many industrial employees who were minimally protected by civil service procedures are now more fully protected by unions. While these developments are perfectly understandable in modern societies, they make the job of the public manager much more difficult. There is the procedural problem of conforming to both civil service and union regulations on hiring, firing, and transferring employees. It is simply that much more difficult to manipulate staff the way the manager might like. In addition, employees must now be dealt with as a bloc, with threats of strikes even against vital services such as police and fire and sanitation. Unlike strikes in most industrial firms, there is no way of doing without those services for more than a short period of time, so public managers and political officials are forced to provide a settlement acceptable to the unions. Although these jobs may be, as in the case of sanitation workers, of very low status, their importance to the community may be such that they will be in a bargaining position comparable to that of physicians in the public service. So not only does the political system lose control over its employees, it also loses control over its own budget.[99]

Political Structure

The political structure of the country can also present significant difficulties in controlling the administration of public policy. Federalism is perhaps the most notable structure inhibiting control. The arrangements of federalism need not be as extreme as those of West Germany, which has most programs of the control government administered by the constituent Länder, but even the less extreme versions of the structure require some administration of programs by administrators not directly responsible to the policy-makers.[100] For example, in the United States most federal social-welfare law is executed by employees of state and local governments, as is most federal education law. This means simply that the control of the federal government is reduced and is left primarily with the rather blunt power of withdrawing federal money from the program. This control has been weakened even more under the Reagan "New Federalism" in which previous categorical programs have been converted into block grants with increasing difficulty in monitoring the use of federal money.

A variant of structure that also inhibits control of administration is the separation of policy-making and executing agencies, as in Sweden.[101] The ministries are held responsible for the formulation of policy, while the boards are held responsible for the execution of those policies. Again, there is a separation that can only make it more difficult to control what actually happens with a policy rather than simply what the policy is on paper.

Culture

We have already outlined variations in culture affecting the success or failure of bureaucratic means of policy execution.[102] We should perhaps remember those variations in the light of what we have been talking about in terms of control of administration. The basic point is that some political systems and cultures lack the normative commitment to public morality and proper administration so important for control of administration. Many, in fact, regard the Western model of bureaucracy as alien and almost immoral. The possession of a bureaucrat's job is not an evidence of public trust or responsibility, but rather an opportunity for the individual and the family. It is the individual who fails to provide handsomely for the family, rather than the individual who does, who will be regarded as immoral in such cultural settings. While Western (or nontraditional) values have certainly spread, they still are not universal, so we must be cognizant when speaking of administrative control of the very different cultural settings in which the problem may occur.

Nonadministration

Finally, nonadministration, just like nonpolicy, is difficult to control. It is much more difficult to control something that does not happen than something that is done improperly. In other words, it is considerably harder to get the bureaucracy to do something than it is to stop it from doing something it shouldn't be doing. This is an obvious restatement of the two dimensions of activity with which we began this chapter. There are few positive checks to force individuals or agencies to make decisions, while there are a number of procedures for stopping them, or for obtaining compensation for an improper decision. Even the political executive, who is presumed to be able to command action, may not be able to command in practice but may only bargain with the myriad of actors all of whom are somewhat involved in executing policy. Even a president vitally concerned about the presence of missiles in Cuba or urban problems in Oakland, or a minister of education concerned about educational reform, cannot command action.[103] The bureaucracy apparently has its own ways of doing things, which means that they will not necessarily be done when executives of government want them done. If presidents and prime ministers have these problems, what about us poor average citizens? The answer is that we have to rely first on the general acceptance of the ideas of "good government" by most of the people whom we employ in the public service, and second, we have to be willing to go to the trouble of using the available political methods when those internal norms do not work as we think they should.

SUMMARY

The basic conclusions of this chapter are actually summed up in the preceding sentence. The control of administration, even in the currently enlarged state of government and bureaucracy, seems to depend on two rather personal characteristics of people. The first is the internalized sense of their proper role on the part of civil servants. This sense of civic responsibility, duty, or even honor may vary across cultures, even within the narrow range of Western governments, but the basic ideas of responsiveness to demands, responsibility to political leaders, and accountability for actions are found in virtually all systems. They may not always be put into effect, but the values are generally understood. Most civil servants appear to accept these values and generally try to put them into operation. If it were not for this widespread acceptance of those values, all the institutional mechanisms of control outlined here would be buried in the sheer volume of maladministration.

The second component of a properly functioning system of administrative accountability and control is the population served by the civil service. In practice, most methods of accountability depend upon individual or group actions to press demands before the mechanisms can go into operation. Thus, responsibility and accountability imply a pair of actors—there must be someone to be responsible to. Even institutional mechanisms within political institutions such as legislatures would be ineffective if politicians found that the population did not care. There would be little or no incentive to expend energy and time. In short, there is simply no means of ensuring proper administration for an apathetic, cynical population.

If we return to the several dimensions of accountability and control with which we began this discussion, we can see that the two are quite well covered by the mechanisms outlined. First, there are a number of checks on bureaucratic institutions but relatively fewer checks on individuals, in large part due to their insulation by the organization. It is sometimes difficult for political institutions to deal with individuals without dealing with an entire organization. Thus, in order to keep the wheels of government turning, many personal actions may yet go unpunished. Likewise, there are any number of procedures for dealing with sins of commission but relatively few for dealing with sins of omission, or simply excessive rigidity. In many cases the "nonadministrators" are technically correct in terms of the rule book but manage to undermine the intent of programs by their adherence to the letter of the law.

It is clear from earlier chapters that the role of public bureaucracy in making public policy is on the increase. Therefore, the questions of accountability and control become even more crucial as bureaucracy grows in power. Trends in government and society would appear to make control both easier and more difficult for future generations of citizens and politicians. On the one hand, the spread of mass education and the media makes it easier for the population to be informed about the actions of bureaucracy. Legal changes in the requirements for publicity in several countries are making information more widely available. Mass education may also mean that the public bureaucracy will be drawn from a broader spectrum of the population and therefore have both greater empathy with the problems of citizens and a better understanding of the public's conception of bureaucracy. Finally, recent events in a number of countries—the United States, Japan, West Germany, and Italy are examples—have led their populations to be concerned about what happens in government and to be more willing to question the activities of public officials. If such healthy skepticism does not develop into cynicism and a rejection of the political system as immoral and essentially unjust, then it can help to promote effective popular control over bureaucratic behavior.

At the same time, there are several developments promoting greater insulation from control for the bureaucracy. In addition to the increasing size of bureaucracy and the complexity of the tasks it undertakes, the rising affluence of most Western populations has been associated with a growing demand for publicly provided goods. There may therefore be a feeling that goods and services produced through the political process may be superior to those privately provided, and therefore less questioning of the actual costs and benefits of public programs. In addition, a number of personnel practices in the public service may tend to insulate the bureaucracy further. In particular, the growth of public employee unions may limit the ability of managers to control personnel. Finally, there appears to be an increasing tendency to hive off and depoliticize public services. This is in part a reaction to the popular revulsion over politics mentioned above, in part due to the increasing involvement in services with some market characteristics, and in part a means of cutting obvious costs. In either case, depoliticization is in most cases simply a formula for bureaucratic power.

In sum, the pressures for greater accountability seem stronger than those for greater insulation. We may expect more public concern and involvement in public affairs. How effective this will be will ultimately depend upon the willingness of the population to persist in pressing its demands and using the mechanisms available to it. There is the danger that short-run failures may produce enduring cynicism and a long-term "tuning out" of the population from the affairs of government. The numerous institutional mechanisms discussed here are available to aid in the search for responsibility, but in the long run responsibility in government can come only from the interplay of responsible officials and citizens.

NOTES

1. See Carl J. Friedrich, "Public Policy and the Nature of Administrative Responsibility," in *Public Policy*, Friedrich and Mason, eds. (Cambridge, Mass.:

Harvard University Press, 1940); Herbert Finer, "Administrative Responsibility in Democratic Government," *Public Administration Review* 1 (1941): 335–50.

2. A useful summary for the United States is W. W. Boyer, *Bureaucracy on Trial* (Indianapolis: Bobbs-Merrill, 1967).

3. Some indication of the volume is given in R. G. S. Brown, *The Management of Welfare* (London: Fontana, 1975), pp. 104–6. Also, Committee on Tribunals (Franks Committee), *Report, Cmnd. 218* (London: HMSO, 1957). Also, in the United States, the Social Security Administration now handles over 4 million cases each year.

4. Even on appeal, the facts found in the administrative hearing are generally the facts of the case (in the U.S.), with decisions being overturned on points of law.

5. Anthony Downs, *Inside Bureaucracy* (Boston: Little, Brown, 1966), pp. 132–33.

6. The latter case is one in which, although the welfare officers are operating within their legal authority, their actions so violate many people's conceptions of the role of the bureaucracy that they have brought the place of the welfare system into question.

7. Richard Crossman, *H. C. Debates*, 18 October 1966, vol. 734, 55, col. 51.

8. See the Introduction and chapter 4.

9. Eugene Bardach and Robert A. Kagan, *Going By the Book: The Problem of Regulatory Unreasonableness* (Philadelphia: Temple University Press, 1982).

10. Dwight Waldo, *The Administrative State* (New York: Knopf, 1948). United States Civil Service Commission, *History of the Federal Civil Service* (Washington, D.C.: Government Printing Office, 1941).

11. One important exception is West Germany, where senior civil servants are indeed identified politically and where, as the "purges" of 1969 showed, changes in governments may also involve changes in civil servants. See N. Lehmann and Renate Mayntz, *Personal im öffentlichen Dienst* (Baden-Baden: Nomas Verlag, 1973), chap. 11.

12. For reviews, see Henry Parris, *Constitutional Bureaucracy* (London: Allen & Unwin, 1968); Ari Hoogenboom, *Outlawing the Spoils* (Urbana, Ill.: University of Illinois Press, 1968).

13. We gave some indication of the structure of incentives in chapter 3, with the basic finding that few people are attracted into the public service because of the ability to do things to or for society but rather more often are attracted by social conditions or monetary rewards.

14. Hugh Heclo, *A Government of Strangers* (Washington, D.C.: The Brookings Institution, 1977).

15. See Renate Mayntz, "German Federal Bureaucrats: A Functional Elite Between Politics and Administration" (Paper presented at Conference on the Role of Higher Civil Servants in Central Government, Madrid, Spain, December 1980); Marie-Christine Kessler, *La politique de la haute fonction publique* (Paris: Presses de la Fondation Nationale des Sciences Politiques, 1978).

16. Hugo Young, Sarah Hogg, and Jan Connell, "Thatcher's Mandarins," *The Sunday Times*, 11 July 1982, p. 17.
17. Friedrich, "Public Policy."
18. See Nils Herlitz, "Publicity of Documents in Sweden," *Public Law* 17 (1958): 54–59; Sigvard Holstad, "Sweden," in Donald C. Rowat, ed., *Administrative Secrecy in Developed Countries* (London: Macmillan, 1979), pp. 29–50.
19. Stanley V. Anderson, "Public Access to Government Files in Sweden," *American Journal of Comparative Law* 3 (1973): 419–473.
20. Roger Choate, "The Public's Right to Know," *Current Sweden*, no. 93 (Stockholm: Swedish Institute, 1975), p. 4.
21. For a general review see Rowat, *Administrative Secrecy in Developed Countries*.
22. See *Departmental Committee on Section 2 of the Official Secrets Act of 1911*, Cmnd. 5104 (London: HMSO, 1972); Jonathan Aiken, *Officially Secret* (London: Routledge and Kegan Paul, 1971).
23. This "facelessness" and anonymity is also quite closely related to the constitutional principle of ministerial—as opposed to civil-service—responsibility for all public acts of the ministry. This principle is, however, being modified significantly. See Maurice Wright, "Ministers and Civil Servants: Relationships and Responsibilities," *Parliamentary Affairs* 30 (Summer 1977): 293–313.
24. Downs, *Inside Bureaucracy*, pp. 88, 92–97.
25. Germany has an extensive arrangement of this sort through the disciplinary courts. See K. E. von Turegg, *Lehrbuch des Verwaltungsrecht*, 4th. ed. (Berlin: DeGruyter, 1962), pp. 339ff.
26. One interesting account is Richard N. Billings and John Grierga, *Power to the Public Worker* (New York: Luce, 1974). See also Alan Edward Bent and T. Zane Reeves, *Collective Bargaining in the Public Sector* (Menlo Park, Calif.: Benjamin/Cummings, 1978).
27. Leonard Reed, "Firing a Federal Employee: The Impossible Dream," *Washington Monthly* 9 (July 1977): 14–25.
28. See chapters 5, 6, and 7.
29. It may still be better to clean one's own house than to be caught.
30. Peter M. Blau, *The Dynamics of Bureaucracy*, 2nd. ed. (Chicago: University of Chicago Press, 1963), pp. 137–193.
31. Ezra N. Suleiman, *Elites in French Society: The Politics of Survival* (Princeton: Princeton University Press, 1978), pp. 140–144; William M. Evan, "The Inspector General in the U.S. Army," in *The Ombudsman*, ed. D. C. Rowat (London: Allen and Unwin, 1965), pp. 147–152.
32. Charles Peters and Taylor Branch, *Blowing the Whistle: Dissent in the Public Interest* (New York: Praeger, 1972).
33. Edward Weisband and Thomas M. Franck, *Resignation in Protest* (New York: Viking, 1975).
34. There is one inspector general in each cabinet-level department, with several others handling complaints from other executive agencies.
35. See chapter 5.
36. Mark V. Nadel, *The Politics of Consumer Protection* (Indianapolis: Bobbs-Merrill, 1972); James E. Anderson, "Economic Regulatory and Consumer

Protection Policies," in *Nationalizing Government*, Theodore J. Lowi and Alan Stone, eds., (Beverly Hills, Calif.: Sage, 1978), pp. 61–84.

37. See Ruth Link, "Consumers Take the Initiative," *Current Sweden*, no. 78 (June 1975); Richard C. Leone, "Public Interest Advocacy and the Regulatory Process," *Annals of the American Academy of Political and Social Science* 400 (March 1972): 46–58.

38. This concept has been subject to much unfavorable analysis, especially in Daniel Patrick Moynihan's *Maximum Feasible Misunderstanding* (New York: Free Press, 1969).

39. James L. Sundquist, "Coordinating the War on Poverty," *Annals of the American Academy of Political and Social Science* 385 (1969): 46–48.

40. See a series of articles in the *Times* (London), 9–13 February 1976. Also, "Shaky Start to Participation," *The Economist* 258 (13 March 1976): 128. Norman Dennis, *Public Participation and Planner's Blight* (London: Faber & Faber, 1973).

41. John D. Montgomery, "The Populist Front in Rural Development: Or Shall We Eliminate the Bureaucrats and Get on With the Job?" *Public Administration Review* 39 (1979): 58–65.

42. See Michael Lipsky and Margaret Levi, "Community Organizations as a Political Resource," *Urban Affairs Annual* 6 (1972): 177–95.

43. See chapter 6.

44. Geoffrey Marshall, "The Techniques of Maladministration," *Political Studies* 23 (1975): 305–18; K. C. Wheare, *Maladministration and Its Remedies* (London: Stevens, 1973).

45. For a discussion of the relative budgetary powers of a number of parliaments see David Coombes et al., *The Power of the Purse* (London: Allen and Unwin, 1976); For Britain see Ann Robinson, *Parliament and Public Spending: The Expenditure Committee of the House of Commons* (London: Heinemann, 1978).

46. An important counterforce has been the development of the Congressional Budget Office in the United States as an independent source of economic and budgetary analysis. This office is especially significant when the presidency and Congress are controlled by different political parties. See Allen Schick, *Congress and Money* (Washington, D.C.: The Urban Institute, 1981).

47. Morris S. Ogul, "Congressional Oversight: Structure and Incentives," in Lawrence C. Dodd and Bruce I. Oppenheim, *Congress Reconsidered*, 2nd. ed. (Washington, D.C.: Congressional Quarterly, 1981), pp. 317–31.

48. Winfried Steffani, "Amerikanischer Kongress und Deutscher Bundestag— ein Vergleich," in *Parlamentarismus*, Kurt Kluxen, ed. (Köln: Kiepenheim & Witsch, 1967), pp. 230–46.

49. This is a particular problem for legislation passed by the European Parliament or legislation that comes from the European Commission. Another committee monitors those sources of law and informs Parliament of possible conflicts with British laws or customs.

50. See chapter 5.

51. See Walter Gellhorn, *Ombudsmen and Others* (Cambridge, Mass.: Harvard University Press, 1967); Donald C. Rowat, ed., *The Ombudsman: Citizen's*

Defender (London: Allen and Unwin, 1965); Frank Stacey, *The Ombudsman Compared* (Oxford: Clarendon Press, 1978).

52. The Finnish and New Zealand ombudsman is clearly given this power, while the Danish and Swedish have gained the power largely through accretion and custom. See, for example, I. M. Pedersen, "The Danish Parliamentary Commissioner in Action," *Public Law* 115 (1959): 116–20; G. Langrod, "Le controle parlementaire de l'administration dans le pays nordiques: le rôle de Ombudsman en Suede, en Finlande et au Danemark," *Revue administrative* 12 (1959): 664–73.

53. Gellhorn, *Ombudsmen.*

54. Stanley V. Anderson, *Ombudsman Papers* (Berkeley: Institute of Government Studies, 1969).

55. Frank Stacey, *The British Ombudsman* (Oxford: Clarendon Press, 1971), pp. 307–310; William B. Gwyn, "The Ombudsman in Britain: A Qualified Success of a Government Reform," *Public Administration* 60 (1982): 177–95.

56. Paavo Kastavi, "Finland's Guardians of the Law," in Rowat, *Ombudsman,* pp. 58–74.

57. West Germany has only an ombudsman for military affairs, while Sweden and Norway have a separate military ombudsman. The Danish and Finnish ombudsmen receive complaints on military affairs. The New Zealand ombudsman and the procurators in the communist countries generally do not handle military affairs. The ombudsmen in virtually all these systems have the right to receive complaints from prisoners, although few are received except in the Scandinavian countries. The Soviet procurator also is involved in prison inspection.

58. Gellhorn, *Ombudsmen,* pp. 45–46, 65–66, 217.

59. Ibid., pp. 420–39.

60. Charles L. Clapp, *The Congressman: His Work as He Sees It* (Washington, D.C.: Public Affairs Press, 1963), pp. 75–84; Morris P. Fiorina, *Congress: The Keystone of the Washington Establishment* (New Haven: Yale University Press, 1977); Richard Fenno, *Home Style: House Members in Their Districts* (Boston: Little, Brown, 1979).

61. Basil Chubb, "Going Around Persecuting Civil Servants: The Role of the Irish Parliamentary Representative," *Political Studies* 11 (1963): 272–86; James D. O'Donnell, *How Ireland Is Governed* (Dublin: Institute of Public Administration, 1977), pp. 38–39.

62. E. L. Normanton, *The Accountability and Audit of Governments* (Manchester: Manchester University Press, 1966); "Public Accountability and Audit: A Reconnaissance," in B. L. R. Smith and D. C. Hague, *The Dilemma of Accountability in Modern Government* (London: Allen & Unwin, 1971), pp. 311–46.

63. Frederick D. Mosher, *The G.A.O.: The Quest for Accountability in American Government* (Boulder, Colorado: Westview Press, 1979); Harris, *Congressional Control,* pp. 135–52.

64. Normanton, *Accountability.*

65. This problem is particularly acute in Italy, where the budget merely limits the amount to be spent rather than funds a program. See articles by Valerio

Onida, Vittorio Mortara, and Sabino Cassese in Coombes, *Power of Purse.*

66. This is most notable in Germany under the Economic Stability Law of 1967. Also, the ability of the French government to put a budget into effect without approval of Parliament severely reduces the "power of the purse" in that system.

67. See George A. Steiner, "Problems of Implementing Program Budgeting," in *Program Budgeting,* David Novick, ed. (New York: Holt, Rinehart & Winston, 1969), pp. 328–47.

68. ———, *Value for Money Audits* (London: Royal Institute of Public Administration, 1982).

69. Mosher, *The G.A.O.*

70. Rune Premfors, "Sweden," *Efficiency and Effectiveness in the Civil Service* (House of Commons, Treasury and Civil Service Committee, 8 March 1982).

71. Steffani, "Amerikanischer Kongress."

72. Hugh Heclo, *A Government of Strangers* (Washington, D.C.: The Brookings Institution, 1977).

73. See Ezra Suleiman, *Politics, Power and Bureaucracy in France* (Princeton: Princeton University Press, 1974), pp. 137–54. Leo Moulin, "The Politicization of Administration in Belgium," in *The Mandarins of Western Europe,* M. Dogan, ed. (New York: John Wiley, 1975), pp. 163–86. Lehmann and Mayntz, *Personal im öffentlichen Dienst.*

74. Sir John Hoskyns, "Whitehall and Westminster: An Outsider's View," in *Fiscal Studies* 3 (1982): 162–72.

75. F. Tannenbaum, "Politica y administracion publica en Latinoamerica," *Foro Internacional* 4 (1963): 243–59; Jackton B. Ojwang, "Kenya and the Concept of Civil Service Political Neutrality: A Case of Silent but Determined Politicization," *Indian Journal of Public Administration* 24 (1978): 430–40.

76. Jerry F. Hough, *The Soviet Prefects: The Local Party Organs in Industrial Decision-Making* (Cambridge, Mass.: Harvard University Press, 1969), pp. 149–77.

77. See, for example, Pierre Lalumiere, *L'Inspection des finances* (Paris: PUF, 1959); Suleiman, *Elite in French Society.*

78. Peri E. Arnold, "The First Hoover Commission and the Managerial Presidency," *Journal of Politics* 38 (1976): 46–70; James G. March and Johan P. Olsen, "Organizing Political Life: What Administrative Reorganization Tells Us About Governing" (Paper presented to convention of the International Political Science Association, Rio de Janeiro, August 1982).

79. The Committee on the Civil Service (Fulton Committee), *Report, Cmnd. 3638* (London: HMSO, 1968); Committee on the Control of Public Expenditure (Plowden Committee), *Report, Cmnd 1432* (London: HMSO, 1961); John Garrett, *The Management of Government* (Harmondsworth, Middlesex: Penguin, 1972).

80. Royal Commission on Financial Management and Accountability, *Final Report* (Ottawa: Minister of Supplies and Services, 1979).

81. As, for example, in Norway following the Kings Bay coal disaster. See John Higley, Karl Erich Brofuss, and Knut Grohalt, "The Top Civil Servants and the National Budget in Norway," in Dogan, *Mandarins,* pp. 252–54.

82. See Arthur M. Schlesinger, Jr., *The Coming of the New Deal* (Boston: Houghton Mifflin, 1959), pp. 521–27.

83. See, for example, *The Reorganization of Central Government, Cmnd. 4506* (London: HMSO, 1970); Richard A. Chapman and J. R. Greenway, *The Dynamics of Administrative Reform* (London: Croom Helm, 1980).

84. A summary of these problems and the reactions of the "reform movement" in the U.S. is given in York Willbern, "Administration in State Government," *The Forty-Eight States: Their Tasks as Policy Makers and Administrators* (New York: American Assembly, 1955), chap. 5.

85. Richard Neustadt, *Presidential Power* (New York: John Wiley, 1960); Heclo and Salamon, *The Illusion of Presidential Leadership*.

86. "Who is Responsible for Caring for the Poor?" *Congressional Digest* 52 (August 1973): 195–224.

87. Perhaps the most obvious case of this conflict was between President Lyndon Johnson and William McC. Martin, chairman of the Federal Reserve Board of Governors, in 1964. Similarly, President Reagan and Chairman of the Federal Reserve Board Paul Volcker have not always agreed on monetary policy.

88. See, for example, Renate Mayntz and Fritz W. Scharpf, *Policy-Making in the German Federal Bureaucracy* (Amsterdam: Elsevier, 1975), pp. 42–45.

89. R. E. Wraith and P. G. Hutcheson, *Administrative Tribunals* (London: Allen and Unwin, 1973), pp. 43–70, provide a description and enumeration of tribunals in the United Kingdom. See also Z. M. Nedjati and J. E. Trice, *English and Continental Systems of Administrative Law* (Amsterdam: North Holland, 1978).

90. F. F. Ridley and J. Blondel, *Public Administration in France* (London: Routledge & Kegan Paul, 1964), pp. 148–59; Nedjati and Trice, *English and Continental Systems*, pp. 36–40.

91. Friedrich, "Public Policy."

92. Warren F. Ilchman, *Comparative Public Administration and the "Conventional Wisdom"* (Beverly Hills: Sage, 1971), pp. 35–38.

93. See chapter 2.

94. See, for example, Bernard Gournay, "Un Groupe dirigant de la Societé francaise: les grands fonctionnaires," *Revue Francaise de science politique* 14 (1964): 215–42; Suleiman, *Elites in French Society*.

95. See, for example, the evidence reported in chapter 2.

96. Don K. Price, *Government and Science* (New York: Oxford University Press, 1962), pp. 95–123; Michael D. Reagan, *Science and the Federal Patron* (New York: Oxford University Press, 1969); Elizabeth Morrissey and David F. Gillespie, "Technology and the Conflict of Professionals in Bureaucratic Organizations," *Sociological Quarterly* (1975): 319–32.

97. W. H. Robson, "Ministerial Control of the Nationalized Industries," *Political Quarterly* 40 (1969): 103–12, 494–96; Maurice Garner, "Auditing the Efficiency of Nationalized Industries: Enter the Monopolies and Mergers Commission," *Public Administration* 60 (1982): 409–28.

98. Of perhaps more relevance to the readers of this volume is the "hiving off" of scientific and educational organizations such as the National Science

Foundation or the University Grants Committee (UK). On attempted congressional control of the NSF see *Science* 188 (1975): 338–41.

99. Sterling Spero and John M. Capozzola, *The Urban Community and Its Unionized Bureaucracies* (New York: J. Dunellen, 1973).

100. In general, however, the central government is able to extend its control over the *Länder*. See Konrad Hesse, *Der Unitarische Bundesstaat* (Karlsruhe: Miller, 1962).

101. Pierre Vinde and Gunnar Petri, *Hur Sveriges Styres* (Stockholm: Prisma, 1975), pp. 84–89.

102. See chapter 2.

103. See Graham Allison, "Conceptual Models and the Cuban Missile Crisis," *American Political Science Review* 63 (September 1969): 701–6; Jeffrey Pressman and Aaron Wildavsky, *Implementation* (Berkeley: University of California Press, 1974).

CHAPTER 9

PUBLIC ADMINISTRATION IN THE 1980s

Administering public programs has never been an easy task. The very nature of government programs—their diffuse goals, unmeasurable or even unidentifiable benefits, and their politicization—make effective administration difficult. But the administration of public programs has become even more difficult in the 1980s. This increasing difficulty is a function of several different aspects of the economic, social, and political environments within which administration is being conducted. The most important factor affecting administration is the real—or perceived—scarcity of resources available to the public sector. The "go-go" days of the 1960s are now long past, and even the confused economic picture of the 1970s may appear more hospitable to political leaders having to make decisions about revenues and expenditures in the early 1980s. What is most disconcerting about the economic problems of the 1980s is that, unlike other recessions during the postwar period, there is apparent agreement that there is no short-time solution and there is likely to be an extended period of slow or nonexistent economic growth.

But it is not just the state of the economy that makes administration difficult. Citizens have become increasingly wary of the power of the "bureaucracy" over their lives, and even in countries with histories of strong and relatively benevolent government (Sweden, the United Kingdom) there has been some reaction against bureaucracy and administration. This resistance to public organizations is at least in part a function of the failures of past policies and programs, which in turn produce skepticism about the efficacy of any "new" programs. The weakness of economic management is chief among these failures.

Finally, the increasingly centrifugal nature of government and its complexity make administration more difficult. Public organizations are tied directly to private sector organizations, so that citizens may wonder whether the organizations are acting in the "public interest." Furthermore, within the public sector itself, there are so many organizations that affect the administration of a single program that interorganizational politics complicate the administration of what is apparently a simple program.

SCARCITY AND ADMINISTRATION

For most of the countries in the world, scarcity is a basic and continuing fact of life, while for the majority of Western countries it is a more recent phenomenon. The long-term scarcity facing almost all Third World countries creates massive problems for public program administrators in those countries. The uncertainty of the budgeting and planning process, combined with the simple fact that there are not enough resources to meet legitimate needs of the population, makes trying to manage these economies and societies very difficult for even the most capable administrator.[1]

For the Western world, the constraints of scarcity have been reimposed after several decades of rapid and sustained economic growth.[2] This has required an adjustment in policies and policy-making styles premised on such growth. For political leaders, scarcity has meant that instead of only distributing good news, they must take part of the blame for the poor shape of economies. For public administrators scarcity has meant adjusting the internal functioning of their organization, their relationships with clients, and their expectations about the future of their programs. Administrators who once would make a name for themselves by expanding their programs must now try to protect their images by restricting growth or even by careful pruning.

One fundamental factor that has changed is that economic growth can not be relied upon to fund ever-increasing numbers of programs and ever-increasing salaries for civil servants. Money may not be the only—or even the best— means of motivating civil servants, but it certainly does not hurt.[3] When the real incomes of civil servants begin to decline—as they have done—then it is also likely that morale will also decline. The decline in morale may be even more pronounced when the civil servants must also deliver programs providing reduced benefits to clients. It is quite probable that a feeling of failure and alienation from the program, and even from the political system more broadly, will be generated by such a combination of reductions. Those workers will have been denied both the direct rewards of their salary and the indirect rewards of providing services to clients in ways that they and the clients would both prefer. Consequently, the (very difficult) task of administrative leaders is to provide alternative sources of satisfaction for workers.

The denial of some of the satisfactions of employment is not made any easier by the threats of cutbacks and terminations of organizations that have become more common during the 1970s and 1980s. It was conventional to assume that government organizations were immortal, but the events of the 1980s do not support such a contention.[4] In the United States the Reagan administration had discussed the termination of the newly created Departments of Education and Energy, as well as a number of lesser agencies. In the United Kingdom a round of "quango bashing" has resulted in the elimination of several hundred small quasi-governmental bodies. Even in Sweden, the paragon of the welfare state and Big Government, organizations have been terminated and cut back severely. In virtually all countries one of the reactions of government to increasing demands for expenditures and decreasing real revenues has been to eliminate employees or whole organizations. The difficult task for managers, therefore, is to manage these cutbacks in manners that produce minimal disruption for remaining organizations, workers, and clients. This is especially important given that government experiences functional termination much less frequently than program or organizational termination.[5] That is, even though some employees and organizations may be eliminated, government will continue to provide some of the same types of services, and mechanisms must be found for consolidating or reorganizing the implementation of the programs without completely upsetting the routines of government.

Levine offers some guidance for "cutback management" in the public sector.[6] A first decision that any manager must make is whether to resist cutbacks or only to smooth the transition from the more affluent to the less affluent mode of service delivery. These strategies may be quite different, for the rigidity that may be generated in a pitched battle against retrenchment may make any subsequent cutbacks more difficult or may lead to the total elimination of the program rather than just a cutback. Likewise, a manager must decide what the sources of his or her difficulties are. Strategies will be very thorny if the source of the difficulties is entirely economic, as compared to problems that stem from changes in the demand for the service being rendered or in the political support available to the organization. In the case of economic decline it may be more productive to attempt to resist the change and displace greater cuts onto other organizations, whereas when there is a decline in support more may be gained by making the transition as painless as possible. Neither of these options may be palatable for managers bred on years of growth and expansion, but they may be the only options open.

Thus, management in the 1980s has become—and may well continue to be—the task of attempting to produce results with dwindling real resources. This will require capable managers, but the dwindling of resources and the declining competitive position of public sector wages may mean that those managers cannot be attracted to government.

INCREASING CHALLENGES TO GOVERNMENT AND ADMINISTRATION

Not only does the economic environment generate difficulties for administrators, but citizens themselves do not represent the pliant population that they once did. This increasing difficulty experienced by administrators appears related to a number of factors. One is simply the size of government itself. Some citizens feel themselves disadvantaged by the "growth of government" and consequently do not feel like accepting the dictates of that government. Such a reaction may be specific, as individuals refuse to honor certain types of laws and regulations, for example, tax laws; or it may be more general, as some citizens attempt to withdraw from the monetized, regulated economy to a simpler life.[7] Even in the absence of these extreme reactions citizens may simply be less willing to accept laws and regulations, and may try to avoid rather than evade taxation and other laws.

Associated with the size of government is the complexity and interactions of many laws and regulations. An individual in a modern society is affected by a range of policies, some of which may be contradictory or mutually canceling. The number of individual bureaucracies making rules about any industry or any type of behavior may be so large and so sufficiently uncoordinated that the individual feels that if government does not know what it wants, then why should the citizen attempt to figure it out for them.

Also, citizens have seen it all before. An administrator attempting to implement a "new" program may find that in fact it is really a program that has been tried previously—and failed. Frequently governments appear to rediscover solutions that they have previously rejected, especially when there are changes in governments and the institutional memory is at least partially lost.[8] Even when there is not a return to a rejected solution, a number of changes in a policy area may generate cynicism and an unwillingness to accept any programmatic changes. This problem has been especially pronounced in social policy, where change after change has been advertised as *the* solution to the problems of the poor, but where each program is actually just another milepost in a long journey attempting to solve those problems.

Finally, many policies simply have not worked or have not produced the intended effects.[9] Further, many that have worked may appear inefficient and excessively clumsy. Many of the complaints directed against regulations as mechanisms for producing certain desired benefits of the society have been that direct prohibition of activities may not be as efficient as incentives or tax-based mechanisms. Consequently, several alternatives to direct public intervention have been proposed.

One of the most commonly mentioned alternatives to direct intervention is replacement with tax incentives, especially in the area of environmental regulation. Instead of prohibiting pollution or setting maximum allowable levels, firms would be taxed according to the amount of pollution that they emitted. This would provide the firms with an incentive to clean up their plants. Further, given that more efficient firms could better afford to pay the effluent taxation, they could become more profitable relative to less efficient firms, and the utilization of resources in the economy as a whole would be improved.

A more extreme approach to the problem of perceived governmental inefficiency and clumsiness would be to reprivatize the public activities in question. That is, instead of having government administer the program at all, it could be returned to the private sector, albeit with some public control and regulation. In principle, almost all public sector programs could be provided through the private sector, and some reprivatization is already well under way in the United States and other countries. Even some traditional defining functions of government, for example, fire and police protection, could be provided—and have been provided—by the private sector.[10] Some extreme positions hold that even items such as public streets should be sold off to private firms. There is no guarantee, however, that this would satisfy more than the ideological preferences of such advocates. As many public services involve the granting of monopoly rights, for example, a street, there would be no more competition than there was when the service was in the public sector. Further, many of the inefficiencies found in the delivery of government services may be functions of large-scale organization as much as functions of large-scale organization in the public sector.

But it is not just the preferences of citizens that have changed. The attitudes of employees—again whether in the public or the private sector—are different than they were prior to the 1960s. Large organizations have traditionally depended upon the willingness of employees to accept the authority of organizational superiors, and to accept the correctness of the rules and procedures of the organization. Most workers are no longer willing to accept this degree of control in an unquestioning fashion. Rules and orders now require explanation, and workers expect to be involved in the making of policy that affects their work. This involvement may produce, in the long run, improved performance, as it gives employees more of a commitment to the goals and procedures within the organization. This has been especially true in Japanese organizations, and to a lesser extent in Scandinavian organizations. But the process of adjustment for managers who have not been accustomed to dealing with employees in this manner may be difficult. Management has ceased to be conducted by authority and is increasingly a process of explanation and discussion. Interestingly, this is true even in public sector organizations that have been most authority-oriented, for example, the military.[11]

COMPLEXITY IN ADMINISTRATION

The point above concerning privatization of public functions relates to another salient feature of administration in the 1980s that makes the job of the public sector manager more difficult. This is the increasing complexity of the "implementation structures" within which those managers manage. One of the aspects of that complexity is the increasing degree of fusion between the public and private sectors. The second aspect is the degree of complexity that exists within the public sector itself.

Traditional liberal social thought has made the distinction between state and society, with the former serving as the embodiment of the legitimate authority of the latter, so long as basic contractual or natural rights were fulfilled.[12] In the 1980s, the arbitrary distinction between state and society does not have much validity in the majority of industrialized societies. Similarly, extensive differentiation of state institutions may not have occurred in most less industrialized societies and certainly is not true of socialist governments.

In the first place, the public sector is making increasing use of the resources and capabilities of the private sector. A large number of public programs are implemented by private organizations. These range from the announcements made by cabin personnel in airplanes requiring passengers to buckle their seat belts to professional organizations deciding who should and should not be given the right to practice the profession. A more complex pattern of private enforcement of public policies is the wide-scale utilization of agricultural organizations to implement public agricultural policy.[13] The implementation of these laws typically involves a local organization dividing among its members an acreage allocation determined centrally. Finally, private organizations are used to provide services that might otherwise be directly provided by public employees. For example, in the United Kingdom the government contracts with the Law Society to provide legal services to the indigent. Governments contract to obtain a variety of goods and services, but contracts such as the above are significantly different. They enable—and require—an organization to act in the name of government in order to implement a law. Government by contract is government at one remove, and the problems of accountability and control central to the understanding of public administration become even more pronounced (see chapter 8).

Second, not only does government adopt private methods for the achievement of its purposes, but the private sector has become quite adept at using the public sector for its purposes. We have already discussed some of the means by which this occurs. In general, the division of government into a number of "subgovernments," a feature of almost all developed societies, means that it is difficult for elected leaders to exercise coordination and control. The expertise located within each of these segments of government, combined with the strong political linkages between organizations in the private sector and those in the public sector, makes the exercise of coordination and control even more difficult. Government in a bureaucratic age has become government for a number of purposes—some of them contradictory—rather than government that speaks with a unified voice attempting to achieve a limited range of objectives.[14]

Finally, government itself has become increasingly complex. Some of this complexity stems from the fact that government is doing so many more things than it was doing even at the end of World War II. And even when an organization is created in an area that government has allegedly not been involved in previously, it will likely have some relationships with existing organizations. And given the political environment in which public organizations are created, there is an even greater probability of overlap and duplication. Dozens of federal organizations are involved to some degree in health policy in the United States, and there is not any political system that has been capable of resolving problems of duplication and overlapping jurisdictions. Public administration has never been the simple command system assumed by some traditional treatments of the problem, for example, that of Woodrow Wilson, but the level of complexity has been increasing significantly. The "implementation structures" that a public organization now faces include a number of central agencies, other line agencies, and private organizations.[15] As the complexity and the size of the public sector have increased, central organizations such as those concerned with budgeting, personnel, etc. have in turn attempted to impose greater central control. Likewise, as scarcity has become a more important feature of contemporary administration other organizations are more prone to compete for resources. This all amounts to a much more complex system of administration and of policy making than would have been found even in the 1960s.

MANAGING IN THE 1980s

Management in the public sector has never been easy, but it is even more difficult in the 1980s than it was previously. Scarcity, changing social and cultural values, and increasing organizational and interorganizational complexity all make it more difficult to accomplish things through the public sector. But, paradoxically, it becomes even more important for those in government to manage effectively. Scarcity, as well as imposing constraints on managers, makes their skills more valuable. There is the simple need to get the most out of each dollar, pound, or rupee of public money.

As noted, one of the many responses to the demands for greater efficiency and effectiveness in government has been the attempt to reprivatize many public services. However, in the long run this may have the effect of reducing the effectiveness of government, with little short-term economic savings. As government loses control over functions considered to be public, it may lose the ability to effectively direct the society; it may lose the steering ability that constitutes the root of the word government. Short-term cost effectiveness may be limited, for many of the monopoly characteristics of public provision may be present in private provision, and this limited saving may be purchased at the expense of long-term alienation and ineffectiveness. Government may lose the ability simply to govern by authority and may have to resort to intervention by more obtrusive and more expensive mechanisms.

In addition to coping with scarcity, managers will have to confront declining morale of workers and perhaps of clients. Arguably, changes in organizational formats and managerial styles have not kept pace with changes in society. Employment in large-scale organizations is more common in the economy but is less satisfying for many—if not most—workers. Managers may therefore be in the position of trying to obtain improved performance from disaffected workers in order to provide reduced services to disgruntled clients. Organizational forms that involve workers and clients to a greater extent have been experimented with but continue to be experimental, and there remain a number of organizational problems simply in motivating and rewarding employees.

Public management in the 1980s, in almost any country one would want to consider, may require extraordinary patience and skills. And, more importantly, it may require an extraordinary conviction that the quality of life can be enhanced by collective action. It will further require the conviction that administration is not the "mere application of the law" but rather is a vital component of the governmental process with a tremendous—and often untapped—potential for assisting in the creation of a better economy and society.

NOTES

1. Naomi E. Caiden and Aaron B. Wildavsky, *Planning and Budgeting in Poor Countries* (New York: John Wiley & Sons, 1974).
2. Richard Rose and B. Guy Peters, *Can Government Go Bankrupt?* (New York: Basic Books, 1978).
3. See pp. 84–88.
4. Herbert Kaufman, *Are Government Organizations Immortal?* (Washington, D.C.: The Brookings Institution, 1976); Brian W. Hogwood and B. Guy Peters, *Policy Dynamics* (New York: St. Martin's, 1983), table 4.1.
5. Peter deLeon, "A Theory of Policy Termination," in Judith L. May and Aaron B. Wildavsky, *The Policy Cycle* (Beverly Hills, Calif.: Sage, 1978), pp. 279–300.
6. Charles H. Levine, "Organizational Decline and Cutback Management," *Public Administration Review* 38 (1978): 316–25.
7. Rose and Peters, *Can Government Go Bankrupt?*
8. Hogwood and Peters, *Policy Dynamics*, pp. 261–4.
9. Sam D. Sieber, *Fatal Remedies: The Ironies of Social Intervention* (New York: Plenum, 1981).
10. E. E. Savas, *Privatizing the Public Sector* (Chatham, N.J.: Chatham House, 1982).
11. Franklin D. Margiotta, *The Changing World of the American Military* (Boulder, Colo.: Westview, 1978).
12. P. E. Kraemer, *The Societal State* (Meppel, The Netherlands: J. A. Boom, 1966).
13. John T. S. Keeler, "Corporatism and Official Union Hegemony: The Case of French Agricultural Syndicalism," in Suzanne D. Berger, ed., *Organizing Interests in Western Europe* (Cambridge: Cambridge University Press, 1981); Clemens Pedersen and P. H. Knudsen, "Landbrugets organisationen andelsbe-

vaegelsen," in Landsbrugsradet, *Landbruget i Danmark* (Copenhagen: Landsbrugsradet, 1977), pp. 99–139.

14. Guy Peters, "The Problem of Bureaucratic Government," *The Journal of Politics* 43 (1981): 56–82.

15. Benny Hjern and Chris Hull, "Implementation Beyond Hierarchy," Special Edition of the *European Journal of Political Research*, June 1982.